THE CONTROL FACTOR

Our Struggle to See the True Threat

Bill Siegel

D1516986

Hamilton Books
A member of
The Rowman & Littlefield Publishing Group
Lanham · Boulder · New York · Toronto · Plymouth, UK

Copyright © 2012 by
Hamilton Books
4501 Forbes Boulevard
Suite 200
Lanham, Maryland 20706
Hamilton Books Acquisitions Department (301) 459-3366

Estover Road
Plymouth PL6 7PY
United Kingdom

Library of Congress Control Number: 2011944571
ISBN: 978-0-7618-5816-4 (clothbound : alk. paper)
ISBN: 978-0-7618-5822-5 (paperback : alk. paper)
eISBN: 978-0-7618-5817-1

Cover art by Dan Romer.

Dedicated to

the memory of my mother
whose smile and inimitable ability
to make everyone around her feel deeply valued
are permanently seared into my heart

and

to my father
who has taught and given me so much
by being the extraordinary man he is.

Contents

Preface

As a child born in the decade following World War II, visual records of the rise of Adolf Hitler, the transformation and destruction of Germany and the Holocaust brought forth a specific fascination for me. Knowing of the horrific end, I puzzled endlessly over the question, "How could they not see what was coming?" Decades later, the question has still not been satisfactorily answered. Worse, the lessons do not appear to have been adequately learned.

While we are condemned to repeat the history we do not remember and learn, the repetition is rarely obvious until historical analogies are drawn afterwards. Unfortunately, in an age in which devastating destruction can be brought about by very few, we cannot afford not to learn. Still, so much is working upon all of us to ensure that we do not timely recognize and confront the threats we face.

This book attempts to approach the problem from a somewhat different angle. Perhaps the most critical premise is that we collusively avoid taking responsibility for clear perception as that would entail us acting in ways which might disrupt our various fantasies about who we are and what are values ought to be. Instead, we tend to assume a false responsibility—that for the behavior of those who truly threaten us—to create the illusion that we are adequately addressing the problem. Yet a fantasy solution is no solution at all, and by its nature tends to bring about the very consequences it seeks to avoid.

The device utilized here is to posit the "Control Factor," that effort our minds engage in order to keep us blind. The Control Factor is an active process constantly at work within us that needs to be tamed and, ultimately, converted from a destructive force into an ally. Unfortunately, such undertaking takes effort. In this age where Americans repeatedly choose to trade the immediate pain necessary to correct past actions (including, for instance, excessive debt and spending, failing educational system, weakened foreign policy, etc.) for a much more painful future, it is difficult to call upon the discipline necessary to address the destructive tendencies of thought and perception within our individual minds.

The book is divided into three parts: The Threat, The Control Factor, and The Inner Jihad. Many readers well familiar with the intricacies of and issues concerning Islam may be comfortable quickly moving through Chapter 2, "Our Islamic Enemy."

The process of publishing a book takes significant time. Consequently, many of the examples within the book will soon, if not already, age. Nonetheless, the book is not about a historical construct but a mental one. Examples are used simply to stimulate the reader's interest in finding and creating other ones to familiarize himself with his own Control Factor and process of avoiding seeing the threats we face. Hopefully, as examples age, the reader will practice his Inner Jihad by seeking newer ones.

Events occurring following the completion of the book have only amplified suggestions made within it. The Arab Spring has proved to be the "fantasy" the book proposes. The rise of the Muslim Brotherhood as a prominent (if not ultimately to become the prominent) force in the Middle East, as well as its influence upon our government, is ever more apparent. Anti-Semitism is increasingly expressed in forms unparalleled since World War II. The Palestinian leadership has only more thoroughly demonstrated the futility of any expectation that it will ever recognize a Jewish state of Israel. Our Islamic Enemy's working solidarity with the Far Left—both with global ambitions—extends beyond overlapping goals into shared strategies, tactics and actions. Iran's existential threat to America and our values grows more pressing as it remains essentially ignored.

Again, history's repetition is not precise. Goebbels, goose-stepping and gas chambers may not be the symbols of the next iteration of horrific destruction. Unleashed hatred has a vast palette from which to choose in expressing itself. Yet, if we remain blind to how far down the road we have already traveled toward the next human experiment with massive transformation and annihilation, our nation may not be afforded the luxury of future hindsight.

Acknowledgments

I wish to acknowledge with deep gratitude the support of many who made this book possible.

First, my dear friend Dr. Herbert London, whose own writing I so greatly admire, for his encouragement and counsel and for his "agenting" the publication.

I am grateful to Julie Kirsch and Lindsay Macdonald at Hamilton Books for overseeing the project and being such a delight with whom to work.

I am thankful for the editing assistance from Patti Pierucci, Christine Brim, Ned May, Dymphna, and Peter Petre who, in limited time, helped give form and life to the book.

I am indebted to Donald White, Dorothy Albritton and Vicki Swope for all of the copy editing and formatting. Also to Monte Farber, Amy Zerner, and Dan V. Romer for their artwork. And a most special thanks to my assistant, Charlotte, for helping with everything!

On a more personal note, my special thanks to my brother and his family for so greatly enriching my life.

In no way can I repay the many people who have taught and inspired me, many of whom I am so honored to call my friend. They are all heroes in helping us all see what is staring us in the face, including: Ayaan Hirsi Ali, Ambassador John Bolton, Steve Emerson, Dr. Mark Gabriel, Frank Gaffney, Joel Gilbert, David Horowitz, Dr. Zudhi Jasser, Bernard Lewis, Lewis Libby, Dr. Herbert London, Irshad Manji, Itamar Marcus, Cliff May, Andy McCarthy, Daniel Pipes, Claudia Rosett, Robert Spencer, Shelby Steele, Ibn Warraq, Congressman Allen West, Diana West, and Bat Ye'or.

Most importantly, not a single page would have been written without the love, support, wisdom, encouragement and guidance of Monica. I cannot thank you enough for the lessons you give me everyday.

Introduction

May 1, 2010

Around six-thirty on a breezy spring evening, a 1993 Nissan Pathfinder with dark-tinted windows is left parked in New York City's Times Square, the tourist-filled heart of the city. With its engine running and hazard lights blinking, in minutes the vehicle begins to smoke and emit popping sounds. Street vendors alert the police who dismantle four explosive devices in the burning SUV—combinations of propane, gasoline, and fireworks that together formed a large car bomb. Had it fully detonated, scores of people would likely have been killed or burned.

The official response is as unsettling as the incident itself. That night, New York Mayor Michael Bloomberg suggests that the bombing attempt could have been the work of right-wing American extremists. "If I had to guess 25 cents," he tells CBS's Katie Couric later that night, "this would be exactly that: homegrown, or maybe a mentally deranged person, or somebody with a political agenda that doesn't like the health-care bill or something. It could be anything."

While Bloomberg was saying he was unsure what this act was about, his statements suggested he was certainly clear what it was *not* about: an Islamic terror attack. Nonetheless, two days later, Pakistani-born Faisal Shahzad was picked up at JFK International Airport trying to flee the country. Following the arrest, Bloomberg kept up the spin, urging New Yorkers not to go overboard with suspicions of Islam. He added, "We will not tolerate any bias or backlash against Pakistani or Muslim New Yorkers." (Shahzad had no such compunctions. At his trial, he declared, "Brace yourselves, because the war with Muslims has just begun.")

November 2, 2004

Theo Van Gogh bicycles to work in the early morning hours in Amsterdam. A great-grandson of the painter Van Gogh's brother, and an accomplished documentary filmmaker, author, and actor, Van Gogh is a respected member of Amsterdam's arts community. Mohammed Bouyeri, a 26-year-old Dutch-Moroccan citizen, accosts him, shoots him eight times with a handgun, tries to decapitate him, and stabs him in the chest. Finally Bouyeri flees after attaching a note to Van Gogh's body with a knife. The note threatens the life of Ayaan Hirsi Ali, a former Muslim and member of the Dutch Parliament with whom Van Gogh has been making a film on the treatment of women in Islam, *Submission*. Hirsi Ali continues to receive credible death threats and needs to live under tight security.

January 1, 2010

In the early evening of this New Year's Day, a 28-year-old Somali armed with axe and knife breaks into the Aarhus, Denmark home of Kurt Westergaard, who is looking after his five-year-old granddaughter. Westergaard barricades himself in a bathroom that has been heavily fortified in the event of just such an attack. As the assailant batters on the door with the axe yelling, "We will get our revenge!" Westergaard pushes a "panic button" that summons the police. They come quickly and, after being attacked with the axe themselves, shoot the perpetrator in the knee and place him under arrest.

Westergaard had created one of twelve cartoons chosen by the newspaper *Jyllands-Posten* to accompany a story about the fear of retribution felt by artists when depicting Islam. His cartoon showed the Prophet Mohammed with a bomb in his turban. The story ran without incident in September 2005, but months later, his cartoon became the flash point for riots across the Middle East. Danish embassies were torched and their flags burned while death threats were hurled at those associated with the newspaper.

The European response to the attacks on Van Gogh, Westergaard, and other critics of Islam has been as paradoxical as Michael Bloomberg's reaction to the car bomb in Times Square. In Denmark and other nations, major efforts were launched to tighten blasphemy laws and censor any insults to Islam—in effect answering Muslim violence by chilling and criminalizing free speech.

August, 2010

New York City authorities grant permission for the construction of a Muslim community center and mosque near the World Trade Center, touching off a storm of debate. Not only is the site within blocks of the Ground Zero; the building in question is an unholy monument to the 9/11 attack. Mohammed Atta flew American Airlines Flight 11 toward the North Tower at such speed that the landing gear ripped from the plane, crashing through the roof at this very location.

One side of the debate about the building of the mosque argues that America stands for freedom of religion and that the owners are entitled to build it on their property in accordance with local regulations. The other side agrees that while the right exists, to build the mosque would be an insult to the families of victims, as well as a symbol of victory to Muslims worldwide who would choose to see it as such.

The mosque's most visible advocate and intended leader is Imam Feisal Abdul Rauf. Labeled in the liberal media as a 'moderate Muslim,' Rauf wraps himself in benevolent words such as "healing" and "outreach," and has written a book, *What's Right with Islam is What's Right with America*, that promotes mutual understanding. Few people realize that the same book in its Islamic edition carries a very different title promoting the expansion of Islam through the U.S.: *A Call to Prayer from the World Trade Center Rubble: Islamic Dawa in the Heart of America*. Rauf has made statements rationalizing the 9/11 attacks such as his comments on CBS's *60 Minutes*, "U.S. policies were an accessory to the crime that happened. We have been an accessory to a lot of innocent lives dying in the world. . . . Osama bin Laden is made in the USA." More chillingly, Rauf separately proclaimed, "Those who are hostile to us now will see their children and grandchildren become Muslims in the future."

As reports surfaced of these remarks and other facts, more and more people questioned the imam's intentions and purposes for the mosque. Polls showed some 70 percent of Americans opposed to building it where planned.

When *Time* magazine weighed in on the controversy, however, it chose a strangely sympathetic angle: "Is America Islamophobic?" its August 2010 cover story asked. Author Bobby Gosh alleged that Islamophobia is "taking root" in "places all over the country." He likened it to a new anti-Semitism, arguing that fear and prejudice are to blame for many of the difficulties Muslims face in America. Islamophobia is, in short, America's fault.

January, 2008

U.S. Army Reserve Major Stephen Coughlin, a lawyer and Joint Chiefs of Staff intelligence officer, has produced a 300-page thesis entitled, *To Our Great Detriment: Ignoring What Extremists Say About Jihad*. In it in he makes a compelling case that U.S. military decision-making is severely compromised because we have allowed Muslim apologists to shape our leaders' understanding of Islam. His elaborately researched presentation using authoritative Islamic legal source materials demonstrates, for those unfamiliar, the true workings of *Shariah* or Islamic law. Coughlin zeroes in on Ikhwan al-Muslimeen, the Muslim Brotherhood, an 83-year-old confederation that now encompasses organizations in more than 80 countries under the motto "God is our objective, the Koran is our law, the Prophet is our leader, *jihad* is our way, and death for the sake of Allah is the highest of our aspirations." Coughlin, warning Pentagon and other federal officials, observes that members of Muslim Brotherhood associated groups have been able to influence military officials and other U.S. government and academic institutions. The pictures they paint of Islamic aspirations and goals, he warns, are far milder than what authoritative Islamic writings and legal sources proclaim.

Not long after he submits his report, the Pentagon repositions Coughlin after Heshim Islam, a Muslim aide to Deputy Defense Secretary Gordon England urged his firing. Denouncing Coughlin's repositioning an act of intellectual cowardice, LTC Joseph C. Myers, an Army Advisor to the Air Command and Staff College, echoes Coughlin's warning that allowing America to be guided by the false narratives of Islam puts us in grave danger of failing to understand our enemy. Many who suspect a serious infiltration of deceptive Muslim guidance into our government and society voice support for Coughlin, but to no avail. Rather than investigate Coughlin's claims, authorities turn him into the enemy and try to remove his narrative from the public discourse. Ultimately, Coughlin's contract is allowed to expire without renewal.

July, 2010

Objecting to the promotion of General David Petraeus to command U.S. and NATO forces in Afghanistan, the largest assembled block of UN member states in the world, the Organization of the Islamic Conference (OIC), protests in its July 2010 *Monthly Bulletin*: "Petraeus wrote an anti-Islamic manual." The complaint refers to the counter-insurgency manual Petraeus developed in 2006 for advancing "the surge" in America's war in Iraq. In it he refers to "Islamic insurgents," "Islamic extremists," and "Islamic subversives," which the OIC now attacks as being "in direct contradiction to the U.S. military's war-fighting doctrine" and as "anti-Islamic." Bizarrely, the OIC made its point: President Barack Obama's chief national security adviser for counter-terrorism, John Brennan, subsequently issued a policy directing U.S. officials to avoid using language that connects Islam to terrorism.

These disparate events cited above illustrate the workings of a psychological process that endangers us all. It is labeled here the "Control Factor." *It is that creative part of our minds that actively and continuously seeks to assure us that the threat we feel, see, hear, and think about is largely under our control, when it in reality is not.* These examples represent three distinct levels of the Islamic threat: from blatant terrorism, to the seemingly innocuous infiltration into and manipulation of Western society from within, to the pressure exerted upon us by international institutions.

We have not yet learned to confront the threat from Islam fully and effectively at any level. While we have made significant strides in combating terrorism, it remains a relentless and growing threat. And we are at a loss as to how to stop the slow and carefully executed "Trojan Horse" plan to propagate anti-American expressions of Islam *within* America under the protection of constitutional freedoms, especially when they are assisted from *without* by the efforts of Islamic nations and international institutions.

Instead, just as Mayor Bloomberg instinctively sought to downplay the attempted terror bombing and ensure that New Yorkers and Americans across the country remained calm, the Control Factor safeguards our internal comfort, constantly reframing, reformulating, and reprocessing our perceptions and beliefs in order to create a sense of control, despite the clear fact that we are *not* in control.

January, 2011

The "Day of Wrath" protests in Cairo, Egypt, were seemingly steered by a small group consisting of a Google executive, some opposition leaders, and a representative of the Muslim Brotherhood. Protesters initially demanded reforms, but the goals ripened into the demand for the resignation of President Hosni Mubarak.

Western reporters heralded the protests as peaceful and accentuated the optimism inherent in the narrative of *the oppressed ruled overthrowing the despotic ruler*. Trumpeting the extraordinary role that Twitter, Facebook, and other social media played in this political transformation, the media amplified the hope that young Muslims attuned to modernization will create a more liberal and democratic Egypt and ultimately transform the entire Arab world.

Mubarak made a starkly different argument. He warned that if he did not keep a firm hand on leadership, the Muslim Brotherhood would take hold of the nation and all would be for the worse. Sure to be lost, Mubarak predicted, were the liberal reforms he had just begun to institute and the comparatively low unemployment rate Egypt had achieved under his rule. The press largely attacked his position as a self-serving ruse.

As the United States weighed in, declaring that Mubarak "must go," it sought to qualify the reputation of the Muslim Brotherhood and console Westerners about the Brotherhood's potential emergence. The Director of National Intelligence, James Clapper, declared, " 'Muslim Brotherhood' . . . is an umbrella term for a variety of movements, in the case of Egypt, a very heterogeneous group, largely secular, which has eschewed violence and has decried al-Qaeda as a perversion of Islam. . . ." He continued, "[T]here is no overarching agenda, particularly in pursuit of violence, at least internationally." At the same time the director of the CIA, Leon Panetta, declined to call the Brotherhood radical; instead he maintained that, like most other groups and like Islam in general, it simply contains extremist elements.

Exactly a week after Mubarak resigned, the Muslim Brotherhood made itself heard. In a move recalling the triumphal return from exile of Ayatollah Khomeini in the Iranian Revolution, the 84-year-old cleric Yusuf al-Qaradawi made his first public appearance in Egypt in 30 years, addressing a crowd the *New York Times* estimated in excess of one million in Cairo's main square. (Interesting to note: Brotherhood operatives refused to allow to participate the Google executive who had become the symbol for how the protests would bring about a more Westernized and democratic Egypt). An enormously popular figure on the Al Jazeera network, Qaradawi is in effect the Muslim Brotherhood's spiritual leader. He has prayed publicly for the opportunity to kill a Zionist, has said he awaits the conquest of the Al-Aqsa Mosque in Jerusalem and has pressed to have Egypt's three-decades-long peace treaty with Israel overturned. He did not wait long to stoke the revolutionary turmoil in neighboring Libya, three days after his first appearance issuing a fatwa stating that any Libyan soldier who can shoot dead embattled leader Muammar Qaddafi should do so "to rid Libya of him."

Having been banned from entering from entering the United States and Great Britain and denounced by other clerics, Qaradawi is anything but secular, as Clapper might suggest, and has a well articulated agenda to advance *Shariah* throughout Egypt and the world. One wonders if Clapper and Panetta, who occupy the most important intelligence positions in the U.S. government, had ever bothered to read the Constitution of the Muslim Brotherhood of Egypt, which states that a primary goal is "establishing an Islamic state that will apply Islamic law in a practical way, and the Muslim Brotherhood will be the guardian inside the territory of this Muslim state, and the Muslim Brotherhood will work to export this Islamic system internationally" (Gabriel translation). Clapper and Panetta either demonstrated utter ignorance of Qaradawi and the Brotherhood, perhaps the largest Islamic group in the world, or had some overriding interest in attempting to disguise the Brotherhood's essence.

* * * * *

America in the twenty-first century is facing an extraordinary number of challenges, many of which appear to be without precedent. Rapid advances in technology, interconnectedness, global investment, and information sharing have made many things in our lives that once helped us feel safe and that we took for granted now seem less secure. Consequently, many more Americans are experiencing great anxiety about their futures.

Predictably, beliefs about how to confront these challenges are extremely varied. In a time when America's president is using the rhetoric of "inclusion" and "coming together," these divergent beliefs often make consensus too difficult a task. The country finds itself split into factions and polarized, with citizens often entering the ring of public discourse solely to try to knock out the other side.

How we deal with new challenges is governed at least as much by beliefs and emotions as by reason. Our inner coping mechanisms, and how we confront them, contribute as significantly to our perception of the challenges as does external reality itself. Only when we learn to effectively manage these mechanisms and the styles of thinking they generate will we be able properly to preserve, support, and advance our exceptional nation and treasured principles of freedom and liberty.

This is of critical importance in America's interaction with Islam. The threat from those who, under Islam's banner, seek to destroy the Western world is so frightening that Western minds have adopted a wide variety of psychological defenses to deal with our fear. In doing so, we falsely convince ourselves that we are in control of a battle that is rapidly getting beyond our control. This is the Control Factor at work—that continuously *active* part of our minds that keeps us at every moment locked into perceptions that create the false sense that we are in control, or at least able to regain control if needed.

Critical to our long-term survival is an honest and comprehensive examination of exactly how we bury our fears rather than courageously face, fight, and defeat them. Just as Muslim apologists like to refer to "*jihad*" as an internal struggle against those thoughts, lusts, and appetites that thwart one's deepest spiritual goals, so must each of us in the West look inward at the thoughts and beliefs which keep us from seeing the struggle in which we are engaged for what it really is—a war which has been declared on us. Thus, the necessity for *America's Inner Jihad*. Only when a critical mass of Americans see this clearly will we learn how to fight and win this war.

In truth, we are in a war—a Holy War, as defined by the enemy itself. We are unsure how to defend ourselves in such a war, much less how to fight it aggressively. This uncertainty, complicated by our asymmetrical adherence to rules and moral codes which our Constitution and national identity impress upon us but which our enemy does not share, has led many to a deep anxiety—a sense of too little control over our present circumstances and exponentially less over future ones. To ease this anxiety, the Control Factor's organizing principle is to recast our perceptions, thoughts, and beliefs to restore the sense of control; that is what it created to do. The self-deception that results is at least as dangerous to us as any enemy weapon.

Unless and until we have the will to recognize the Control Factor and train ourselves to recognize its insidious power, we will become progressively vulnerable to the threat that it obscures. Confronting the Control Factor requires careful introspection, for no two minds delude themselves in exactly the same way. This process is labeled here as our *Inner Jihad*. Only when great numbers of our citizenry engage in it will we be able to confront what we have been seeking to avoid—*that we do not yet know how to fight this war within the context of our own values, morals, and laws.* Until then, our strategies and tactics will be largely ineffective, weakened and undermined by the very Control Factor maneuvers that *appear* to fend off the threat. If we are to have any real hope of winning the war and preserving our nation, the Inner Jihad has to start now.

This is not a book about Islam. It does not explore the great debates about Islam's laws, history, and philosophical premises. (For readers wishing to learn more, there are plentiful resources to explore, including the many books and films cited here and suggested in the bibliography. Much effort has been made to promote these works as they are most valuable for furthering one's Inner Jihad). The focus here, instead, is the destructive pattern of self-deception into which Americans slip when confronted with the Islamic menace, and how to awaken from the comforting illusions we create. The discussion of Islam is limited to reviewing some of its distinguishing features with an eye toward how they mesh with our habits of self-deception. A rich history and body of literature is necessarily generalized and simplified. Religious scholars, historians, and the well studied could reasonably object to some of these necessary simplifications without curtailing their usefulness. Instead, the emphasis here is placed upon the *process* of learning and self-examination.

To help the reader learn to identify, stalk, and neutralize the Control Factor's devious work, there next comes an anatomy of its many techniques, tools, tactics, and maneuvers. For each, many more examples could be cited. Every day—in newspapers, on television, in conversation, online, and elsewhere—we are bombarded by examples of the Control Factor at work. It is most useful for the reader to practice spotting instances as they take place both around him and within his own mind, rather than relying on the specific ones highlighted here.

To be clear, the concept of psychological defenses is, by its very nature, somewhat amorphous. One might challenge the constructs and assertions made in this book with the claim that they, too, are partially the product of thinking steeped in its own defenses. Typically in a psychotherapeutic context, the determination of whether defenses are at work depends upon the subject's ultimate agreement. That is, the criteria for determining whether psychological defenses are active includes to varying degrees whether the subject ultimately concludes that they are. Consequently, part of the value of examining the Control Factor's multitude of maneuvers is to be able to ultimately discover which ones are most at work with each of us.

The final part of the book is devoted to the Inner Jihad. Many of its key aspects are outlined to help instruct and inspire the reader to progress. It is offered in the hope of helping us begin to resolve the paradoxical difficulties and eliminate the self-imposed constraints that presently hobble us.

The German philosopher Ludwig Wittgenstein had an analogy for existential quandaries. The philosophically troubled mind, he said, is like a fly trapped in an upside-down bottle, banging itself incessantly against the glass. The key to escape, Wittgenstein said, is for the fly to look down and see the path by which it flew in. The Inner Jihad against our Control Factors works the same way—it can help us look down and learn to deal with this terrifying puzzle for which we do not presently see a solution. Only by understanding what we have done to get into our own "fly bottle" will we, like the fly, have any hope of getting out—alive.

Part I

The Threat

Chapter 1

America Faces a New Challenge

No wonder Americans feel anxious. The nation confronts ordeals on almost every imaginable front. It struggles with its identity, its place, and its self-image as world leader and lone superpower. Its economic stability is being severely tested. Governmental spending, deficit, and debt have far surpassed the levels with which most anyone would ever be comfortable. China and other rising powers with interests in conflict with ours are asserting themselves in new and growing ways. We face severe challenges in unemployment, energy dependency, education, breakdown of the family, housing, immigration and border control, public health and healthcare, environmental degradation, and more. Such ills compound one another and even threaten to combine in what would be the historical equivalent of a perfect storm. The sense of vulnerability they create makes it seem ever more difficult to change course and rehabilitate.

Nonetheless, and without minimizing the hardships now experienced, the nation has in the past faced severe recessions and depressions, epidemics, natural disasters, foreign wars, large criminal networks, and so on. And, for most of these tribulations, the solutions have been found to lie largely within the country's control. We have gotten into great difficulties only to discover again and again that, given the political will to develop consensus, we can make great strides to address them. While the current levels of debt and deficit present a never before experienced national security threat, the nation has within itself the power to address it. Instead, the rigorous focus on these perils adds to and can often be a partial coping mechanism for dealing with another, even more severe threat, one that uniquely welcomes, thrives upon, takes advantage of and throws fuel on all other vulnerabilities we face—Islam.

Under the banner of Islam forces have assembled that share a clear determination to bring down America and the West. These forces are fast becoming capable of inflicting severe destruction from both outside and within. While America has faced many enemies in the past, enemies with grandiose ideologies, ambitions and pretensions, their ability to realize their goals was restricted—by dependence on centralized forces, by limitations of weaponry, intelligence, resources, manpower and time, and, most importantly, by their love of life and fear of death. Now that has all changed.

The "War on Terror" thus far has split Americans into two camps, each of which has a difficult time relating to the other. One camp regards the wars in Iraq, Afghanistan and elsewhere as well as our domestic struggles with certain Muslim groups and actors as self-contained, unrelated disruptions which would disappear if only managed correctly. "If only" we would address their "root causes" and stop all behavior of our own which "generates" such anti-American hatred, the differences between the warring parties would ease and enough points of agreement could emerge to pave the way toward resolution. Enemies are ultimately all the same, the underlying rationale goes, and we just need to find the proper way resolve the differences that exist between us. Regardless of faith, beliefs can be compromised and reconciled if the correct solution is offered. They will want the same thing, too.

Political correctness is a hallmark of the way this camp describes the enemy. To mention a "war with Islam" has today become virtually taboo. The Obama administration has disallowed the use of "Islam," "terror" and "jihad" in the same sentence, much less in the formation or description of coherent policy. Instead, many of our policymakers derive comfort from the belief that Islam is a "great" and "peaceful" religion which simply has been "hijacked" and distorted by a small number of "crazies."

The opposing camp sees differently—a relentless enemy guided by a vision of world theocracy and bent on the destruction of Western Civilization. This camp believes that America will be compelled to wage a long war with those labeled here as "our Islamic Enemy." As used here, "our Islamic Enemy" is intended to cover the full range of those who, under the banner of Islam, seek our destruction; whether from the supposed "few" fanatical "crazies" to terrorist groups, Islamists, to Salafists/

Wahhabists, Islamofascists, constituencies and rulers of nation states, and perhaps, the states themselves. The defining criterion is the primary devotion to an expression of Islam above all other principles, which the enemy himself believes compels and commands the defeat of all that stands in the way of its expansion until the world is dominated by Islamic law. Given that massive destructive power today is not dependent upon large-scale access to personnel, weapons, or financing, the size of the force is somewhat irrelevant. Whether nation or solo killer, the defining criterion of the enemy is devotion to Islam above all other principles, which the enemy himself believes compels and commands the defeat of all that stands in the way of its expansion until the world is dominated by Islamic law.

The conflict between America's two camps lies not in a disagreement about how to arrive at a state of peaceful coexistence with Islam. Rather, it is the question of whether coexistence should or can be achieved at all.

America of course has had its share of enemies and wars. Filled with their own horrors, the two World Wars, as well as the Korean, Vietnam, and Cold Wars, involved complex entanglements of national and global interests. The enemies were predominantly visible, locatable, state-based, motivated and capable. In every case except the Civil War, the central battlefields have been on foreign soil. German saboteurs presaged 9/11 with their Black Tom attack on New York City in an attempt to prevent us from entering World War I in Europe, not to extend the battlefield to America. Pearl Harbor and six months of U-boat assaults on our Atlantic coast aside, and large numbers of Nazi and Communist spies notwithstanding, Adolf Hitler, Josef Stalin, and Hirohito were still largely unable to bring the battle to us.

Even in the Cold War, despite the persistent fear of atomic attack and serious concerns over communist infiltration, the actual battlefields were in proxy lands. Despite our courageous national character, deep down we knew we could always give up the fight and return home safely if the going got too rough—as we did in Vietnam, Somalia, and Lebanon. As Ayn Rand once said, "In my view, we should fight fascism and communism when they come to this country."[1]

Few other nations have enjoyed such splendid isolation. People around the world have lived for millennia with vulnerable and fluctuating borders. It is indisputably part of the European consciousness to fear invasion. Middle Eastern cultures have until the 20th century lacked the defined borders so familiar to the West and have instead relied on vague tribal boundaries to mark their domains. America's oceans and borders, however, have helped keep our power, status and—in parallel fashion— our national psyche protected and stable.

Things differ today. The threat of terrorism within the homeland, coupled with massive illegal immigration, an overspent economy, high unemployment, a looming threat of inflation, extreme weather conditions, and other elements of the looming "perfect storm," are recent phenomena that have created a type and quality of vulnerability and insecurity unfamiliar to most Americans. For many reasons, including the expansion and global distribution of media, information, technology, connectivity, and weaponry, the threat knows no borders. Our Islamic enemy is motivated, capable and needs no nation state. He is motivated by a religion that is uncompromising and values death more than life. Most significantly, his goal, worldwide submission to Islam and dominion of Islamic law, is not accomplished through the mere acquisition of territory, resources, booty, or bounty. This is a battle literally to "the end."

We tend to equate this threat with terrorism. This assumption secretly affords us great comfort, as it gives us what appears to be clearly defined crimes in contravention to civilized principles which we can subject to familiar forms of retaliation and punishment. As horrific as terrorism may be, we can still imagine ways to confront it, whether through military engagement or criminal prosecution. Both are attempts to "control" the problem. Thus the Bush administration was motivated to declare the "war on terror," and the Obama administration has further narrowed its definition of America's enemy to al-Qaeda and the Taliban.

But too tight a focus on terror obscures the total threat. The enemy is pressing on at least three different levels. Terrorism, or the "Violent Jihad," is only the most visible, familiar and recognizable—covering acts from seemingly random bombings to organized suicide attacks to ongoing operations by al-Qaeda, Hamas, Hezbollah, and other groups abetted by states such as Iran.

A more devious level of threat is the Civilization Jihad, a label taken from Muslim Brotherhood documents. At this level, the Brotherhood and its vast array of associated organizations are working non-violently to push our society to transform itself from within. Violence is abhorred— or at least avoided—at this level as it creates too much backlash, gives the actors too much attention, and belies the claim of Islam to be a "peaceful religion." What's more, violence strips the Civilization Jihad of one of its most important weapons—the claim of victimhood.

The third level of threat is identified as the "International Institutional Jihad"—Muslim-controlled countries pursuing common goals through the United Nations, the Organization of the Islamic Conference (OIC), the Arab League, the newly expanded Gulf Cooperation Council, and other organizations. Such institutions enable different expressions of Islam to develop common sets of principles, helping unite otherwise divergent Muslims move toward the ideal of a single Islamic nation or Ummah. Thus united, our enemies use the institutions to advance their agendas. As the Obama administration proceeds with its "anti-exceptionalism" program, submitting more of US foreign policy to international dictates and approval, this level of threat will assert itself more visibly and profoundly as it gains momentum and success.

When viewed across these three levels or Jihads, the threat we face is revealed as dire because we have no roadmap for how to successfully confront it. Worse, many of our traditional and treasured principles of freedom, justice, tolerance, and individual responsibility handicap us greatly. We have some sense of how to confront terror, especially if, like Obama and Attorney General Eric Holder, we impose the narrative which makes it a criminal justice matter. But fantasizing it as such does not change the reality. And even as a criminal justice issue, our courts are having difficulties: witness the failed attempt to close the Guantanamo Bay military prison. Military force is similarly problematic. We know how to deploy it against conventional armies, but, as seen in Afghanistan, Iraq and elsewhere, we have difficulties against terror-based armies and insurgencies.

Dealing with the Civilization Jihad is more difficult still. Put simply, our Constitution does not protect itself well. Those who seek to use our Constitution to destroy our Constitution may need little more than highly motivated operatives, capital, and extreme patience, all of which are readily available to the enemy.

During the twentieth century, America attempted to address communist infiltration. Despite the McCarthy hearings and legislative actions, the nation never perfected a constitutionally acceptable way reliably to head off well-organized full-scale subversions meant to destroy our system from within. Fortunately, the Soviet Union collapsed of its own weight and the communist threat was, at least temporarily, silenced.

America was central to the formation of the United Nations, as well as many other efforts to bring about global peace, improve of the Third World, and raise international norms and standards. We retained, however, veto rights in order to protect our interests, and held the military supremacy required to push through much of our own agenda. Never was our sovereignty threatened, much less offered up as an ante. Step by step, however, the International Institutional Jihad is grasping the reins as America's power and influence decline. In what John Bolton, former US Ambassador to the UN, denounces as "norming," internationally created standards are being forced upon Europe and even America from without. If a progressive standard or principle cannot be sold domestically in the US, activists first sell it internationally and have international institutions then pressure America to accept it at home. This pattern has emerged across divergent fields ranging from women's rights to the laws of communication, the seas, and space.

The Obama administration itself has gotten into the act, on the issue of gun control. By cooperating with international efforts to extend arms-control treaties to cover small firearms, it hopes to be able to force these controls onto the US population, circumventing the full Congress and the states.

Not too subtly, the administration has edged foreign policy all the closer to placing US sovereignty in the hands of foreign nations and the UN. By adopting the "Responsibility to Protect Doctrine" to justify American military actions in Libya, the administration created a strong precedent for conditioning future actions on the consent of foreign nations and organizations such as the Arab League and the UN.

Our enemy is learning this process so quickly that new restrictions on free speech and other rights are now commonly proposed by such international organizations. While the United States has resisted to date, we are hard-pressed to keep those trends at bay under Obama's seemingly collusive direction.

The events of 9/11 demonstrated the gravity of the threat we face. Yet for most Americans, the threat is simply too frightening consciously to accept and integrate at once. Rather, most Americans have been struggling, in large part unconsciously, with a deep and unfamiliar sense of danger to their lives and to many of the freedoms we take for granted. Thus America's challenge lies in understanding the threat, accepting its reality, and recognizing that we simply do not know how to deal with it adequately—we do not yet know how to effectively fight it within the context of our morals, ethics and laws.

People often define problems to "fit" the solutions they think may apply. Having few solutions, however, to address the three levels of jihadist threat has led us to fail adequately to see, much less define, the problem. In turn, having no firm sense of a solution amplifies our fears. A major challenge, therefore, lies in learning to recognize and accept the danger even as we strive to figure out how to meet it.

Chapter 2

Our Islamic Enemy

Since 9/11, through television programs, films, books, in classes and in general conversation, many Americans have been trying to understand Islam and those who do violence in its name. Much has been added to the reservoir of Islamic study, covering Islamic history, Islamic law, and Islam's various divisions, including the four schools of Sunni Islam, Shi'ism, Wahhabism, Salafism, Sufism, and more. Knowledge of modern Islamic political history, including the rich and relevant experiences of Muslim countries in importing communism, socialism, nationalism, pan-Arabism, Nazism, and other ideologies is extremely important in understanding the events enveloping us. Much history, research and analysis have also been made public about Islamic interest groups and their true underlying objectives, most importantly the Muslim Brotherhood and associated entities including the Islamic Society of North America (ISNA), the Muslim Students Association (MSA), and the Council on American-Islamic Relations (CAIR).

It cannot be over-emphasized how important it is for Westerners to familiarize themselves with such material. In view of the power that our minds exert over our beliefs and opinions, it is important that each of us make an effort to learn and struggle with concepts embedded in Islam, the *Koran*, the *Sunnah,* and the words and acts of the Prophet Mohammed, Islamic history and law. This book, however, is not the forum for even a brief review of this material; instead it will summarize important and unique aspects that help shine light on the workings of the Control Factor.

A major difficulty for the West lies in identifying its enemy:

- Is it a group of people, a pathology, a socio-economic condition, an ideology, a "great religion", or something else?
- How far does it extend—to ad hoc groups of frustrated persons, groups of cultural rebels, adherents of cult-like belief systems, or to all self-proclaimed followers of a "great religion?"
- Does it cross the vast range of languages, origins, ethnic and cultural backgrounds, and political persuasions that differentiate the many Islamic communities worldwide?

What we do know is that the enemy parades under the banner of Islam; Islam is the unifying principle. Consequently, we feel a compulsion to address the modern-day Islamic threat by attempting to figure out what Islam "is." The notion is that if we know what it is, we can decide whether those who attack the West are proper representatives of Islam. If that is the case, we will, in some sense, be more comfortable with the idea that we are at war with Islam. Such a conclusion would also give us a sense of how to respond; anything connected with Islam would seemingly be fair game. (The enormity of this prospect, however, is enough to make most of us want to conclude otherwise.)

Alternatively, if we convince ourselves that what these enemies say and do is different from Islam, we focus our strategies and responses on other factors such as socio-economic conditions, levels of education, or even the amount of freedom and the prevalence of human rights. Thus trying to pin down what Islam "is" in *thought* is really an attempt to gain control over it in *reality*. The fantasy is that simple answers can lighten our burden.

The Family of Islam

Like all major belief systems, Islam has manifested itself in many different ways across a 1400-year time span and a wide variety of cultures and races. This diversity of expression can lend logical support to almost any argument constructed around what Islam supposedly "is." Because there are seemingly contradictory propositions and concepts within the body of Islamic texts and history, people who have little familiarity with the religion can be persuaded that there are widely divergent descriptions of "Islam." Muslim apologists write about the "glory days" of Islam, during which Islam led the world in science, culture and medicine. The days when Al-Andalus flourished, lead them to herald Islam as having been a center for "tolerance" of other religions. The religion is highly misunderstood, they say, and Allah, as many prayers begin, is "most compassionate and most merciful."

Critics can cite historic events and eras to construct a very different narrative of Islam as a barbaric, savage, intolerant, and mindless method of maintaining cultural cohesion. Religious scholars have for ages debated and struggled with the intricate details of applying Islamic principles to the realities of daily life for individuals, families, communities, and governments, leading to vastly divergent conclusions. Apologists typically downplay or reframe to justify—if not ignore—any hint of violence or *jihad* in reciting the history or dictates of Islam.

In this light, it makes little sense to ask what Islam "is." The question merely leads to endless debate. Rather, it makes sense to look at the vast number of ways Islam has expressed itself, and to attempt to identify among those many expressions what German philosopher Ludwig Wittgenstein called "family resemblances." Blood relatives share genetic material but particular features might express in one member and not another. Some relatives might have hazel eyes and a stocky build, while others are more distinctive for their lankiness and curly hair. Indeed, some members may barely appear to be related. What makes it a family is not that there is any one thing in common. What is significant is that we learn ways to group these members for particular purposes.

Wittgenstein struggled as a philosopher with how to stop the compulsion to ask the form of question "what is x?", where "x" is an abstraction such as justice, beauty, or ethics. He believed that the compulsion itself is formulated and nourished by the natural Platonic but improper view that all words "stand for" something—the essence of justice, beauty, or ethics—and that essence is what we communicate about. Wittgenstein ultimately concluded that it is the use of words in life situations (he called them "language games") that gives them meaning and that, in actuality, this philosophical investigation is meaningless, as it takes words out of their normal, real-life contexts in order to seek a presumed but nonexistent archetypal core. Thus the meaning of any word lies only in its use. And since that use is varied, a word's meanings will be united only by the family resemblances, and will have vague and ever-changing boundaries.

One of Wittgenstein's great contributions was to help his students recognize the compulsion to look for the "true meaning" of a word, and the powerful grip this compulsion holds over our thinking. This is the same compulsion that drives us to try to define what Islam "is" so that we may understand and identify the enemy we face and find an easy solution to the threat it poses. As a vital step toward clarity in identifying our true "enemy," it is important that we recognize and resist this compulsion and instead look at the family resemblances across Islam's broad range.

Islam has expressed itself very differently from culture to culture, era to era, and geographic location to geographic location. Stoning or honor killings to preserve family pride may occur in certain Islamic cultures at certain times and be considered a part of Islam while being absent from other areas and times. Female genital mutilation is practiced in certain cultures than in others. The cultural standards of territories conquered by Islam throughout history often have been incorporated into expressions of Islam in those territories. Behaviors of Indian Muslims differ in many ways from those of Arab or African Muslims. Consequently, it is how people, both within Islam and outside, use the term "Islam" and find meaning in such use that underlies our true understanding. It is the overall continuity of these expressions that truly give Islam meaning.

Put simply, Islam is as Islam does.

The "family resemblance" metaphor can be carried a step further. The body of ideas that more or less defines Islam can be likened to genes. Certain sets of ideas might be dominant for some Muslims while remaining dormant in others. A particular group of Muslims might share this package of ideas, while another group has most of those ideas but with variants, and so on. Like genes, shared ideas may or may not be expressed in different ways, times, and combinations. What becomes critical is which ideas are actually turned "on" and when.

Obviously, the most pronounced family resemblance within Islam is that followers call themselves Muslims and tend to perform some combination of various rituals and behaviors unique to the religion. Yet for seriously engaged Muslims, there is a deeper unifying trait: adherence to beliefs and traditions which at their core seek to establish a worldwide devotion to Allah through submission to Islamic or *Shariah* Law. "Islam" means "submission." This aspiration is reflected in each of Islam's key sources: the *Koran*, the *Hadith* (the acts and sayings of the Prophet Mohammed, to whom Islam was "revealed"), the *Sira* (the life of Mohammed), Islamic history, and Islamic law itself. How this objective has been realized throughout Islam's 1400 year history has depended on a variety of factors, including how much power the Islamic community has had, who its enemies have been, its particular needs at a specific time, and so forth. One important lesson to learn and keep in mind: When Islam is a minority in a given territory, it expresses itself in certain forms; when it is in control, it expresses itself in others.

Some Critical Aspects of Islam

Islam is the last of the major Abrahamic faiths, after Judaism and Christianity. Thus it has the advantage of being able to expressly redefine and re-narrate the predecessor religions. The *Koran* and other Islamic literature describe the histories in the *Torah* and the *Bible* in ways which Jews and Christians would never accept. It claims, for instance, that Jesus was not crucified. The Christian texts obviously cannot respond to this since they predate Islam. And, unlike stories in the *Torah* or the *New Testament* which describe peoples no longer in existence or relevant, Islamic descriptions and commands regarding Christians and Jews apply to peoples whose existence continues today.

Evolving last among these religions also enables Islam to define itself as superior to prior religions, destroying any basis for mutual respect or even tolerance. Islam views itself as the only religion in the sense that there is only one spiritual path. Koranic verse 3:85:[1]

> If anyone desires a religion other than Islam (submission to Allah), never will it be accepted of him; and in the hereafter he will be in the ranks of those who have lost (all spiritual good).

It also elevates Muslims above those of other faiths, as in the Koranic verse 3:110, which denigrates 'People of the Book'—Christians and Jews:

> Ye are the best of peoples, evolved for mankind, enjoining what is right, forbidding what is wrong, and believing in Allah. If only the People of the Book had faith, it were best for them: among them are some who have faith, but most of them are perverted transgressors.

Islam was, at one time, clearly the dominant force in the world. Extending its control into what is today Europe, India, China, and Africa, at its peak it's reach was far greater than the Roman Empire. As has been pointed out, Islam functions differently when it is in control than when it is in the minority. The experiences with overwhelming success, leadership, and dominance in the world have fortified this basic expectation of superiority.

Being the last of the Abrahamic religions has enabled Islam in its founding literature uniquely to establish express rules for the treatment of adherents of other religions. This is a subtle yet powerful distinction. While the *Torah* and the *New Testament* (as opposed to subsequent Christian and Jewish writings) have no express commands for dealing with Islam, Islam has compelling dictates for the treatment of Jews and Christians. It makes them second-class *dhimmis*, at best a protected but inferior class to be subjected to taxes, severe humiliation and, in certain contexts, death.

Author Bat Ye'or has written extensively on the humiliations that are prescribed for *dhimmis*, all of which function to burn deeply into the Islamic psyche both the exalted status of Muslims as well as essential disgust for the unbeliever. Across different periods in Islamic history, *dhimmis* were required to wear items or clothing to identify themselves, including arm bands or large crosses worn around the neck. They had to lower themselves physically when passing a Muslim in public. They were restricted from repairing or building anew places of worship and had to carry out their religious practices in private. When paying their special tax, they were often beaten to emphasize how despicable they were and how grateful they should be that their lives have been spared. While the notion of "Chosen People" has often inspired envy and resentment against Jews, Muslim superiority is so deeply embedded in the Muslim mind that it has meant centuries of horror for non-Muslims. And while at times in history the Christian treatment of non-believers was more horrific than concurrent acts by Muslims, this reflected more the political evolution of the Church as distinct from the acts and commands of Jesus and Mohammed.

Much of Islam's history depicts Muslims attacking Jews, Christians and other infidels, as Mohammed himself does in the *Sira*. Significantly, Islamic law is replete with dictates not just for how Muslims are to behave but also for how *dhimmis*, slaves, or other non-Muslims are to behave. This is a crucial characteristic that makes Islam a political ideology at least as much as it is a religious ideology, if not predominantly so.

Much of the world's history arises from the competition of ideas— the struggle for superiority and dominance of a concept, organization, community, nation, or religion over all others. While much of the Western world today promotes human equality as the superior concept, Islam's fundamental principles and its triumphalist goal prevent it from sincerely sharing this value.

Islam declares Mohammed to be the last of the great prophets. Accordingly, those who believe are compelled to accept him as the ultimate role model. According to Bill Warner of www.PoliticalIslam.com,[2] the *Koran* calls Mohammed the perfect Muslim no fewer than 91 times. What is more, Mohammed receives more "air time" than Allah. The *Koran*, which is solely the word of Allah, accounts for only 14% of the writings comprising Islam's two most foundational texts, while Mohammed's sayings and acts (the "Hadith") constitute 86%. The texts stipulate that no one can come later and redefine Islam or countermand Mohammed's revelations, sayings or acts. The possibility of new "interpretations" of Islam is as a result significantly limited by this stricture, as no one can hold comparable credibility or authority to define Mohammed's words or actions.

This dictate is entwined with one even more powerful: The *Koran* is deemed to be the immutable word of Allah. It calls itself unchangeable. Accordingly, Islamic law is necessarily and constantly in conflict with inevitable historical and future development and change both within and outside Islam.

Not unlike (but vastly more consequential than) the debate in US constitutional law between advocates of the "living Constitution" and "strict constructionists," Islamic scholars have long struggled with the tension created by the *Koran*'s self-declaration of immutability. In contrast, the US Constitution makes provision for changes to itself. While reason and challenge (*ijtihad*) were significant during the first few centuries of the evolution of Islam, they have been largely shut down for the past millennium. The immutability of the *Koran*, coupled with Mohammed's status as the last and model prophet, makes any adjustment, evolution, or integration with modernity difficult to achieve and always subject to great debate and resistance.

Historian Daniel Pipes has suggested, for example, that half a millennium ago the three Abrahamic religions all restricted the charging of interest on finance, permitted forced slavery, and treated the sexes vastly differently. Many expressions of Islam continue today very much unaltered, while modernity has brought substantial evolution to Judaism and Christianity.

As unchangeable as is the *Koran*, so must the Muslim be. Since most of the texts present Mohammed and his behavior as ideal, there is little room to deviate. Furthermore, unlike other religions or spiritual practices that present themselves as private expressions of private choice, an adult Muslim is strictly forbidden to leave Islam. And as configured into state law in Saudi Arabia, Iran, Sudan and Somalia, the Muslim apostate who gives up his religion can face capital punishment. Modern-day Jews who frown on others entering Judaism, and Christians who value the individual choice to "accept Jesus," would find wholly unholy the injunction to kill or otherwise punish those who leave their religion.

Even more confounding, the *Koran* teaches that the other major religions were in fact originally Islam and that Jews and Christians distorted what was originally given to them. That is, the *Koran* recasts history to identify prophets including Noah, Abraham, Moses, and Jesus as those who actually gave their followers Islam. Hence Abraham was the first Muslim. The *Torah* was originally the *Koran*. Jesus is redefined not only as being mortal, but not even being the one who died on the cross. (Jesus also plays a major role in Shi'ite apocalyptic ideology. In it, the Twelfth Imam or Mahdi, the Islamic version of the Messiah, returns with Jesus, who exposes Christianity as false and Islam as the one true religion.)

Recasting Judaism and Christianity enables Muslims to claim consistency with, support of, and resonance with the other "Great Religions." It gives the veneer of substantial tolerance of them, while actually bearing little resemblance to them, much less offering any real acceptance of them.

There has long been a dictate to keep much of the life and history of Mohammed out of Western public sight. In particular, there is across Sunni Muslim tradition a ban against picturing their prophet. A consequence (and perhaps objective) of this practice has been to keep Westerners mostly ignorant of who Mohammed was. Today, one who is not Christian nor inclined to examine Christianity nevertheless absorbs a sense of who Jesus was by the innumerable images of and references to Jesus in daily life. Despite the occasional distortion in modern art, most non-Christians retain from these sources a sense of the story of Jesus as a forgiving healer and teacher who suffered greatly on the cross and ultimately was resurrected to demonstrate God's command over death itself. Other than the episode in which Jesus overturned the tables of the moneylenders in the temple, there is little evidence that anger, much less murderous impulses, played any role in his life, psyche or theology.

If asked about Mohammed, most Westerners would likely answer that he was equally benign—a pacifistic healer who lived a "spiritual" life in demonstration of similar principles of love and forgiveness. Mohammed's life, however, was very different from that. The prophet sought and wielded power as a leader, judge, legislator, and military commander. His life involved battles, lootings, murders, executions, and the eradication of rival tribes.

Any full and authentic depiction of Mohammed would show what today would constitute genocide, marriage to a nine-year-old girl, brutality, rape, pillage, torture, hatred, envy and many other acts alien to the biography of Jesus. We would see paintings depicting Mohammed leading raids. We would see Mohammed cutting off the hands and feet of men who had stolen camels. We would see him driving hot nails into the eyes of these thieves and leaving them to die from blood loss and dehydration in the hot desert. We would see Mohammed organizing the digging of trenches so that all 700 males of a Jewish tribe could be lined up, beheaded, and buried in a mass grave.

Sections of the *Koran*, the *Hadith*, and the *Sira* read like horror stories, and to visualize these passages would greatly amplify the shock. The ban on picturing Mohammed, therefore, has helped hide much of what would trouble non-Muslims about Islam.

Mohammed is celebrated as the ideal Muslim, so his acts are, by definition, to be imitated. Most modern Westerners presume that "religion" refers to a body of acts, traditions, rituals, and beliefs designed to enhance the believers spiritually while encouraging peaceful co-existence with all others. They suppose that religion, while mostly a private matter, endeavors to bring out compassion to do what is best for others and to do unto others that which we wish done to ourselves. Such values were foreign to Mohammed. He sought to annihilate those who posed any threat to the expansion of Islam or resistance to its commands. He took for himself that which he desired, and imposed an Islam-versus-the-world duality which sought, in large part, to either dispose of or convert non-Muslims rather than to find common ground and learn to live in mutual harmony.

Dhimmis were of value to Mohammed for the taxes they paid and the labor and knowledge they contributed. So they were tolerated as an inferior class. Nonetheless, this form of tolerance (echoed in apologists' statements like "Islam had in Al-Andalus its glory days where Jews lived with Muslims in harmony") bears scant resemblance to modern civil equality.

Abrogation: A Crucial Doctrine

Mohammed received his first revelations from Allah when he was 40 years old and living in Mecca. During the next 13 years, he tried to recruit those around him into his newly espoused religion, Islam. Since neither Mohammed nor Islam had any power, he could only try peaceably to persuade Christians, Jews and others to join him. Accordingly, some of his revelations during this "Meccan period," as recorded in the *Koran*, utilized compassionate, forgiving and merciful language and ideas that echoed and incorporated elements of Christianity and Judaism. Muslim apologists often refer to these passages when asserting that Islam is a "religion of peace."

Mohammed's final 10 years, however, were radically different. Having recruited only a small numbers of followers (from 70 to 150, depending upon the source), he moved to Medina where he was offered and granted full legislative, judicial, military, and religious power over all of the local tribes. Some of these tribes were primed for a Messiah's arrival by their own religious beliefs. Having obtained such unrestricted power, Mohammed's revelations from Allah during this "Medina period" changed from compassionate and tolerant to warlike and intolerant. Islam was to be spread as aggressively and effectively as possible, and *jihad* now came to more clearly mean a martial undertaking. Understanding both the Mecca and Medina periods is crucial to understanding our Islamic Enemy, for they show how Islam expresses itself one way when it is in the minority and in a completely different way when it has control or the power to obtain it.

The contrast between the Mecca and Medina periods helps shed light on the *Koran*'s apparent contradictions. When questioned by Westerners about hateful and murderous injunctions in the *Koran*, it is common for Muslim apologists to invoke other more loving, forgiving, or merciful passages as representative of what Islam truly "says." Dialogue often ends then and there, as Westerners know little about how to respond. A Westerner will often simply accept the apologist's retort because it is the comfortable resolution.

It is important, however, to understand the Koran on its own terms. Unlike the *Torah* or the *New Testament*, it is not a collection of stories in which the words of God are embedded. Rather, the *Koran* consists solely of the Revelations of Allah; these are Allah's "first person" words and commands. And while scholars and apologists can cook up sophisticated arguments about how to treat these contradictions, the *Koran* gives its own directive in a Sura or section that defines abrogation. Verse 2:106 Allah says, "Such of Our revelations as We abrogate or cause to be forgotten, We bring in place one better or the like thereof" (Picktal translation). Verse 13:39 Allah says "Allah doth blot out or confirm what he pleaseth: with him is the mother of the book." And in verse 16:101 Allah says, "When we substitute one revelation for another—and Allah knows best what he reveals in stages they say, 'Thou art but a forger': but most of them understand not."

Thus Allah himself provides the rule for resolving contradictions: The later revelation abrogates, or cancels, the earlier one. Allah expresses this as an improvement; he sends a better revelation to *replace*, not to co-exist with, what has come earlier. In short, in the event of uncertainty or confusion, the Medina commands abrogate the earlier Meccan ones. By its own terms the Koran should not be understood to contain any contradictions. And this, too, serves to limit those who wish to argue there are varied interpretations of and pathways to modernizing the Koran.

Abrogation is a major tenet of Koranic study as taught today worldwide—most importantly at Al-Azhar University, the Cairo center for Islamic studies whose scholars' opinions today (like those from the Vatican) carry the greatest authority across much of the Islamic world. Since the *Koran* describes itself as the immutable and final word of Allah, efforts to minimize or reinterpret its words are suspect. Rather, abrogation of the peaceable passages (some 114 verses speak of love peace, forgiveness, mercy, and so on) by the martial ones (roughly 123 verses about fighting and killing in submission to Allah) gives clarity to seriously engaged Muslims.

The consequences of these aspects of Islam, above and apart from the actual teachings of Islam, give it unique underpinnings. The emphasis on establishing Islamic totalitarian rule—by force when force is necessary and deemed likely to be victorious—is difficult to disguise. Islam carries within it these core values, and they form part of the belief systems of Islam's leaders as well.

Western dialogue about Islam is informative. We frequently hear and read in the media, as well as in political and private conversation, a proposition that resembles this: "Most Muslims are peaceful (good people, not terrorists, want the same things Westerners do . . .)." Basing their opinions in part on minimal contact with Muslims and statements made by spokesmen for Muslim organizations, along with their own great desire for it to be true, Westerners typically formulate their analyses of Islam-related issues on this presupposition.

Of course it is true that not all (or perhaps even not most) Muslims pose a threat. Most Muslims themselves, however, do not really know what their religion says, as Islam is taught in many non-Arabic-speaking territories, and Muslims often only learn what they have been told by local leaders. Many are Muslim by culture and identity, as opposed to being seriously engaged followers. Many Muslims presumably are not seriously engaged with the core concepts embedded in Islam. Perhaps if Muslims were given the freedom to choose their preferred life, many might opt for a Western lifestyle. Many who are entwined with the modern world tend to limit their engagement with religious practices of Islam and vice versa. Many who transact with the West appear able to relegate any Islamic activities to a more private nature, mirroring Westerners' ability to do the same with their religious behaviors. There is often some suggestion, for instance, that many Iranians and more economically comfortable Arabs throughout the Islamic world may prefer the American or Western lifestyle to rules imposed upon them by their respective regimes.

Decoding Labels

The labels we apply to Islam are also informative, because they obscure as much as they reveal. "Radical Islam," for example, denotes fanatics who have taken, their religion to the extreme, and therefore do not properly represent Islam. Again, Islam is presumed to be one thing, in this case peaceful and similar to Westernized religions, while the radicals distort it to justify their own violent and misguided purposes.

The label "Good Muslim" is often invoked as in, "Most Muslims are good and decent people." From the behavior of such individuals an inference is often drawn about the religion itself—that Islam too is good and peaceful. Yet as described earlier, Islam defines Mohammed's behavior as that of the perfect Muslim, and it is precisely that behavior that the so-called "radicals" seek to emulate. The reader is encouraged to read about the life of Mohammed, the *Sira*, in order to see the vast array of traits, acts, responses, and other characteristics of the Prophet that have become the model for the "Good Muslim;" traits, etc. very different from those that Westerners would label "good" or "peaceful." Thus, while Westerners are drawn to labeling the "peaceful" modernized Muslims as "good," Islam would call the "radicals" and "extremists" the true "good Muslims."

This twist surfaced when Osama bin Laden was given a Muslim burial, reportedly complete with over forty minutes of prayers praising him. (Interestingly, it is debatable whether burying bin Laden at sea when land was more readily available was proper in the first place). Obama said bin Laden was not a "Muslim leader" and many questioned whether that meant he was to be seen as representative of being a Muslim. If not, why the burial and the (at least partially) *Shariah*-compliant treatment of his body? In fact, many Islamic expressions would call bin Laden very much a "good Muslim."

Another Western distortion is embedded in the phrase "political Islam" and the related term "Islamism." These expressions endeavor to separate those who use Islam to guide political acts from those who practice it as a private and personal doctrine. While the distinction has a certain appeal, it attempts to take out of Islam what lies at its core. Islam is inherently political—Mohammed was a leader, legislator, judge, and commander and thus inseparable from what the West considers the "political" sphere. It is inherently economic too. Islamic law controls all aspects of economic life, forbidding the charging of interest, determining taxes and charitable obligations, and explaining how to divide conquered booty and the pay from converts—a primitive wealth redistribution plan. Hence it is difficult to argue that original "true" Islam was private and apolitical, as many Westerners secretly may wish to believe.

"Political Islam" in part attempts to reconcile the conflicting material in the *Koran* and *Hadith*. One such way to resolve, as discussed earlier, is by abrogation; the earlier principle is cancelled by the later one. A slightly different approach, as utilized by Bill Warner, asserts that there are essentially two Korans comprising a dualistic framework. One is religious while the other is political; Warner suggests that Mohammed was a failure as a religious leader but a success as a political leader. Even under this dualistic perspective, in which the contradictions are not to be eliminated but held simultaneously, the political can never be separated out of Islam.

Western defenders of the terrorist group Hamas employ a similar distortion. Muslim apologists have contrived to sell the idea that Hamas has a "charitable wing" and a "military wing." Accordingly, Hamas as a whole should not be held responsible for certain acts performed by the military wing. Westerners somnambulistically accepted this excuse, despite the fact that Hamas's charter makes clear its militant intent. Something similar is embedded in the attempt to separate Islam into a private religious (and presumably peaceable) "wing" and a political or Islamist "wing," while the "charter" of Islam (the *Koran* and other sources) declares clear intentions that apply to all aspects of Muslim life.

When Islam is seen as a totalitarian political ideology which prescribes rules for every area of life, and which aims to dominate the world, the Western notion of "religion" starts to fade. It is no coincidence that many if not most Muslim-majority countries live under some form of dictatorship or despotism. Ironically, while many of these regimes are at least partially secular (and are often despised by their seriously engaged Muslim subjects), they continue the hard-core demand for submission that Mohammed established. That is, Islam has embedded political and civil submission into its adherents' values; submission to what is a secondary issue. Regardless of the content of his revelations, Mohammed was able to use the "religious" aspects of his ideology to establish his political rule. Further, it is this "religious" covering—the assignment of all authority to Allah which has greatly contributed to Islam's longevity.

In contrast, Adolf Hitler, who developed substantial connections with the Arab Islamic world, made at least two critical mistakes resulting in the demise of his own global ambition. First, he launched far-flung military offensives before he had the ultimate knockout weapon—the atomic bomb (a mistake Mahmoud Ahmadinejad seems to be avoiding). As Andrew Roberts also argues in *The Storm of War*, Hitler put ideology above strategy both in marching into Russia as well as needlessly joining Japan in declaring war against the United States.

In contrast to Hitler, Mohammed was careful to contour Islam's commands to fit the relative power base he had assembled at any particular time. Allah commanded Mohammed to fight the Meccans *only* when he had the power to win.

Secondly, Hitler failed to place the ultimate power outside of himself Consequently, when he fell, Nazism all but disappeared. There was no future beyond him on which to place hope. Mohammed, on the other hand, never claimed to be God—he acknowledged his mortality, paradoxically ensuring the longevity of his movement by making himself the human ideal to be mimicked until Judgment Day.

Similarly, Mohammed's decisions were fallible and subject to challenge. This relates to the notion of Mohammed being the perfect Muslim. Jesus, being divine, could not fully be imitated as no one could perform the miracles he did (even though Jesus declared that those that those who follow Him will be able to do even greater miracles). Mohammed, on the other hand, was able to separate power and divinity from his own mortality, encouraging a subsequent and lasting following by serving as a model for what a human can do. Imagine if Hitler had formulated Nazism with a god and series of divine instructions delivered to Hitler and only Hitler, ordering his Nazi followers to do what Hitler did forever. Nazism would certainly present a far greater threat today than it does. (It is interesting to note that the area in which Nazism survived and even flourished to some degree following Hitler's demise was in the Arab-Islamic world.)

Like most charismatic leaders, Mohammed lacked the humility to designate a strong successor, a failing that sparked the schism between Sunnis and Shi'ites that persists to this day. Nonetheless, in large part because of Mohammed's success in placing authority outside himself in a form that would survive him, Islam has thrived. Meanwhile, by establishing himself as the last prophet, Mohammed could unilaterally determine and reveal the use of that power. Any discomfort from a difficult command, decision, or ruling could be alleviated by pointing to Allah. With slight exception, Mohammed could not be wrong except when he wanted or needed to change paths, in which case he could admit to confusion concerning a revelation. No one else, however, had the authority to challenge him because no one else had superior access to Allah. Wrapping what was essentially a full political ideology in religious terms and behavior gave him maximum freedom and support. Similarly, uncloaking Islam from its "religious" orientation as essentially political can be extremely meaningful and revealing for us.

"Moderate Islam" is another curious label. In one sense it suggests the opposite of what many users perhaps intend. That is, it can suggest that Islam "is" something more extreme and that the "moderate" version is something tailored and, consequently, less authentic. Yet, that is precisely the confession that those who most often use the term wish to deny.

Nonetheless, the term reflects a Western impulse to applaud behavior we wish to see while denying the foundational premise that Mohammed's behavior is the Islamic ideal. It suggests that core Islamic values lie in the middle of some presumed scale and therefore the extremes must be discarded. In Islamic terms, however, as with the label "Good Muslim," if any behavior should be called "core" it is that which most closely mirrors Mohammed's.

Nominalizing the wished for behavior of individuals to create an ideology makes no sense in this context. We would flinch if we heard someone refer to "radical" or "moderate" Nazism. We can talk of Nazis who were diehard believers, and those who joined the party only because they were forced to in order to remain employed, be accepted by their community, or simply to survive. We can be certain that Heinrich Himmler would describe a very different Nazism than would the hapless German in the early 1940s, who was only peripherally involved with the party, never wanted to kill another human, and would prefer the "whole thing" to go away. In either case, the principles of Nazism remain as expressed, regardless of one's relation to them.

Even Turkey's Prime Minister, Recep Tayyib Erdogan, has turned away from the phrase "moderate" Islam. In August 2007 he said, "These descriptions are very ugly; it is offensive and an insult to our religion. There is no moderate or immoderate Islam. Islam is Islam and that's it."[3] While many of us often refer to "moderate Muslims"—and there are large numbers of Muslims who shy away from acting in a "radical" manner or believing in any "radical" doctrine—it is difficult to point to any significant example of the actual institutionalization of such moderation. Indeed, while Muslims demonstrate different levels of commitment and dedication to *Shariah* law, many find the very distinction offensive. If "moderation" means "peaceful" and "tolerant," these words would seem to take on different meanings today from those expressed through much of Islamic history.

Curiously, the construct of "moderate Islam" has been intimately connected with the notion that most Muslims subscribe to such a moderate form of Islam. That is, "moderate" often carries along with it the proposition that it identifies the majority of Muslims. Similarly, "extremist" is most often employed to designate a small and hopefully inconsequential group of Muslims. While these terms seek to identify different forms of Islam, they more accurately refer to different levels of commitment and dedication to *Shariah*. Oddly, the same people who tried to claim that the "extremists" are few and represent a small number of "crazies" are often the same ones who like to argue that most Muslims around the world "hate" Americans.

Sacred Lying

Erdogan's bluntness is a rare event. When Westerners delude themselves about Islam, they should not count on Muslims to set them straight. Over the 14 centuries of Islam, deception has developed into a valuable and frequently used weapon, especially in territories where Muslims have little power or control. Islamic texts not only permit dissimulation, deception and trickery, they also sometimes command it. Deceit comes in many forms including the Shi'ite concepts of *taqiyya* (sacred deception and dissimulation), *kitman* (half-truths), and *khodeh* (trickery and deceit). *Adarorah,* meaning "the ends justify the means," has become the Sunni version for permitting or commanding deceit in order to protect the faith. *Taqiyya* will be used here as shorthand for all of these forms as it is the term is the most recognizable in the Western world.

These tactics emanate, in part, from stories of Mohammed. In one, the prophet desires the assassination of an enemy named K'ab. He gives permission to a follower, Bin Maslama, to deceive K'ab by claiming not to be Muslim—a lie that would otherwise bring fatal consequences under Muslim law. The phrase "*jihad* is deceit," from a strong Hadith, is deeply embedded in Islamic consciousness. And it thrives today among the many Muslim apologists who, by portraying themselves as opposed to violence or terrorism, mask deep devotion to Islam's true objectives.

As they generally apply in modern actions, *taqiyya* and *adarorah* give permission to lie whenever and wherever doing so would help advance Islam. After being convicted for his attempt to car-bomb Times Square, Faisal Shahzad was asked by the judge, "Didn't you swear allegiance to this country when you became an American citizen?" The *New York Times* describes Shahzad's response as a smile, "like a boy caught in a fib." The dialog continued:

"I did swear, but I did not mean it."
"You took a false oath?"
"Yes."
"Very well. Is there anything else you want to tell me?"

"Sure," he began, and went on to say, "Blessed be Osama Bin Laden,
who will be known as no less than Saladin of the 21st century crusade,
and blessed be those who give him asylum."[4]

This simple yet poignant example shows how deception weaves its
way into Islamic thinking while demonstrating how powerful a hold Islam's
history has on many seriously engaged Muslims. (No doubt similarly
deceptive oaths were part of the military career of Major Nidal Malik
Hasan, the Fort Hood murderer.)

(An interesting side note is that in Christianity and throughout Jewish history a martyr has been one who suffers death rather than violate
religious precepts; one who tells the truth in the face of torture and inquisition. *Taqiyya* or "sacred deception" essentially alleviates this challenge
for a Muslim by becoming a command or permission, allowing him to
escape such torture so long as his "heart [is] remaining firm in Faith"
[16:106]. Martyrdom in Islam, instead, permits dying in the act of mur-
dering)

Nor is lying reserved for terror acts in the Violent Jihad. Raymond
Ibrahim has reported in Frontpagemagazine.com 6/17/11 how high level
Muslim Brotherhood leader Sobhi Saleh lied on television about not knowing another guest would join him. When the host repeatedly called him
on it he swore to Allah that he was telling the truth. Finally, he was
ultimately understood to be lying and the host reprimanded him for swear-
ing to Allah when lying. Nonetheless, this example over trivial circumstances highlights how the license to lie so long as it furthers Islam is so
easily and widely used.

The mandate for deception in Islam is matched by an equally powerful mandate for truth. Muslims are prohibited from speaking falsely about
their faith. This injunction gives many Muslims difficulty in providing
what many Westerners want to hear: condemnations of terror and assurances that *jihad* is not a core duty of Islam. In an exchange in 2010 with
the writer David Horowitz, a Palestinian woman steadfastly refused to
deny that she supported Hamas or to distance herself from a leader who
had called for Jews to be annihilated everywhere. Her resistance ema-
nated from her belief that she would be killed by Hamas for doing so.
Similarly, Imam Feisal Abdul Rauf during the Ground Zero Mosque
controversy repeatedly declined to answer whether Hamas or the Muslim Brotherhood is a terrorist or extremist organization. Instead he side-
stepped saying, "The issue of terrorism is a very complex question . . .

I do not want to be placed, nor do I accept to be placed in a position . . . of being put in a position where I am the target of one side or another."5

While deception is one response of Muslims to this call, others find great difficulty in denying the Violent Jihad and the duty to further such Jihad. The obligation to speak truthfully about Islam has been fundamental throughout Islamic history and can be brutally enforced. Muslims often live in tremendous fear that other Muslims will declare them blasphemous or apostate for failing properly to define or describe Islam—a long-established principle called "Takfir." Many Muslim communities throughout the world are organized to promote these fears in order to preserve their base.

It must be understood that Islam is typically embedded in a community context. There is often a local mosque (or mosques) with leaders through whom much of the community is taught and informed. As inducement to attend the mosque, Mohammed said that prayer in the mosque is rewarded 25 times more than a prayer offered at home or at the market. Consequently, great power is vested in the imams and other local leaders such that any condemnation by them easily spreads, promoting fear throughout the community. Speaking out against Islam or the interests of the leaders in any fashion often results in alienation and worse. This fear typically generates a passive and quiet community which, in turn, fortifies the leaders' power. Hence, little dissent is likely to be heard from Muslims absent great individual courage.

The West Creates Its Distinctions

Most crucially, the use of terms such as "moderate" and "radical" is not part of Islam itself. If Muslims do not think of themselves as "moderate" or "radical," then why should the distinction exist? It reflects efforts by non-Muslims to understand—ultimately to be able to control—Muslim behavior. Behind each term, though, lie questionable presuppositions. Westerners typically use "radical" simply to connote a willingness to engage in violence, while "moderate" suggests "non-violent" or less violent. In the media and elsewhere the use of the distinction suggests that between "radical" and "moderate" there is a great distance. "Moderates" are sophisticated, emotionally integrated and modern; "radicals" are emotionally immature, less educated and somewhat backward.

Thinking this way is dubious at best. It betrays the Western tendency to assume that the only threat Islam poses lies with terrorism or violent acts, understandable given the shock of 9/11 and other horrors. Terror, however, is merely a tactic, albeit a central one which the Koran seems to abet as in verse 8:12, in which Allah declares he will "strike terror" in the hearts of the unbelievers. It is only one of many ways in which the Muslim may serve Allah and Islamic law. By itself, it does not differentiate Muslims.

Westerners should know this. It is interesting that many correctly point out the inadequacy of the phrase "War on Terror" by noting that it is difficult to battle against a tactic. Yet these are often the same people who subscribe to the notion that a Muslim who is not a terrorist is therefore a peaceable follower of a tolerant faith. That is a dangerous presumption, especially today given the realities of most expressions of Islam and given that the Violent Jihad is only one of three levels upon which the West is threatened.

Believing that "radicals" constitute only a few percentage points of the estimated 1.2 to 1.6 billion worldwide Muslim population gives many Westerners a subliminal sense of comfort. It invites them to split off and project their fear and anger onto the "radicals" while preserving their positive feelings for the "moderate." However, a closer look reveals that the moderation of the vast majority is dubious at best. We frequently are warned that we must not act in any provocative or hostile manner toward Muslims, as that is likely to be used as a "recruitment tool" in radicalizing Muslims. Common sense ought to tell us that if drawing cartoons of Mohammed, or resisting the construction of the Ground Zero Mosque, or publishing photos of bin Laden dead would radicalize Muslims, there must be very little difference or distance between the "moderate" and "radical" to begin with. If the "moderates" are that susceptible and easily persuadable, there is little comfort to be taken in the belief that they would truly align with the West.

Consider again the proposition that "Most Muslims are peaceful and want what we want." Westerners are quick to agree that the statement is true. Yet it is unclear what it actually means, much less how one would prove it to be true. Polls conducted in the Muslim world are often of questionable validity. A test for "peacefulness" (what it means, how to measure. . .) is highly problematic and, given the nature, doctrine, and history of Islam, difficult to trust. Those few polls that have received coverage typically stun the West with how many Muslims support terrorism, the actions of 9/11, and the return of a Caliphate. While the proposition is often used to quell fears in Westerners, it becomes dangerous when it begins to create categories and becomes embedded in Western analyses about Islam.

Over time, the phrase "moderate Muslim" tends to be used to designate a Muslim one in the West need not fear. It is a label to dispel resistance, at best confusing and at worst dangerously deceptive. When any form of that proposition is uttered, one should immediately question the goals of the speaker. Accuracy will typically not be high on the list.

The Allegiance of the Masses

"Peacefulness" has no place in the analysis of former Muslim Dr. Mark A. Gabriel, an educator and writer who studied and taught at Cairo's Al-Azhar University before seeking religious asylum in the United States. A well traveled Egyptian who has memorized the *Koran,* he is familiar with the full spectrum of Muslim beliefs, cultures, and behaviors. Gabriel categorizes Muslims by focusing on degrees of commitment to *Shariah* and other elements of the traditional core of Islam. The emphasis is on *Shariah*, not Western standards for religious behavior.

In one of his books, *Culture Clash: Islam's War on the West*,[6] Gabriel talks in terms of four designations. "Liberal Muslims," which he estimates comprise five percent of the Muslim world, are typically highly educated, do not follow traditions, and desire that Islam be reformed. "Ordinary Secular Muslims" are Muslim primarily by culture. They have little understanding of their religion but strongly identify with it. Gabriel suggests they may constitute 70 to 75 percent of Muslims worldwide.

Gabriel's third category is "Committed Muslims." Members of this group have a deep understanding of Islamic law, desire to see it established in significant measure worldwide, and make a great effort to live by it. Their defining characteristic is that they have not made a full commitment to all of *Shariah*, such as the cutting off of hands for theft, capital punishment for apostasy, mandates of *jihad*, and so on. Gabriel suggests Committed Muslims comprise, perhaps, 15 to 20 percent of Islam worldwide, but account for much higher percentages in repressive countries such as Egypt and Iran.

Finally, Gabriel estimates that the rest, up to five percent, are "Radical" in the sense that they wish to see all of Islamic law applied worldwide and make themselves available to act toward that objective. The Radical wishes to follow Mohammed's dictates and way of life as well as all of Allah's commands of *jihad*.

Gabriel's construct does not account for various "Islams"—radical, moderate, political, and so on. Rather, it categorizes Muslims' various relationships with *Shariah*. While *Shariah* itself is not singular (there are at least four Sunni schools of law and various embodiments of Shi'ite law among others), this approach goes a long way toward giving us clear vision of the threat we face. What is most compelling about Gabriel's analysis is that Committed and Radical Muslims comprise 25 percent or more of the worldwide Muslim population—300 to 400 million people—roughly equal to the total population of the United States. He sees the Committed Muslim as one who knows the Radical is living appropriately and thus, under the right circumstances and pressures, can be easily converted into a Radical. Even more sobering, if Muslim birthrates of recent decades continue, the estimated world Muslim populations of today (1.5 billion Muslims comprising roughly 25% of the world's population) might well grow comprise 40% of the world's population by 2025. Demographic growth is one of Islam's most potent weapons.

This categorization certainly lends a disconcerting and sobering perspective, especially when one realizes that when the time comes for Muslims to choose sides, the commands of Islam make it difficult for *any* Muslim to turn his back on the others. Only a small percentage of Germans and Soviets were zealous Nazis and Communists respectively but when they secured the tools of power they were able to control vastly greater numbers. Many, if not most Germans might have preferred to avoid any conflict, but once World War II broke out, most found it difficult to turn away from the Nazis. Indeed, if any secular or liberal Muslim is forced to choose sides, it is more than likely that he, too, will fall into line with the rest, especially if protection is needed or victory appears possible. In fact, such loyalty is so fundamentally commanded by virtually all expressions of Islam, that one who failed to fall in line would not be able to call himself Muslim. "When you are called (by the Muslim ruler) for fighting, go forth immediately" (Bukhari, 4:52:79 and 42).

We see this pressure manifest already in the fact that many Muslims have difficulty denouncing terrorist groups. Games are often played in which Muslim apologists will renounce violence against "innocent civilians" or even "terrorism" in general. They are often holding back a parenthetical "out," however, as they either will not consider most non-Muslim civilians (particularly those in formerly Muslim lands) truly innocent, or are prepared to use a strained definition of "terrorism" which excludes Muslims acting within their duty of *jihad*. While there has been more than a millennium of debate throughout Islam over whether and when force may be used offensively (and not merely in defense of Muslim lands), these lines are crossed whenever necessary. For example, 9/11 was considered by al-Qaeda and others "in defense against" America's invasion of Saudi Arabia by its having posted troops there. Similarly, all of Israel is frequently deemed an acceptable target under similar reasoning used by Muslim Brotherhood spiritual guide Yusuf al-Qaradawi and others. To many Muslim clerics, no Israeli is considered an "innocent civilian."

In lands controlled by non-Muslims, Islamic communities place even greater pressure on what members should or should not say. Community representatives generally do all the talking. In America, as many as 80 percent of the mosques appear to be under the control of Muslim Brotherhood-associated groups and funded by Saudi Arabia and others in exchange for a commitment to spread Saudi- and Brotherhood-dictated expressions of Islam. In a peer-reviewed study[7] of 100 mosques in the United States conducted by the Center for Security Policy's David Yerushalmi and Mordechai Kedar, it was found that 81% promote *Shariah* and essentially incubate *jihad*. 58% invited imams known to promote Violent Jihad as guests and 51% had texts on site rated as severely advocating violence. This creates an extremely pressure filled environment with which it is difficult to disagree. Western leaning Muslims who publicly speak their minds or attempt to promote "moderate" views face extreme ostracism or worse.

Other critics have followed Mark Gabriel's lead. Andrew McCarthy, Frank Gaffney and his "Team B," Stephen Coughlin and many others have all zeroed in on the underlying goal of advancing *Shariah* as the critical characteristic marking our potential enemies. This approach will likely be refined over time. Yet it goes a long way toward providing a powerful lens in the search for those who are hostile to the West.

The Language of Islam

Obviously, 1400 years will produce a rich variety of interpretations and meanings of words. Different words such as *jihad*, for instance, will take on different connotations and nuances when defined in one culture, school of law and time period versus in another. Time can also differentiate shades of meanings as a word's usage purifies along with the development of the cultures in which it is use. This is simply how language and meaning evolve. Nonetheless, core concepts emerge with words over time. And critical to the Control Factor analysis, many vital words take on different meanings when used in the West as opposed to within Islam.

The idea of "peace" in Islam, for instance, is very different from that used in the West. In Islam "peace" can come only in the future when Islamic law rules the world. It is in this sense that Muslim apologists are able to speak of Islam as a religion "of peace" as that is its end goal. Yet the meaning differs profoundly from common Western usage, which envisions peace as conflict-free co-existence in the present. For Muslims, peaceful co-existence with non-Muslims is a temporary state that can last only until Islam is able to fully assert itself and eliminate any control by infidels. Just as Mohammed would enter into only a 10-year peace accord in his famous Treaty of Hudabiya—an agreement he broke two years later once he had assembled enough power to conquer Mecca— Muslim thought places little value on long-term accommodation with non-believers. "Peace" for seriously engaged Muslims is only a tactic for winning the ultimate war.

Thus while the West looks with great excitement at the possibility of peace between Israel and the Palestinians, leaders of Hamas and Fatah argue over how such a "peace" might fit within their mutual plans for the eradication of Israel.

In his documentary *Farewell Israel,* filmmaker Joel Gilbert explores the meanings of two Arabic words for "peace." *Salaam* generally denotes the absence of conflict, as in a truce whereas *sulha* means full reconciliation and more closely resembles Western concept of "peace." Gilbert shows that Arabs use the former to describe their conflict with Israel because there is no place in Islam for the latter—ultimate reconciliation. Even former Egyptian President Anwar Sadat, when making his "peace treaty" with Israel, avoided any reference to true reconciliation or *sulha*.

While the more than thirty-year "peace" or "truce" between Egypt and Israel has been of enormous mutual value, its frailty is visible in the wake of Egypt's recent revolution where threats of tearing up the treaty are now frequently bandied about. For the first time since the Camp David Accords, Egypt has opened the Suez Canal to two Iranian warships. And since Egypt controls the supply of natural gas to Jordan, we may also see Egypt blackmail Jordan into repudiating its own treaty with Israel. More than one month after the Egyptian gas pipeline into Israel (which also serves Jordan, Lebanon, and Syria) was blown up and subsequently repaired, gas has still ceased to flow regularly. Egypt has already opened its border with Gaza, a border it had worked with Israel in the past to control. In Israel's neighborhood "peace," especially between Muslims and non-Muslims, by Islamic definition, is fragile.

Any "real peace" between Muslims and non-Muslims will likely suffer the same frailty. As Bernard Lewis writes, "According to the jurists, the natural and permanent relationship between the world of Islam and the world of the unbelievers was one of open or latent war and there could, therefore, be no peace and no treaty."[8] Against this backdrop, the words become more understandable. Between Muslims, *Sulha* suggests full reconciliation following a temporary dispute. Thus, a husband and wife can reach reconciliation which is intended to last unconditionally. Any *Sulha* with non-Muslims, however, is always conditional and limited; conditioned upon Muslims becoming strong enough to reset terms and limited in time.

Imam Feisal Rauf, the original front man for the proposed Ground Zero Mosque, underlined this distinction in a letter to *The New York Times* in 1977. Commenting on Sadat's visit to Israel, Rauf called on fellow Muslims to "give peace a chance." But he alerted them to the critical message from the Prophet Mohammed, "After a state of war with the Meccan unbelievers that lasted for many years, he acceded, in the Treaty of Hudaybiyah, to demands that his closest companions considered utterly humiliating. *Yet peace turned out to be a most effective weapon against the unbelievers* (italics added)." Just as Mohammed used the peace to rearm, so do the Palestinians during recesses between "Intifadas." Added Rauf prophetically, "In a true peace it is impossible that a purely Jewish state of Palestine can endure . . . In a true peace, Israel will, in our lifetimes, become one more Arab country, with a Jewish minority."[9]

The imam's assertion is of a peace with what filmmaker Gilbert calls the "Diplomatic Strategy against Israel."[10] As Gilbert shows in his documentary, Jordan's King Abdullah proposed acceptance of Israel in 1947 because it would position the Arabs to take control later. Gilbert also cites Cecil Hourani, adviser to the former Tunisian President, who in the mid-1960s advocated three objectives: containment of Israel by territory and demographics, weakening and "de-Zionizing" Israel, and the final transformation of Israel into a Muslim state. It is this formula, according to Gilbert, that guided Egypt and Sadat subsequently and gives context to Islamic talk of peace that so often confuses the West.

Indeed, Gilbert goes on to show how the Camp David Accords between Egypt and Israel carried a different meaning for each side. With Israel and the West, the hope was for full reconciliation leading to permanent mutual tolerance.

For Muslims, however, a different context is given. In 1977, Israeli President Menachem Begin sought to trade the Sinai which it had captured in 1967 back to Egypt for "peace." Sadat subsequently traveled to Israel to make a historic speech in front before the Knesset. At prayers the night before, his mission is described "the journey of salaam." What Sadat says the following day is that he is looking for a "permanent peace based on justice." The words *peace* and *justice* are coupled no fewer than seventeen times. "Peace can not be worth its name unless it is based on justice." Critically, what many in the West did not understand is that "justice" here means full compliance with Islamic law.

What would "justice" entail? Sadat made it clear: the complete withdrawal of Israel from Arab territories acquired after 1967, including Arab East Jerusalem, and the creation of a Palestinian state with the full right of return for all Palestinians. Meanwhile, he declined every opportunity to affirm Israel's legitimacy as a state. And showing the true intent of the long term plan, Sadat made the traditional offering of *dhimmi* status Islam requires to conquered Jews saying, "We accept to live with you in permanent peace based on justice. You want to live with us in this part of the world? In all sincerity, I tell you, we welcome you among us with full security and safety." Jews heard this as a negotiating ploy in a simple land-for-peace transaction. Muslims, however, heard it as a first step toward regaining the territory called Israel.

These are the goals. While Sadat eventually entered into the Camp David agreement in which he accepted much less, at the signing he never mentioned "peace;" he never called for *sulha*; he simply suggested *salaam*, that there be "no more war."

The war between believers and non-believers does not cease until it ends as described in the *Koran* and the *Hadith*—with total victory after the last Jew has been killed. Mohammed frequently referred to *jihad* as the "unfinished battle." *Jihad* is similarly described in the 1979 Pakistani military treatise, *The Quranic Concept of War*, as "a continuous and never-ending struggle waged on all fronts including political, economic, social, psychological, domestic, moral and spiritual to attain the object of policy. It aims at attaining the overall mission assigned to the Islamic State, and military strategy is one of the means available to it to do so. It is waged at individual as well as collective level; and at internal as well as external front."[11] And today our Islamic Enemy is saying it clearly and loudly.

To put it succinctly, the inevitable outcome for those who do not want or value peace is war. And while countries such as Jordan and Egypt have enjoyed decades-long peace accords with Israel, their interlude of peace is in large measure a result of having been brutally defeated in conventional warfare by Israel. There is much evidence of the frailty of peace should conditions change in the surrounding Arab-Islamic world, including the unrest leading to the ouster of Egypt's President Mubarak. Peace may rapidly vanish should Israel no longer appear to have overwhelmingly dominance, either in conventional warfare or war through other means.

"Freedom" is another concept that differs significantly, and seemingly irreconcilably, in its meanings for Islam and the West. To Westerners it represents the ability of the individual to make critical decisions in his life and to accept responsibility for their consequences. Freedom in this sense discourages blame and victimhood.

By contrast as Joel Gilbert shows, "freedom" for many Muslims means the escape from the tyranny imposed by foreign unbelievers. The opposite of "tyranny" is "justice" which, as we have seen, means the guidance of Islamic law. Tyranny is also sometimes described as *jahiliyyah* or "ignorance of Allah." *Jahiliyyah* is ultimately to be transformed into the "freedom" to submit to Islam and *Shariah*.

This difference underlies the tension witnessed during the Cairo protests over President Mubarak's rule. While many Westerners saw in the protesters a desire to mimic and embrace the West's notion of freedom of the individual, at least some Egyptians, including those of the Muslim Brotherhood, were demanding something very different altogether: freedom from the tyranny of Mubarak and the opportunity to live in a *Shariah*-dominated community.

Seen through Western filters, this is not freedom but subjugation. Yet to many Muslims spiritual fulfillment and relief are to be found in submission to decisions dictated by Allah and the Ummah, not those determined by the individual. To be clear, "Islam" means "submission" and when given the choice, seriously engaged Muslims see freedom in submission. This is part of the reason why Islamist candidates have enjoyed overwhelming success in Middle Eastern Islamic nations where democratic elections have recently been introduced. As the Islamic world begins to experiment with different elements of democracy, it is necessary to remember that what *freedom* means to Muslims is not what it means to most Westerners.

On 6/9/11, scholar Andrew Bostom elaborated on this difference when describing that following the Egyptian revolution, Muslim Brotherhood leader Mohammad Badie confessed that the Brotherhood intended to form a political party called the Freedom and Justice Party or Horeya and Adala.[12] "Horeya," Arabic for "freedom," Bostom's post tells us, differs greatly from Western notions of freedom and means "being perfect slavery" to the demands of Allah. While the West expects (or hopes) individual freedom of choice and democracy to emerge from the Arab Spring, Islam provides no choice at all for the individual to decide his ultimate political arrangement; Allah does that.

And as *democracy* itself plays an increasing role in the Middle East, its usage becomes even more telling. To many in the West, it refers to a complete system of liberal institutions that function not only to assess the will of the people but to ensure that it is protected and carried forward. It refers to a deeply entrenched and relied-upon system for allowing people to voice their wishes while securing through legislative and judicial machinery the means to protect and manifest those wishes.

Yet to others, "democracy" simply refers to the mechanism of elections. As various Muslim nations experiment with democratic systems, they tend to import this more simplistic notion. They recognize that Islamic law and history often place serious emphasis on "consensus," but it is a far cry from the complex tradition of liberal Western democracy. Rather, it is Allah, as voiced through *Shariah*, who establishes law, not man.

It is worthwhile to examine Andrew McCarthy's analysis in *The Grand Jihad* and other writings of the connections between Islam and the Far Left. To summarize, McCarthy sees the origins of the connections in similar devotions to a collective or general will—for Muslims expressed through *Shariah*, for the Far Left as expressed through Jean-Jacques Rousseau's "social contract," and in both cases, "social justice." In short, freedom in both cases is essentially the freedom to submit to the state, since *Shariah* embodies the state, and is at complete odds with the individual liberties guaranteed by the Constitution of the United States.

Uncertain Before Allah

Another subtle yet powerful notion in Islam has to do with future certainty. Regardless of any "sinful" behavior in this life, other religions and practices typically afford followers the ability to see a pathway to future peace, either with or without God. Christianity, in many of its modern formulations (excluding Calvinism, for instance), offers redemption through the acceptance of Jesus as savior and relief from guilt through confession, indulgences, and other traditions. Judaism offers rituals of atonement and other repentant acts to address the guilt for any sinful behavior of its followers, always holding out the possibility of God's forgiveness. Eastern religions provide similar functions to assuage guilt that man inevitably generates and experiences.

Islam, by contrast, is markedly short on forgiveness. While Mohammed's early teachings sometimes refer to a compassionate and merciful Allah, *the god who hates* is overwhelmingly dominant, as made clear by Wafa Sultan, a non-religious Syrian Muslim psychiatrist who chose that phrase as the title of her book.

Worse, Muslims are born into an agony of uncertainty. A Muslim is taught that his fate is fixed at birth yet will remain unknown to him throughout his life. Simultaneously, he is taught to seek Allah's favor and obey Allah's laws despite his predetermined fate. This affords little comfort that anxiety or guilt can ever be assuaged.

There is, however, one clear escape from this psychological bind: death as a martyr in *jihad*. Verse 4:74 says "Let those who sell the life of this world for the Hereafter fight in the cause of Allah. To him who fighteth in the cause of Allah—whether he is slain or gets victory—soon shall We give him a reward of great value." Dying in *jihad,* in the service of Allah, is a guarantee—the only one—of avoiding the horrors of hellfire and of gaining entry into paradise. While many non-Muslims are tempted to explain the recruitment of terrorists by the external circumstances of their lives (poverty and lack of opportunity for education, advancement, marriage or sexual fulfillment), Islam's ability to induce anxiety necessitating a pathway to relief may be the strongest motivation and one which goes unexamined. To a Muslim in difficult circumstances, whether physical or psychological, with little certainty about his future and some deep sense of guilt, dying in *jihad* can easily become a fitting solution. It certainly sheds light on the susceptibility of those steeped in Islamic beliefs to various forms of martyrdom.

War to the End

Islam divides the world's territories into two "Houses." The territory controlled by Islam is called "The House of Islam" ("Dar al-Islam"). The rest of the world is called "The House of War" ("Dar al-Harb"). Infused throughout Islam is the notion that it is perpetually at war. This "War of the Houses" has been raging since Islam's inception, and has gone through two great periods or "jihads." The first began with Mohammed, and by the end of Islam's first century Dar al-Islam covered more territory than the Roman Empire at its peak. The second *jihad* reached its peak in the 1600s with the Caliphate of the Ottoman Empire, after which Dar al-Islam began a 400-year decline.

When Islam has the power to advance, it does so. When it lacks power, it effectively puts the war on hold until it can be successfully resumed. Islam's renewal over the past century has caused some to argue that a "Third Jihad" is in progress today. Unlike modern Western cultures, Islam functions on such a long-term time scale that the war is never finished. And most seriously engaged Muslims have a palpable sense of time and history which informs their vision.

As Sheikh Ahmed Yassin, founder of Hamas, once said, "We have to be patient because Islam will spread sooner or later and will have control all over the world. Patience will shorten the journey of Islam."[13] That journey finishes only when the world has been fully subjugated to Islam.

Islam often obtains control of territory through violence. In the words of Frank Gaffney and his Center for Security Policy's Team B writers, the prior stages can be reframed as "pre-violent" times awaiting the proper power to obtain victory through violence. Alternatively, Islamic literature frequently refers to the "unfinished battle" which conveys an endless preoccupation with a war not completed until final triumph.

Furthermore, by defining defeats as setbacks rather than losses, Islam designates territory that was under Islamic control at any time as Islamic land *forever*. The House of Islam has stretched from Spain to India and beyond at various times. (Possession, having occurred at least once, is 100% of the law for Islam forever). Accordingly, significant parts of Europe and elsewhere are considered Islamic, despite the long absence of Muslim control. This notion underlies the calls by many Muslim leaders and terrorists to "reclaim" Israel as well as European lands that were at one time Islamic. This amplifies the martial essence inherent in the War of the Houses, which cements many Muslims into the perspective of never-ending war.

The aggressive force we face today is predominantly an Islam governed by a violent set of ideas and beliefs—an Islam that despises Western ways and seeks to restore the "sanctity" of Allah and his wishes throughout the world. Replete with hatred, intolerance, envy, deception, and grandiosity, it mandates the resumption of war whenever the balance of power shifts in its favor. None of this can credibly be denied.

Additionally, there are the Islamic expressions that appear on the surface to turn away from violence. While these expressions seem to dovetail nicely with Western concepts of peaceful and private religious experiences, many could not be further from that truth. Instead, as part of the Civilization Jihad, such expressions, including those uttered by infiltrators of the West and America under the Muslim Brotherhood umbrella of organizations (CAIR, ISNA, MSA, etc.) referred to in the Holy Land Foundation trial as "unindicted co-conspirators and/or joint venturers," share the same goals as those which utilize violence. The difference is one of strategy and appearances, not of substantive ideology, objective or aspiration. At their cores and in their hearts, these apparently "peaceful" expressions are ruthless, vicious, and lethal to our American way of life.

Most expressions of Islam carry with them these core aspects that can make it difficult to integrate with a Western society; these elements cannot be wished away by Western minds. Islam has positioned itself to take advantage of its different moral foundation. In simple terms, Western Civilization moved in large part from "An Eye for an Eye" to "Turn the Other Cheek." In contrast, Islam's core ideas move it back to "Submit or I'll Slit Your Throat."

Islamic true believers who seek to destroy the West and impose *Shariah* worldwide through a central Caliphate or Imamate pose a real, immediate, and serious threat. Many other Muslims who in their current circumstances would not choose to be at war with the West, would nonetheless fall in behind the Islamic forces if conventional war broke out. Loyalty to Islam reigns supreme for all seriously engaged Muslims, and the dangers associated with being labeled non-Muslim (Takfir) are too intimidating for many Muslims to deny. As *Koranic* verse 4:115 states: "And whoever contradicts and opposes the Messenger (Muhammad) after the right path has been shown clearly to him, and follows other than the believers' way, We shall keep him in the path he has chosen, and burn him in Hell—what an evil destination!"

Indeed, as Dr. Gabriel suggests and most Westerners wish to believe, few Muslims are active terrorists and many hopefully do not wish to see Western society destroyed. While it is difficult to get a clear sense of numbers of those who truly pose a threat to Western Civilization, numbers are less relevant when destruction can be so easily created today by so very few. To be preoccupied in searching for numbers is itself a trap. The fact that the many Muslims living under strict authoritarian rule fear to speak out publicly, and the important role that deceit plays in the Muslim world, both make a meaningful investigation virtually impossible. Rather than count numbers, we should ask why we feel numbers are so important. For even if we can believe the numbers are small, can we rest comfortably in the certainty that there is no true threat?

Nor is rigorous categorization necessary. Those who pose a threat, Islamists, Salafists, Twelver Shi'ites, al-Qaeda, Wahhabists, and the like, are our enemy because they have declared themselves to be so. It is not our responsibility to define or number them—it is theirs. To be clear, our enemy is not Islam per se—in part because the construct "Islam is . . ." has little utility for us. Rather, we face an enemy that, under the banner of Islam, seeks to destroy what America and the West hold dear, and to force what remains of the West to submit to *Shariah.*

Some Westerners wish to believe our enemy consists of very few, while others see it as uniting large numbers. Those who have been comfortable with the terms such as "jihadi enemy" assume that the threat is limited to participants in the Violent Jihad and disregard the greater numbers active in the Civilization Jihad and the International Institutional Jihad. Whatever the numbers, whether a tiny band of 12 individuals or a community of more than one billion, whatever the method of categorization, the Muslims who threaten us and identify themselves as defenders of Islam and enemies of the West are, for purposes here, appropriately identified as *our Islamic Enemy.*

Chapter 3

Two Battlefields and America's Inner Jihad

Since 9/11, Americans have questioned whether Islam is a "peaceful" religion. Many have accepted the idea that it is.

This conclusion is in no way easy to reach. It is the product of wishful thinking, fear, and denial of abundant evidence to the contrary. Those who wish to believe Islam is like all other religions must explain to themselves why *jihad* is a core duty for all Muslims. The word means "struggle;" in the *Koran* and throughout Islamic law, literature and history, with few exceptions, it refers to the struggle to spread Islam and Islamic law. It is so central to Islam that it is often referred to as the "sixth pillar," alongside—and more central than—prayer, pilgrimage, fasting, charity and declaring the *Shahada*, the affirmation that "There is no God but God and Mohammed is His Messenger."

In seventh-century Arabia, most struggles were military and violent in nature. Accordingly, *jihad* refers almost universally throughout the *Koran* and *Hadith* to a martial and violent effort to ensure the spread of Islam. Establishing and securing *Shariah* is the essential duty of *jihad*, and historically violence has been the primary method of executing that duty. There is, to be sure, a concept of *jihad* by *dawa*—spreading Islam via proselytizing and peaceful conversion. There is also, as witnessed today, *jihad* via peaceable infiltration into a non-Islamic culture until such time as enough power is accumulated to effect a takeover. This is the "Civilization Jihad," or as author Robert Spencer labels it "Stealth Jihad." Others have used phrases including "Gentle Jihad," "Soft Jihad," or "Pre-Violent Jihad." By any name, "Civilization Jihad" aims quietly to use the freedoms of a culture in order eventually to gain enough power within that culture to usurp and eventually destroy those very freedoms, with the ultimate goal of establishing *Shariah*.

Across 1400 years of Islamic history, *jihad* has been defined in multiple ways. Nonetheless, the essence of *jihad* (and the essential feature of its many family resemblances) is the struggle to make the unbeliever or *kafir* ultimately submit to Islamic law. Bill Warner calculates that 64 percent of the *Koran* is devoted to "unbelievers." Throughout Islamic history, Muslims have offered the kafir the choice between death and submission whenever they had the power to do so. For "People of the Book" (Jews, Christians, and, later, Zoroastrians), submission could also be accomplished by accepting the diminutive *dhimmi* status and all that it entails, including paying a special *jizya* tax and enduring extreme humiliation. Essentially, by accepting *dhimmi* status, the *kafir* agrees to submit to Islam in exchange for his life (not unlike a mafia-imposed protection scheme).

When Muslims have little power, they often refer to all non-Muslims as "brothers" or *kuffar*. (Some uses of *kafir* and its plural, *kuffar*, exclude People of the Book, as well as those who "mistakenly" misbelieve. It is used here, however, rightly or wrongly, to include all non-Muslims). When Muslims have controlling power and the Islamic hierarchy is in place, however, certain non-Muslims become *dhimmis*, and all cease to be "brothers." The institution of *jihad* may extend to include any act that advances this submission, so that giving money to jihadi charities, or spreading deceptive ideas of Islam, or converting *kuffar* through persuasion can each satisfy the Muslim duty to *jihad*. Nonetheless, the overwhelming use of the term *jihad* throughout Islamic law and history has been martial and violent.

Muslim apologists and deceivers, however, try to convince Westerners that *jihad* refers instead to each individual's spiritual struggle to control his thoughts, beliefs, appetites and lusts. (This definition does apply credibly within some small Islamic groups such as Sufis and Ahmadis). This spiritual definition is based chiefly in a single obscure utterance in the sayings of the prophet Mohammed, a text that is considered to be "weak" or of limited authority. (Even Muslim Brotherhood founder Hasan al-Banna said this was "not authentic hadith.") In this *Hadith*, the Prophet, having successfully returned from battle, is said to have stated that now that the *lesser jihad* (the battle) is won, it is time to face the *greater jihad*, or internal spiritual work. In other words, while battling the unbelievers has been important, the real struggle lies in combating temptations in our minds and bodies that divert us from full devotion to Islam.

Inner discipline is certainly a core idea in all religions and spiritual practices. And it is certainly true that Muslims, like all believers, must fight their own internal resistance to the ideas and rituals that define their faith. In this sense of course, *greater jihad* is a meaningful component of the overall concept of *jihad*. But it is hardly the dominant concept. The story is used to disguise the fact that the overwhelming use of *jihad* is the martial concept of battling the *kuffar* to spread Shariah, not the self. Bill Warner estimates that *jihad* is used in connection with war in 97 percent of the Bukhari Hadiths, with only 3 percent in any sense connected to the spiritual struggle with one's self. There is no mention of such *greater jihad* in the *Koran* at all.

There is, however, indeed a central role for this concept *for us* as a reminder that there are two interdependent battlefields upon which we must fight:

1. The physical, often military, battle with our enemies over territorial and legal control and,
2. The internal, mental battle with the parts of ourselves that harbor our fears and distort our perceptions and beliefs.

The second, internal battlefield is the focus of this book. It is where we must confront our own terror, the fear that impels us to treat our Islamic Enemy as benign and deny the threat it presents.

It has become fashionable to criticize the phrase "War on Terror" as it appears to be a fight against a tactic on the physical battlefield and fails to address the more subtle and often more effective ways of spreading Shariah.

The phrase is fully appropriate, however, on the internal battlefield as it describes the battle we all must engage. *We must make war against our own internal terror.*

Operations on these two battlefields must be complementary in order to be most effective and efficient. Rather than run away from and be driven by terror, we must learn to face our fears directly and look beyond them with clarity. This is the "Inner Jihad"—the struggle properly to direct what transpires in the theater of our own minds—and it must be fought constantly and courageously so that we may wage the external or physical war that lies ahead.

Although Muslim apologists claim that *jihad* directs Muslims to look inward, that injunction is most needed today by Westerners who have focused so much on the external world that we have lost the balance and anchor we need in our internal worlds. The Inner Jihad we must fight in our own mental theaters is unfamiliar to us. Most of us simply think our thoughts without awareness or introspection. Our thoughts run constantly and commingle with our interactions with the world. Most often, our thoughts run *us*. Psychotherapy cultivates an awareness of thoughts to strip them of the power they can hold over us. Similarly, many spiritual practices, particularly in the Eastern disciplines, attempt to slow the mind and detach us from our thoughts in order to free us from their limitations. The Inner Jihad aims to do the same in the face of a true real-world threat.

The true "War on Terror" is the one we must fight within our own minds. It lies in stark contrast to the approach often taken to date designed to teach us that we have nothing to be afraid of. This is the approach proffered by many on the Left in the West: dismiss our fears rather than confront them. Instead, we must dismantle the mental obstacles that keep us from being aware. We must battle the Control Factor and live with, respect, and learn from our terror, so that we can marshal its force to help defeat that which truly threatens us. Courage, the old adage says, is not acting in the absence of fear, it is acting despite and along with fear. We must seek not to avoid our terror but, rather find ways to confront our enemy despite and in full recognition of it.

America's approach to the Inner Jihad must be diligent, not unlike that of a devotee of any spiritual practice. Our minds, beliefs, thinking patterns, and styles of emotional response must be monitored and stalked aggressively in order to train ourselves to remain on the path. The Inner Jihad, or struggle on the inner battlefield is essential in order to refine and define the focus necessary to adequately confront the challenge that our Islamic Enemy brings to us on the external or physical battlefield. It is a key to victory.

Chapter 4

The Horror Film

Imagine the progression of Islam's modern interaction with the West as an archetypal horror film. In horror films, there is some form of threat— a monster, a virus, an alien, an oversized animal, or simply a human gone mad. The critical characteristic of the threat is that it seeks our complete submission or destruction and its nature precludes reasonable or rational compromise. In short, it has no *conscience* in the Western sense of the word, and experiences no moral dilemma in bringing about our demise.

The typical horror film also has a specific and recognizable arc. Much of the beginning of the film is spent familiarizing the audience with the normal life of the key characters. Rapport is carefully built between the audience and the main characters, in part by displaying the characters' flaws as a prelude to their coming into play later when difficult moral choices need to be made. The main character often has a scarred past, some significant failure, emotional wound, or ethical shortcoming, revealed in the service of establishing the character as "human."

The film slowly introduces evidence of the particular threat that will create the drama. We may see people dying of an undetermined cause or suffering damage from some unknown animal, disease, psychotic killers, environmental force, and so on. While the audience knows a threat lurks, the characters are initially oblivious to the extreme challenge to their existence that lies ahead. Worse, an active effort is made to ignore the early evidence, explaining the initial violence or destruction as part of the status quo and normal daily expectations. Meanwhile, the characters attempt to continue their daily lives as usual.

The violence intensifies as the film progresses, bringing with it with greater shock and surprise. The characters typically split into factions, each having different ideas, beliefs and explanations of what is actually occurring. Some characters remain oblivious and insist nothing out of the ordinary is happening. They are the early victims. Others notice something is wrong but have little motivation to figure out what is happening, much less do anything about it. Others convince themselves there is nothing to be concerned about and demean those who are worried.

Eventually others zero in on a specific source but believe the threat is harmless and attempt, in vain, to interact with it. Others start to grasp the danger but underestimate the threat's danger and ability to destroy. They employ ineffective weapons or other measures and are readily eliminated themselves.

Other characters attribute familiar values and motivations to the threat and attempt to appease, negotiate with, or persuade it to give up on its nature or goals, only themselves to meet with rapid death.

While the audience understands the gravity of the situation, much of the film depicts the struggle of the characters to accurately perceive and then to fully assess and accept what they face so that they have a chance of developing effective responses. At a certain point, the characters must accept and *admit that they do not know how to fight* the threat before they can effectively embark on a path to adapt and learn. That realization and admission alone generates great panic among the characters but is a necessary step in developing any adequate response.

It is this delay in awareness, understanding and comprehension that creates dramatic tension. As the film proceeds, the threat adapts, evolves, and progressively learns how to overcome the barriers and defenses that the characters have put in place. As the threat closes in on the main characters, the horror ratchets up. If the threat is a being, it may start to invade the characters' personal space. If it is a biological threat, it may enter the main characters' actual bodies. Meanwhile, the characters remain foolishly blinded to the full dangers they face. They are consistently "behind the curve" in securing their own safety which creates the core of the horrific drama.

The tension in the movie focuses on whether the characters will wake up in time to take advantage of whatever resources remain available to them. The frustration the audience feels is amplified by the fact that had the characters understood what they faced earlier, they would have been better prepared to handle it.

Even more terrifying, in the typical horror film, the threat cannot be assuaged with civilized practices. The threat frequently does not speak our language or understand our ways. There is no way to communicate, plead, or negotiate with it. Familiar civilized solutions become no solutions at all. Rather, in a well-executed film, the threat is so implacable and relentless that the characters (and, by identification, the audience) can never rest comfortably; they can never get control of their circumstances or destiny.

Metaphorically, we are engaged today in the initial scenes of our own long-term global horror film with its own threat—our Islamic Enemy. From one angle, the threat lies with certain Muslims and their activities. From another angle, the threat appears as a virus of thought, embedded in certain expressions of Islam, which spreads by various means to those believers whose "immune systems" have been compromised and whose ideological genetic makeup can be activated under the proper conditions. What drives the horror film is the experience of being out of control. Similarly, this notion that we are not in control of the threat posed by our Islamic Enemy is devastatingly disruptive to the American mind and is what necessitates the Inner Jihad.

The horror film typically builds upon this tension until a critical point is reached, the key point moment that marshals an all-out fight or survival. More on this later. Meanwhile many of us are still struggling to perceive the threat clearly, going through many of the stages common to such films. Our film is real, however, and the need to understand the Control Factor and all that it does to keep us from that critical moment is why the call for our Inner Jihad is urgent.

Part II

The Control Factor

Chapter 5

The Control Factor—Paths of Denial

While watching the horror film, the audience understands that the suspense will be over within a few hours. Knowing there is a time limit to the tension and an eventual end to the film allows the audience to succumb more easily to it and become absorbed in the terrifying experiences.

Not so with a real threat to our security. In fact, it is extremely difficult for the American mind to remain in such a state of insecurity, danger, and terror that our Islamic Enemy poses. Instead, our minds are geared to eliminate as efficiently as possible any horrifying experience and re-establish the sense (or illusion) that control exists or is obtainable. That part of the mind tasked with eradicating the experience of losing control is labeled here "the Control Factor." While we are inclined to regard our perceptions and beliefs as passive, the Control Factor is something we do; it is an active and creative process. It is also a process that is ongoing and constantly re-occurring; just when one thinks it has been subdued it tends to spring back into action. When challenged, the Control Factor will seek to combat any obstacle and keep its perceptions and beliefs alive.

Consequently, our "Inner Jihad" is our individual battle against our Control Factors and all of the ways in which they operate in our mental theaters.

The Control Factor logic is premised upon a relationship between the physical world and our internal mental states. Since a stable external world helps steady and calm our internal worlds, we unconsciously presume that the converse is true—that easing our minds will help stabilize the external world. Many of us spend most of our time unaware that there is even a difference. Our internal stresses and emotional dramas often stem from the ways in which we perceive and interpret the world. And these stresses can in turn influence our external-world interactions. We may not realize that while reality creates perception, perception, in turn, helps create reality. Much of the challenge of psychotherapy and spiritual practice concerns learning to distinguish between the two, to disentangle them when necessary, and, ultimately, change one to better influence the other.

Our minds are programmed to protect the perceptions and beliefs with which we navigate the world. We weave narratives, storylines, and "histories" to solidify these understandings and establish a sense of security. When these protective or defensive ideas are seriously threatened, the result is fear, alerting the system that there is a challenge. And the human mind is capable of tolerating only a limited amount of fear.

The Control Factor operates independently of and is not a measure of one's "intelligence." People of very different levels of education and IQs are equal targets for the Control Factor. In fact, it is often the brightest who are best able to generate new and creative ways to assist the Control Factor in keeping themselves and those who listen to them oblivious to the threat immediately in facing them. Consequently, those who do see and face the threat are often bewildered by how so many supposedly "brilliant" people—from the educated "elite" to media voices to politicians to university professors and so on—are completely unaware of the most obvious danger around them. Further, "intelligence" becomes a tool of the Control Factor: "if this or that educated and articulate person fails to be concerned about the threat, why should I?"

The Control Factor mobilizes a panoply of psychological defenses against this fear, including the many "D's": Denial, Distortion and Delusion, to name a few. In an overarching sense, all Control Factor tools are forms of denial. The Control Factor fills our minds with premises, presuppositions, beliefs, images, and narratives that deny the reality of the threat we face and the fear it causes.

The critical attribute of the Control Factor is that it is an *active* mechanism. We prefer to believe we are passively perceiving and interpreting ideas and events as they arise, but familiarity with Control Factor maneuvers shows us just how complicit our minds are. Ultimately, we must awaken to these processes and assume responsibility for them.

To battle our Control Factors, we must become aware of its many weapons, tactics, and strategies. Brief examples of each defense or maneuver can help us understand the power and pervasive influence of the Control Factor. Some maneuvers will strike the reader as familiar, while others may seem foreign or abstract. Each individual's Control Factor employs the particular tools it needs.

It is intended that the experience of reading through an assortment of Control Factor mechanisms will enable the reader to develop a perspective from which he can more easily become aware of his own Control Factor. These specific categories and examples are meant chiefly to guide the live process of recognizing one's own Control Factor at work.

Denial

While all Control Factor maneuvers constitute some form of "big D" denial, the denial of simple facts is perhaps the most obvious and common process. When Osama Bin Laden gave his warnings before 9/11, or when Mohammed Abed al-Salem—who founded the Palestinian al-Jihad in the early 1980s—warned in his book, *The Missing Commitments*, that "the Islamic invasion is coming to Rome,"[1] most looked the other way and never registered the threat.

More recently, as the Egyptian revolution of 2011 progressed, many Americans, including high-level policy makers, believed the Muslim Brotherhood to be a welcome peaceful organization that would contribute to positive change in the Arab world and relations with the United States. Yet just months earlier, the new Brotherhood leader, Mohammed Badie, stated (as quoted in Barry Rubin's article entitled "Muslim Brotherhood Declares War on America: Will America Notice?"):[2]

> Arab and Muslim regimes are betraying their people by failing to confront Muslims' real enemies, not only Israel but also the United States. Waging Jihad against both of these infidels is a commandment of Allah that cannot be disregarded.

The CIA's budget is how much?

Various types of denial can link together in progression. There is an overarching sequence of denials that employs a variety of perceptions of our Islamic Enemy. One may first presume that Islam does not say or stand for what it manifestly does and, consequently, ensure that he never investigates Islam itself.

Next, one may deny that Islam has anything at all to do with the multitude of terrorist acts committed around the world. This kind of denial was evident during the infamous Beltway Sniper shootings in fall 2002 in and around Washington, DC. Immediately after snipers John Allen Muhammad and Lee Boyd Malvo were arrested, we learned they were Muslims. Shortly after that, we learned they had made many statements in support of *jihad* and the 9/11 terrorists. Almost as soon as this horrifying information became public—that a pair of Muslims had, just one year after 9/11, indiscriminately attacked and killed innocent Americans—the Council on American-Islamic Relations (CAIR), aided by a media establishment that was already deeply limited by its own Control Factors, warned the public not to assume that Islam had anything to do with the killings, despite all the evidence to the contrary.

Following the arrests of Muhammad and Malvo, CAIR's Nihad Awad quickly issued this ludicrous statement: "Police reports indicate the suspects acted alone, based on their own motivations. There is no indication that this case is related to Islam or Muslims. We therefore ask journalists and media commentators to avoid speculation based on stereotyping or prejudice. The American Muslim community should not be held accountable for the alleged criminal actions of what appear to be troubled and deranged individuals."[3]

Despite the snipers' statements, and later graphic jailhouse drawings in which they clearly demonstrated that they were acting as Islamic-inspired terrorists, the public bought this explanation with simple-minded ease. So thoroughly did the Control Factor work in the case of the Beltway Snipers that to this day it is widely believed that they were just two disgruntled men living on the edge, isolated gunmen with family problems that set the stage for their murderous spree. Even evidence presented, gathered during their trials, which showed that the snipers had been sheltered by jihadi groups in the United States with numerous ties to terror, merited no more than passing mention in the media.

Another stage in the sequence of denials consists of sweeping conclusions that no matter what Islam actually commands, it must be reinterpreted to mean something else today. Christianity and Judaism have modernized, after all. Since Islam too is a religion, and a "great" one as well, it presumably must have had its "reformation."

The tendency is to believe that there could not possibly be that many Muslims who subscribe literally to Islam's commands, and that "extremist" or "radical" Muslims cannot organize in any meaningful manner.

There may be terror attacks, even extreme ones such as 9/11, but these are separate criminal acts to be handled in precisely the manner Attorney General Eric Holder insists—within our criminal justice system. Further, there is a tendency to believe that those committing such acts can never succeed in their political aims against the strong law-and-order nations of the West.

Denial is often "flagged" by language we use. Ordinary "if only" constructions, for example, often accompany the fantasy that the Islamic threat is controllable: "If only Bush had not been president. . . ." "If only we engage the Islamic enemies and show them our peaceful intent. . . ." "If only we had demonstrated respect for our allies. . . ." "If only we would eliminate the root causes of Islamic hatred towards us. . . ." "If only the Israelis weren't so belligerent. . . ." and so on.

The critical function of these "if only" propositions is to assign blame to America, Israel, or George W. Bush, making them the causative agents who are in control. We take comfort in declaring that we have caused the current situation because such a declaration implies that we can therefore change it. That is exactly what the mind needs to believe in order to maintain its stability. Hearing the phrase "if only" should always set off an alarm that some Control Factor move that shifts responsibility is at work.

A similar linguistic "give-away" is the phrase "needs to." How many politicians, pundits, and media personalities will say "Iran needs to understand this or that" or "China needs to understand that Islamic terror is a threat" or "Mubarak needs to resign" and so forth? These statements show arrogance on the part of the speaker for presuming the subjects do not actually understand the matter at hand. More importantly, the moment the speaker makes such claims, he temporarily comforts himself with the thought that once the subject does what he "needs to" do, the threat will abate. The language provides the illusion that control is obtainable.

As with the early scenes of the typical horror film, America for years ignored Islamic terror abroad, dismissing it as a "foreign affair." Then, after 9/11, many took comfort in denying that there was any real threat beyond that presented by a small group of criminals hiding behind an Islamic banner. Indeed, recasting Islamic terror as criminal activity has animated much of the US response. By doing so, President Obama and Holder are returning us in large part to our pre-9/11 state: denial of the dangerous war in which we are actually engaged.

Perhaps the most elemental denial lies in simply ignoring the enemy's words. Disregard for the *Koran*, the *Hadith,* and the formal texts of Islamic law as well is all too familiar. For 30 years, the Islamic Republic of Iran has announced it is at war with America and seeks the elimination of the State of Israel. Arguably the most influential anti-Western "Islamist" of the twentieth century, Muslim Brother Sayyed Qutb, has made clear that Islam's central war for 1400 years has been with the Jews and other non-believers who have been enemies of Muslims since the beginning of Islam. Many fatwas, including those issued by Osama bin Laden, have also declared war on America and the West. Westerners typically just close their ears. When pressed, they attribute alternative meaning to the words. Some insist the words are exaggerations and do not reflect real intentions. Others say the words are nothing more than "tough talk" from terrorists—suggesting that those who truly understand the subtleties of diplomacy know to discount such displays.

"Slay them (the unbelievers including Jews and Christians) wherever ye catch them," the *Koran* states in verse 2:191 (Ali). It is but one of many commands used to incite war against non-Muslims. And in verse 9:5 (Ali): "Then fight and slay the pagans wherever ye find them, and seize them, beleaguer them and lie in wait for them. . . ." Verse 8:12 (Pickthal) adds, "I will throw fear into the hearts of those who disbelieve. Then smite the necks and smite of them each finger."

The 9/11 attacks were an obvious manifestation of the Koranic command "to strike terror into (the hearts of) the enemies of Allah" Verse 8:60 (Ali). Yet in the aftermath of the attack, with evidence to the contrary, President Bush used language suggesting Islam is not what it declares itself to be. "I believe that Islam is a great religion that preaches peace,"[4] he said to Al Arabiya with the World Trade Center rubble still smoldering in the background. He appealed to Muslims not to let "the propagandists hijack their religion to murder innocent people."

Similarly, Osama bin Laden's 1998 fatwa against the United States could not be clearer: "The ruling to kill the Americans and their allies—civilians and military—is an individual duty for every Muslim who can do it in any country in which it is possible to do it."[5] These are plain, simple and loud proclamations made by those who follow Mohammed. Only the Control Factor's masterstroke—denial—makes this difficult to comprehend.

Many Westerners likewise ignore the charters and writings of Palestinian factions such as the PLO, Fatah and Hamas, which explicitly call for the destruction of Israel, and the words of the Prime Minister of Malaysia, who regularly denigrates Jews as the deceitful rulers of the world. The same avoidance occurs when Muslims in America declare that Islam will conquer the land and *Shariah* will rule, or when Muammar Qaddafi states that Islam needs no weapons to conquer Europe within decades, as demographics alone will do the job. The same is true of events across the Islamic world, where Westerners refuse to pay attention to the words of their enemy, particularly those made in the enemy's own language to his own constituents. This avoidance is pure early-stage horror film behavior.

What is more, while the Islamic Republic of Iran pursues development of nuclear weapons, we completely disregard the very words of the Preamble to that nation's own constitution.[6] A section qualifying its armed forces reads:

An Ideological Army
In the formation and equipping of the country's defence forces, due attention must be paid to faith and ideology as the basic criteria. Accordingly, the Army of the Islamic Republic of Iran and the Islamic Revolutionary Guards Corps are to be organized in conformity with this goal, and they will be responsible not only for guarding and preserving the frontiers of the country, but also for fulfilling the ideological mission of *jihad* in God's way; that is, extending the sovereignty of God's law throughout the world (this echoes the Koranic verse: *"Prepare against them whatever force you are able to muster, and strings of horses, striking fear into the enemy of God and your enemy, and others besides them"* [8:60]).

Similarly, the Preamble makes clear the intent to expand *Sharia* globally:

Islamic Government
The plan of the Islamic government as proposed by Imam Khumayni at the height of the period of repression and strangulation practiced by the despotic regime, produced a new specific, and streamline motive for the Muslim people, opening up before them the true path of Islamic ideological struggle, and giving greater intensity to *the struggle of militant and committed Muslims both within the country and abroad.* (italics added)

And later in the Preamble:

> With due attention to the Islamic content of the Iranian Revolution, the Constitution provides the necessary basis for ensuring the continuation of the Revolution *at home and abroad* (italics added). In particular, in the development of international relations, the Constitution will strive with other Islamic and popular movements to prepare the way for the formation of a single world community (echoing the Koranic verse: *This is your community, a single community, and I am your Lord, so worship Me* [21:92]), and to assure the continuation of the struggle for the liberation of all deprived and oppressed peoples in the world.

Denial preys on our inability to realize that in a post-Enlightenment world we do not know how to deal with a large, powerful, well-financed, and politically astute effort to destroy America as we know it and transform it into a *Shariah*-based Islamic nation. The lessons from the Cold War are largely inapplicable, especially in an America that has substantial progressive multicultural/pluralistic tendencies. With Soviet-style Communism, there was a locatable center that could be held responsible for its operations. The absence of a centralized Islamic state, or of a Caliphate, has been an advantage for the enemy, because there is no fixed base against which to retaliate. And while our Islamic Enemy shares a unified overarching goal, there is great disunity among its many factions and sects. In the Cold War we employed a mutual-assured-destruction strategy that does not apply well to our Islamic Enemy. There was an address for the Communists to which a response could be directed, and an organization with a hierarchy from which to obtain responses. This is not true of Islam today. We have limited experience with this type of enemy. Denial deeply embedded by the Control Factor leaves us all but blind to the fact that there are no easy or comfortable answers to the three-level Jihad that is being conducted against us.

To some extent, we know how to conduct police operations to confront terrorist bombings. More than 10 years after 9/11, we have been able to thwart dozens of potentially large-scale acts of terrorism through good pre-emptive police and investigative work. Some of the failures of terrorist acts have been due to a combination of citizen alertness and the relative incompetence of terrorist actors like the "shoe bomber" of 2001 and the Times Square bomber 2010. More significantly, we are blessed with many brilliant, hard-working, expert law enforcement personnel who have performed magnificently.

Our criminal justice system is able, in certain cases, to deter and penalize some of those who act against us. For example, the Times Square bomber, Faisal Shahzad, was quickly brought to justice and sentenced to life in prison just a few months after his attempted bombing. Nonetheless, our justice system cannot adequately handle the complex issues that our Islamic Enemy forces upon us. The difficulty that even President Obama has encountered in closing the Guantanamo Bay facilities makes this clear.

We also know how to launch Navy SEAL operations to kill Osama bin Laden and conduct a "Surge" in Iraq when we reach a political consensus that permits us to do so. Our sophisticated military, unmatched in the world, is able to engage and overrun an opposing military and has shown at times great success with counter-insurgency and counter-terrorist techniques. It can also help disrupt domestic terrorist activities.

Yet, as discussed elsewhere, reframing the dangers that face us to fit into such categories helps create the illusion that we can effectively confront them all. What we consistently deny is the larger picture—that none of these defenses are adequate to confront and combat the true threat of our Islamic Enemy. At his sentencing in October 2010, the Times Square bomber warned Americans, with a smirk: "Brace yourselves, because the war with Muslims has just begun."[7] Americans still do not know how to respond to this sort of clearly expressed threat, and that generates such intense fear and panic that the Control Factor is immediately summoned to quell those feelings.

Distraction and Deflection

Distraction is another simple but potent technique we use to insulate ourselves from the severity of the threat we face. On a mundane level, some of us are simply unable to stay in a conversation about any Islamic threat. We change the subject, hang up the phone, or walk away. The Control Factor works in so many ways that these responses often escape notice.

Even George W. Bush, who of currently living presidents appeared to understand best the true nature of our Islamic Enemy, encouraged distraction in the wake of the 9/11 attacks. "Go shopping," he urged the nation, in an attempt not merely to show the enemy that he had not succeeded, but to distract Americans and deflect their attention from the horror of the deeds. As will be seen with most defenses, they create exactly what they set out to avoid. By encouraging us not to let the "radicals" disrupt our lives, Bush (and the Control Factor) ultimately led us to even greater disruption later.

Apologists for Islam often use distraction when confronted in conversation with evidence that Islam is other than the "peaceful religion" they suggest it is. How often do we hear someone respond to an inquiry about the nature of our Islamic Enemy by drawing an irrelevant analogy? "Well, Bush did the same thing," or "It was our CIA that created al-Qaeda," or "America/Israel is occupying their lands." An oft-used tactic has been to refer to the 1995 Oklahoma City bombing, the one modern terror incident in which a connection to Islam has yet to be sufficiently demonstrated and accepted. This move was used extensively during the 2011 House of Representatives hearings on Muslim radicalization; many who objected to the hearings argued that since the Oklahoma City bombing of 1995 did not involve Muslims, it is "racist" and discriminatory to connect terrorism to Muslims. (It is unclear how this is "racist" as being Muslim has nothing to do with race). An inordinate amount of time in the hearings was wasted on demagoguing this very claim. Muslim apologists and those steeped in denial frequently divert a conversation by asserting there is no connection between terror and Islam because there seemed to be none in a particular case.

Irrelevant analogies to the history of the Catholic Church and Judaism are yet another way to divert substantive discussion about Islam. We hear references to the Crusades, the Inquisition, murders in the name of Christ, God's commandments for the killing of the Amalekites in the *Torah*, and more. These references are used as debating strategies so that current concerns about Islam can be ignored. For example, Osama bin Laden frequently applied the term "crusader" to modern-day Christians, and by extension, Americans, implying that their goal is to impose a Christian dictatorship on Muslims. With this claim, he and his followers sought to distract us from seeing their own plan to impose an Islamic Caliphate—a situation in which the ostensible "crusaders" become the real victims of an Islamic "crusade."

Distraction is also used on a broader policy level. Despite Iran's having clearly stated that it is at war with America, and, despite its connection with most of the world's terror attacks since the beginning of the Khomeini revolution 30 years ago, America has consistently focused its attention elsewhere. The media and US government have tended to separate the struggle with the Iranian government from those with terrorist groups such as al-Qaeda, Hezbollah, and Hamas, partly because of the fiction that the sectarian conflict between Sunni and Shi'ite Muslims bars their working together against common enemies, specifically the United States and Israel. This ignores the fact that Hezbollah is an Iranian creation and that Iran has made substantial contributions in recent years to Hamas.

Iran's connections with al-Qaeda, and specifically with 9/11, have been largely ignored in the media. The 9/11 Commission Report touched briefly on the links. Unfortunately, the Commission came across critical evidence just days before the publication of its report. While it stated that "a senior Hezbollah operative visited Saudi Arabia to coordinate activities there"[8] and that this operative shared flights in and out of Iran with some of the 9/11 hijackers, it addressed the evidence primarily by calling for further investigation by the government into Iran-al-Qaeda- Hezbollah coordination.

While the government has yet to proceed, a federal lawsuit brought by victims of the 9/11 attacks in the Southern District of New York (Havlish, et al. v. bin Laden, et al.) has pushed the inquiry further. Critical evidence surfaced in the case which had not been thoroughly examined by the 9/11 Commission according to reporter Ken Timmerman—specifically a six-page classified analysis which "referenced 75 distinct source documents, including electronic intercepts, the crown jewels of US intelligence gathering at the time." While the Commission did not have time to review these documents, Timmerman concludes they had led President Bush to remark about Iran: "They're harboring al-Qaeda leadership and we've asked that they be turned over to their respective countries."[9] (Timmerman also notes that Bush backed his CIA director in asserting that there was no "direct connection" between 9/11 and Iran.)

According to the lawsuit (in which three 9/11 Commission staff members submitted affidavits and evidence from three former Iranian intelligence officers never reviewed by the Commission was entered), Iran allegedly used Hezbollah operative Imad Mughniyah and others to assist in the planning and preparation for the 9/11 attacks as well as to assist al-Qaeda leaders to escape from Afghanistan in the face of US post-9/11 attacks. Other assertions include: Iran has been aiding Sunni organizations since the beginning of the Islamic Republic in 1979; Mughniyah and a high-level Iranian Revolutionary Guard officer traveled to Sudan to meet with bin Laden; Mughniyah trained al-Qaeda operatives in the

1990s in special camps in Lebanon and Iran; the 9/11 plan was based on a pre-existing Iranian plan to use planes to attack US buildings. Iran's involvement was expressly approved by the nation's Supreme leader and overseen by his office, the intelligence ministry, and the al-Quds Force of the Revolutionary Guards. Iran had installed flight simulators for the aircraft used in the attacks and provided training, weapons, money and other support for future terror operations. While this is only one side of the evidence, the case has been in the courts since 2002. Nonetheless, the Control Factor prefers to distract us and cause us to continue to perceive Iran as a threat distinct from, and even expressly at odds with, al-Qaeda.

More recently, in March, 2011, with Tunisia, Egypt, Bahrain, and Syria in upheaval, the Obama administration avoided direct observable involvement, much less military action. Instead, it opted to take limited military action in Libya. The engagement was framed in terms of a "humanitarian" effort to save civilians from anticipated slaughter from Libyan leader Muammar Qaddafi, even though the most vulnerable "civilians" were active revolutionaries, allegedly including al-Qaeda and Muslim Brotherhood operatives. While Obama's policy seemed disjointed—taking action in Libya and remaining on the sidelines elsewhere, it seemed that Libya afforded him the opportunity to establish a precedent for the future use of the "Responsibility to Protect Doctrine" that members of his administration created and so highly favored. This doctrine, which advocates intervention when a ruler is abusing his people, requires the approval of the international community. Hence, for Obama, he can turn over US policy, and consequently sovereignty, to the UN and other international organizations: if the Arab League approves, as it did with Libyan intervention, the US will proceed. Critically, it will provide Obama with an excuse for not taking action elsewhere—the international community did not approve. Meanwhile, as Libya absorbed public attention and US and NATO resources, the nation's attention was deflected from the more dangerous and threatening changes occurring in Egypt and elsewhere. Great drama can be generated by the dethroning of a regime (be it that of Saddam, the Taliban, Mubarak, or Qaddafi) yet attention quickly fades with the more difficult work of stabilizing the country.

A more subtle Control Factor distraction tactic is to become consumed with the search for "root causes" and "explanations" of terrorist behavior. The national media follows this path every time there is an act of terrorism or extreme violence. When US Army Major Nidal Malik

Hasan, a Muslim psychiatrist, went on a shooting spree at the Fort Hood Army post in Texas in 2009, killing 13, he shouted "Allahu Akbar!" as he pulled the trigger. He identified himself on his calling card as a "soldier of Allah" and frequently proselytized for Islam. He had given classroom presentations in which he described suicide bombers as heroic, suggested that Muslim soldiers should be released as "conscientious objectors," cited Koranic verses such as "And whoever kills a believer intentionally, his punishment is hell" (4:93). Yet pundits almost immediately found reasons other than Islam for his rampage, blaming it on his fear of being deployed to Afghanistan and being compelled to fight against fellow Muslims. He was "alienated" from the Army and society, CBS News reported. He may have been taking "Army-administered medication,"[10] the Huffington Post explained. Many explanations were floated, but when Hasan's stated goal of jihadism was mentioned, we were warned against "jumping to conclusions" and admonished to look elsewhere for causes.

Reasonable-sounding connections can be made between violent acts and poverty, lack of education, hopelessness and so on. However, the terrorists who have emerged to date have mostly been educated and middle class, people who certainly had reason to hope for a bright future. Yet some apologists, such as University of Chicago professor Robert Pape, go so far as to assert that there is little relation between terrorism and Islam, in particular extremist interpretations of Islam. In a 10/18/10 *Foreign Policy* magazine article entitled "It's the Occupation, Stupid," Pape postulates instead that suicide bombings are caused by US occupation and oppression.

Of course, various important correlations can be drawn between specific factors and the many who voice rage at the West and America; and there are many who do. Some point to Arab populations enlarged by the demographics of youth who are disoriented by the interaction of a modernized world with traditional cultural values; especially as these youths travel and use the internet and become more aware of the rest of the world. Sexual frustration among men who are unable to secure a marriage necessary for sex is also described. Much is also written about the lack of meaningful political institutions in the Arab world other than those controlled by corrupt rulers who have taken the country's wealth for their own and distracted revolt by focusing attention elsewhere on Israel or America. Everything politically "modern," from socialism to nationalism to secularism that has been tried has failed and when the

West engaged, it left the Arab world with Israel and war torn territories unable to lead themselves forward such as in Afghanistan after the retreat of the Soviet Union. What was "modern" is deemed "Western" and, worse, "American."

The consequences of these frustrations, envy, and political emptiness are often argued to be a rush to the benefits that "fundamentalism" brings. These include a manageable simplicity to the burdens and responsibilities of modernity, an opportunity to voice political objection under the protection of religious claims where political parties are otherwise forbidden to exist, and a path to success, identity, and meaning. The structure of these ideas is to suggest that the "root" causes of the threat we face with all its power and rage really emanate from something other than Islam; instead, Islam, an otherwise flexible, tolerant, and workable body of ideas and principles, is twisted and "hijacked" both intentionally and/or unconsciously, to solve these seemingly larger and more powerful challenges. "If only" we could have the clarity to see and the maturity and motivation to act, we could, through assisting the Arab world, pressing moderation, and creating conditions for political institutions that recognize dissent, solve the conditions of their rage and the supposed abuse of Islam would disappear from lack of need.

In fact, the opposite argument has merit. Expressions of Islam can be plausibly considered as the cause of poverty, ignorance and minimal opportunities throughout much of the Islamic world. Corruption pervades in many of the political structures. Capital is used to pay for weapons at the expense of other services. Sexual repression and the abuse and domination of women are major contributing factors. Bans on musical and artistic expressions and, to a large extent, comedy (especially self-effacing humor) compound the oppression. Koranic injunctions to turn away from the materialism of "this world," subordinating individual advancement to the demands of the faith and community can all be argued to be "root causes" of the dissatisfaction of many Muslims worldwide.

Imam Feisal Abdul Rauf, of Ground-Zero-mosque notoriety, has argued that Islam's ban on interest and usury has much to do with why Islamic-controlled nations generally have been less developed than those in the West. Additionally, while oil has made many Arab-Islamic countries rich and brought their economies into the modern world, it has done so at major cost: the so-called "Oil Curse."

Excluding Islam from this "root cause" analysis is the work of the Control Factor. Simply put, Islamic expressions are so intimately tied up with the many cultures throughout the Arab world (and other Islamic controlled territories) that it is senseless to think in terms of addressing "root causes" apart from Islam in its many expressions. More importantly, the relevance of these "explanations" lies not in their truth or falsity but in their usefulness as distractions. They serve mainly to obfuscate the simple fact that Islam is the central organizing principle at work. Instead, the fantasy goes, "if only" we address these "causes" of Muslim woes, we can regain control over the terror in our own minds.

Deletion

Deleting relevant facts or considerations is a powerful weapon not just for apologists but for the Control Factor itself. When the Muslim Democratic Congressman from Minnesota, Rep. Keith Ellison, appeared on Bill Maher's *Real Time* show in March, 2011,[11] Maher, an atheist who belittles all religions, tried to corner him by pointing out that the *Koran* "instructs observant Muslims to despise non-believers." Ellison replied that Maher needed to put Koranic statements in context and to learn more about the "complex" *Koran*. He then asked Maher about other lines in the *Koran* such as "Anyone who takes a life, it's as if he killed the whole world" and "anyone who saves a life, it's as if he saved the whole world." (5:32) Ellison also cited the oft-used Koranic phrase "there is no compulsion in religion."

Predictably, Ellison was leaving out a great deal. Verse 5:32 does indeed employ the words Ellison described but it is Ellison who left out the context. Shi'ites generally treat the "killing" it describes as a "spiritual killing," relating to the crime of apostasy. That is, if you take someone out of the faith, your crime is as severe as if you have killed all mankind. Conversely, keeping someone within the faith makes you a savior.

Sunnis, on the other hand, often interpret this killing as physical but reach a very different principle than Ellison recites. The context for the passage is that Allah, having seen Cain slay Abel, viewed it as a crime against humanity. He then instructed the Jews not to kill anyone *without acceptable reason ("unless it be for murder or for spreading mischief in the land")*. With these words Allah is commanding Mohammed to follow this same rule he had given the Jews in earlier times and which the Jews subsequently failed to obey (5:32):

On that account: We ordained for the Children of Israel that if anyone slew a person—unless it be for murder or for spreading mischief in the land—it would be as if he slew the whole people: and if any one saved a life, it would be as if he saved the life of the whole people. Then although there came to them Our messengers with clear signs, yet, even after that, many of them continued to commit excesses in the land.

It must be understood that Allah is claiming that Islam was given to the Children of Israel via Moses and other messengers. Therefore, the passage is to be understood to apply to Israelites as *Muslims* who kill other Israelite *Muslims*. The injunction here is to prevent a Muslim from killing another Muslim. It has been interpreted in this way throughout Islamic history from the revered Koranic interpreter Ibn Kathir to those who teaching at Al-Azhar University today. Ellison failed to tell Maher's audience how the verse is often taught to Muslims—especially those who should concern us most.

The context is further revealed in the following verse which helped form the basis of the Islamic injunction against *Harabah*, "highway robbery," and later was applied more broadly to fighting, acting, or speaking against Allah, Mohammed, and society as a whole (5:33):

The punishment of those who wage war against Allah and His Messenger, and strive with might and main for mischief through the land is: execution, or crucifixion, or the cutting off of hands and feet from opposite sides, or exile from the land: that is their disgrace in this world, and a heavy punishment is theirs in the Hereafter.

Some have tracked this verse through various *hadith* to conclude that Allah was admonishing Mohammed for having dealt even more brutal and barbaric punishment to eight highway robbers (driving heated nails through their eyes and leaving them to die in the desert, as we have seen). Far from forbidding killing, these verses are seen to justify brutal criminal punishments. In Saudi Arabia, for instance, crucifixion for highway robbery has occurred twice in recent decades while Amnesty International has reported 90 judicially commanded amputations in the last two decades of the twentieth century. If there is any notion here of preserving the sanctity of life, it lies in Allah's restricting the punishment to include *only* these methods. This paints a very different picture of Islam than the life-affirming version Ellison described.

Interestingly, the exception in 5:32 ("unless it be for murder or for spreading mischief in the land") has in many cases exceeded the rule. Osama Bin Laden and all others engaged in the Violent Jihad have justified their actions as being in response to America's killing of Muslims, the occupation of Saudi lands, and so forth. Similarly, the Cairo Declaration of Human Rights expressly prohibits killing innocent people *except for Shariah-prescribed reasons*. The verse offers absolutely no protection against Muslims engaged in any of the three levels of Jihad.

So while Ellison tries to use this verse to show how killing is absolutely forbidden, many Sunnis invoke it as *license* to justify killing non-Muslim criminals and those who fight against Muslims—precisely what prompted Bill Maher to question the religion in the first place.

Of course, Ellison can hardly be expected to point out that throughout Islamic history, law, and literature, killing and torturing non-Muslims is often commanded; such behavior is anathema in other major religions today.

Furthermore, Ellison tries to qualify the famous phrase "there is no compulsion in religion" to mean mutual tolerance. In essence, he is trying to say "We Muslims do not require you to follow Islam anymore than you require us to follow your religion."

> Let there be no compulsion in religion: Truth stands out clear from Error: whoever rejects evil and believes in Allah hath grasped the most trustworthy handhold, that never breaks. And Allah heareth and knoweth all things. (2:256)

In fact, while this has been one interpretation accepted during different historical periods, for many the verse signifies something different. First, it has been deemed abrogated by a variety of later verses that force non-Muslims to either convert, become *dhimmis* in certain cases, or die.

> . . . then fight and slay the pagans wherever ye find them, and seize them, beleaguer them and lie in wait for them in every stratagem of war; but if they repent, and establish regular prayers and practice regular charity, then open the way for them: for Allah is Oft-forgiving, most Merciful. (9:5)

Yet, even in its original, unabrogated form, Ellison again leaves out the verse that follows which supplies the very context Ellison claimed Maher so desperately needed to learn:

Allah is the Protector of those who have faith: from the depths of darkness He will lead them forth into light. Of those who reject faith the patrons are the evil ones: from light they will lead them forth into the depths of darkness. They will be companions of the fire, to dwell therein (For ever). (2:257)

The critical concept here is that if one does not follow Allah, he will be subjected to the eternal fire—hardly the modern concept of mutual tolerance. Christianity, from Constantine through Justinian prior to Mohammed's life had, to varying degrees, forced subjects to follow and not to leave its religion, often through punishment by death. While such "compulsion" was often even more severe during periods of Church history, it has been expunged from modern Christianity. It still has a hold, however, in many Islamic expressions.

Yusuf Ali's footnote is also helpful. It explains that compulsion is incompatible with religion for what we might call conceptual reasons (as opposed to behavioral ones). First, it suggests that faith is meaningless if induced by force; in essence it is not true faith. In addition, anyone truly of goodwill would clearly recognize the greatness of Allah and not need any persuasion. Finally, it states that Allah's protection is continuous. In essence, the notes reduce "there is no compulsion in religion" to a tautological notion that a true believer, by definition, would never have to be forced into belief, exalting Islam to the exclusion of other religions. It is a statement about how great Allah and Islam are, not a statement about how Muslims should treat or tolerate non-Muslims. While this verse has been subject to various interpretations throughout centuries, and while Ellison's tactical use of the phrase is common and familiar today, it employs deletion in ways that render it deceitful.

Detachment

Escape is, perhaps, the most predictable response to an overwhelming peril—not just in the physical world but in the mind as well. Emotional detachment accomplishes many of the Control Factor's objectives. Separating ourselves from any identification with the threat is easy. After all, most Westerners have an advantage: ignorance of Islam, few relationships with Muslims, and minimal contact with Muslim lands. This leaves us emotionally disconnected from Islam's goals, beliefs, stories, and desires. Dismissal of all things Muslim as something from "over there," an area in which we should not be present in the first place and that which does not enter into Western daily life, helps us avoid the threat by imagining it is elsewhere. If we cannot at a minimum place ourselves within the Islamic narrative and emotionally connect with our Islamic Enemy, we cannot comprehend, much less experientially sample, the true degree of danger which threatens us.

Conversely, those who have seen and physically experienced Islamic terrorism first-hand—for instance New Yorkers and 9/11 survivors and their family members—those who have difficulty detaching, are among those who are most aware of their own Control Factors. Firefighters and police officers who pulled bodies from the rubble of the World Trade Center, parents and spouses who heard the terror in the voices of their loved ones as their planes were about to go down, everyday people who were forced to flee the clouds of debris that roared through the city streets—all know firsthand what Islamic terrorism feels like, and are generally less able to detach and are less susceptible to other Control Factor maneuvers.

Detachment can be aided by disassociation. This is commonly deployed when claiming an unjust "guilt by association." Whether it is revealing government relations with associates of Muslim Brotherhood affiliated entities, or tying Obama to Louis Farrakhan, the leader of the Nation of Islam, or to alleged PLO associate Rashid Khalidi, the Control Factor is quick to ignore many obvious facts under the legalistic notion that one is innocent until proven guilty, and that mere association does not transfer guilt. These are true principles that define our legal system, but we are not engaged in any legal action. The Control Factor uses this tactic of disassociation to obfuscate much of what common sense tells us.

We might also include under detachment the ridiculous principle that we can placate the enemy by purging words such as "*jihad*" and "war on terror" from our lexicon and barring their use by government agencies. Although this practice began during the Bush administration, the Obama administration has taken it to euphemistic extremes—labeling the offensive in Libya as "kinetic military action." The European Union, likewise, has tabooed "Islamic fundamentalist" and "*jihad*," purging them from its official handbooks.

Unfortunately, detaching from words does little to eliminate the veracity of their meanings. And as we will later see, any effort to appease or request a change in the behavior of our Islamic Enemy in exchange for these moves will instead invite only more hatred and disrespect.

Displacement

Another weapon wielded by the Control Factor involves displacing the enemy. Rather than maintaining focus upon the true threat, the Control Factor seeks scapegoats. Many people have turned President Bush, Vice President Dick Cheney, "neocons," or Israel, into the villains from whom they believe we need protection. Bush became the purveyor of torture at Guantanamo Bay, not the leader of a free people defending themselves against terror. Similarly, in order to identify a new villain, the media equated waterboarding with the chopping off of limbs, gouging of eyes and the mass slaughter of innocents.

The secret benefit of this maneuver is that one can experience himself venting his anger and fear toward someone who will not retaliate; unlike the real enemy, scapegoats are safe targets. Simultaneously, the fantasy affords some sense of empowerment through the illusion that one is actually confronting an enemy. It feeds the belief that we can restore order and stability to our world and, hence, to our minds. Since we elected Bush to be our leader, we can change that and return to stability. A great deal of President Obama's campaign appeal was the subliminal suggestion that a "change" from Bush in and of itself (with no clarity about what was to substitute) would make for "better world."

Anti-Semitism and scapegoating are well-explored subjects and there is no need to review them here. Nonetheless, they are the age-old prototypical examples of displacement of the true enemy. Charging that the Israel lobby is behind the war in Iraq or that a Jewish cabal—reminiscent of the fantasy elaborated in *The Protocols of the Elders of Zion*—caused 9/11, are but a small sampling of how the Control Factor can misdirect our focus and comfort the mind. Unfortunately, this Control Factor tactic has, today, become embedded within our university system; students' attitudes are shaped by the teaching of a reconstructed history designed to scapegoat Jews, Israel, America, and the West in general. The film *Crossing the Line*, along with www.campus-watch.org, are just a few of many sources tracking this dangerous phenomenon.

Discoloration

It must be emphasized that very little in the real world is as "black" or "white" as our minds wish to make it appear. The displacement of an enemy sometimes contains an element of truth; otherwise displacement would not work as a mental defense. Nonetheless, it is the very same need to avoid a harsh and chaotic internal world that so excessively distorts a displaced enemy. Removing shades of meaning so that "everything Bush" is deemed evil while "everything Obama" is touched with grace has dominated a great deal of our political discourse. Disregard for complexity and the fact that most events and issues are multi-determined leads to an inappropriate blindness.

"Bush Derangement Syndrome,"[12] a phrase coined by conservative commentator Charles Krauthammer, is an interesting case in point. It identifies one of the most frequently used Control Factor devices in which everything wrong or threatening is ascribed to George W. Bush. It involves most of the "D's" including denial, distortion and distraction. It discolors him as well. In 2006, following an unsuccessful attempt by terrorists to hijack an airliner out of Great Britain, an anti-war activist commented in *The New York Post*: "Hoping to kill 3,000 people at one shot? Wouldn't that have been lucky for Bush?"[13] The Islamic Enemy was displaced by many onto Bush, whose entire identity was discolored into the simple blackness of evil. For many people, nothing he could do could mitigate their enmity.

Similarly, when Iran (where "Death to America" is a constitutionally implied ideal) reportedly assists US forces in Afghanistan in the effort to track down Osama Bin Laden, or when Saudi Arabian intelligence alerts US intelligence to potential terror plots, discoloration leads many to minimize these nations' threat to us, or even to regard them as our allies. Consequently, the Control Factor allows us to feel less concerned about Iran's nuclear program or Saudi Arabia's control of the oil markets. Following the killing of bin Laden, the US relationship with Pakistan has been called into question. While Pakistan had been considered an ally in most public descriptions, it is no longer easy to overlook all it has does in direct contravention of US interests. (Interestingly, this Control Factor maneuver is often manipulated by the intentional sending of conflicting messages. It is a potent weapon of our Islamic Enemy.)

Conversely, modern intellectual thought takes great pride in all of the "grays." It often relishes complexity and nuance to such an extent that problems requiring clarity are often fuzzed with excessive shadings. Often a deep exploration of the "grays" yields plenty of ideas and more ways to define and frame an issue, yet results only in showing how the fundamental conflict repeats itself at both the general and specific levels—like the famous fractal patterns of the Mandelbrot set which at higher levels of magnification reveal repeated versions of themselves. The Control Factor uses the full range of grays to obscure true threats; dangers that ultimately require the lucidity and conviction of black and white, good vs. evil. Incessantly dissecting the shades of terrorism, of "radical Islam," of jihadi motivations, often leads one away from understanding what should be crystal clear. Detailed analyses and delineations can frequently lead to fascinating perspectives and insights and make for compelling articles and speeches. Yet such insights, by shunning simplicity, can result in paralysis.

As described earlier, Islam encompasses numerous disciplines, sects, beliefs and rivalries. Yet a common thread is *jihad*. "In the Muslim community, the holy war is a religious duty, because of the universalism of the (Muslim) mission and the (obligation to) convert everybody to Islam either by persuasion or by force, the other religious groups did not have a universal mission, and the holy war was not a religious duty for them, save only for purposes of defense," wrote renowned Islamic scholar Ibn Khaldun in the fourteenth century. "Only Islam is under obligation to gain power over nations."[14] While that statement applies as strongly today as ever, much time is expended exploring gradations, qualifications, and exceptions, in an effort to minimize, deny, and defeat its clear principle.

An indication of this process is the word "conversation." Politicians and media personalities, to demonstrate their grasp of the intricacies of various issues, often declare, "We need to have a national conversation about. . . ." Often the effect is to delay until some future date recognition of the clarity that is staring us in the face. And often, those advocating such "conversations" already believe their position is correct and are simply allowing the Control Factor to use the appearance of complexity to obfuscate simplicity. (And often, when those "conversations" do take place, little is accomplished other than the participants applauding themselves for engaging in such effort).

The issue here is not that things are black and white on the one hand or multicolored on the other. What is critical is the use that is made of either perspective. Perhaps the simplest of examples lies in how we view the Muslim populations in the Western world. For certain purposes they can be viewed as uniform. From a different angle we can observe significant differentiations among a wide variety of communities, citing vast ethnic, cultural, and religious differences. We can make important distinctions, for instance, that American Muslim populations seem to be better-educated and from higher economic classes than European Muslims. Yet the relevance of either perspective is determined by its purpose and the Control Factor makes good use of both perspectives for its own purposes.

On the internal battlefield—the stage in the mental theater of war—things are as we "cast" and "script" them. Stories can be as simple or complex as we choose. Our vulnerability lies in becoming stuck in one style of narrative so that others are not available to us. Sometimes a full appreciation for the "grays" or color gradations leads to effective responses, while simplicity leads to thoughtless mistakes. In other circumstances the moral clarity and simplicity of "black and white" is precisely what is needed, especially when difficult action is required. Wisdom often lies in knowing which is necessary, and any restriction on the freedom to see through both perspectives is often evidence of discoloration by the Control Factor.

Delusion

A related move is to delude ourselves about the true nature of our enemies. Ignoring the abundance of declarations and proclamations, the Control Factor magically transforms despotic or theocratic rulers—who have irrefutable records of supporting terrorism and committing extreme human rights violations—into civilized, morally acceptable leaders desirous of diplomatic engagement through which mutually beneficial understandings and arrangements may ultimately be reached.

Of course, those deep in the grip of their Control Factors sometimes pay lip service to identifying tyrants like Saddam, Ahmadinejad, Arafat, Assad, Nasrallah and others as problematic, uncooperative, and even "evil." Yet such attacks are often immediately qualified with statements and explanations excusing these despots, preventing our own leaders from taking the necessary actions to confront them. To many people, in fact, it was the failure of George W. Bush to respond appropriately to these leaders that caused them to act the way they did.

Similarly, President Obama absurdly declared in 2010, "I am committed to doing everything I can to support Lebanon and ensure it remains free from foreign interference, terrorism and war,"[15] completely disregarding the political realities of that country.

Popular entertainers express many of the delusions lurking in our culture. We hear rants from the likes of comediennes Joy Behar or Janeane

Garofalo that equate Islamic and Christian extremists. Similarly, many well-known voices expressed dismay in advance of Congressional hearings on Muslim radicalization in America. The facts showed there was ample cause for concern and for the hearings. Steven Emerson of the Investigative Project on Terrorism reported, for example, that more than 80% of terror convictions since 9/11 involved "radical" Islam, and that Muslims, who represent less than 1% of the US population, are defendants in 186 of 228 cases listed in 2010 by the Justice Department.[16] Yet many people attacked the hearings for not simultaneously covering Christian, neo-Nazi, or KKK terrorism as well supporting the delusion that there is a rational equivalence.

Like denial, delusion is ubiquitous in the world of the Control Factor. The Control Factor's very existence is based on the delusion that there is no serious threat and that we are in control.

Distortion

The Control Factor also distorts our perception of the enemy's organization. Our minds seek a central focus which enables us secretly to imagine how the conflict will end. Following 9/11, the easiest course was for Westerners to focus on Osama Bin Laden or the Taliban. Similarly, nations or nation-states attract our attention, so we focus on Iran or Saudi Arabia or Pakistan. Yet part of the power of our Islamic Enemy lies in his ability to thrive without any such centralizing agent, especially as he spreads through new territories, including America. Enemy actors in widely dispersed locations are taking on authority so that the hunt for a few critical targets will do little to extinguish the threat. It must be noted that many of the enemy's factions were never connected in the first place, and developed in an ad hoc fashion, so that a centralized core never existed. Instead, as in horror films, the "disease" seems to have a life of its own.

The Obama administration has reconfigured the scope of our enemy to al-Qaeda and its affiliates, thus simplifying the target. It has also designated "terrorism" as the only behavior of our Islamic Enemy that must be confronted and overcome. As his assistant for Homeland Security and Counterterrorism, John Brennan, stated on May 26, 2010, at the Center for Strategic and International Studies:

> The reality, of course, is that we never have been and will never be at war with Islam. After all, Islam, like so many faiths, is part of America.

Instead, the President's strategy is clear and precise. Our enemy is Al-Qaeda and its terrorist affiliates. For it was al-Qaeda who attacked us so viciously on 9/11 and whose desire to attack the United States, our allies, and our partners remains undiminished. And it is its affiliates who have taken up al-Qaeda's call to arms against the United States in other parts of the world. The President's strategy is unequivocal with regard to our posture. The United States of America is at war. We are at war against al-Qaeda and its terrorist affiliates.

This approach, which embodies multiple Control Factor moves, focuses and limits our political mission. It comforts us that the mission is achievable and the enemy can be surmounted through the appropriate and measured use of military strength abroad and judicial action at home. Nonetheless, by narrowly circumscribing our Islamic Enemy, Obama is distorting the true danger in order to soothe our anxiety and ignorance.

Fareed Zakaria, *Time Magazine* Editor-At-Large and CNN host, reinforced the distortion in a May 2, 2011 posting entitled *Al Qaeda is Over*.[17] Zacharia argues that bin Laden's death means the end of al-Qaeda which was simply "an idea and an ideology, symbolized by an extremely charismatic figure in Osama bin Laden." History, says Zacharia, shows "that the loss of the charismatic leader—of the symbol—is extraordinarily damaging for the organization." Finally, given the backdrop, in which the "Arab Awakening" is occurring, he concludes that al-Qaeda is out of the picture.

Even the Obama administration could not subscribe to such a rosy view. Less than a month later Secretary of State Hillary Clinton, discussing strained relations between the United States and Pakistan, stated, "We have reached a turning point. Osama bin Laden is dead but al-Qaeda and its syndicate of terror remain a threat to us both. We both recognize that there is still much more work required and it is urgent."[18] Furthermore, it is certainly not always true that eliminating the charismatic leader spells the death of the movement as was seen most recently in the 2004 Israeli assassination of Hamas leader Sheikh Ahmed Yassin. The result was unquestionably a strengthening of Hamas.

Nonetheless, the critical maneuver here lies in Zacharia's conclusion, which echoes the core position of Brennan and the Obama administration. While acknowledging that ad hoc terrorism, such as that of the Somali pirates will continue, he essentially argues that bin Laden's death ends the ideology which served to lure the Muslim world into a threat against the West. This belief that the "existential" threat is over—by limiting the real threat we face to al-Qaeda—is a pure example of the Control Factor at work.

Obama made this same move with respect to Israel in his second speech on the Middle East, at the US State Department during May, 2011.[19] He described Israel's security concerns in terms of children being "blown up on a bus" and having "rockets fired at their homes." These were recent events and were typical of Palestinian terror. Additionally, he itemized Israel's security needs as follows: "to prevent a resurgence of terrorism, to stop the infiltration of weapons, and to provide effective border security." This construct was repeated, verbatim, in his speech days later to AIPAC. As horrific as terrorism is and has been for Israel, and as needed as those security steps are, the greater threat to Israel which Obama was avoiding is existential—the threat of being destroyed through full warfare by its Arab and/or Iranian enemies. Limiting the security concerns to terrorism distorts and understates Israel's vulnerability.

This process is particularly compelling given how hard we find it to imagine a solution to terrorism that is consistent with our morals, military strengths, and constitutional limits. Not having a solution readily available entices us to redefine the problem until a solution appears. Limiting terror to that which our courts might be able to address, especially in cases of foreign terrorists, is a result of distortion. When Obama announced that 9/11 mastermind Khalid Sheikh Mohammed would be tried in New York City in a civilian court, he was sending a message that the terrorists are, in reality, no more of a threat than common criminals, distorting the truth that their agenda—unlike that of common criminals—is to bring the entire world into compliance with Islam.

Another frequently advanced notion is "if only" the West would cease its occupation of Muslim lands, Islam would shift its focus and aggression away from us. The Control Factor here first gives us comfort that retreat is possible, as if our Islamic Enemy simply wants the West to vacate the Middle East. It is certainly true that in some expressions of Islam, a distinction is made between "offensive *jihad*" into lands not already under Islamic control, and "defensive *jihad*" against the occupation of Muslim lands. When this distinction becomes inconvenient, however, it is easily circumvented by reframing offensive actions as defensive in nature.

Importantly, even though Shi'ites typically discourage offensive *jihad*, it remains a critically serious threat with the Iranian regime, whose main figures believe wholeheartedly in the return of the "Twelfth" or "Hidden" Imam. The End Days so sought after will be signaled when the Twelfth Imam, who since 874 has been in occlusion, returns to rule. Some "Twelvers", including Iranian Supreme Leader Ali Khamenei and President Mahmoud Ahmadinejad, believe that they have a duty to help bring about the return by creating the conditions of world chaos that are said to signal the reappearance of the Twelfth Imam.

The main body of Shi'ite jurisprudence had for centuries reserved the authority to wage war for the Twelfth Imam. According to Ayatollah Mahmud Taleqani, however, modern jurists, along with Ayatollah Khomeini, have reinterpreted this to mean only that the authority of a "just" ruler is required. In any event, since Ahmadinejad claims he is in touch with the Hidden Imam, he can claim that he is acting on direct orders should he desire to wage offensive *jihad*.

More ominously, as far back as 1986 under Ayatollah Khomeini, the Islamic Propagation Organization summarized the then contemporary view: "yet, there are certain Islamic scholars—(certain Fuqaha) who hold that the existence of a powerful Islamic government with sufficient force and power is enough for Muslims to declare war on the defying infidels and if the Muslims are sure to win, then under such circumstances, too, offensive *jihad* is permissible."[20] As described in *Jihad and Shahadat*, a collection of essays edited by Mehdi Abedi and Gary Legenhausen, this position was a minority view at the time. Today it seemingly offers a rationale for the regime to wage any war that Iran has the power to win. Once Iran obtains nuclear weapons, it clearly has enough power to win a first strike war. Regardless, Iran continues its march towards these weapons unimpeded by the "international community."

It is true that Islam has splits and sects, the most well-known of which is the division between Sunni and Shia. The hatred between the two is deep and long-lived. It is a fantasy, however, that they are too filled with animosity ever to cooperate. To the contrary, there is a long history, including a rich present, of their working together in the face of a common enemy, and nothing unites them more than the possibility of destroying both the United States and Israel as well as tyrannical leaders of Islamic states who do not satisfy Islamists' demands.

Iran and Iraq despite their long-standing antipathy and mutual aggression have aided each other in battles against the United States. Even now, with Iraq officially considered a US ally, Iran has a strong political presence there and a history of supporting Iraqi insurgents. Iran's his-

tory of working with al-Qaeda in various capacities along with its dominating assistance to Hamas indicate that the Sunni-Shia split will always
defer to a common enemy like the United States, the Great Satan, or
Israel. And, as Iran attempts to gather regional power at Saudi Arabia's
expense, many Sunni Muslims and nations will be expected to hedge
their bets and subordinate any sectarian conflicts to the necessity of hitching
their wagons to the rising Iranian presence.

There is a *hadith* in which Mohammed (foreseeing that Islam would
have many expressions) states that "my community will be split up into
seventy-three sects" and later, "Seventy-two of the seventy-three Muslim sects will go to hell; only one of the sects will be in Paradise, it is the
majority group." (Dawud book 40, number 4579 and 2.0427; 2.14.2705;
8.1480; 3.35.4255) While it will be interesting to see how each sect
explains itself to be the correct seventy-third one, this concept places
great pressure on sects to unite so that a majority can emerge. More
importantly, no higher goal exists in any Islamic group than the establishment of Islamic law throughout the world. That is the unifying principle of all Islam, and the Control Factor does all it can to keep us from
recognizing it.

Demonization

The accusation of "Islamophobia" has been a key element in the early
scenes of our horror film. Focusing on the real enemy can be so frightening that some, instead, focus inward on that very fear that the enemy
understandably provokes. This demonization, by first displacing the enemy inside of ourselves, has taken root in much of the West, as the UN,
the International Criminal Court, and various other political entities
throughout Europe and Canada try to criminalize speech that defames or
simply insults Islam.

Dutch parliamentarian Geert Wilders has been prosecuted for producing the film *Fitna*, which simply juxtaposes Koranic commands with
film footage of Islamic terror. The appropriate and justified fear of our
Islamic Enemy thus becomes hateful, and anyone who expresses it is
deemed the villain and humiliated for it. Jihadists cannot have stated
their goals and ambitions more clearly than they have in recent years.
Nonetheless, "Islamophobes" who correctly understand these goals are
deemed the real problem; their correct interpretation and understanding
of Islamic commands is seen as an "insult" to Islam.

Demonization is often entwined with other distortions. Former London Mayor Ken Livingstone actually asserted that Muslims were being demonized in exactly the same way Adolf Hitler demonized Jews, being labeled as vermin and worse. While Jews have long been true victims of our Islamic Enemy, many people found Livingstone's comparison compelling. Even more outlandish, the United Kingdom recently considered banning all discussion of the Holocaust in its schools because the subject "offends" Muslims who take the position that it never occurred. Similarly, most readers are familiar with the efforts by Mahmoud Ahmadinejad in UN and other public appearances to ridiculously charge the US and Israel for virtually every evil on the planet. Such demonization has unfortunately become common parlance in the halls of the UN.

This tool is very similar to the trend developed in America following the election of Barack Obama. As more and more Americans became disenchanted with Obama, those seeking to protect him began a campaign to attack any dissent as "racist." While the tactic had some initial traction, it was so overused that it soon proved the opposite—that the accusers were themselves the racists. Reducing all dissent to racism was an indication that it was the *accusers'* minds that were seeing race everywhere and projecting it onto their targets. When Rep. Joe Wilson shouted "You lie" during President Obama's speech in 2009, it was followed by accusations of racism. "I guess we will probably have folks putting on white hoods and white uniforms again," said Rep. Hank Johnson. "That's the logical conclusion if this kind of attitude (against Obama's policies) is not rebuked."21

For some who employ this form of attack, it is *their own* racism and race-based perceptions of the world that are exposed. For decades, many liberals have organized their lives so intently around the proposition that racism continues to be a (if not *the* most) critical issue in America, that they have developed a dependency on this perception to keep their lives in order. At some point, however, it is the race baiters that should be labeled "racist," since it is they who infuse racism into every situation. The "log" is in their own eyes. Those who charge "Islamophobia" distort in the same way.

The above are just a few of the Control Factor's many moves. The Control Factor typically deploys a number of these tools simultaneously, and many of them overlap. Just as the threat in the horror film is constantly learning, adapting and evolving new strategies, the Control Factor's weaponry is similarly evolving into more complex iterations. It is critical for each of us to slow down and examine his or her own Control Factor's moves to learn how it operates. In that context, there is always much more to examine.

Like displacement, for instance, switching aggressor/victim roles is a common Control Factor tactic. Labeling President Bush and Israel as terrorists, beyond its self-evident absurdity as displacement of the enemy, gives the illusion that the true source of our problem is identifiable, locatable and, consequently controllable. "One man's terrorist is another man's freedom fighter" is the relativist's use of distraction to engage in this maneuver. Similar devices include what Benjamin Netanyahu referred to as the "reversal of causality,"[22] a tactic which flips the cause (or provocation) and response so that our enemies are afforded an explanation for their behavior as well as compassion and understanding. They are said to be simply reacting to our evil treatment of them.

These moves are some of the simple building blocks upon which more complex and nuanced Control Factor operations are based. Labeling each maneuver will help us identify and therefore gain some control over the Control Factor. Eventually, we reach the point where the Inner Jihad becomes fully internalized. At that point categorization becomes second nature, if not unnecessary.

Chapter 6

The Control Factor—The Need to be Liked and the Game of Guilt

The Control Factor is adept at zeroing in on our emotional needs precisely because it is a part of our mind. Many of its weapons are built out of its awareness of just how much the West values and takes pride in the appearance of emotional control and how much it wishes to be liked by others. Hence, the Control Factor finds its way to guide many of the ways in which we think we are demonstrating to others just who we are. At this level, many of the basic maneuvers are combined with emotional content to form larger "units" of behavior.

Attack Emotions

A critical Control Factor tool lies in the attack on emotions themselves. We saw some of this in the charge of Islamophobia where one's concerns and fears about Islam are turned against him so that he is to feel guilty about holding such fear. Similarly, on a larger level, we often hear about the "politics of fear" or "fear mongering," when a politician or party is accused of frightening voters to obtain their votes. The Bush administration was frequently cited by Democrats as abusing the threat of terrorism to this end, as were various Republican candidates during the 2008 election. Some Democratic presidential candidates and congressmen went so far as to claim that there was little or no real threat from terrorism other than that which was generated by the Bush administration.

Meanwhile, President Obama has freely exploited fear and anger in his attacks on Republicans, Tea Party attendees, and conservative media

figures. During his campaign he was famously overheard to belittle conservatives as those who "cling to their guns and religion" to assuage
their fears. His coterie has subsequently attacked those opposed to illegal
immigration as being anti-immigrant, racist, and afraid of anyone unlike
themselves. He has raised class warfare to new heights and has amplified
global warming fears in order to push through his wealth-redistribution
agenda. He successfully passed his health care reform legislation by playing on the fears of the elderly and stoking the anger of the uninsured to
generate the demand that health care be transformed from a luxury to a
right. And his backers have employed "Medi-scare," airing a television
commercial showing an elderly woman in a wheelchair being thrown off
a cliff to dramatize opponents' proposed adjustment to the Medicare entitlement. Fear was and is one of his most effective tools.

Another example of this duplicity over fear-mongering is the climate
change debate. Despite some evidence that "man-made" global warming
is a politically motivated hoax, the Obama administration held a conference on "environmental justice" in 2010. "Climate change has the potential to accelerate and intensify extreme weather events which threaten
the nation's sustainability and security,"[1] according to a statement released by the Department of Homeland Security, which sponsored the
conference. Criticizing fear-mongering is often a disguise for those who
most use fear-mongering to their own advantage.

Anger has also become a prime target. As with the charge of
"Islamophobia," liberal progressive attacks on "crazy teabaggers" and
"gun-toting conservatives" (and virtually anyone enraged by what they
view as Obama's radical policies) attempt to punish any emotional response that doesn't comply with their agenda—essentially creating "Emotional Dhimmitude." Needless to say, these same progressives' own
emotional outbreaks are fully overlooked when they organize, protest,
and boycott against a president's or governor's attempt to limit the power
of public labor unions or enforce laws against illegal immigration. They
are frequently the very persons who hold deep hatreds for anyone who
disagrees with their liberal agendas. As writer Ann Coulter has argued,
the assassinations of the last century have all been done by liberals. While
the media creates an image of crazy, ignorant right-wingers to both fear
and be angry at, the image more appropriately fits the long list of progressive liberals that have been politically active for decades.

Freedom of expression has been greatly compromised by this Control Factor tactic. The simple message is that one's emotional discomfort

with a policy reflects one's own emotional inadequacy and has no relation to the policy itself. This attack on emotions has been extremely effective in selling the narrative that people who fear or are enraged by Islam are the *real* problem.

Grandiosity

While Westerners treasure the principle of the human equality, it often masks a sense of grandiosity. We have a tendency to view the non-Western world as innocent victims. Self-conscious about our material advantages, we want to see ourselves as sensitive to and concerned about the needs of the rest of the world. Yet this posture often emanates from a deeper sense of superiority. Until we overcome this arrogance, we will be stuck on the losing side of arguments that present other countries, and particularly those of our enemies, as victims deserving of our favored treatment.

Grandiosity is not the same as American exceptionalism. The latter emanates from a faith in America itself and the principles upon which it was founded. Grandiosity emanates from its opposite, a deeper insecurity that is often derived from idea that America has failed, does not deserve what it has achieved, or worse, is the source of all evil in the world. Many Americans unfortunately confuse the two and paradoxically reject any true faith in America, for fear of being seen as unduly grandiose.

Grandiosity often creates a false sense of power that can lead to submissive *dhimmi* behavior while American exceptionalism often generates the confidence to assert power when truly required. That is, when faced with the fears our Islamic Enemy creates, grandiosity leads us to believe that since we are so much better, we can easily afford to give in here or there in order to accommodate the inferior "other." American exceptionalism leads us to value and therefore do all that is necessary to protect who we are. Again, the distinction lies in the use made of each.

The controversy surrounding the proposed Ground Zero Mosque is an interesting case in point. New York Mayor Michael Bloomberg scolded those who asserted American exceptionalism in objecting to the mosque by reframing the conflict as a "religious freedom" issue. Protecting religious freedom is what makes us "better," according to the mayor. Yet religious freedom was never the issue in this case; the mayor reflected the millennium-old behavior of *dhimmis*, wrapped in Control Factor grandiosity.

Grandiosity is also observable in the generalizations of Muslims we create in our minds. Many imagine "Muslims" as vulnerable, in need of protection, unintellectual, if not stupid and emotionally volatile. This is true even of those whom one would expect to promote equality—the most vocal supporters of Muslim rights often harbor the deepest disparaging views of them as individuals. Such typecasting is insulting and shows a grandiose sense of being "better than" others. But it remains unexamined, even unconscious, as the Control Factor directs us to look everywhere else.

The film *Generation Zero* by Citizens United makes a related case that the generation that has taken power in recent decades was conditioned to narcissism by post-Depression era parents determined to prevent their children from suffering as they had. Through the '60s a self-centered focus on the individual led to a generation that cut itself off from the wisdom of its ancestors and believed it had the answers its parents lacked. Sacrificed was the core sense of value of a citizen to the nation. In its place, or to justify this change, the generation became attached to the narrative that America at its core is evil and much is needed to correct it. Who better to do so than this generation that viewed itself as uniquely gifted to understand America's errors? Needless to say, seriously engaged Muslims employ this narrative as well.

Grandiosity is extremely dangerous, as it is so difficult to admit within oneself. Many in the media, through whom we learn a great deal about world news and events, tend to be deeply trapped in their own grandiosity, with little recognition of how formidable a force it is within them. This grandiosity is often transferred, intentionally or not, through the descriptions of news events making it easy for the Control Factor to simply embellish, absorb, and utilize it.

Western Shame and Guilt

A related and more powerful tool lies with the politics of shame and guilt. This ploy involves the notion that "if only" we make ourselves feel ashamed enough and "if only" we act guilty enough, we can, in effect, earn the return of the stability and control we so desperately need and miss. This is the basis of Shelby Steele's concept of "White Guilt," explained thoroughly in his brilliant book of the same title. What lies buried in this concept is that since we determine when and how to open up the valves of shame and guilt, we control and determine the outcome—the control the Control Factor is created to generate.

The post-Vietnam period is often described as a low point in America's experience. The generation now in power was shaped by it; many of its members grew up viewing their country as evil. The resulting sense of shame or disgrace, often unconscious, drives us to say to the world in effect, "We ask you to forgive us so that you will like us and not retaliate against us." Showing penitence, we imagine, enables us to regain the sense that we are safely in control—that the world is not threatening because we have brokered a form of forgiveness for our sins.

The same dynamic was evident in the endless post-9/11 questioning of "Why do they hate us?" and its related formulations:

- "If only we solve the Muslim poverty and desperation. . . ."
- "They attack us because of our occupation of their lands or our CIA's overthrow of their rulers."
- "Our greed for and manipulation of oil is causing this."

In fact, America's gestures of self-hate and self-flagellation can be viewed through this lens as an unconscious and cowardly attempt to accept responsibility *for our enemy's behavior*—again so that we can comfort ourselves that the threat is controllable. Simply put, self-blame is a powerfully addictive way to create a mental sense of order and control, despite and at the expense of, the seemingly horrid pain of guilt and shame.

Not long after taking office, President Obama gave an interview on Arab television to confirm the Muslim view that America is the real problem. "America was not born as a colonial power," he said, somehow implying that we became a colonial power, aggressively annexing other states just as quickly as we could overpower them. "We sometimes make mistakes. We are not perfect,"[2] he added, not simply to demonstrate his grasp of the obvious but to emphasize our *causal* role.

We also employ self-blame to appease our allies. Some Americans have saturated themselves in the disgrace they believe the George W. Bush administration brought upon the nation. Before Obama's election, we frequently heard the charge that America must heal or "re-weave" its relations with its allies. After his election, Obama went on a world tour of shame, apologizing for all American sins. Fortunately, Obama so drastically overplayed this Control Factor technique that he might have inadvertently diminished its effectiveness for the future. And oddly, despite his campaign calls for properly respecting our allies, Obama has "slapped" those allies (from the United Kingdom, to France, to Japan, to South Korea, to Poland, to Israel, and even the Mubarak regime) while "kissing" and bowing to our enemies.

Again, this entails another grandiose view disguised here as respect, wherein we are presumed fully responsible for the direction a relationship with another country takes. Absent completely from this perspective is any responsibility assigned to our "allies" when they fail to cooperate with us—or when they abandon us altogether. During the Iraq War, for instance, many Americans allowed themselves to ignore the fact that France and Russia, among other nations, put their own duplicitous economic interests ahead of their "friendships" with us. And while Bush was improperly castigated for going to war with Iraq "for oil," France and Russia were truly preventing enforcement of UN sanctions against Iraq in order to obtain Iraqi oil. As famed journalist Claudia Rosett reported, the UN's Oil for Food program turned out to be a monstrous scam through which many of our "allies" sabotaged our efforts.

Secretary of State Hillary Clinton embarked on a campaign to "reset" our relationship with Russia—conveying the foolishly weak position that we need to first earn back Russia's goodwill. We face the same bind today with "allies" that have undermined our attempts to establish meaningful sanctions against Iran. Nonetheless, the Control Factor insists that the United States has a unique responsibility to allies which takes precedence over other concerns.

The politics of shame is designed to keep our own behavior in check. It derives from the idea that if we control our behavior, our Islamic Enemy will control its own in response. It keeps us in the submissive *dhimmi* state with respect to our Islamic Enemy. We feel shame for our "savagery" in battling our enemy, prompting us to identify psychologically with the primitive characteristics of our enemy. We feel shame for failing to uphold the ideal that all are "equal" in God's eyes, and for failing to forgive Islam for its past. (This shame over our lack of forgiveness presupposes the erroneous notion that like Christianity, Islam has eliminated savagery and war from its core ideology.) We feel shame for neglecting to portray the Islam of today in all of its "magnificence." We feel shame for experiencing instincts of self-defense and aggression against the threats our Islamic Enemy poses.

President Obama has been the offender-in-chief when it comes to shame over American ideals. In early 2010 he ordered the American flag taken down from our relief center in Haiti following the devastating earthquake there. "It would send the wrong message," Obama said apologetically, despite the fact that Americans gave more than any other nation to help the Haitians, and the fact that every other nation providing relief in Haiti flew its flag.

Shame functions as both a cause and consequence on what could be called the "wheel of fear." Fear leads to shame for harboring fear, which leads to self-destructive behavior commanded by the Control Factor, which leads to greater fear, and so on. Appeasing the enemy, keeping silent about the enemy, being submissive to and exaggerating the status of our enemy, failing to assert force when necessary are all self-destructive behaviors motivated by shame on this wheel of fear. In essence, it means accepting the status of dhimmitude in exchange for the illusion of being protected and safe; protected from the shame that the Control Factor created in the first place.

Guilt offers a similar "buried" attraction. Certainly there is a place for guilt in relations, both interpersonal and diplomatic. People and countries do "wrong" things and appropriate guilt can lead to behavior that re-establishes (or "resets") relations and deters future improper behavior. Guilt functions well in a context in which all parties recognize and share similar values.

The *politics* of guilt, however, is an abuse of these impulses. While guilt can cause great suffering and feel burdensome, it often functions as a powerful lure. The attraction lies in the promise of future relief from a presumed moral deficiency or lapse. Yet, as with all Control Factor processes, since the entire drama is operated by us, we secretly control its power. As much as we might feel or believe we are suffering guilt due to our "foolish ways," we often actually prefer this to the underlying terror we would experience in the absence of guilt.

By indulging our Western Guilt, we believe that we are on a path toward absolution. Unfortunately, this is illusory—our Islamic Enemy has no intention of granting such a pardon. Despite President Obama's many apologetic gestures toward Muslims at home and abroad—including support for the construction of the Ground Zero Mosque and, incredibly, the statement that America could be considered "one of the largest Muslim countries in the world"—our Islamic Enemy still denounces him and promises to destroy America, along with its President. In fact, following the "Arab Awakening," many in the Muslim world have become even more vocal and demonstrative about these views and intentions. A Zogby International analysis for the Arab American Institute Foundation, *Arab Attitudes, 2011*, found that Arab approval of the US after Obama's efforts was lower in most countries than under Bush and less than 10% across the Arab world. Showing one's own self-respect, rather than begging to be liked, is more often the successful path toward approval in the Arab world.

In many ways, the presumed basis for guilt is irrelevant. Western Guilt is fueled by many narratives: stripping the less developed world of its resources without paying a "fair" price, massive injuries to the earth's climate and ecological balance, the degradation of other nations' and cultures' identities, values and sovereignty, the globalization of market capitalism to the detriment of non-Western peoples, and more. It provides the basis for the *game of guilt,* which is played in order to obtain whatever concessions can be extracted by whoever is playing the part of the "aggrieved party." The Control Factor pays little attention to the narratives' validity. Rather, attracted to and excited by the game, the Control Factor has us suit up and commence playing without any sense of the facts or the rules that must be followed.

Guilt functions most rationally when a weaker counterpart is the "aggrieved." With Steele's White Guilt, whites tended to behave as if guilty and make concessions to blacks in exchange for the supposed restoration of a moral high ground—from which the whites can continue to dominate. The game was played for concessions, as blacks were incapable of restructuring society directly.

The housing crisis that led to the financial crisis of 2008 was created over decades in large part by the narrative that blacks were being prevented from having their piece of the American dream. The concession for this presumed example of America's evil was to push through regulations that pressured banks to make risky loans they otherwise could not justify. The Community Reinvestment Act led to an explosion of precarious lending as the risk of these loans was ultimately transferred to investors and then the taxpayers. As with most defenses, the White Guilt led to the very result it seemingly sought to eliminate—a tragic setback in the housing market with extreme hardship to blacks (and, of course, others).

In the game of guilt, however, where our Islamic Enemy *does* have substantial power to severely disrupt the status quo, Western concessions only invite more mischief.

A simple Western concession made to our Islamic Enemy was the release and return of detainees at Guantanamo Bay to their native countries, or their transfer elsewhere. It has been estimated that 25 percent of all former detainees have resumed terrorist activity. In December 2010 the National Intelligence Office confirmed that 150 out of 598 prisoners released have re-enlisted as jihadists.[3] Granting concessions only resulted in more of the same destructive behavior.

In the game of guilt, we believe we can dissociate ourselves from our supposed "evil ways" and regain our moral compass and authority "if only" we demonstrate how well we now understand our prior foolishness. Furthermore, we convince ourselves that the rest of the world will match our behavior with an equally civilized and respectful response. Borrowing from Steele, this can be labeled "Western Guilt." It is one of the Control Factor's most powerful weapons, and, when applied to the war with our Islamic Enemy, it creates the sense that there can be a reasonable and comparatively painless resolution to the struggle—simply own up to our sins and make whatever reparations are necessary, and then control and order will be re-established. Unfortunately, Western Guilt has the opposite and unintended consequence of inflaming and motivating, rather than pacifying, the rage of our Islamic Enemy. Our demonstration of what the enemy considers weakness only emboldens him in his cause.

The so-called "Black Hawk Down" episode is a simple demonstration of the enticement of weakness. In 1993, 18 US soldiers were killed when two Black Hawk helicopters were shot down by Islamists—organized by Osama bin Laden—in Somalia during a UN-sponsored humanitarian mission. President Bill Clinton pulled US troops out of Somalia shortly after the incident, prompting Osama bin Laden to scornfully label America as a "paper tiger." The withdrawal only emboldened al-Qaeda and its affiliates to attack much bigger targets.

A similar phenomenon can be seen in the psychology of the "sadistic-masochistic relationship." The appeasement actions of the masochist tend to push the sadist toward even more extreme demands. From a "systems" perspective, this type of relationship feeds off of increasingly more aggressive behavior, with the dominant partner doomed to make demands that become untenable and impossible to satisfy—ultimately leading to termination of the relationship. Relations with our Islamic Enemy often involve sadistic behavior by that enemy. At that point, any gesture of appeasement on our part leads not to a quieting of their demands, but to their intensification.

The Control Factor's use of guilt infects our policy decisions in subtle ways as well. It creates a powerful compulsion to restrict our behavior by moral and legal precepts that are often not shared by our enemy. We take great pride in our moral "superiority," and the notion that we will not stoop to the enemy's primitive level. When the "violations" occurred at Abu Ghraib, many people responded with intense self-hatred and fury, none of which our enemy applies to himself. Again, as demanded by the Control Factor, this places us at cause; our presumed moral violations are what "set them off." It also places the presumptive solutions—punishment, guilt, recompense—in our hands so that we can again feel some sense of restored order and control.

Again, a critical component of the game of guilt is the premise that our action created the rage and fury in the "aggrieved." But often the aggrieved party is given the signal to act with rage precisely because it receives a tip from the guilty party that the game is on. It was the American press that set off the Muslim rage response to Abu Ghraib by framing the affair as a gross injustice. Similarly, the protests of enraged Muslims in response to the famous Mohammed cartoons publication occurred months after publication and only as part of a well-organized campaign. The rage exhibited was anything but the spontaneous act it was made out to be, but that did not matter. The signal was given.

Westerners have become so used to being conscious of any words or acts that in any manner imply a racial bias that we have learned to preemptively shut them off before they manifest themselves. Similarly, we feel that anything that can possibly be interpreted as "anti-Muslim" needs to be suppressed. In censoring our thoughts and behavior in this way, Western Guilt suggests, we can secretly regain control over our enemy. The essential lesson that the Germans learned following World War II began with this admirable fight against racism. The result of Hitler's racism, the mass murder of six million Jews—comprising two-thirds of Europe's Jewish population—became a source of intense shame and guilt for Germans in the post-war years. Any implication of racism or anti-Semitism was immediately suppressed and removed, at least from public view. Over time, however, this effort expanded into an overarching resistance to war itself in any form other than resistance to dictators and radical ideologies, again an effort to control their own behavior.

The same applies to America's so-called "torture" of enemy combatants. Putting aside the many legal fallacies involved in the debate concerning "torture," the psychological need for Americans to attack themselves lies, in part, in a false and almost superstitious sense of "who caused what." If we act properly, the thinking goes, so will the enemy (or in the worst case, we can feel good about being good losers. Note that this is independent of arguments concerning whether torture is an effective technique and apart from any positive value derived from treating prisoners "humanely.") This proposition enables us secretly to believe that our Islamic Enemy, unlike the threat in a horror film, is like us and can ultimately be dissuaded from its goal.

Israel has been endlessly trapped in the game of Western Guilt. The fully anti-Israel agenda of the United Nations has had no difficulty finding Israel at fault for the eternally "aggrieved" Palestinians. The United Nations Relief and Works Agency (UNRWA) was originally established in 1949 as a "temporary" entity to assist Palestinian refugees following the 1948 war the Arabs started in reaction to the formation of the state of Israel. (Jewish refugees of roughly equal number involuntarily cast out of surrounding Arab countries meanwhile settled in Israel with no such assistance program). Oddly, UNRWA has remained active for over half a century because of the strength of the game of Western Guilt. No matter what Israel does, the rules require that it is framed as victimizing "defenseless Palestinians."

The United Nations and many of its members need the game to continue. Rulers of many Arab nations maintain control over their population by casting Israel as the demon responsible for all of their ills. A common move of authoritarians throughout history, it diverts focus away from the failings of their own leadership to deliver satisfactorily to their subjects. The Palestinian leadership feeds off of the rewards extracted from the assignment of guilt to Israel, and the more such concessions are granted, the more dependent upon them the leaders become. Meanwhile many Israelis would rather continue the game, horrific as it is, than risk the uncertainty that would initially result from ending it. Such is the deepest reason why, despite so many different political views among Israeli leaders for decades, there has been a largely unconscious collusion to continue the game. As discussed in greater detail in Chapter 9, the lure of the game is addictive, and the parties hold onto their roles with the same fervor that any addict hoards his drug.

White or Western Guilt usually involves large wealth transfers. Whether it is directed at Great Society programs or aid for lesser-developed countries, much of the game of guilt revolves around extracting money. Nor is this limited to guilt over perceived racism. For those who do not believe in the principles of "climate change" and "global warming" as human-generated phenomena, the entire structure of the debate utilizes Western Guilt to justify a climate change debt obligation—a magically created liability to perform wealth transfers to other countries and internationally based organizations. Great sums of Western aid to Islamic-controlled countries, including Palestinian entities, have been obtained through similar pressure. Oddly, while US laws have been amended to prohibit the funding of terrorist organizations, the US State Department continues to fund Palestinian organizations which clearly meet the conditions outlined under the ban. The attraction of Western Guilt promises a moral leveling, but if one "follows the money" there is much else to be observed.

The UN's Oil for Food program, which turned into an international scandal, is a prime example of Western Guilt misdirected. Established in 1995 to allow Iraq to sell oil on the world market in exchange for food, medicine and other needs for Iraqi citizens—without allowing Iraq to fund its military—it ended in chaos in 2003. It was born of Western Guilt over sanctions imposed on the Iraqi government. Billions of dollars were diverted from the Iraqi people into the hands of Saddam Hussein and his corrupt regime, not to mention UN officials. It served as tragic proof that when the West attempts to pay for its guilt, the money often ends up in the wrong hands.

Playing the game of guilt requires seeking out reasons to feel guilty. A favorite of the Far Left, metaphorical "dogs" are released in order to sniff out any reason possible to convict America. Often, as seen with curriculums in high schools and universities, significant distortions, even lies, are proffered through years to establish a basis to hold America responsible for all misery experienced in the rest of the world. Much of Obama's connection with the young and the Left lies with his refined ability to express why we have much to feel guilty about. The game requires identifying the victims and identifying with the victimizer. Again, the seduction of the game lies in believing that by accepting responsibility for being the victimizer, the path to regaining control is within grasp. The attraction is so strong, however, that the game simply is set to continue indefinitely as its rewards greatly outweigh its costs.

The most significant challenge with Western Guilt is ending it. *The game of guilt itself gives us no indication of how and when it is to terminate.* When is enough enough? When has enough punishment or redemptive behavior occurred? Is six or seven trillion dollars' worth of Great Society programs, generating a level of American debt which today threatens the solvency of the nation, sufficient to end white guilt? Perhaps not, as some blacks continue to call for reparations for past slavery and act as if America is at square one in addressing its racial past. When has the United States paid in full for its "involvement" in the 1953 overthrow of Iranian Prime Minister Mohammed Mosaddegh? When have the "abuses" at Abu Ghraib been fully redeemed? When is America relieved from its guilt for having "created" jihadists to fight the Soviet Union in Afghanistan, only to leave following the Soviet withdrawal?

When will Western Guilt be satisfied? Generating guilt is easy. Ending it is the hard part, especially for those who have invested so much in learning to play. With guilt, the Control Factor can wreak havoc, precisely because the attraction to it is so fundamentally powerful and there is no roadmap to stop it.

Bad Faith

Borrowing another concept from Steele, bad faith becomes a powerful weapon for the Control Factor. Intimately connected with "White" or "Western Guilt," in a *Wall Street Journal* opinion piece entitled, "A Referendum on the Redeemer,"[4] Steele described Obama as caught in the role of redeemer rather than leader. Essentially, Steele tags Obama as a child of the American counterculture of the '60s which views America as "characterologically evil"—racist, sexist, greedy, environmentally insensitive and imperialistic. In the face of such deep flaws, "bad faith in America" became the virtuous unifying drive through which the counterculture claimed moral authority.

Steele's argument regarding Obama is that bad faith became a rationalization for the use of American power—to undo our own evil impact. Hence bad faith replaced American exceptionalism as the core self-image among this generation, and steered our leaders away from traditional leadership. Rhetoric such as "corporate greed" has replaced the "spirit of entrepreneurship;" charges of racism where none exists are rampant; and Obama's belief that "at some point, you've made enough money" has replaced "equal opportunity for all."

This maintenance of a deficient and evil self-image plays heavily into the Control Factor's arsenal when dealing with our Islamic Enemy as well. It assists us in blaming ourselves for the acts of the enemy, searching for redemption, and pushing for greater and greater accommodation as required of all *dhimmis*. And it begs, by contrast, not only to protect but also to elevate our Islamic Enemy in both subtle and deliberate ways as the price of our redemption.

Just as the game of guilt gives no instruction on how it is to end, Steele describes bad faith as putting Obama—and by extension all of us—in the "position of forever redeeming a fallen nation rather than leading a great nation." Fighting the compulsion of Western Guilt and bad faith is among the most difficult challenges of the Inner Jihad.

Show the World

Western Guilt, shame, bad faith, and grandiosity converge in one of the Control Factor's most tempting techniques: the compulsion to demonstrate how good we are. We hear this in responses such as, "We have to show the world that we are better than they are," or "In supporting the Ground Zero Mosque, we are showing them how we respect the freedoms (which they do not) and hope they will get the message." We see this in individual behavior, such as Joy Behar's stunt of walking off the stage of "The View" to demonstrate dislike of Bill O'Reilly's perspectives on the building of the Ground Zero Mosque—a response more motivated by personal ego and identity than the realities of the underlying assertion. We see this in the pseudo-emotional sympathy many on the Left act out—often in such a rote and rehearsed fashion that they themselves forget they are manufacturing emotions—in order to display ostentatious identification with the sufferings of Muslim "victims."

The act generally betrays an even greater underlying anger which, when the Control Factor loses its ability to cover it up, demonstrates the terror that gives rise to the Control Factor in the first place. Regardless of one's opinion on the use of torture, the response to the publicly-released photos of Abu Ghraib was animated by more than legal issues. Most of us would agree the behavior of the prison guards was despicable, unacceptable, and destructive to America's cause. But the almost uncontrollable anger and panic with which many responded is oddly absent when these same persons witness the overwhelming horrors committed by our Islamic Enemy. Rather, when we "Show the World" how horrified we are, it often reveals to observant eyes the displaced underlying terror which it seeks to mollify—in typical horror-film fashion.

The grandiosity is self-evident. Thinking that we are better than others is not the essence of American greatness. And presuming that we need to demonstrate that we are better comes from an insecurity that flies in the face of American greatness. This is where Western Guilt enters. In order to justify the grandiosity, some deficiency must be presumed to begin with. All "Show the World" approaches are stoked by a presumed position of moral disadvantage, thereby requiring us to earn back respect. As with other Control Factor tools, this manufactured moral low ground is still secretly better than facing the true nature of what confronts us.

The next question becomes "Who is watching?" This reveals even more grandiosity, as if our minds project a stage in which the rest of the world watches in judgment, and we live or die by virtue of the verdict—another failure to differentiate the internal and external battlefields. Remember: defenses often create the very thing they set out to defend against. While this combination of grandiosity and Western Guilt attempts to re-establish some moral high ground, it merely ends up supporting our Islamic Enemy.

President Obama seems to spend much of his time in "Show the World" mode. His approach to addressing the Libyan revolution was held hostage to his need—from his own perspective and that of the Far Left—to demonstrate how he would comply with "international community" standards and the "Responsibility to Protect" doctrine he seeks to promote. Making no real effort to consult with Congress, Obama avidly sought UN and Arab League approval for the establishment of a No-Fly zone. (This is an important result of the International Institutional Jihad). He also tried to convey the impression that America was not "leading" the operations despite all evidence to the contrary. Interestingly, as with most defenses, his attempt to execute a Control Factor move backfired. Despite an outcome that many consider at least initially positive, all that he really showed at the time was how disorganized, weak, and strategically flawed we were.

Far Left pundits such as MSNBC's Rachel Maddow have argued that hostility from our Islamic Enemy exists because of America's promotion of "a narrative."[5] This narrative, Maddow explained on her show in the spring of 2011, holds that America is at war with Islam; she then applauded Obama for making great efforts to change it. While this may sound logical, it once again carries the buried premise that we control the enemy's perceptions. Maddow fails to understand that our Islamic Enemy controls his own perceptions and uses this "narrative" precisely as a weapon to coerce submission from us—as demonstrated by Maddow's own behavior and world view. That realization is too discomforting, however, for much of the Left. It prefers the illusory control afforded by the belief that "if only" we can "Show the World" a little more, our enemies will respond. Unfortunately, they are the ones pulling our strings, not the other way around!

"Show the World" is intimately tied up with the fantasy of the "international community." The concept is the subject of untold numbers of books, theses, and studies. For our purposes, however, it is significant that a neutral description has been hijacked by a Far Left agenda. The concept when used by the Control Factor typically involves a benevolent community of nations that has, to varying degrees, been disadvantaged by America. It imagines a world which has had its resources stolen and desires only to return to a world that delivers "social justice." The idea packs a full wallop of Western Guilt with America as the universal villain.

An honest look around, however, would show not a true "community" but a disorderly assemblage of nations that each has its own interests and acts in ways that effectively deny any notion of community. As long as the Control Factor has America to demonize, it can hold out the promise of paradise to come with the community of nations as an inducement to get America to tap dance for approval—to "Show the World" how desperate we are to protect our illusion of control. Golda Meir recognized the dangerous power of this Control Factor move when she famously declared, " Israel will not die so that the world will speak well of it."

Whenever we hear a variant of the phrase "We must show the world," our Control Factor alarms should light up with full intensity. Showing the World is not about celebrating or demonstrating American exceptionalism; it is about escaping responsibility for a situation we would rather not confront.

The "Peaceful Muslim" Disclaimer

A related Control Factor move has developed into a generally accepted unit of behavior. As more and more of us struggle with the threat that our Islamic Enemy presents, many have felt compelled to qualify their statements concerning Islam with a disclaimer which typically includes the following:

> There are approximately 1.5 billion Muslims in the world. Most are peace-loving people who want the same things we want—to raise their families in peace and to afford them the opportunities that we all desire. I even know some Muslims or have some as friends. They are not terrorists, nor should they be feared. In fact, they should be celebrated for their rich heritage in the name of diversity and we should do everything possible to make sure we do not accuse them of being terrorists or posing any other kind of threat to us.

This disclaimer has become as standard as the cigarette warning label. It is always presented as fact, although no one can point to any polls or to an acceptable and reliable method for testing it. As such, it more closely reflects a collective wish among those who use it, rather than a report on the behavior and intentions of Muslims worldwide.

Most often the purpose of the disclaimer has little to do with facts and more to do with statements about the speaker himself. As with "Grandiosity" and "Show the World," the disclaimer is frequently intended to convey various subtexts, including "I am not a racist, but rather possess the intellectual capacity to differentiate between peaceful and other Muslims;" "I have credibility because I have Muslim friends;" "I am qualified to make this or that distinction because I see the larger picture;" "I harbor no fears about Islam," or "Please don't attack me; I am not attacking you." There are many variations, but they typically operate on behalf of the Control Factor to quell fear.

Clearly, one of our Islamic Enemy's greatest assets is the difficulty the West has identifying precisely who is part of our Islamic Enemy and who is not. As stated earlier, our "Islamic Enemy" is not defined by numbers or territory, and could include a small or large population. The difficult issue concerns not the actual numbers, but who should have the responsibility for identification. To date, that burden has been subsumed by the West rather than being transferred back to the Islamic world, all to the great detriment of the West.

Mimicking the American philosophy of law, the West starts by presuming that all Muslims are peaceful and similar to us until proven otherwise. And such proof is generally limited to after-the-fact evidence of the first level of threat—terrorism or the Violent Jihad. While this model dovetails gracefully with Western principles of guilt, this issue is not about crime or legal presumptions; it concerns identification. Instead, the burden of identification should be shifted back to where it belongs—the Islamic world itself. It is the Muslims, not non-Muslims, who should be held responsible for clarifying who they are and what they stand for.

The Bully Laughs

Even more serious is what could be called our "Three Stooges" policy response to Iran's drive to become a nuclear weapons state. An archetypal comedic riff goes something like this: A bully takes a shot at a weaker subject. Instead of responding in kind, the weakling threatens that if attacked again, he will fight back. The bully, far from being deterred, is enticed to strike again. The routine continues indefinitely as the weaker subject repeatedly refuses to fight back. We laugh because each of us deep down is all too familiar with the shame of such weakness and the results that such an ineffective response causes.

Another comic example comes from *Monty Python and the Holy Grail*[6] in which the "Black Knight" bars King Arthur from passing through. After threatening "None shall pass," and "then you shall die," a fight ensues. The king cuts off one of the knight's arms who says "'tis but a scratch" and "I've had worse." When the king cuts off the other arm, the knight calls it "just a flesh wound." After the king has cut off both of the knight's legs, reducing him to a stump on the ground, the knight continues his foolish rants, "alright, we will call it a draw . . . I'll bite your legs off," still acting as if he is still a threat to the king who has moved well past.

Instead of directly confronting Iran's violations of international agreements when they occurred, and in lieu of drawing lines in the sand and sticking with them, US policy has consistently looked the other way: substituting the vacuous threat of future action for meaningful determined action today. As with the Stooges, this merely invites more bullying. In contrast, the one time Iran appeared to pull back on its anti-American efforts followed President Bush's march into neighboring Iraq in 2003—his act of standing up to Saddam next door. Being presented with more than 100,000 troops on the other side of its border with Iraq, in addition to substantial troops on another border in Afghanistan, gave temporary pause to the Iranian regime's anti-American machismo. It was then that Iran was reported to have assisted the United States in its war in Afghanistan and to have temporarily halted its nuclear program, while its Supreme Leader, Ali Khamenei, is arguably said to have issued a form of fatwa, albeit highly disputed and invalid, that condemned nuclear weapons under Islam. Even the Iranian Revolutionary Guards reportedly moved large sums of money out of the country—mostly to Dubai, which contributed greatly to that emirate's then rapid investment development— in anticipation of a US invasion. Bush, however, was unfortunately unable to sustain the necessary political will at home to pursue an aggressive policy to take advantage of this chink in Iran's armor. As Iran subsequently realized it held the upper hand, it quickly renewed its pronuclear and anti-American efforts.

Having failed to stop Iran's race to obtain nuclear weapons, and despite making statements that Iran must not be allowed to obtain nuclear weapons, the Obama administration is now paving the way for a new policy of "containment" of a nuclear Iran. Worse, by submitting US policy concerning the Libyan revolution to UN approval, Obama has set a precedent that will shelter him from having to take any serious military action against Iran—it is clear that Russia and China have too many joint interests with Iran to approve any use of force against it. Thus, Obama's "Responsibility to Protect" doctrine effectively takes the use of force off of the table without Obama's having to suffer the political consequences of such a move. With the hopelessness of the Three Stooges and the ridiculous optimism of Monty Python's "Black Knight," the administration is suggesting: "No worry, if they, as a nuclear power, ever attempt to cross this latest line, then we will unleash our force against them!"

This is pure Control Factor foolery. The argument is made that force is not being used against Iran *now* in order to stop Iran from obtaining the bomb, because we either fear Iran's response will be too aggressive, or we are concerned about the collateral damage our own aggression might cause. Yet, the threat of a *later* strike as part of a containment strategy lacks any credibility. Iran will be better able to respond forcibly once it has the bomb, and we would face even greater dangers of collateral damage. It may well never need to use its bombs as its leverage alone will enable it to extort unimaginable concessions from the rest of the world. On the other hand, given the regime's deep desire to bring about the return of the Mahdi, which is preconditioned upon the creation of worldwide chaos and the destruction of Israel, the unprovoked offensive use of such weapons should never be discounted. Nonetheless, Obama's Secretary of State Hillary Clinton and heralded "containment" advocates such as Jimmy Carter's Zbigniew Brzezinski, speak optimistically as if this approach makes eminent sense—just as would Monty Python's foolish good knight. As time progresses, however, our opportunities to effectively deploy force in any meaningful manner quickly fade.

A simple variation exists with the US relationship with Pakistan since 9/11. It is obvious that Pakistan, at best, has been duplicitous, if not our clear enemy. Nonetheless, because US policy makers believe we "need" Pakistan, we have deluded ourselves as to what we could expect from the Islamic nation. As Congressman Allen West, an Army Lieutenant Colonel who served in neighboring Afghanistan, likes to say he learned on the inner city streets of Atlanta where he grew up: if you keep telling someone that you need them, they will "roll you over."

Recap

As stated at the outset, all of the Control Factor weapons work together, overlap, and in some sense constitute denial and delusion about the reality we face. They all help to create, as former prosecutor and author Andrew McCarthy titled one of his extraordinary books, a "willful blindness." In the horror film, denying the true nature of the threat—whether it is a monster, a biological phenomenon, or an insane person—is the essence of the initial scenes.

Simply put, we do not control all of our circumstances, so the desire to believe we do necessarily denies much of our experience. Yet the denial is blunt and straightforward when we fail to take heed of the words of an enemy who tells us he will wipe Israel off the map, end Western Civilization, not rest until Islam controls the world, and worse. While our Islamic Enemy is adept at the practice of deception (*taqiyya*), he is often stunningly straightforward about his intentions. Simple denial is similarly at work when we refuse to understand the long, violent, and intolerant history of Islam, or to recognize that our repetitive attempts at "diplomatic solutions" consistently fail. Calling Islam a "religion of peace" in which a few "crazies" have hijacked a religion based on living in harmony with the non-Islamic world is to delude ourselves about Islam's very rich and complex history as well as its set of totalitarian, us-against-them martial principles.

Distortion, deletion of material facts and displacement of the enemy all contributed to the report years ago that more than 80 percent of Britons believed Bush was a greater terrorist than Bin Laden and al-Qaeda.

Similarly, Bush was constantly characterized as a "warmonger" in his "rush to war" with Iraq, despite having spent more than 15 months pursuing all appropriate avenues, including engaging the United Nations, continuing President Bill Clinton's policy of pursuing Iraq regime change, consulting with and getting consent from Congress, achieving greater than 73% public approval, urging enforcement of the prior war's ceasefire agreement, and providing Saddam Hussein with a final exit strategy. Bush, often characterized as a "religious extremist" whose fanaticism somehow equaled that of the enemy, became one more expression of these mechanisms.

Conspiracy theories about 9/11 are perhaps the most extreme examples of Control Factor displacement and distortion. Unable to accept the existence of the enemy in any form whatsoever, a surprisingly large number of people bought into the ridiculous notion that the Twin Towers were brought down by a government operation. The Control Factor manipulates perceptions so easily that believers can only see evidence that comports with the theory. To them, al-Qaeda did not attack us, the buildings were clearly pre-arranged for internal detonation (either by Israel's Mossad or Vice President Dick Cheney himself the night prior), the Pentagon was actually hit with a missile, and an airplane did not crash in Shanksville, Pennsylvania. Making the enemy "us" is pure displacement, but the extreme twisting of the facts is an example of almost pathological distortion. Perfectly obvious facts become imperceptible precisely because the mind needs to believe that our government was at cause. If so, it is at least possible to change it and therefore restore internal harmony. Just as Josef Goebbels taught that the bigger lie has a better chance of being believed, so has the Control Factor operated to make many Americans willingly accept what is clearly absurd.

Equalizing blame or fault, a form of moral relativism and moral equivalence, is another insidious technique used by the Control Factor. Saddam Hussein's treacherous activities, when not ignored entirely, were often overlooked or justified by the notion that America once supported him—as if this carries an equalizing weight. Offensive Palestinian acts are ranked equally (at best) with Israel's defensive responses. Human rights groups will freely attack so-called American "abuses" of women, illegal immigrants or gays, for instance, yet refuse to comment on, much less act against, truly severe abuses of these groups in the Islamic world. Secretary of State Hillary Clinton's 2010 report to the United Nations on

America's own human rights violations failed to elicit a similarly self-berating disclosure from the Islamic world.

This process, similar to distraction, can easily be observed in domestic politics. Many Obama supporters, when questioned about the seeming incoherence in his policies, will immediately respond by shifting the focus back to something Bush did years before. And Obama, like many Leftists, has often subliminally equated American "atrocities" with those of our enemies. It is easier and safer to place the evil within ourselves than to truly face it where it thrives. Self-inflicted Western Guilt is, indeed, a powerful force.

In short, Control Factor efforts to get them to like us are, like all psychological defenses, doomed to create the opposite. Essentially, our Islamic Enemy is *just not that into us!*

Chapter 7

The Control Factor—Mistaken Identities

Remember, we are dealing here with the internal battlefield. This is the stage within our minds on which we play out all of our individual dramas and stories. Just as Mohammed had full power over Medina, each of us, whether we are aware of it or not, fully controls this stage play. We are the writer, the director, the production manager. We are the exhibitor who chooses whether to run the horror film, or instead, the happy musical or comedy.

We are also the casting director. We choose the characters to play the various parts on this stage. In doing so we select or embody them with a wide variety of qualities and characteristics that we think work best for the story. Sometimes these characters accurately reflect those in the physical world they seek to portray. Often, they do not.

Some of the most insidious Control Factor operations involve these mistaken identities. That is, to reduce anxiety, we often change our perceptions to either make others look like us or, by assuming aspects of others, make ourselves believe we understand others. This shows up in the multiple uses of projection and introjection as well as in our attempts to negotiate with those who simply do not wish to join in.

Projection and Introjection

Perhaps more powerful than any of the "D" defenses is projection, one of the most ubiquitous and difficult to control psychological weapons in the Control Factor arsenal. Typically we project onto others qualities or behaviors we are unable to accept in ourselves. For example, I perceive in you negative aspects that I perhaps unconsciously believe I have but am unwilling to admit to myself. Control Factor projection serves other functions as well. For example, we project many of our positive beliefs and characteristics onto our Islamic Enemy, believing he desires peace, responds cooperatively to diplomatic efforts, lives up to agreements honorably, regards warfare against non-Muslims as something to be avoided unless absolutely necessary, and views generosity as a sign of good will, to be matched rather than exploited.

When we believe the enemy wants what we want, we are stepping into dangerous territory, creating the groundwork for a hopeless cycle of appeasement which has proven suicidal from Adolf Hitler to Mahmoud Ahmadinejad. Appeasement begins with the presumption that the enemy is just like us. In particular, it presupposes that the enemy does not really want to go to war, just as the appeaser is doing all he can to avoid war. The appeaser assumes that the enemy must fear him as much as he fears the enemy and that the enemy has some identifiable goal, such as territory or resources, which can be satisfied in some mutually acceptable (if costly) manner. After projecting all of this onto the enemy, the appeaser deals with the enemy in the very way he prefers to be approached—with reason and civility. The appeaser expects to be satisfied by the enemy through simple and quick negotiations to end the potential nightmare.

Typically, however, the enemy is fundamentally different from the appeaser, which is precisely why the projections do not work. The enemy becomes acutely aware that the appeaser is unable to assess the situation clearly and is willing to give up almost anything rather than initiate or continue a conflict. Consequently, like all Control Factor defenses, this projection brings about the very result it seeks to avoid. This is no different from the horror film character who approaches a deranged human or monster with offerings of food, expecting the monster to become peaceful, only to find himself consumed as the ultimate meal. These are projections of our habits of thought (on the internal battlefield), and they influence our interactions with the enemy (on the external battlefield).

Projection seems to play a profound role particularly with secular Europeans. A significant percentage of Europeans find any faith or belief in a radical religious ideology that entails world domination and violence intellectually offensive and, therefore, only likely to be found in the few. Many such European intellectuals simply project their same point of view onto Muslims, for instance, and conclude that only a few could possibly buy into any extremist objective. They simply do not believe that any significant number of Muslims could believe in such an ideology. This particular projection of their own views is one of many that serves to keep much of the European population blind to the incredible advance Islam has made in full view.

In similar fashion, we take into our minds representations or *introjects* of the enemy. We imagine what the enemy is truly like, thinks, desires, judges, etc. But we forget that it is we who create these introjects. We make these mental constructions to fit our own needs for psychological comfort, and they literally begin to take on a life of their own within our minds. Since they are made up of our own psychological and emotional characteristics, and embody a mixture of our own values, rarely do they accurately portray our actual enemies. Once we have given these introjects or constructs life within our minds, however, the Control Factor utilizes the power we have assigned them, keeps them alive and strong, and uses them to its advantage.

Consequently, as these introjects build, mature into more complete objects, and become more familiar to us, they start to control our understanding of the enemy. We assign our own values, codes of conduct, priorities, and wishes for peace and cooperation to them. Since we create them, they *are* actually like us. This is what feeds the presupposition of the appeasers that our enemy can be negotiated with. It is no wonder that many Westerners conclude that Islam is a "peaceful religion" and that "most Muslims are peaceful people who simply want to live in harmony with those of other religions." This is the rosy scenario that Westerners have created for themselves. Whether these words are true or not, those who utter them have in some sense placed themselves in the shoes of an imagined Muslim and wrapped this introject in their own wishes and desires.

In turn, the Control Factor then has us internally interact with the introjects we have created. The more the introject is engaged within us, the greater the sense of familiarity we have with it and the more real it seems. In short, we accept as real that which we have created and with which we have frequent internal interaction. For example, most Westerners have no interest in a world subjected to *Shariah* law in anticipation of the final Islamic Day of Judgment. Consequently, this is not internalized or assigned to an introject and therefore is often not recognized as a goal of real Muslims.

During the first day of the Homeland Security Committee hearings on Muslim radicalization in America chaired by Representative Peter King, the Democrat members of Congress challenged the basis for the hearings. Most were minorities, black and Hispanic, and insisted that the hearings should have covered other groups such as the KKK and neo-Nazis. Whether simply a political ploy or a serious concern, these members were using their experiences in "protecting" blacks for decades and casting (projecting onto) Muslims as if they too share the same sensitivities and experiences. Meanwhile, two Muslims claiming to represent vast numbers of Muslims were sitting in front of the members as witnesses in full disagreement with these Democrat members and their implicit characterization of the Muslim community as oversensitive, fragile, unable to distinguish true inquiry from a political "lynching" and so on. The Democrat members refused to accept or even acknowledge what the witnesses were telling them. Clearly, many of these black "leaders" are simply reluctant to turn over their position as "lead vocalists" for black victimization to Muslim leaders and seek to prevent a separate emergence of a Muslim minority that does not depend upon them. Any power found in their arguments lies mainly in the nature of these projections.

These Control Factor ploys are found in Obama's Iran policy. Despite overwhelming evidence of the Iranian regime's intentions to obtain nuclear weapons, and despite numerous violations of international law by the regime, Obama has relied on the public's desire to view the regime as reasonable, with more bark than bite. One can frequently hear the Control Factor utter statements especially among media "elites" such as "Iranian President Ahmadinejad does not really believe what he says, he is just a shrewd negotiator," or "The government can be deterred if given the appropriate 'carrots'," or "The regime has many fractures and is at heart just as reasonable as we are." The Control Factor's inappropriate projections and introjections are leading us into grave danger.

The Cairo protests of 2011 that resulted in the demise of Hosni Mubarak's presidency were led by an odd combination of internet-savvy youth, labor union advocates, and Muslim Brotherhood members. Much of the Western press, however, chose to see the protesters as persons quite like us, all of one intention, all seeking individual liberty in Western terms. The same projection affected the media characterization of the early days of the Libyan revolution. When Muammar Qaddafi claimed the rebellion was incited by al-Qaeda, the media cast this as just another insane remark from a disturbed leader. It only took a week or so to obtain evidence that it was the media, not Qaddafi, that was hallucinating about who the rebels were. Projection of Western wishes had as much to do with these media characterizations as did any realistic or responsible assessment.

"Splitting" is an intimate part of the projection process. The Control Factor often splits off negative aspects of Muslims we wish to ignore. It then attaches those attributes either to another displaced enemy or to an introject. For instance, it might strip the qualities of hatred and brutal disregard for human rights from our Islamic Enemy and attach them to ourselves. We thus become the unforgivably ruthless prison guard at Abu Ghraib, the savage violator of human rights at Guantanamo who viciously employs torture, the tyrannical occupier, or the horrific soldier who uses too much force. Alternatively, it may attach them to Bush and Cheney, whom we, in turn, split off from ourselves. The rage and viciousness inherent in some jihadic behavior is often seen split off from jihadists and transferred to the "right wing" or Christian militias in an amateurish attempt at equating the two.

Another move lies in claims by the Muslim Brotherhood associated groups, such as CAIR, that any criticism of them or of Islam by any government entity is what fuels recruitment of Muslims into radical groups. The underlying premise is that America is at war with Islam and if Muslims become aware of this they will become enraged and join the battle to defend Islam. However, it is these very Brotherhood entities that are seeking to enlist as many Muslim followers as they can in the Civilization Jihad they are pressing. It is also these groups that support the very narrative they claim is victimizing them by urging Muslims not to work with the government, to fear the FBI, to never talk with a government agent without obtaining legal counsel, to distrust the government, and so on. Nonetheless, these underlying goals are split off from the Brotherhood we "cast."

Splitting might be a part of the answer to that troublesome question among conservatives, "Why are so many Jews liberal Democrats who ultimately act to the detriment of Israel?" (apart from the old joke that reform Judaism is simply Democrat politics with a few noshes thrown in). Israel, exalted as the Jewish homeland, represents an ideal throughout most Jewish expressions of religion and culture. Western Jews' own personal failures can lead them to split off those shortcomings, project them onto Israel, and then look to punish Israel for any indication of its failing to meet those very same ideals. This unfortunately also encourages the rest of the world to hold Israel to higher standards than any other state.

Westerners, in responding to terror attacks, often presume and fear that their retaliation might be as despicable as the attack itself. Besides displacing fear and anger, this move employs an identification hidden in splitting. All of a sudden, politicians and media voices rush to warn us against preemptively unleashing attacks against all Muslims which would make us seem uncontrollably rageful, racist, lacking discernment and full of cruel intentions. Yet these are precisely the characteristics we are reluctant to identify in our Islamic Enemy and have split off from it. While jihadists cite the *Koran*'s "Fight the Pagans wherever ye find them and seize them, beleaguer them, and lie in wait for them" (9:5) and "Strike terror in their hearts" (8:60) and statements that Allah has "cursed" (5:13 and Bukhari 5.725 and 6.175) the Jews and will turn them into apes, monkeys, swine, and idol worshipers because they are "infidels," (5:60, 2:65, 7:166) we seem determined to forget that Muslims can be rageful in their service to Allah, cruel in their choice of weaponry, and infinitely racist. Images of the beheadings of Daniel Pearl and others are quick to leave our minds.

The Control Factor here secretly makes us feel more similar to an otherwise incomprehensible and all too fearsome enemy. This helps us quell our fear. Regardless of how one views the activities at Abu Ghraib or Guantanamo, or civilian trials for enemy combatants, the mental maneuver here—demonizing ourselves—narrows the gap between our nature and culture and that of the enemy. The more we secretly believe we are similar to our enemy, the more we believe the enemy is secretly like us, and the more we are able to anticipate a peaceable resolution to conflicts. Remember: in the horror film it is often the obvious and vast difference between the threat and ourselves that brings about such indescribable terror.

Projection can be observed in the enemy, as well. In its most base form, our Islamic Enemy, steeped in its own hatred, projects that hatred onto the West, depicting the West as uncontrollably engaged in a hate-filled endeavor to destroy the Muslim world. More conceptually, as described earlier, Osama bin Laden's labeling of America as embarked upon a crusade to establish Christianity throughout the world was also a projection of the goal bin Laden holds in his mind, a *jihad* to conquer the world and establish global *Shariah*. One often needed only to listen to what Yasser Arafat would accuse Israel of doing to get a true glimpse of what he was planning for Israel. He would make claims about Israel's plans to attack, to destroy historical evidence of Palestinian history, to indiscriminately terrorize Palestinian civilians, to abuse Palestinian children, all of which he was intending to or would subsequently do to Israel. Calling Jews racists is also an obvious example. More recently, following Sunni suicide bombing attacks against Shi'ites in Iran, the speaker of the Iranian parliament, Ali Larijani, placed blame on the United States and Israel, stating: "They are the only ones capable of such terrorist attacks."[1] All the while, Iranian Revolutionary Guards were behind many such suicide attacks throughout Iraq and elsewhere.

Similarly, the enemy is frequently heard to cite America as the true terrorist, a violator of human rights bent on world domination, a ruthless murderer and deceiver. In October 2010, Palestinian Authority Prime Minister Salam Fayyad accused Israel of being behind an arson attack on a mosque in Bethlehem, representing "part of a policy of state terror, which the Zionist apartheid state is carrying out against the Palestinians."[2] It is clear which polity has a policy of terrorism. The Islamic world is replete with hate-spewing sheikhs and imams regularly making charges against the Western world—especially America, Israel, and Jews— that are filled with projections of their own impulses and desires, if not actions. And few things resemble Apartheid as much as the Muslim-*dhimmi* relationship.

The new Supreme Guide of Egypt's Muslim Brotherhood, Muhammad Badie, said in a provocative sermon on October 6, 2010, that the Zionist movement "knows nothing but the language of force, so the Muslims must meet iron with iron, and winds with even more powerful storms."[3] No nation in history has ever voluntarily suspended and resisted its use of force more than Israel. It has done so since its creation to its grave disadvantage precisely in an effort to elicit from its Islamic Enemy any language other than force. Rather, it has been Muslims throughout history who have shown that they know only the language of force. Still, Badie's projection is too useful for him to abandon.

Perhaps most devastating is the projection that is interwoven with the language of Nazism. Palestinian leaders have led a media effort to turn upside down the historic tragedy of Jewish genocide so that Israelis are now described as behaving like Nazis themselves. Palestinian media frequently claim that the Israelis are conducting a Holocaust-like extermination of Palestinians with imagery reminiscent of the Nazis, including cartoons for children depicting mass murder in trenches and comparing Palestinian checkpoint lines with those at Nazi death camps.

This type of projection ignores the important history of the Nazi-Islam relationship. The systematic Nazi extermination of European Jews has roots in the Muslim genocide of Armenians earlier in the twentieth century. More importantly, Nazi leaders worked with the Grand Mufti of Jerusalem, Haj Amin al-Husseini, in planning the extermination of Jews. The Mufti, who famously met with Hitler, was also befriended by Adolph Eichmann, with whom he visited Auschwitz to observe techniques of mass murder. With Heinrich Himmler the Mufti formed his own 40,000-member Bosnian Muslim SS force that served the Nazis during the final years of the war.

The Mufti continued to be a significant Islamic force after the war and was reputed to be a distant relative of Yasser Arafat. He kept up his relationships with many Nazis who survived the war. As Matthias Kuntzel describes in *Jihad and Jew-Hatred*, the fundamental anti-Semitism that formed the core of European fascism was transferred, via the Mufti and the Muslim Brotherhood, to many Islamic-controlled countries, and became a foundation for much of our Islamic Enemy since that time.

Projection that inverts reality is seen also in Mahmoud Abbas' challenging the fact that Jerusalem had a Jewish Temple 2,000 years ago. It echoes in Palestinian Arab Prime Minister Salaam Fayyad's remark: "Jerusalem is our people's religious, cultural, economic and political center,"4 which he then uses to justify Palestinian control of Jerusalem.

In fact, the notion of the "Palestinian people" is a fiction created by Arafat and his "comrades." As the Palestinian Media Watch and others including Frontpagemagazine.com's Steven Simpson describe, it was the Romans in the early 2nd century, fed up with Jewish revolts against the empire, that named the Jewish dominated land of Judea "Syria Palestina" after the Jews' ancient enemy, the Philistines, in order to insult the Jews who nonetheless still constituted more than a majority. And despite the two major *jiahds* by which the Arabs conquered the lands today called Israel, they had little interest them. And when the British took over lands on both sides of the Jordan River from the Ottoman following World War I and divided them up, the term "Palestine" was "revived as a quasi-political entity ruled by a British governor" according to Simpson.5

During the next period, the term was used *by Jews* for newspapers and organizations such as the "Palestinian Post" and the "United Palestine Appeal." Arabs considered the term Zionist. It was not until the early 1960s when Arafat formed the PLO that the term was co-opted for use by Arabs. Simpson quotes the leader of a PLO splinter group, Zuhair Muhsin, as saying in a 1977 interview with a Dutch newspaper:

> The Palestinian people does not exist. The creation of a Palestinian state is only a means of continuing our struggle against the state of Israel for our Arab unity. In reality today there is no difference between Jordanians, Palestinians, Syrians and Lebanese. Only for political and tactical reasons do we speak today about the existence of a Palestinian people, since Arab national interests demand that we posit the existence of a distinct Palestinian people to oppose Zionism.
>
> For tactical reasons, Jordan, which is a sovereign state with defined borders, cannot raise claims to Haifa and Jaffa, while as a Palestinian, I can undoubtedly demand Haifa, Jaffa, Beer-Sheva, and Jerusalem. However, the moment we reclaim our right to all of Palestine, we will not wait even a minute to unite Palestine and Jordan.

Even Arafat admitted in 1974 in the New Republic, "What you call Jordan is actually Palestine." Simpson notes that Arabs began utilizing the term with the formation of the PLO in 1964 when both the West Bank and Gaza were occupied by Jordan and Egypt respectively; clear proof that the goal was the extermination of Israel itself, not those territories, as Israel did not control them until after the 1967 war.

The simple truth—that the Jews have a multi-millennia-old identity centered upon Jerusalem and its Temple, while the Palestinian identification with Jerusalem and Judea and other lands was a fabrication made largely by Yasser Arafat—is turned on its head in the lessons taught daily to Palestinian children and today taken as common knowledge by many across the world. In August of 2011, a Palestinian Authority (Fatah) television documentary concerning Palestinian Authority plans to build Arab residential homes at the plaza for the Jews' Western Wall twisted history in stating, "They [Israelis] know for certain that our [Palestinian] roots are deeper than their false history. We, from the balcony of our home, look out over [Islamic] holiness and on sin and filth (Jews praying at the Western Wall) in an area that used to have [Arab] people and homes. We are drawing our new maps. When they [Israelis] disappear from the picture, like a forgotten chapter in the pages of our city's history, we will build it anew (residential area). The Mughrabi Quarter will be built here (on the Western Wall Plaza)."[6]

Projection takes an even more extreme form in constantly repeated allegations of a Jewish conspiracy to invade and destroy Islamic lands. Despite the reality of Mohammed's treatment of the Jewish tribes of Medina, including mass murder, and his later attacks on Jews in Kaybar and elsewhere, this genocidal drive is thrust out of Muslim minds and projected onto the Jews or Israelis. Throughout Islamic history—from the first two major *jihads*, beginning with the prophet Mohammed himself, to the modern version of the "blood libel" (in which Jews were falsely accused of using children in religious blood-letting ceremonies), to the infamous conspiracy of the Elders of Zion (another false accusation charging the Jews with planning global domination), to current charges made in ranting sermons by imams throughout the world—projection of the Islamic drive to destroy Jews is constantly in evidence. It was the Grand Mufti who in a Nazi broadcast in 1944 from Berlin to the Arab world famously commanded, "Arabs, arise as one man and fight for your sacred rights. Kill Jews wherever you find them. This pleases God, history, and religion. This saves your honor. God is with you."[7]

The Israeli-Palestinian conflict has from the beginning been driven by such projection. In 1956, the Grand Mufti of Egypt, Sheikh Hasan Ma'moun, issued a fatwa signed by leaders of all four Sunni Schools which summarizes what underlies *jihad* against Israel: the projections of the Muslims' own imperative to take back Muslim land, hatred for the other, and a deliberate plan in the form of *jihad* to accomplish his goal. Islamic scholar Andrew Bostom presented excerpts from this fatwa in his May 13, 2011 *American Thinker*[8] article:

> Muslims cannot conclude peace with those Jews who have usurped the territory of Palestine and attacked its people and their property in any manner which allows the Jews to continue as a state in that sacred Muslim territory.

> [As] Jews have taken a part of Palestine and there established their non-Islamic government and have also evacuated from that part most of its Muslim inhabitants . . . Jihad . . . to restore the country to its people . . . is the duty of all Muslims, not just those who can undertake it. And since all Islamic countries constitute the abode of every Muslim, the Jihad is imperative for both the Muslims inhabiting the territory attacked, and Muslims everywhere else because even though some sections have not been attacked directly, the attack nevertheless took

place on part of the Muslim territory which is a legitimate residence for any Muslim.

Everyone knows that from the early days of Islam to the present day the Jews have been plotting against Islam and Muslims and the Islamic homeland. They do not propose to be content with the attack they made on Palestine and Al Aqsa Mosque, but they plan for the possession of all Islamic territories from the Nile to the Euphrates.

Such projections are as vital, entrenched, and active today as they were when Ma'moun issued his fatwa. They effectively keep the Israeli-Palestinian conflict alive because they afford the Arab Muslim little flexibility to change. The combination of intense hatred and the drive to follow the commands of Islam, bundled and distorted through projection, make the possibility for a Western-style peace difficult for the Arab Muslim to envision.

Humiliation plays an important role in many Islam-dominated cultures. The *Koran* and other Islamic works are filled with language that devalues human life unless one lives up to the highest ideals and dictates of Allah. In these writings Allah's attitude toward man is frequently colored by hate and disgust, and Arab culture amplifies this mindset. Then, in its own defense, the Islamic mind projects this humiliation and self-loathing onto any enemy it can find to absorb it.

Humiliation has also served as an explanation or excuse for Muslim behavior. The general narrative is that the Arab-Islamic world suffered great humiliation following the end of World War I. Its humiliation grew even more profound following the creation of the Israeli state, referred to by Muslims as the *Nakba* or "catastrophe." Even Obama, in his 2011 Middle East speech, cited humiliation as an effect of tyranny: "It's the same kind of humiliation that takes place every day in many parts of the world—the relentless tyranny of governments that deny their citizens dignity."9 The narrative leads to a recommendation that the dignity of the Muslim be reinstated however possible in hopes that once the humiliation is allayed, its projection onto non-Muslims will stop as well. While this is a coherent approach in certain cases, it fails to take into account that expressions of Islam which pit Muslims against the world come as much from within as without.

In 2010, *South Park,* the Comedy Central TV series, mocked the prophet Mohammed in one of its episodes. A "radical" Islamic web site responded by issuing a threat against the lives of the show's creators. Next, the Council on American-Islamic Relations (CAIR) stepped in. A Muslim Brotherhood front organization tasked with selling to America a civilized, peaceable, and modernized image of Islam, CAIR, declared an unindicted co-conspirator and/or joint venturer in the 2008 Holy Land Foundation trial, suggested that the website had been infiltrated by enemies of Islam. Yet CAIR itself has been suspected of this very activity—legally infiltrating parts of the US government, law enforcement agencies, the judiciary, and other institutions to obtain important information, to spread lies about Islam in order to facilitate deeper Islamic penetration into American society and to control the dialogue between the government and Muslims; all in service of the Civilization Jihad. CAIR, ostensibly established to create peaceful relations in America, was founded by central figures from Hamas, an organization designed to ensure that there would be no peaceful relations with Israel.

When listening to our Islamic Enemy, one should always ask whether what it says more truthfully applies to it rather than to us. Put otherwise: We have found the enemy and he is that of which he accuses us!

The Business Transaction Model

Projection and the mistaking of identities solidify into what is called here the "business transaction model," recasting all conflicts as transactions to be completed with traders on each side.

Any conflict is resolvable through effective negotiation—that is often the approach of people who view themselves as sophisticated, experienced business negotiators. The Control Factor readily puts this perspective to work. As business-negotiation devotees learn the facts of a particular struggle—for example, the Iranian quest for nuclear weapons or the Israeli-Palestinian conflict—they typically conclude that there should be little difficulty in coming up with a fair and just solution. How many times have we witnessed newcomers to Middle East disputes show confidence that they can talk sense into the two sides, invariably to meet with failure? Believing himself to be a specially gifted intermediary, Senator John Kerry was said to be trying to insert himself into dialogue with anyone who would see him. How many others have we seen who believe the same?

President Obama perhaps shared this grandiosity as he developed his approach to the Israeli-Palestinian conflict early in his presidency. It is tempting to think one is specially gifted in solving these problems, as one is inclined to view the conflict as the "business" of dividing up territory and assets. One can be easily seduced into believing there is always a just way to do that. But historian Bernard Lewis perhaps put it best when he said that if the conflict is a question about real estate, there can be great hope for a solution. But if it is about the existence of Israel itself, a solution will not be achieved. Indeed, with much of our Islamic Enemy, the underlying question is the existence of non-Islamic peoples and territories—specifically, Israel and a homeland for the Jews in what Muslims declare to be exclusively Muslim land. Similarly, as Benjamin Netanyahu said in his historic speech to the US Congress in May, 2011, "You see, our conflict has never been about the establishment of a Palestinian state; it's always been about the existence of the Jewish state. This is what this conflict is about."[10] Hence, the business transaction model is dangerously deceptive, and consequently ineffective.

The Control Factor also has us minimize the importance of the Islamic concept that once land is Islamic it is always Islamic. This lies at the foundation not just of Hamas and Fatah (who simply disagree as to the best way to reacquire the "occupied" Islamic land called Israel) but of Islamic thought across the Muslim world as well. It is not so much sympathy for the supposed victimized Palestinians that unites Muslims in the "cause." No other Arab country will take them in, much less even pretend to not disfavor them. Rather, in many cases, it is the desire to see Islam reassert its dominance over what it considers its own territory. Consequently, the notion of trading away such lands in any serious business transaction sense is difficult for many Muslims (especially those that control the outcome of "peace" negotiations) to indulge and is what makes this model counterproductive to the West.

Part of what makes the business transaction model seductive is the apparent obviousness of the solution. We frequently hear "experts" say that "everyone knows" the proper resolution to this or that situation; the art then lies in coaxing one party or another to get there. Consequently, we hear how "everyone knows" that North Korea or Iran has to give up their nuclear weapons; we just have to figure out and apply the right carrots and sticks.

This dynamic was trumpeted in Obama's second Middle East speech. Obama used the familiar "everyone knows" construct: "What America and the international community can do is to state frankly what everyone knows—a lasting peace will involve two states for two peoples. . . ."[11]

He continued by outlining terms, including a return to "the 1967 lines with mutually agreed swaps." He made it sound so sensible and clear.

Interestingly, in laying the groundwork for Obama days prior, *New York Times* columnist and Obama "adviser" Thomas Friedman wrote that Israel "needs to" make a deal and that Netanyahu was to blame for the lack of any resolution to date. "Israel needs to use every ounce of creativity to explore ways to securely cede the West Bank to a Palestinian state,"[12] he added placing the burden upon Israel. Again, peace was a transaction in the making that simply needed the proper creative solution.

It all sounds so reasonable to the Control Factor. That is, until Netanyahu made it clear first that the proposed "borders" (themselves random as they were ceasefire lines and never intended to be final territorial boundaries) are indefensible and that settling upon borders before deciding the future of Jerusalem and the right of return made no sense. Nor do "mutually agreed swaps" add anything to the equation as the parties are left with the 1967 lines in the event that no exchange can be agreed upon. Netanyahu also pointed out the obvious—that while peace can be obtained only through negotiation, negotiation can only be achieved with a true partner who seeks peace. And it is clear that Hamas, as well as double-talking Mahmoud Abbas, had no interest in peace, much less the existence of a Jewish state. (Curiously, Friedman had also written, "I have no idea whether Israel has a Palestinian or Syrian partner for a secure peace that Israel can live with." If Friedman did not know the answer by then, perhaps he should not have been advising Obama.)

Simply put, sophisticated business transaction model wisdom and strategy are useless when one party's goal is the annihilation of the other. Still, viewing complicated differences as resolvable through transaction negotiations is powerfully comforting to almost everyone as it reinforces the fantasy that our Islamic Enemy is really just like us. That is precisely what makes this Control Factor move so insidious.

This powerful and frequent use of projection, introjection, splitting and other means for conflating identities resembles a powerful hypnotic device sometimes referred to as the "Confusion Technique." Once the mind is confused as to who's who and what identities have been broken off and mixed up, it is highly motivated to accept the first forcefully asserted seemingly rational explanation proposed. The Control Factor is best positioned to serve up that explanation.

Chapter 8

The Control Factor—Fantasy World

The Control Factor fuels more fantasies than the entire library of Hollywood's horror films. These fantasies entail different combinations of Control Factor denials and maneuvers, packaged with emotional content and rolled up in convenient narratives which can be more readily digested and more easily and predictably shared with and disseminated to others. Our minds constantly run these fantasies on the internal stage and actively create new ones to fit our Control Factors' needs. Just a few favorites are explored here.

The "Lone Superpower" fantasy, for instance, imbues America with a grandiose sense of its power. It is somewhat a myth, though, because no country today can fully force its will on others. While America's shared superpower status with the Soviet Union divided the world in a way that gave tremendous clout to each, the collapse of the Soviets did not mean that their power flowed to the United States. In fact, many today speak of America's fast and marked decline, comparing it to Britain's in the twentieth century.

The Control Factor, however, uses the "Lone Superpower " fantasy to provide us with the false comfort that our vulnerabilities are easily manageable, or to blame us for the world's problems, which then become ours to solve. In each case, we are in control. Yet the limitations of our power are increasingly apparent. Despite the fact that our military has performed superbly in Iraq and Afghanistan and the fact that Special Operations have achieved remarkable results, including the killing of Osama bin Laden, its utility in battling our Islamic Enemy is trending down. As nuclear weapons spread, particularly to Iran and subsequently perhaps through Arab lands, our threat of conventional military action is at least partially neutralized. And as US's deficit issues have grown, especially under a Democrat administration, actual expansion of military weaponry is certain to decline. (While military expenditures have increased over the past decades, much of that has gone into bureaucracy as distinct from weaponry and support.) As interest on it national debt owned by China alone finances roughly 80% of China's rapidly rising military budget, and as China invests heavily in the Middle East and other regions vital to our Islamic Enemy, US ability to project power will diminish. Of course, reinforced by the US, Israel, and other Western countries' dominance in innovation, the "Lone Superpower" fantasy is comforting. But in reality, especially in light of the "perfect storm" of other priorities the nation faces, it will become ever less dependable.

The "Lone Superpower" fantasy is closely tied to another narrative to which Americans cling: that America is always strong enough and its constitutional foundation is secure enough to withstand any external challenge. The strength gained from the Founding Fathers and Abraham Lincoln, along with our leaders in the World Wars, has mutated into a "Big Daddy" fantasy in which America is presumed not only able to provide for all, but to protect itself against all. While we have demonstrated ample might in warfare, the fantasy is also being applied to threats from within—for instance, that America can and will always absorb rather than be absorbed.

This fantasy has allowed America to lull itself into a deep trance, sleeping through a threatening infiltration by our Islamic Enemy into all aspects of our culture. America's borders are wide open, its government and other institutions are beginning to be influenced by if not filled with those who ultimately seek to destroy it, its educational institutions are dominated by multicultural and relativistic philosophies that erode traditional American identity, and its economic system is being abused to such extent that restoring it may not be possible. While the American Muslim population is currently small, it is being assisted by a rapid rate of global demographic expansion as well as by its joining of interests with America's Far Left. Meanwhile, the Control Factor promises us that everything will ultimately "work out." After all, it is America.

This fantasy is not limited to affairs involving our Islamic Enemy. It also blinds us to the activities of China, Russia, and many other non-Islamic nations. Nonetheless, it is most dangerous when it distracts us from the stealthy infiltration of jihadists into our society. As each step occurs—a change in law, a cultural provocation permitted, the election of a politician, or the appointment of a judge associated with the Muslim Brotherhood—the Control Factor reassures us that all is acceptable; worse, each step encourages another. If full, Violent Jihad ultimately emerges, we tell ourselves we will still be strong enough to fight and rid ourselves of it. Because our focus has been restricted to the Violent Jihad on the terror level, we expect that when the "pre-violent" Jihad converts to violence, Big Daddy will be fully able to protect us. The Control Factor fails to inform us by then it will be too late.

Barack Obama likes to play into the Big Daddy role. He often adopts a stern facial expression and deepens his voice as if he is the "daddy," disciplining those who have gone astray. We see this attitude in his demand that the Iraqis or Afghans learn to be responsible for their own security. How does he do this? By disciplining them with the threat to remove US troops by certain dates. Similarly, his responses to Wall Street, the BP oil spill, the messes in banking and automobiles, and so on, have taken the tone of a father chastising a wayward, undisciplined child in order to "teach" a lesson. He implores them to "get their acts together" and insists he will remain on top of them until they do. Tellingly, however, Obama seems able and willing to play this part with our allies or those over whom he has authority. When Obama needs to deliver true "tough love" to our Islamic Enemy, the Control Factor sends this talent into hiding.

Obama has also craftily manipulated a variation of this fantasy that grips many on the Left: that bureaucrats are best able to step in and fix the difficult problems we seem patterned to avoid year after year. This notion is central to the Progressive movement as ignited by President Woodrow Wilson to whom Obama appears ideologically bound. Obama staffed tens of "Czars" to oversee regulations he wanted instituted. He appointed commissions and offloaded onto them the appearance of authority and competence to solve various problems. Needless to say he frequently ignored the advice of many whose prestige he used for political advantage such as Paul Volker, Warren Buffett, and most detrimentally his bi-partisan National Commission on Fiscal Responsibility and Reform led by Alan Simpson and Erskine Bowles, preferring instead to operate privately through his "Czars." When Obama finally announced his "plan" for deficit reduction in 2011, he suggested that should our national debt exceed a certain level, he would then have another commission of experts determine the proper actions to take, just as a panel of experts will be tasked under "Obamacare" to decide the best allocation of resources in end of life care. The Control Factor is quick to buy into the notion that our problems are best solved by a group of bureaucrats or, as Herb London likes to say, a "fraternity of experts."

This is particularly dangerous when it concerns our Islamic Enemy. Muslim outreach efforts, coupled with bringing Muslims into the administration and letting Muslims instruct our government officials about Islam is a way to satisfy the desire to know that the right group of "experts" is on top of the situation. Yet this Control Factor maneuver has allowed the very wrong "experts" to infiltrate and guide our government, especially in furtherance of the Civilization Jihad. This fantasy explains in part how Stephen Coughlin can be stopped from giving our military a full exposition on Islamic law while those associated with Muslim Brotherhood groups are assigned to educate our military, intelligence operatives, local law enforcement, and others.

A related theme lies with the "Don't Worry, Our Courts Won't Allow That" fantasy. When Americans are pressed to curb speech that insults Islam, or to allow terror training camps on private property so long as local rules are complied with, or to accommodate *Shariah* practices in public areas, the question is begged: "When will all of this cease?" Will anyone be able to stop what author Andrew McCarthy and others have called "creeping *Shariah*" before it is too late? As Islamic law inches into non-Muslim-controlled territories, each incremental step seems fair and relatively harmless on its own—not worth the aggravation and negative response that opposing it will generate. During early advances of *Shariah* in America, such steps have been accepted in the hope that our courts will ultimately keep our culture intact.

Our courts, however, have moved somewhat sharply toward liberal, progressive, multicultural tolerance. At the same time, the system is over-burdened and unable to respond with a unity of purpose. And as "the creep" gains momentum, it becomes more difficult to reverse. In late 2010, the "Don't Worry, Our Courts Won't Allow That" fantasy was shattered with one rap of the judge's gavel. It happened in Oklahoma, where a federal judge put on hold the implementation of a ballot measure—already passed by the voters—banning state courts from considering Islamic *Shariah* Law. In early 2011, a Florida judge permitted a private mediation to employ *Shariah* as both parties had agreed to it in advance. While this decision may comport with common American principles of private contract law, our *stare decisis* system based on precedent can easily expand the scope of the ruling over time. As precedents build and resulting *Shariah*-based behaviors become more commonplace, the ability to reverse or even curtail such expansion will decline. While it is a soothing fantasy to expect our courts to protect us in the long run, it is unclear whether they will have the capability and motivation to do so. Judges, after all, have to confront their own Control Factors as well.

Americans love the "We Are So Awesome" fantasy. Stemming in large part from ignorance—as well as the belief that throwing money at people tends to silence their grievances—this notion suggests that the modern Western world embodies everything that the Islamic world could possibly want. It suggests that the War of the Houses can be quieted "if only" we assist the Islamic world toward economic progress and growth. Although vast numbers of Muslims worldwide enjoy material and other comforts associated with Western culture, and aspire to more of them, the idea that our Islamic Enemy will respond to Western-style opportunity is complex and questionable.

It is well understood by now that the 9/11 terrorists were neither impoverished nor poorly educated. More support per capita has been thrust for decades upon the Palestinians, particularly those in Gaza, than any other group in the world, with little to show for it. Still, the Control Factor marshals this fantasy toward its goal of convincing us that our enemy will be tamed, satisfied, appreciative, and redirected from his true goals if we simply help him become a little more "like us," a little more "awesome" himself. The truth is, we are not so "awesome," and to our Islamic Enemy we are despicable and must be destroyed, not emulated.

In the "Assimilation" fantasy, Americans distinguish "our" Muslims from those in Islamic countries. We are frequently told that American Muslims are well integrated into American culture and thereby pose no threat to American values. It is true, for instance, that many Muslims in America have obtained more education and higher status than those in Europe; that some Muslim immigrants have come precisely to escape *Shariah*; that other Muslims may share in our identity and values and enjoy our freedoms and wealth. Nevertheless, the overwhelming long-term Muslim migration tendency is to disengage and form separate communities, as we have seen throughout Western Europe. There, decades-long efforts to foster multiculturalism and protect the identities of Muslim minorities have prevented assimilation from occurring naturally.

Following the establishment of more than seventy-five *Shariah* courts in the United Kingdom and "No-Go zones" in Britain and other European countries—with accompanying violence, hatred, and economic underperformance—many European leaders have declared multiculturalism a major failure. To paraphrase Abigail Esman in *Radical State*, how does a Somali boy relate to a Dutch girl in a miniskirt? The same question applies in Dearborn, Michigan. *Shariah* principles do not easily adjust and assimilate into a modern host culture. As Islam accumulates power, it begins to form clearly defined Muslim neighborhoods and to make cultural demands.

The goal, of course, is to gather enough power to begin to advance *Shariah's* "creep." *Shariah* courts are starting to get a foothold in America as well, with initial versions receiving approval in Richardson, Texas, and others proposed in California and Minnesota. Similarly, US law has been shifting both to accommodate Muslim behavior and to restrict anti-Muslim expressions. The Center for Security Policy's *Shariah Law and American State Courts* study[1] examines fifty appellate court cases in over twenty-three states that have already attempted to address conflicts between *Shariah* and US law.

The "Assimilation" fantasy has America in its grip. It may keep us sleeping through a very real and dangerous trend. Consider, for example, so-called "Muslims of the Americas" terror training camps in several dozen locations across the United States. These are isolated communities of predominantly American-born black Muslims where Pakistani Sheikh Gilani's military and terror training program is taught and practiced. By and large their members are impoverished, many relying on welfare benefits funded by American taxpayers. The American Dream has been supplanted in these camps by the Islamic ideal of "take what you can from the infidel," a sad demonstration that many Muslims, even when born on American soil, will resist assimilation into the American system.

Such resistance is more than cultural; it is deeply embedded in and prescribed by Islam. In verse 5:51 of the *Koran*, Allah commands: "O ye who believe! Take not the Jews and the Christians for your friends and protectors; They are but friends and protectors to each other. And he amongst you that turns to them for friendship is of them. Verily, Allah guideth not a people unjust." In 5:55 Allah continues, "Your real friends are no less than Allah and His messenger, and the Fellowship of Believers . . ." The fourteenth-century Islamic scholar Ibn Tamiyah extended this notion, declaring, "Muslims should not mix with anyone else, and if they do they should be killed as well."[2] In 1998, Osama bin Laden amplified the idea: "Every Muslim, from the moment they realize the distinction in their hearts, hates Americans, hates Jews, and hates Christians. This is part of our religion. For as long as I can remember, I have felt tormented and at war, and have felt hatred and animosity for Americans."[3]

In a sense, Westerners have assimilated Muslims on the stage of their own minds. Quick as we may be to play the "Assimilation" fantasy in our mental theatres, we should not expect to see it replicated on the physical battlefield. It runs counter to too much of what Islam has stood for 1400 years.

President Obama likes to invoke the related storyline embedded in the "Universal Values" fantasy. It refers to values that supposedly unite us all globally, suggesting that walls between us can be easily brought down. Similarly, there is talk of "universal human rights." Yet Western, post-Enlightenment values are still more correctly viewed as unique rather than universal; no such rights exist. Mutual toleration is far from universally valued. For millennia, man's instincts have been savage, competitive, and based on the necessity of survival. If any value approaches universality, it is the one exhibited by our Islamic Enemy—the quest for superiority and domination—quite the opposite of what this fantasy proclaims.

A 2009 Zogby International poll[4] of the Arab world, taken subsequent to Obama's Cairo speech, demonstrates this reality. The poll identified Venezuela President Hugo Chavez as the world's most popular leader. The runners-up were Syria's Bashar al-Assad, former French President Jacques Chirac, and Osama Bin Laden. It is clear that the "universal values" thus expressed are not the same as those imagined by Obama. While we can play word games with "human rights" and "gender standards" to maintain the fiction that bridges are being built, until fundamental differences between the West and Islam are directly addressed, no "universal" value can ever emerge.

Candidate Obama tapped into Americans' "Savior" fantasy. Because we are so unprepared to live with the constant uncertainty and sense of danger our Islamic Enemy poses, we gravitate to leaders who we think can relieve our unrest. Part of Hillary Clinton's appeal during the Democratic presidential primaries in 2008 was the subliminal, if not explicit, suggestion that she could return us to the "safety" we had in the 1990s under the Clintons. Obama appealed to voters as a man who could speak

with non-Americans in a new way. For many, he became a "Messiah."
His nomination speech, in which he declared "this was the moment when
the rise of the oceans began to slow and our planet began to heal,"[5]
played to the fantasy.

We look for saviors in nations hostile to us as well. Years ago, many
"elite" thinkers believed Iran's former president, Mohammed Khatami,
would become a "reformist" and usher in a major change in national
objectives. The "Savior" fantasy was applied again to Mir Hussein
Mousavi, when in 2009 he almost "defeated" President Mahmoud
Ahmadinejad. In both cases, Control Factors wrongly projected onto
these candidates the persona of a true agent of change who wanted peace
with the West and would deal responsibly with it. Any clear-eyed investigation would reveal that these "saviors" were firm supporters of the
Islamic Republic's constitution, nuclear program, and Revolutionary
Guards.

The hope vested in words such as "reformist" or "moderate" often
greatly overestimates the reality. Hillary Clinton famously remarked about
Syria's President Bashar al-Assad, "Members of Congress of both parties who have gone to Syria in recent months have said they believe he's
a reformer."[6] When Assad succeeded his father, many expected him to
bring about reforms. Clinton herself made a major effort as Secretary of
State to pull Assad and Syria away from the lures of Iran. Assad did
nothing of the sort, of course, and when the 2011 spring rebellion came
to Syria, this "reformer" turned the guns on his own people, slaughter-
ing protesters in the street. Yet even months later, Obama and Clinton
continued to believe Assad could and might even change.

Another perversely magnetic figure for the West is Palestine's
Mahmoud Abbas. The alleged financier of the Munich Olympics terror
killings and a Holocaust denier, Abbas can speak to a Western audience
and make Westerners feel optimistic about Israeli-Palestinian peace. As
was true of Arafat, however, one need only listen to what Abbas says to
his own people in Arabic to realize he is no such "moderate." (The
Palestinian Media Watch has catalogued this material in detail and all
Inner Jihadists are encouraged to review this site in detail). Nonetheless,
many in the liberal media continue to refer to him as a partner in peace
and a man poised to make peace with Israel—"if only" Israel would
change its ways and act reasonably. *Washington Post* columnist Eugene
Robinson, on MSNBC's *Morning Joe* program, called Abbas "the best
thing Israel had."[7] It is the Control Factor that keeps those like Robinson

fantasizing that Abbas could be a friend of Israel who will transform Hamas "if only" Israel would give him what he needs.

A related fantasy emerged after the 2003 Iraq War, as tensions concerning Iran's nuclear advance accelerated. *New York Times* writer Thomas Friedman introduced a distinction related to our dealings with the Iranian regime. His counsel was to focus on changing regime behavior, not changing the regime.[8] This call became the rallying cry not only of State Department policymakers but of the liberal media "elites" as well. In this case, when employed by the Control Factor, it served to calm the worries of those who feared President Bush might "cowboy" our way into a military confrontation with Iran. The recommended approach, however, demonstrated extreme arrogance and naiveté by feeding the fantasy that the United States had the power and skill to coax the regime out of the very behavior that defines the core of its principles. It was a pleasant whimsy and served these media elites and the Control Factor well by helping to deter Bush from engaging in any forceful manner with the regime. It was foolish policy however.

Years later, as Iran's march to nuclear weapons has proved unstoppable by any form of engagement, negotiation, or even sanctions, "changing regime behavior" has been shown to have greatly strengthened Iran's hand. "Changing the regime," on the other hand, would have led to different results and is regaining some favor in the public eye—if not employed too late. Such fantasies, regardless of Friedman's skills in selling them, can be extremely dangerous to our ultimate survival.

The "Let's Start from the Beginning" is another common fantasy about the Middle East. This rallying call somehow ensnares us repeatedly. It allows us to erase all memory of failed diplomatic attempts—and to forget why they failed—without regret, much less any learning. Instead we take a deep new breath and announce "Now we are serious" so that we may begin anew. Like a fourth-quarter pep talk, it marshals every Control Factor element and motivates us to want to sit down, put all our differences on the table, and once and for all come to some reasonable terms for settlement. After all, the fantasy declares, "We all *do* want peace, don't we?"

Sadly, not everyone *does* want peace, particularly not our Islamic Enemy. Yet, the call for a final "grown-up" negotiation embodies the assumption every negotiation that preceded it somehow lacked the timing, the urgency, the wise hand, and the reasonableness to achieve peace. This is completely out of line with the reality of history, but that does not interfere with the grip this narrative has over many Control Factor slaves. Andrew McCarthy, in "The Grand Jihad," humorously nails this fantasy by questioning how many times the West would allow Yasser Arafat to "resell his 'I renounce terrorism' carpet."[9]

Each time the "war" with our Islamic Enemy ratchets up a notch, the West looks with fresh hope to resolving the Israeli-Palestinian conflict, as if that were the key to pacifying the Muslim world. Unfortunately, it is this very fantasy of beginning again that ensures that nothing new results.

On June 3, 2010, on CNN's "Larry King Live," referring to the attempted breach of the Israeli-Egyptian blockade of Gaza, President Obama said, "I think what's important right now is, is (sic) that we break out of the current impasse, use this tragedy as an opportunity so that we figure out how can we meet Israel's security concerns, but at the same time start opening up opportunity for Palestinians, work with all parties concerned—the Palestinian Authority, the Israelis, the Egyptians and others—and—and I think Turkey can have a positive voice in this whole process once we've worked through this tragedy—and bring everybody together to figure out how can we get a two-state solution, where Palestinians and Israelis can live side by side in peace and security."[10] Many Americans who voted for Obama, especially the young ones, actually thought they were hearing something new from the White House. This is, however, simply the same fantasy being replayed, in long hypnotic sentences that push the listener to respond, "Yes, we can!"

Obama's history as a law school lecturer and community organizer has helped him create a "blackboard" style of leadership. He is so used to describing, analyzing, and solving problems on a blackboard that he has based his entire approach to communication on the classroom. And since so many of the critical voters he needed to appeal to have been students with little non-academic experience, this style helped to easily establish rapport. Not only does his approach presuppose that he is smarter than his student audience, it feeds the hope that we finally have elected someone "smart enough" to solve our problems. Reciprocally, once Obama spells out his solutions—as vague and filled with platitudes as they are known to be—his followers tend to believe all will be fine. Hence, when he adopts the "Now Its Time to Get Serious and Finally Solve This Peace Problem" attitude, his followers are easily swayed. Unfortunately, Obama is a coach skilled perhaps in the x's and o's of academic playbooks but with little sense of—much less playing time in—the game itself.

As much as we may wish that a call for a fresh start would yield results, we often do so when we are most reluctant to study why all prior attempts have failed, and face up to what is really required. We have seen efforts in the past decade alone by Bill Clinton, Dennis Ross, Condi Rice, Tony Blair, "the Quartet," and George Mitchell, fail to advance the Israeli-Palestinian "peace process." Meanwhile, having voluntarily withdrawn from Lebanon, ceded the Gaza strip, and suffered two intifadas, Israel has the full threat of Hezbollah and Iranian-funded Hamas staring it down and is all the closer to having a non-negotiated Palestinian state forced upon it. Instead of realizing that neither Hamas nor Fatah has any intention for "peace," the Control Factor seeks to have Israel just finally "get serious."

Intimately connected with this fantasy is the notion that diplomatic advances indicate fundamental changes. That is, the Control Factor is swift to conclude that if some arrangement for a cessation of hostilities is reached, the problem is significantly resolved; once Hitler has signed, Chamberlain can celebrate. Obviously, even our worst diplomats are not foolish enough to fully believe this, but there is, nonetheless, a great tendency for the Western mind to allow this temptation to creep in.

For instance, despite decades of "peace" by virtue of an extremely beneficial Egyptian-Israeli treaty, it is nonetheless true that many Egyptians, including the major voices at Al-Azhar, regard Jews as their true nemesis and a major cause of their hardships. This is not to assert that Westerners blithely assume such a treaty does anything more than assist order in a troubled region. Nor does it in any way downplay the enormous benefits obtained by all parties from the treaty for at least three decades. The Control Factor, however, is astute at creating and magnifying impressions that greater changes within the minds of our Islamic Enemy have been made. Just as treaties under Mohammed were intended as temporary cessations of struggle in order to afford time to rebuild, our Islamic Enemy today engages in the same subterfuge. As history has demonstrated, our Islamic Enemy is no respecter of treaties. And as the Cairo protests of 2011 commenced, the first policy challenged by many of the protesters was the treaty itself. Needless to say, if our Islamic Enemy ultimately obtains control of Egypt, the treaty will be threatened.

A film entitled *Miral* was released in 2011 with a substantial promotional effort. The film depicts the struggles of a Palestinian woman in

Israel. When the filmmaker, Julian Schnabel, was asked by Charlie Rose about why he made the film, his responses focused on describing the Palestinians as a "forgotten people" and how they "need to be heard." He seemed to suggest that Israelis lack the requisite empathy to be able to "care about" the Palestinians and called Israel's continuing to build settlements "the root of the impossibility of making peace in Israel."[11] His hope is that when the Palestinians are understood, empathy felt by the West will lead the West to take a new and more just approach to the "Peace Process" such that peace will finally be achieved.

The film and Schnabel's noble intentions and noteworthy cinematic accomplishments aside, the promotional tour should be entitled "Control Factors Gone Wild." First, the notion that peace has eluded the Palestinians because those in the West simply have not understood their plight is again shifting cause and transferring responsibility away from them. "If only" Israel was made, in one way or another, to recognize its folly and change its ways, then the problem would disappear.

More absurd, the Palestinian people have been the most remembered and publicized "victims" for half a century. More money has been spent on them and more political time and focus than any other claimed "refugees" in history. More effort by the supposed Israeli victimizers has been expended on helping them, employing them, and caring for their sick, their terrorists, their criminals, than ever occurs naturally, even between non-hostile peoples. No Muslim peoples do as much to respect the sanctity of life, especially of one's supposed enemy, as does Israel. Those in Rwanda or Darfur, the Kurds in Northern Iraq who have gone the longest without a homeland, and others throughout the Arab world and Africa would be grateful to have a fraction of the attention that has been the sport of the Palestinians for decades. Still, we are urged to "remember" the "forgotten."

Again, this is not a comment about or review of the film. Rather, it is about the explanations generated by the Control Factor to keep us stuck in Wittgenstein's fly bottle.

Especially dear to the young but throughout the West is the "We are Racists" fantasy. We dream that racism should and will be eradicated from the world. Yet those who adhere most to this fantasy often are in the grasp of the Control Factor-inspired presupposition that other nations—especially the less-developed countries—are kinder, more equitable, and generally more decent than the West. These assumptions are never questioned, although there is little to support them. They are simply fed through our legal and educational systems and digested without thought.

We feed the "We Are Racists" fantasy by introjecting the vile and racist instincts we witness throughout the rest of the world. (Shelby Steele's *White Guilt* magnificently documents this process as it pertains to black and white Americans.) Instead of seeing the world as it is, we make ourselves the racists. We then feel obliged to "show the world" not only that we know how despicable we are, but that we are intent on ridding ourselves of such racism.

This fantasy has a powerful grip on liberal Westerners, yet it is patently ridiculous in the face of our Islamic Enemy. Islam elevates the "Ummah," the community of Muslims. Everyone else not only is inferior, but also threatens the purity of the Ummah and must be dealt with accordingly. While not based on traditional "race", but rather on qualification as a Muslim, our Islamic Enemy manifests the behavior characteristic of the Nazis, the KKK, and other racist groups. The connection was spelled out clearly in the 1920s by the Grand Mufti of Jerusalem, Amin Al-Husseini. Islam, he said, is vehemently against Jews, who are seen as most vile in every regard. Then he added, "in the struggle against Jewry, Islam and National Socialism are very close."[12]

By introjecting our enemy's racism, we avoid the dangers of and responsibility for condemning and confronting our Islamic Enemy. While Islam embodies this racist nature, the Control Factor distracts us by using our own valued principles to condemn ourselves. It is testimony to the power of the Control Factor that so many fall under this fantasy's sway.

The search for fault within, American self-hate and our compulsion to accept blame for others undermine our foreign policy. Regardless of our culpability if any, the compulsion to accept blame entails the secret fantasy that we can control the threat facing us. When our enemies express rage at us, whether or not we provoked it or contributed to it, the Control Factor urges us to accept responsibility and offer some measure of recompense. The hope is that the enemy will see us for who we are, attempt to establish rapport and peace with us, and reward us in return. This is, after all, how civilized Westerners would approach an enemy they did not wish to inflame.

The search for fault within is intimately connected with the promotion of "The End of War" fantasy. Like Francis Fukuyama's "end of history" proposition, this fantasy attempts to deliver us from the realities of the present to a dreamed-of future where war is no longer a tool for conflict resolution. This fantasy engenders a reaction to any military or aggressive action as inexplicable and unjustifiable. When the Bush administration used force against our Islamic Enemy, many on the Left found not only that the decision was wrong, but that *any* decision to use force was unpardonably primitive. It was an "embarrassment" that many on the Left tried to apologize for.

These are just a few of the fantasies that rear their heads when we are faced with the threat from our Islamic Enemy. At their core they simply package combinations of Control Factor moves into bigger dramatic narratives. As these fantasies are tested and relived again and again, they weave themselves deep into our culture. We are constantly generating new iterations of these and other fantasies which in turn further embed. Over time, protected and promoted by the Control Factor, they become increasingly difficult to isolate and dismantle. They become our truths.

* * * * *

Having described some of the many techniques the Control Factor uses, it is helpful to observe some in practice. In March, 2011, Deputy National Security Adviser Denis McDonough made the following statement:[13]

> President Obama recognizes that through our words and deeds we can either play into al-Qaeda's narrative and messaging or we can challenge it and thereby undermine it. We're determined to undermine it. For example, we know there are many different reasons why individuals—from many different faiths—succumb to terrorist ideologies. And there is no one easy profile of a terrorist. But based on extensive investigations, research and profiles of the violent extremists we've captured or arrested, and who falsely claim to be fighting in the name of Islam, we know that they all share one thing—they all believe that the United States is somehow at war with Islam, and that this justifies violence against Americans. So we are actively and aggressively undermining that ideology. We're exposing the lie that America and Islam are somehow in conflict. That is why President Obama has stated time and again that the United States is not and never will be at war with Islam.

Let's look at just a few of the moves encapsulated within this statement:

- While McDonough correctly states that our words and deeds have consequences, his words do exactly what they set out to avoid—they play into al-Qaeda's narrative. Bin Laden made clear that he viewed America as soft, weak, and afraid to meet the challenge which al-Qaeda poses. In the mind of our Islamic Enemy, McDonough's words simply confirm Bin Laden's claim.

- The statement limits to terrorism the threat we face. Yet terrorism is only one level of the threat and al-Qaeda is just one piece of the terrorism pie. Narrowing the problem in this way gives us the illusion that through military and law-enforcement actions we can keep the dangers contained.

- McDonough subtly equates Islamic terrorism with "violent extremism" in the same way that members of Congress equated Muslim acts with those of the KKK and neo-Nazis during the Muslim radicalization hearings. The notion that violence is the problem and that violent behavior is a symptom of underlying conditions gives us great comfort, fostering the delusion that if we change those conditions, we can limit the violence.

- The implication is that America is essentially racist against Muslims, treats all Muslims as evil, and is therefore conducting a war against Islam. It is this war that, in turn, is to blame for terrorism. Thus McDonough transfers responsibility from the Islamic Enemy to Americans. And the transfer is conducted through Islam's own narrative of victimhood—the essence of the addiction/enabler dance (next chapter). Since America also gave birth to the KKK and other violent movements, it is America that must look at itself in the mirror. Our enemy has been displaced onto us.

- A thread of grandiosity runs through McDonough's words. He plays on the fantasy that, Obama-style, we can elevate ourselves above the problem, ascertain its true cause, and adjust our responses accordingly. By limiting the problem to the bad impressions Muslims are forced to have of America, causing them, in turn, to become terrorists, the "Lone Superpower" fantasy subtly suggests that we do not necessarily have to fight this problem because we all know that when push comes to shove we can win any real war. All we need to do now is win hearts and minds. Taking this posture does nothing more than telegraph our reluctance and inability to confront the challenge directly.

- McDonough's central premise is that America and Islam are not "in conflict," and are compatible systems. This sleight of mouth simply ignores the essence of both parties' belief systems.

- He asserts that America is not at war with Islam—while failing to note the simple and obvious fact that our Islamic Enemy is at war with us. Our enemy has declared it to be so, and fights under the banner of Islam. The fantasy embedded in McDonough's words is that if we comfort our Islamic Enemy, he will absolve us of our historic and current guilts and live peacefully in mutual tolerance with us. But we know, of course, that the game of guilt gives us no instructions for when it is to end or how we are to end it. It is designed to continue indefinitely.

- While McDonough denies that we are at war with Islam, President Obama goes a giant step further: he denies that we would *ever* be at war with Islam. Yet to say "we will *never* be at war with Islam"—words Obama has spoken both before and after the killing of Osama Bin Laden—is to send a message of unconditional surrender before even beginning to fight. This declaration amounts to accepting dhimmitude and is one of the most self-destructive Control Factor moves that exist.

Chapter 9

The Addiction/Enabling Dance—
The Transfer of Responsibility

When simple Control Factor moves have been developed and practiced, then infused with emotional content, and then combined and focused into larger fantasies and narratives that appear internally consistent and perfectly appropriate, the Control Factor has prepared and equipped us to enter into the type of relationship with our Islamic Enemy that furthers its goals.

Consequently, we and our Islamic Enemy have been locked in what shall be called the addiction/enabling dance. Central to many Control Factor mechanisms is the notion that we are responsible for the behavior of the enemy. Not only do we introject aspects of the enemy so we may blame ourselves, we also introject *responsibility* for the enemy's actions and emotions. By believing we are to blame, we stoke the fantasy that the enemy and our circumstances are other than they are and that, since we caused the situation, we can always change it when it becomes necessary. Remember: at the core of the horror film is a threatening enemy that, despite all of our efforts to dissuade, comes after us relentlessly and seeks our demise.

It is common for today's politicians or executives to make the statement "I take full responsibility for. . . ." by which they mean little more than, "There, I've said it, now let's move on," without any further consequence. That behavior, however, does not begin to constitute acceptance of responsibility as required by the Control Factor. *Responsibility* in the context of the Inner Jihad means full liability for the creation and consequences of the action.

Our psychological need to take on responsibility that does not belong to us has debilitating consequences. It confuses our agenda. And, as stated previously, all psychological defenses, on some level, create or enhance the very danger they seek to diminish or avoid. More importantly, the Control Factor does not work in a vacuum. Our enemy gladly accepts and performs his complementary role by transferring to us responsibility for his actions and emotions, thereby avoiding it himself. The result resembles a classic addiction/enabling relationship wherein one party's destructive behavior is supported by another's assistance. This addiction/enabling dance typically involves progressively more extreme steps as time progresses. The addict's need grows stronger as his tolerance to the substance increases, the rationalizations appear more and more justified, and the attachment between the addict and enabler becomes more firmly cemented. Consequently, over time, the relationship becomes more destructive for both parties and all the more difficult to unwind. Such has been the case for decades as we in the West have effectively *taught* our Islamic Enemy to transfer responsibility to us.

A defining element of addiction is blame: other people, in essence, have caused the addict's behavior. Similarly, this is a defining aspect of our Islamic Enemy. Osama Bin Laden blames the presence of US troops in Saudi Arabia; Mahmoud Ahmadinejad blames the Zionist enemy or America, the Great Satan; Palestinian Fatah and Hamas leaders blame the occupation of so-called "Palestinian" lands, long checkpoint lines, building of settlements, and so on; all as justification for terrorist activity throughout the world. Imam Rauf stated shortly after 9/11, "United States policies were an accessory to the crime that happened."[1]

The corollary of blame is victimhood. The mindset of our Islamic Enemy is steeped in victimhood, in part filtered down from Mohammed himself, in part because it is an effective tool in spreading *Shariah*. It is no stretch to describe the Palestinian identity—to the extent it makes sense to talk of Palestinians as a "people"—as one of victimhood. In *Palestine Betrayed*, Efraim Karsh details how the narrative of Palestinian history is framed passively in terms of all that has been done to Palestinians rather than portraying them as active creators of the situations in which they find themselves. They describe themselves in victimized terms, and their description is amplified by the dialogue and actions of the United Nations and other international aid institutions. Indeed, fairly or not, they have secured for themselves over many decades enormous sums of money by parlaying this identity. Using victimhood they have been able to elicit sympathy. Victimhood also permits and justifies hatred which in turn justifies violence and terror. Victimhood also suggests the right to revenge, and the greater the underlying anger and hatred, the more justified and extreme the retaliatory violence. Such is the drama not only of the Palestinians but all Islamic "victims," from al-Qaeda to Muslim Brotherhood members to at least some Libyan rebels. It sits at the center of the addiction cycle as well.

This "addiction/enabling dance" mimics certain child/parent behaviors. As children grow, parents attempt to teach them to take on greater responsibilities. A resistant child will often whine, sulk, retreat or provoke a fight in order to avoid such change. Effective parenting eventually requires a "tough" stance that ceases pampering the child until he learns to take responsibility and show respect for the rights of others. To the extent the parent fails to establish strong boundaries, the child will exploit the parent's own fears, leading to even more childish behavior.

As addicts increase their addictive behavior, their rationalizations become increasingly more detached from reality. Comedian Flip Wilson's "The devil made me do it" routine was a comic expression of this very serious aspect of alcoholic behavior. To make their behavior appear justified, addicts must stretch the truth far and wide.

Some of the core ideas within Islam help facilitate such addictive behavior. The world in Islam has been divided into two parts—that which is under Islamic control, known as "The House of Islam" (*Dar al-Islam*), and that which is not, labeled "The House of War" (*Dar al-Harb*). Note the operative word is "war." It is expressly *not* called "The House of That with Which We Seek to Live Side By Side in Mutual Respect and Tolerance." Such a worldview creates an immediate, primary, and centrally focused enemy almost irresistibly inviting blame to be placed outside of oneself. After all, it is only the existence of non-Muslims and their lack of submission to *Shariah* that delays Judgment Day and the coming of Paradise. All *kuffar* are to blame for this delay which, according to a famous *hadith*, will not occur until the last Jew hiding behind a rock and tree is exposed by that rock and tree and killed. Supported by various other core Islamic ideas, this roadblock to Paradise incites a compulsion to blame which can fast become a habit as strong as any substance addiction.

When confronting the House of War, the seriously engaged Islamic mind always formulates what it is doing *as a response to* or participation in this war. Since the core of Islam affords the Muslim mind no way in which to view the non-Islamic world other than as an enemy, it tends to be locked into a warlike framework. There are few sensible interpretations and punctuations of events that can be agreed upon with the non-Islamic world that are not reminiscent of the playground accusation: "You started it!" That is, a Muslim will rarely admit being at fault for his actions in relation to non-Muslims. Rather, his behavior is framed as a function of the House of War's occupation of Islamic lands, genocidal attacks against the Muslim world, insulting of Mohammed or Muslim sanctity, and so on. Any non-Muslim justification for those same acts, such as the historical basis and need for a Jewish homeland, basing requirements for soldiers to protect Kuwaiti Muslims from Iraqi Muslims, or supporting free speech as a valued component of exporting knowledge and information, is considered irrelevant. Just as an addict will easily accept a narrative of his life as victim of events around him, Islam's entire frame of reference with respect to the non-Islamic world invites—virtually requires—a similar stance. And just as the Control Factor thrives on the use of "projection," the Islamic mind projects its own march to war onto non-Muslims, viewing non-Muslims as a threat seeking to destroy Islam and to prevent its ultimate vision from being manifested. This makes conflict resolution in the War of the Houses virtually impossible, absent eradication of one House by the other.

The story of the Prophet Mohammed's life, behavior to which seriously engaged Muslims are to aspire, is replete with accounts of others who simply got in the way of his spreading Islam. Unlike Judaism, which tends to internalize blame and seeks to take care of itself on its own, and unlike Christianity which at its core (and despite much Church history to the contrary) attempts to forgive those who get in its way, Islam trains Muslims to view others through the lens of the House of War—as infidels who must be converted, subjected to dhimmitude, or killed in order to bring about Judgment Day.

Note, most importantly, the focus here is on the actions of the other, the unbeliever, rather than on themselves. This makes blame seemingly irresistible.

Addicts have a difficult time changing, largely because so many of their beliefs are built on deeply implanted destructive assumptions. Attempts to simply talk them out of their behavior are generally futile as the addict can only assess a new possibility by reference to those old assumptions, a process that leads to a dead end. Consequently, it is difficult for an addict to learn from his mistakes and losses. A similarly restrictive notion in Islam—and certainly not uncommon in the history of other religions confronting failure—is that defeat of Allah's warriors is caused because Allah seeks it, primarily to punish Muslims. This began with Mohammed's first major defeat in battle at Uhud, from which the lesson was drawn that Allah was angry at his Muslims and brought about defeat to teach them their error.

This thinking has pervaded the Middle East throughout the twentieth century as Islam endured numerous defeats. Beginning with the fall of the Ottoman Empire, continuing with poor choices to align with the Nazis and later the Soviets, our Islamic Enemy was primed for what became its greatest humiliation yet, the defeat, time and again, at the hands of its most vile and despised enemy, Israel. These defeats have sounded a rallying call among our Islamic Enemy to return to even greater obedience to Allah and *Shariah*. Even Hitler is regarded throughout the Islamic world as having been sent by Allah to punish and eradicate the Jews, and his defeat was meant to provide incentive for Muslims to finish the task. Again, instead of defeat providing an opportunity for new learning and change, it has, as with the addict, fortified the very presuppositions that keep in place the addictive drama.

These are just some of the ideas embedded in Islam that help facilitate an addiction to blame and victimhood. For our Islamic Enemy, there exists a never-ending battle which places the locus of all difficulties elsewhere. "If only" he can get his enemy to submit to Islam, the Muslim can progress toward obtaining ultimate peace.

Addictive behavior, however, is also dependent on the enablers. And this is precisely the role from which the West needs to extricate itself. Enabling is the function that frames and informs our views of our Islamic Enemy, views nurtured by our education system, amplified by our media, and shaped by our political, business, and intellectual leaders and institutions. It is our contribution to that which threatens us the most.

Enablers support the addict's transfer of responsibility by accepting it for themselves. As addicts assign blame, enablers find ways to accept it (or, at least, support the addict's fixation of blame elsewhere). They make endless excuses for the addict and attempt to qualify or redefine the addict's behavior to others. For more than half a century the United Nations has created a unique definition of "refugee" in order to continue to funnel money to Palestinians without demanding an end to their terrorist activities. That organization and other international legal institutions have consistently placed responsibility for any conflict on the Israelis by willfully overlooking all provocative acts of violence by Palestinians against them. Buying into Israeli Prime Minister Benjamin Netanyahu's "reversal of causality," the United Nations has institutionalized the never-ending search for resolution anywhere other than with the Palestinians, who are never held fully responsible for their failed society, for their acts of terror, or for the consequences of those acts. In short, the enabler accepts that the alcoholic drinks because the enabler or someone else makes him do so.

Western media facilitates this enabling by downplaying many of our Islamic Enemy's defining aspects. While seriously engaged Muslims understand that they are in the "war of the Houses," the media have substituted a narrative of denial and distortion hinging on the unchallenged assumption that Islam has evolved into modernity. Or as Bill Warner characterizes the story, "That was then, this is now. . . ."[2] Along with this comes the rationalization that to see Islam otherwise is to be judgmental and that the enabler is at least as guilty as the addict. Warner further describes the story as, "We don't need to be judgmental; the West and Christians have done worse."

Hollywood itself has become a key enabler. As described in the Investigative Project on Terrorism's documentary, *The Grand Deception*, numerous films have been pressured or protested in order to control how Muslims are depicted. These include *The Siege, Executive Decision*, and *True Lies*. Similarly, following complaints, the villains in Tom Clancy's *The Sum of All Fears* were changed from Palestinian Muslims to Neo-Nazis in an act of enabling appeasement.

The Grand Deception also points out that the Metropolitan Museum of Art withdrew images of Mohammed from its Islamic collection. (This is soon to be reversed.) Publishers as well participate, such as when a novel centered upon Mohammed and his young bride was stopped over concerns about offending Muslims. Similarly, another publisher declined to include the actual Danish cartoons themselves in a book about those images.

Enablers often accept their roles because they have a boundary-free concept of virtue. They typically judge themselves by what they believe their actions demonstrate—a virtuous self-sacrifice through the acceptance of all responsibility for the addict's condition. They believe that they are winning moral credit through their seemingly selfless support of the addict. This is the essence of Western Guilt and Steele's "White Guilt," and because it is often so entrenched in the experience of the enabler, it is difficult for him to change his behavior. For the addict to have any hope of healing he often must "hit bottom;" yet this possibility can also threaten the very moral fiber of the enabler.

Enablers frequently believe that they can talk the addict out of his addiction. They often believe that their own sensitivity and care give them a unique skill such that "if only" they can have the right "conversation" with the addict, they will be able to turn him around. But while enablers typically believe their case is special, it rarely is. This grandiosity is its own reward for the enabler, and we often see it when we endlessly seek out "negotiations" for a "peace process" or "mutual understanding." That is why "peace" negotiations similarly fail. It is what drives the "Let's Start From the Beginning Rally Call" fantasy.

Enablers are easy marks for emotional blackmail. The psychological investment they have in the Control Factor makes it difficult for them to dictate the terms of their relationship with the addict. Meanwhile, addicts develop a wide variety of maneuvers to hold the enabler in place. Consider this exchange in a 2010 CNN interview with Imam Rauf. In response to a suggestion that he back down from building the Ground Zero Mosque, he replies, "If we move from that location, the story will be that the radicals have taken over the discourse. The headlines in the Muslim World will be that Islam is under attack."[3] Posing as a truly concerned American, Rauf continues,

> And I'm less concerned about the radicals in America than I'm concerned about the radicals in the Muslim World. The danger from the radicals in the Muslim World to our national security, to the national security of our troops. I have a niece who works in the army serving in Iraq. The concern for American citizens who live and work, travel overseas will increasingly be compromised.

Many Westerners have been befuddled by exactly this tactic in the years since 9/11.

The language describing our battle with our Islamic Enemy is entirely consistent with our enabling. The now comfortably familiar and never-ending "Peace Process" appears to be a mature and well thought-out road to a mutually satisfying "peace." The process itself, however, has been little more than common criminal extortion and should more aptly be labeled the "Extortion Process." In this seemingly endless dance, the Palestinians act out their rage and extract concessions from Israelis, who feel forced by international pressure to regard or accept each act of Palestinian terror as having been the result of Israeli injustice. If the Israelis give back this or that, then, they are assured, "peace" will be forthcoming.

Everywhere else, when someone hands over something of value in exchange for the cessation of violence, the West labels it "extortion" and treats it as a criminal act. And ultimately, recurring extortion can only lead to war. This is why the "Peace Process" has always been not only the "Extortion Process" but also the "War Process." Nonetheless, Yasser Arafat and Mahmoud Abbas's Palestinians have for decades used terror to extract concessions from Israel in exchange for the cessation of that very terror. Peace, in reality, has long been "off of the table." We seem to have forgotten the fact that Anwar Sadat was assassinated upon entering into a peace agreement with Israel. This is precisely the intensity and danger that underlies Netanyahu's call for Abbas to say to his people, "I will recognize a Jewish state," and why it is so difficult for him to do so. Our Islamic enemy makes it very difficult for any peace agreement to be made. None of the requirements for peaceful co-existence reveal themselves in this extortion behavior, yet the West continues to believe that "peace" simply requires a better negotiation between the parties—the "business transaction model" meets the "Lets Start From the Beginning Rallying Call."

Not only is "peace" inappropriately employed, so is "process." Peace, when not utilized as a reward, can be achieved instantly. Western democracies constantly negotiate difficult issues without ever resorting to the threat of violence. To infuse a "process" into the situation is to promote the very narrative that serves the addict's purposes; primarily to ensure that little is changed. Nonetheless, for decades both sides with the help of many other nations have manifested the very endless drama the word "process" suggests.

Obama's extensive efforts to control other language of our conflict with our Islamic Enemy might seem on the surface to help dampen the hatred so deeply infused. In US government-speak, the "overseas contingency operations" has replaced "war on terror," the new term for terrorism itself is "man-caused disasters," and "Islam" is barred from being joined with "terrorism" and "*jihad*." Such absurd euphemisms, however, are little more than the enabler refusing to identify the addict for who and what he is. Choosing comfortable and productive language is often an important step in mediations between like-minded parties.

Manipulating language in an effort to "gaslight" the population about the threat it faces is an entirely different matter.

What is critical to grasp here is that the enabler is as committed to his acceptance of responsibility for the addict as the addict is committed to transferring it.

Addicts are, in part, defined by their very inability to successfully manage their internal worlds, particularly impulses of anger and hatred. While our Islamic Enemy is adept at expressing great love for Allah, Mohammed, and his Muslim brothers, what animates and resonates more deeply is profound unaddressed hatred. To be clear, hate is hardly unique to our Islamic Enemy. It sits very comfortably within many other groups and, perhaps, exists in most of us in varying degree. Jamie Glazov's *United in Hate*, for example, well describes how hate is the ingredient that binds today's Far Left and our Islamic Enemy.

Nonetheless, hate is expressly commanded by Mohammed. The *hadith* of Abu Dawud, Book 40, Number 4582 says, "The Prophet (Peace Be Upon Him) said: The best of the actions is to love for the sake of Allah and to hate for the sake of Allah." The same has also been popularly referred to as "the strongest bond of faith" and "the highest degree of faith." Hatred is not simply a consequence of circumstance that develops within the Muslim mind, it is elevated as something to be admired and indulged as there is much that Allah hates.

Hatred has, throughout history, been emotionally seductive. It organizes and focuses our internal disorder. It can give us purpose and meaning. It dispenses energy. And, like the game of guilt, it digs in for the long haul. As long as its object endures, hate continues. Consequently, it is a perfect "substance" for abuse.

Western civilization obviously looks with disfavor upon any showing of hate. It burdens the hater with the responsibility for controlling his hate. Our Islamic Enemy, however, thrives upon its hatred for the infidel and feeds off of it. As a result, in relation to the West he is compelled to point the focus elsewhere, away from the hate to its possible causes or explanations for it. That shift, that transfer of responsibility for the difficult-to-manage hatred—enables the dance to continue. Whether argued by the addict or reinforced by the enabler through excuses and otherwise, the lure of hate is difficult to remove.

When a pastor in America seeks to burn a copy of the *Koran*, the Muslim world responds with a hate-filled outburst. General David Petraeus has argued that such an act causes Muslim hatred. The general is a true

American hero who deserves much of the credit for America's success in Iraq and, more recently, Afghanistan. Burning the *Koran* is likely stupid, undignified, and counter-productive. It does not, however, in any way excuse the hatred manifested in response. Accepting a causal relationship is a powerful Control Factor maneuver which, itself, is so seductive it seems to come "naturally" to us. Our Islamic Enemy's hate, however, is simply in search of such an excuse for expression.

(Interestingly, the Investigative Project has reported that a representative of a Muslim Brotherhood associated group said in a private meeting with other members that burning is the *proper* way to dispose of an old *Koran* and therefore, "Islamically," should not be of any concern. Nonetheless, he advocated not telling Pastor Jones or others of this because they might then come up with other provocations.)

True victims have no power. The victimhood claimed by our Islamic Enemy, however, is a thin veneer over extortion and intimidation. It is a powerful weapon and is used as such. It puts its opposition on the defensive by shifting the focus to the claimed injustice. Palestinian Media Watch is an organization that monitors the messages the Palestinian Authority sends out to its population. The incitement to violence is practically a constant, despite the Palestinian Authority's repeated "commitment" to cease such activities. Mahmoud Abbas, in another example of absurd projection, had the audacity to attack PMW with the very same charge—incitement to violence—casting the Palestinian Authority as the victim and attempting to shift attention to PMW.[4] He claimed that PMW's reports on the Palestinian media were themselves causing violence and hatred against Palestinians. Similarly, the Obama administration and Civilization Jihadists have claimed that any negative statement about or criticism of Islam fuels recruitment and radicalization. By asserting this, they enable the enemy to extort from the American public and government silence, passivity, acceptance, funding, and a refusal to directly address the threat we face.

Consequently, underlying much of the treatment of our Islamic Enemy is the notion of "the Fragile Muslim." The fragility refers to a sensitive and unstable internal state which can be triggered by the most meager of actions. Meanwhile one who is fragile has an excuse for failing to take into account even the most reasonable needs and wishes of others. Addicts frequently adopt this façade and enablers buy into it. Any behavior that can be interpreted as aggressive, firm, upsetting, or hostile on the part of the enabler—from publishing a cartoon of Mohammed to killing Osama bin Laden to building settlements in Jerusalem—will often be countered with even greater aggression, to be excused, in turn, as expected from such a fragile being. The "Fragile Muslim" myth has been extensively and collusively employed by both parties in the addictive dance.

Enablers are also assisted by the political language of the media. We are told of the "Arab street," the "mainstream Muslim," and the "Muslim world" as if they were entities capable of expressing a unified position. These terms are most often used to intimidate enablers. We often hear that should the West take a particular action, the Arab street will rise up, or terrorize, or otherwise make trouble for the West. Yet we never hear of the Muslim world as a singular entity rising to condemn an act of terror or join hands with the West to demand a cessation of all struggles. The arrogant and grandiose imagery thus created and then left unexamined in the minds of Westerners is that of an enraged swarm of mistreated, underdeveloped souls who are otherwise unable to help or protect themselves without the enabling actions the West supplies—similar to the classic narrative of "noble savages."

This can only wreak havoc and anxiety on its target. This form of language serves to threaten—much like a child's tantrum or adolescent's rebellion—and holds enablers hostage, making them much like battered wives, afraid to act aggressively against the addict.

Similarly, words such as "innocent" and "civilian" are twisted to sound to Westerners as if they coincide with Western usage. We frequently hear of Muslim respect for innocents, and that the murder of or terror against civilians is prohibited under Islamic law. Yet the definition of "innocents" is often restricted, with Koranic justification, to exclude virtually anyone who can in any way be connected with a source of blame. For example, any Westerner who is deemed to have any connection whatsoever with a Western occupying force (such as a construction worker assisting US armed forces in building roads in Iraq) is stripped of all civilian status or innocence. (As discussed earlier, 5:32 is used by many to permit killing when done to one who has spread "mischief in the land.")

Remember that in the horror film the characters typically do not speak the same language as the threat (a monster, an alien, etc.) so that the ability to communicate is substantially curtailed if not eliminated.

In the addict/enabling dance, words are often asymmetrically applied. We use the language of "feelings" to describe Muslims in such statements as "The Arab street is embittered," or "Palestinians feel the pain of the occupation," or "Efforts must be undertaken so that the Muslim world can gain confidence and trust." Meanwhile the West, America and Israel are typically depicted in action words. This is precisely the dance dynamic: The addict *feels* the consequences of the enabler's *actions*. In contrast, the addict's actions, as well as the enabler's feelings, are deleted from the narrative. One of the few positive outcomes of the Ground Zero Mosque debate was that, for perhaps the first time, the *feelings* of non-Muslims were allowed to take precedence and the *actions* of Muslims in provoking such feelings became the focus of debate. Responsibility began to be transferred back to where it belongs.

Addicts typically take forward steps only to fall back periodically. Yet the enabler hails any sign of improvement as a victory in order to believe that real progress is being made. This fuels the "We Are Close" fantasy that has often influenced Western policy toward the Islamic world. The addict, however, is finely attuned to this response and uses it to perpetuate his addiction.

Such fantasy, so entrenched in the "Israeli-Palestinian conflict," has pervaded US dealings with the greater Arab world, as well as with Iran. Despite overwhelming evidence and experience with the Assads in Syria who thwart American goals whenever possible, the State Department has constantly upheld the notion that Syria can be turned into a major ally. Even after the assassination of Lebanese Prime Minister Rafik Hariri allegedly at the order of Syria, President Obama continued the courtship, restoring ambassadors and sending Senator John Kerry as an envoy.

More recently, when Cairo protesters forced the ouster of Hosni Mubarak and claimed they desired a democratic state, much of the West treated it as "Mission Accomplished." But while Westernized democracy may have appeared close at hand, the actual changes that resulted were orchestrated by the Muslim Brotherhood. The Brotherhood kept up the appearance—so desired by its Western enablers—that it is not a powerful force, announcing, for example, that it was not interested in putting up a candidate for the presidency. But the Brotherhood knew full well that the first president following a revolution faces an almost impossible task and is often destined to fail. Instead, it has been disguising its grab for power by seeking control of the critical ministries that will directly influence much of Egyptian society. It has also aimed at an increasing number of Parliament seats. The Investigative Project News report of 6/28/11 described how the Brotherhood had formed a new party, the

Freedom and Justice Party, to function as a political wing which initially denied it sought power.[5] It subsequently stated it sought no more than one third of the seats, later to increase to that target to 35-40%, and finally to 50%. The article says Mohammad Badie stated that if the Brotherhood were to seek full control, it could obtain at least 75% of the seats.

In addition, the Brotherhood ensured that Article 2 of the Egyptian Constitution, which requires that "Islam is the religion of the state and that *Shariah* be the principal source of legislation in the land," was retained in the new version adopted after Mubarak's fall. There followed a debate over whether the elections should precede or follow the finalizing of a new constitution. While some take that as a hopeful suggestion that more Western influences might be incorporated, it is clear that *Shariah* will in all cases be protected and that arguments are simply over how much more the Brotherhood might be able to push into the document.

Similarly, Control Factor victims have found hope in the notion that an apparent Brotherhood split by some youth members and others will diminish the power of the Brotherhood as a whole. Yet, as the IPT article suggests, the split shows as much how uncommitted to democracy the organization truly is as it seeks to prevent its own members from forming separate parties. While Western enablers were afforded the illusion of great strides being made toward their notions of freedom, the future of Egypt may soon be recognized as an addict's great fall backwards, once the Brotherhood gathers up the reins.

Ken Timmerman, in a 1/31/2011 *Newsmax* article, reports that Obama met with two Brotherhood members in the White House two months prior to his Cairo speech (at which he seated Brotherhood dignitaries in the front rows).[6] Timmerman cites the Egyptian army newspaper *Al Masry al-Ayoun* claiming the Brotherhood members assured Obama that a Brotherhood government in Egypt would "abide by all agreements Egypt has signed with foreign countries" and said they would support the United States in its efforts to fight terrorism and support democracy. Yet, as Timmerman points out, since the Brotherhood does not recognize Israel as a country, agreements with it are not covered by the assurances. And since the Brotherhood does not consider Hamas and Hezbollah to be terrorist organizations (and refers to al-Qaeda attacks on US forces as "resistance" and not terror), it has no intention of standing up to any of these organizations. Whether or not Obama understands the language manipulations here, his response throughout the entire "Arab Spring" fantasy has been pure enabling.

There is also a destructive transfer of responsibility *within* Islam. The female holds an important yet psychologically revealing position within Islam: she is held fully responsible for the lust that any male feels. When that lust is deemed shameful and sinful, responsibility is transferred to the woman or to the satanic forces that are believed to inhabit her. Essentially nothing is to be the object of deep love more than Allah, Mohammed, and Islam, and anything that diverts that passion must be blamed and punished.

Of course, this transfer evolved culturally, and exists in many non-Muslim cultures as well. Nonetheless, it has been fully institutionalized within many expressions of Islam so that women are not merely second-class; they are essentially despised. *Shariah* dictates that a woman who has been raped can be held responsible for it—and often punished by death—if she fails the almost impossible task of producing four witnesses. According to Islamic law, a woman's testimony is worth half that of a man. Men are allowed up to four wives, although Mohammed, even though considered no different from other men, allowed himself thirteen. What is considered criminal pedophilia in modern times in the West was admired in historical Islam: Mohammed became engaged to his last and favorite wife when she was six years old, and married her when she was nine.

If women were to be assigned responsibility for sexuality and its psychological consequences, they would have to be punished for it. Female genital mutilation existed in many cultures independent of Islam, but as the latter matured, the two became entwined in many expressions of Islam. Denying women pleasure, establishing dominance in enforcing such rituals, and forcing women to be symbols of shame and disgust all resonate with many other aspects and dictates of Islam. That a man's honor is held in major part by a woman is hardly limited to Islamic cultures. Yet as with the Mafia (which had its roots in Islamic Sicily), it has become deeply institutionalized within Islam. Should a woman improperly lose her virginity or be raped, for instance, the injury is not to the woman but to the honor of her family. Holding women responsible for that which men wish to deny in themselves is projection "gone wild," and epitomizes the transfer of responsibility for behavior and emotions which characterizes our Islamic Enemy.

It is not uncommon for the seemingly most pious of all religions to be caught in sexual scandals of various types. The same holds true for the most Violent Jihadists. Anwar al-Awlaki was arrested while in the

United States for soliciting prostitutes. Bin Laden's hideout contained a vast pornography library. These incidents, however, only touch the surface of a powerful psychological force at work.

CBS reporter Lara Logan was brutally attacked during her coverage of the 2011 Cairo protests. She was sexually molested by a mob of Egyptian men for at least half an hour before a group of Egyptian women saved her and eventually brought her to the military to be taken away to safety. This was not simply the consequence of overcharged libidos or economically frustrated unmarried men. This assault was a telling expression of the deep hatred for and fear of women and female sexuality that lies at the heart of many Islamic expressions.

Enabling is the Control Factor's most potent strategy. When enabling is used, all of the Control Factor tools or defenses are deployed. As long as the media and educational institutions place the West as the "root cause" of our Islamic Enemy's behavior, we will be supporting the very behavior we seek to eliminate. Each time we blame ourselves for the treatment of prisoners at Guantanamo Bay, or the CIA overthrow of Mohammed Mossedeq of Iran in 1953, we reinforce our tendency to enable. Whenever we unduly accept responsibility for the behavior of our enemy, we ensure that its threat will only continue to grow stronger.

The addict/enabler dance must be stopped. Yet it is often as difficult for the enabler to give up his enabling as it is for the addict to relinquish his addiction, precisely because the enabler wrongly believes his actions and feelings are appropriate. This mistaken belief embodies the very difficulty the West has experienced as it attempts to find an acceptable way to deal with the threat our Islamic Enemy poses.

Obviously, it is difficult for addicts to cease their behavior. When the Palestinians were offered a deal from Ehud Barak under the auspices of Bill Clinton, a deal more lucrative than they ever could reasonably have expected, Yasser Arafat could not help but turn it down. Instead, he immediately resumed in full force the terrorism he had supposedly condemned. The lucrative corruption in which he engaged, and the power he gained by feeding his people our Islamic Enemy's hateful visions, were too good to give up.

For more than 60 years following the formation of the state of Israel, the Palestinians have said "no" to every peace deal offered them. Hatred of Israel is a mass addiction. Stated in modern terms, *the Palestinians are just not into a Jewish state!*

This reaction was also seen in connection with Iraq war of 2003. As soon as American Far Leftists saw that victory was possible through the military offensive and the subsequently arranged elections, they sought to declare defeat. They called for the immediate withdrawal of all troops from Iraq, a move that, as was obvious to all, would destroy any chance for long term self-determination by the Iraqi people. Addicted to hatred of America, they could not tolerate any sign of success—for George W. Bush by name or for their own country at core.

And in early 2011, when Mubarak, Qaddafi, Assad, and others were under siege, a narrative circulated the Arab world that freedom and democracy might follow and that terrorism might no longer be welcome. This was too much for Hamas, a true addict which could not tolerate the prospect of withdrawal. It immediately commenced rocket assaults out of Gaza to draw attention back to Israel as the region's primary villain. A Brotherhood subsidiary now backed in large part by Iran, Hamas also began planning a second flotilla challenge to Israel. Provoking Israel to use force resembles the behavior that addiction therapists call a "cry for help"—though in this case, the action is more a prelude to the cry of "Allahu Akbar!"

The killing of Osama bin Laden was also a case in point. America had so effectively trained al-Qaeda to expect measured and guilt ridden actions from it that, when it changed course and acted abruptly, many Muslims worldwide responded angrily. With bin Laden in hiding, the relationship had, on one level, settled into a comfortable and stable dance. Removing such a profound symbol of the addictive ideology in such a startling and unanticipated manner predictably triggered large scale hostile reaction throughout much of the Muslim world. When the addictive substance is taken away from the addict without his consent, tantrums are the most likely response.

Enablers have immense difficulty separating from the addict. This entails not just uprooting the relationship with the addict but re-evaluating much of the thinking and presuppositions that have supported that relationship. This is especially difficult for enablers because it seems to require a reversal of much of what the enabler has previously considered moral, ethical, and even loving in that relationship.

The enabler's fundamental instinct is to find a solution within the moral and ethical structure it has already been applying to the relationship. Unfortunately, there is no way to readjust the relationship while staying under this same moral "umbrella," since it is precisely those same morals and ethics that the addict is refusing to share or fundamentally accept. Only by acting against those instincts can the enabler effectively reorient his relationship, and possibly change the addict-enabler dance. Ultimately, the enabler must accept that "tough love," or that which on the surface appears to him heartless and even immoral, is necessary both to protect the enabler and prevent the further transfer of responsibility from the addict to him.

This conflict was also observable in America's behavior following the killing of bin Laden. As an enabler, the Obama administration anticipated discomfort with the killing across much of the Muslim World. Its instinctive reaction was to make a show of dhimmitude; a demonstration of guilt and concern that it might have acted disrespectfully in the eyes of some Muslims. Thus Bin Laden's body was washed and buried within 24 hours of his death, in partial compliance with Muslim rituals. (Since bin Laden died on land, burying him at sea did not conform to Islamic law which permits sea burials only if the death is at sea and there is no alternative site on land. Of course, there may have been other considerations involved in the decision. Attorney Alan Dershowitz pointed out in the *Wall Street Journal* that the burial at sea destroyed direct evidence of how bin Laden was killed.[7] Others assert that no country would accept bin Laden.)

The burial confused those Muslims who view bin Laden as an apostate unworthy of treatment as a Muslim. Obama himself called bin Laden not a Muslim leader but a murderer of Muslims. And if bin Laden was instead one who stands to properly receive the gifts Allah promises those who die in *Jihad*, why would his enemy honor him? The compulsion of the enabler often clouds the reasonableness of his actions.

Nonetheless, Obama barred the release of any pictures of bin Laden's body, arguing that we need not "spike the football." An enabler is often petrified whenever he takes initial steps to change the dance. Why needlessly antagonize the addict? Let's make the changes slow and comfortable for the addict. Such rationalizations often hide the underlying fear that gives rise to the dance in the first place and to the Control Factor as well.

Further, bin Laden was reportedly given formal Muslim prayers as part of the naval ceremony. As Islamic scholar Andrew Bostom pointed out in a post on 5/7/11, the required prayer service includes the reading of the *Fatiha* or first *Sura* in the *Koran*. The Sura, Bostom writes, "includes an eternal curse upon Jews and Christians. . . ."[8] All of these *dhimmi* behaviors are typical of enablers who seek to restore the prior balance once something has happened to shake up the addict. The addict will necessarily respond as well, as did many Muslims worldwide, to insist upon it.

Perhaps the most basic example of enabling can be seen in the Obama administration's prohibition against coupling the words "Islam" and "terror" and against associating Islam with terrorists despite the obvious facts to the contrary. Avoiding any "insult" to Muslims is little different from a battered wife defending her alcoholic husband to the police as a kind and lovable man who simply had a bad day or who beat her because she provoked him. The approach is an attempt to avoid facing the harsh realities—that Islam is intimately connected with the violence and terrorism that is committed worldwide in its name and, also and more concerning, with the many non-violent efforts to destroy and rebuild Western society in submission to Islam.

Instead of forcing the Muslim world to explain and defend itself, the West has chosen the enabling function of acting as its defender. The media are filled with non-Muslims who incessantly beat the drum of "Islam is a religion of peace." Irrespective of the truth or falsity of that claim—much less whether it conceptually even makes sense, or whether Islam even constitutes what we term a "religion"—it reveals more about the enabler than it does about Islam or Muslims. These cases resemble the enabler who says of her alcoholic son following another in a long series of arrests for drunk driving and assault, "He's a very good boy at heart who simply had one drink too many and was talked into it by friends." At a certain point, the child must demonstrate and prove to others exactly who he is and is not. It is *his* responsibility.

The West seeks to protect its sense of moral authority by behaving with the Islamic world as if it, the West, has been guilty of exploiting the Islamic world. While an alcoholic's enabler believes he is helping the alcoholic, he is actually reinforcing the addiction. Similarly, when the Control Factor convinces us that we are properly engaging our Islamic Enemy while maintaining what we consider the moral and ethical high ground, we are often just reinforcing the very perceptions and behaviors of that enemy, accepting rather than deflecting its projections. As the enemy obtains more and more powerful weapons, this reinforcement leads us into greater peril.

President Obama brought enabling to the world stage when he embarked upon his global "Apology Tour." He set out to demonstrate to the

Muslim world that America understood it had acted poorly in the past, making mistakes and failing to live up to the ethical code that he, Obama, would have preferred to see. He called America "arrogant," and in doing so, was asking forgiveness. This enabling behavior is precisely what Islam demands of its *dhimmis*, and Obama, far from moving Muslims closer to some imagined state of mutual tolerance with the West, demonstrated how much closer America had moved toward submission to Islam. In fact, by presupposing that his mere apologies have the power to sway our Islamic Enemy, Obama demonstrated arrogance as well as ignorance. And with each step of more intensive enabling behavior comes an increase in the addictive behavior. In effect, announcing that America was prepared to be more *dhimmi*-like invited our Islamic Enemy to assert itself even more. Obama's efforts were a clear failure: as with all psychological defenses, enabling accomplishes only what it sets out to prevent. The impulse to accommodate the unaccommodatable only makes accommodation more difficult.

Some historians argue that Islam has shown great "tolerance" of other religions at times. Indeed, certain Islamic powers at certain times treated Jews more civilly than did certain Christian powers of the past. However, nothing resembling the *modern* concept of mutual tolerance occurred. If fully understood (see Bat Ye'or's extensive work on the subject), the quality of life of a *dhimmi* would shock even the most liberal conscience. *Dhimmi* status is tolerance turned upside down: it is what Jews, Christians, and others have been forced to do at the mercy of Islam rather than what Islam has done for them. To argue otherwise is to so abuse our common-sense notion of "tolerance" as to make it meaningless.

Addict and enabler live by two different sets of rules. There is an "asymmetry gap" between what is allowed for the addict and what is allowed for the enabler. Furthermore, their dance is based first upon establishing and then maintaining this gap so that, as the music plays, the addict moves and the enabler dutifully keeps in step. It is the addict who leads while the enabler follows. To stop the dance, the gap must be made to close. This requires the enabler to take the lead, often in what is called "tough love."

To the enabler, tough love feels like cruelty, because it entails letting the addict reach a painful enough "low" that he is motivated to pull himself together. Tough love for those of us engaged in the Inner Jihad will feel equally cruel and counter-instinctual, as it will require us to contravene certain moral and ethical standards we have placed upon ourselves. But just as in the horror film, we will have to realize that we are under such an extreme threat that we must better learn to first protect ourselves.

Viewed from a different angle, the enabler typically "feels empathy for the addict and defines this feeling as positive evidence of his own value; a martyrdom in its own right. This empathy is experienced as painful but the pain is more truthfully the initial response to the challenge of separating from the addict; a defense against withdrawal and closing the gap in the dance.

There is an old "joke" about a bear hunter who tracks a bear, shoots his gun and misses. The bear chases down the hunter, beats him up a bit but then walks away, believing he has taught the man a lesson. Angry at his mishap, the hunter returns the next day with a more potent firearm, tracks down the bear, but misses again. Annoyed once more, the bear chases him down, finds new ways to beat him up yet again walks away. The hunter becomes even more enraged by his own defeat, his suffering, and the envy he feels that the bear is so much more powerful than he is. He purchases an even more high-powered weapon guaranteed to destroy his target in one shot. He tracks the bear a third time, fires and once again misses. The bear runs him down, picks him up by the collar and says, "You are not really in this for the hunt, are you?"

The simple "dirty little secret" inherent in the addiction/enabling dance is that it (as with the Game of Guilt) is geared never to end. The Arab war against Israel (which Ruth Wisse correctly points out is more accurate than "the Israeli-Palestinian conflict" that draws a false equivalence between the two sides and fails to recognize the true hateful martial intentions and participation of the Arab world) is merely an early step in our Islamic Enemy's march and is extremely illuminating as it shows many of the addict/enabling dance steps. The entire relationship is not targeted to end in "peace" as Westerners mean by that word. Remember, "peace" to our Islamic Enemy comes after the world has been rid of all Jews and other non-believers.

While Obama declared in his September 22, 2011 speech to the UN that "peace is hard," the truth is that peace can be very easy if both sides truly intend it. While the poorly named "Peace Process" has had its stops and starts over the years, there are many simple stops and starts that could have easily led to Western peace. Mahmoud Abbas could stop using terror, stop funding terror, stop claiming Israel is the cause of all of his peoples' misery, stop playing the part of victim, stop rewriting history where Jews are Nazis and the Holocaust never occurred and stop teaching Palestinian children to hate and to aspire to be martyrs killing Jews. In essence, stop hating.

Similarly, there is much he could start such as reaching out with open hands to resolve differences, start preparing his people for peace, start asking how he can work with Israel in developing his economy, start demonstrating simple acts of mutual tolerance and demonstrate that mutual "peace" is what he is seeking, start teaching Palestinian children through the media he controls to value all life equally, to still respect those who do not share the same beliefs and to treat them as they have been demanding to be treated themselves. Most fundamentally, start declaring that the Jews are entitled to their own state on the contested land and start recognizing their right to exist.

While the Palestinian leaders have, for years, objected to Israel's construction of a wall to protect its people, the more insidious barrier to peace is the Wall of Hate our Islamic Enemy has constructed to keep in place the addiction/enabling dance. A Western leader, seeking Western peace, should declare, "Tear down that Wall of Hate, Mr. Abbas, and let us march together toward peace."

All of this can be easily done but for another "dirty little secret." There is such a deeply entrenched envy and hatred for Jews and Israel that rage and victimhood continue to be more preferable to the humiliation, fear, and panic that will emerge once they are afforded the freedom they so adamantly claim they desire. It is the transfer of responsibility that structures the addiction/enabling dance precisely because accepting that responsibility appears too unmanageable to the addict. Lacking skills, a recent history of success and a clear vision of how to function in the modern world, a chaotic hell is destined to break out in the minds of the Palestinians, especially when their envy is so likely provoked by some of the world's greatest advances staring right at them from neighboring Israel. When faced with having to accept full responsibility for his condition when truly granted "freedom," the addict will fight to dance on. This same force will have profound influence upon the results of the so-called "Arab Spring" as well.

No one describes this predicament as elegantly as Shelby Steele in his writings about his own dealings as a black man when released from "oppression," as well as in his talks and writings about the Middle East. Simply put, freedom is terrifying until it is somewhat mastered. Remain-

ing a victim is so much easier. To help disguise the response, the object
of the deep envy is displaced resulting in envy for the real victimhood
their so-called "oppressors" actually have endured. What better strategy
to eliminate the pain of envy than to deny the victimhood the Jews have
endured for thousands of years and in particular in the Holocaust and
absorb it as one's own identity? As Steele might describe, the Holocaust
"steals" their victim legitimacy which must be reacquired through the
lies and denials that have by now permeated the fundamental teachings
and understandings of the Arab world. And as Ruth Wisse argued in the
early 1990s, did they not steal literally

> through usurped Jewish symbols and history? They say they are the
> Arab diaspora, longing for their homeland. The PLO writes a "cov-
> enant," a sacred document like the one in the Torah, that promises the
> land of Israel to them, the Arabs. They launch a ship called the Exodus
> to draw attention to Arab plight. They claim to be suffering a holo-
> caust at the hands of the Jews. They initiate the United Palestine Ap-
> peal, with the map of Israel as its logo. A spokeswoman of the Pales-
> tinian Arabs . . . holds up the picture of a dead Arab girl as the
> Palestinian "Anne Frank."[9]

Add to this the entire self-description as victims of a Nazi occupation and
all that that entails, such as the Palestinian Authority media's claim that
"the conditions of our Palestinian prisoners are worse than the Auschwitzes
of the Nazis where Jewish detainees were held."[10] The "Nakba" or "catastrophe" that was the formation of the State of Israel has become the
horror to out-horror the extermination of almost an entire race of people
in the minds of millions, if not billions, of Muslims. Is it any wonder
that, time and again, Arafat and Abbas have rejected overly generous
peace deals? As the bear might say to them, "You are really not in this
for the peace and freedom, are you?"

Put otherwise, freedom, not peace, is tough. The Arab world has
consistently failed with various imported political systems following the
fall of the Ottoman Empire . Unfortunately, hate and envy (not to mention oil) have been our Islamic Enemy's greatest resources and strategies
for coping with the pain from what stares them in the face. While hate
has served to motivate, it has become an addictive substance trapping the
world in a dangerous drama. All of the goodwill offerings by the West to
assist with such freedom have been overshadowed by the powerful demands of this addiction. The West can help with real aid but only when

the addict truly wants help and can use it to serve the development and mastery of freedom, not the addiction itself. And that is precisely why the West must learn to distinguish its own enabling from true assistance.

In simplest form, responsibility is the flipside or underbelly of freedom. One does not come without the other. Freedom is difficult to manage, especially for those who have never tasted it before. It must be learned and takes time, as America's history demonstrates. Just as addicts try in every way to pass responsibility for themselves onto others, those confronted with newly found freedom remain tempted to transfer responsibility elsewhere. Perhaps counter-intuitively, they seek to hold onto that which keeps them bound in preference to accepting the responsibilities required by greater freedom. It is, however, as detrimental to our own freedom to enable and accept that transfer of that responsibility as it is to their endeavor to acquire and manage their own.

Ending the transfer of responsibility requires us to stop accepting blame for much of the hardship in the Islamic world. It requires us to cease applying different standards of behavior to the enemy than we apply to ourselves. It requires us to punish rather than reward improper behavior, even though such actions may lead, at least initially, to even more chaotic behavior as our enemy tries to test our convictions. It means that when we make mistakes, including mistakes in war that are common in all wars, we cease to berate ourselves and merely march forward knowing that we will do better next time. It means calling a stop to the game of guilt in all of its forms. It means we must be prepared to punish the enemy, when appropriate, without hesitation or self-doubt. It means we must demand of the enemy that he accept our moral and ethical precepts, should he desire any constructive relationship with us. And finally, it means we convince the enemy that the old game is over and maintain our position until our adversary has fully accepted and learned its lesson.

It means the dance has ended.

Part III

The Inner Jihad

Chapter 10

The Inner Jihad—What We Don't Know

The Control Factor has a relentlessly powerful grip on our perceptions and beliefs. In the absence of adequate tempering, it can run wild, much like the "ego mind" in Eastern spiritual practices. We need an equally potent arsenal of tools to loosen this grip. Of course, an active Inner Jihad on our internal battlefield in no way guarantees success on the external battlefield. Rather, the value of the Inner Jihad and its subduing of the Control Factor lies in freeing up our potential to create more effective and efficient solutions. Indeed, one of the Control Factor's objectives is to limit our perception of choices to precisely those that further its own aims. The Inner Jihad counters by clarifying our identity and purpose and empowering and licensing us to act. These changes can, in turn, bring substantial gains on the external front.

It is important to understand that the Inner Jihad is optimistic. It is the opposite of "fear-mongering." While the Control Factor is fueled by fear of the actual threat which, in turn, keeps us blind, the Inner Jihad faces that fear with strength resulting in clarity and resolve. And it is only upon this strength that realistic hopes for the future can be built. The American DNA is made for this task and the Inner Jihad should be approached with the confidence that is derived from centuries of American successes.

The Inner Jihad does not strategize over how to conduct the external war. It is not a policy-making function. It does not instruct on whether to bomb Afghanistan, send Predator drones into Pakistan, set up No-Fly Zones over Libya, blockade Gaza, kill or capture bin Laden. Nor does it determine whether to waterboard or give Miranda warnings to enemy combatants. It does not argue for attacking Hezbollah sites before or after bombing Iranian nuclear positions. Nor does it argue for a particular treatment of homegrown terrorists or specify constitutionally acceptable means to confront the Civilization or Stealth Jihadists.

Instead, it sets out to clear the mental blocks that often get in the way of formulating clear and acceptable strategies by showing us the external threat for what it truly is. It guides us to step away from our dance with our Islamic Enemy, to unwrap each of the fantasies that have such a profound grip upon us, and to scrutinize and reverse the simple distortions and denials that are the Control Factor's building blocks by substituting clear perceptions of the enemy as it truly is. Because the Control Factor reflects the individual nuances of each mind, each Inner Jihad will travel its own unique course. Nonetheless, certain guidelines and principles apply widely to all of us.

Admit We Do Not Yet Know How to Fight

The early steps in any addiction treatment require recognition that the addict does not know how to successfully change. The same is true for us as enablers stuck in the Addiction/Enabling Dance the Control Factor orchestrates. Accordingly, the first step in the Inner Jihad is to clear the mind of any presumption that we know how to fight the war with our Islamic Enemy. We have become too comfortable and any hint of change sets the Control Factor off. Believing that there is an easy solution leads the mind back to denial and displacement. The enemy becomes someone within our own ranks who is fighting ineffectively: our problem would be easily solvable but for Bush's incompetence, Obama's pro-Muslim leanings, the CIA's use of torture, the failure to send enough troops to Fallujah and Afghanistan, permitting Guantanamo prosecutions, our crippling energy dependence, and so on.

Only when we accept that these types of explanations serve to hide the truly frightening realization that there is a real enemy aiming for our destruction can we come to terms with our ignorance of how to proceed. Only when an addict truly understands how dangerous his habit is and fully appreciates the costs of continuing does he have any chance of reversing course and beginning anew.

The West is at the beginning of what could be a long and tortuous learning process. It has yet to develop a coherent, comprehensive, affordable, and morally acceptable approach to fighting the war. Much will need to be tried on the physical battlefield and much will fail. To paraphrase a famous adage: War plans never survive the first contact with the enemy. Trial and error will rule, despite our best efforts to eliminate any chance for error.

Rendition, waterboarding, Predator drone bombing, and other acts may or may not prove effective. Some Muslim outreach, hiring Muslims to critical law enforcement positions and creating laws that bend to the demands of *Shariah* will likely prove counterproductive. Engagement and partnership with Muslim groups have been tried for years in the United Kingdom and Europe with mixed results at best. Efforts intended to counter the radicalization of youths by supporting Civilization Jihadist groups might superficially appear to support a move away from violence, but at the cost of giving increased legitimacy to these organizations.

The increasing power of the Organization of the Islamic Conference nations presents unprecedented complications for us, especially if our economic power in the world continues to decline. The OIC's agenda will be increasingly advanced as China and Russia form and deepen alliances with Iran and other oil-producing members of the OIC. The replacement of the dollar as the world's reserve currency and other shifts under consideration would likely be devastating for us as we become a major target for the OIC and others. Failed diplomatic engagement with hostile nations and support for the overthrow of previously cooperative rulers has opened the Middle East to new and untested governance and relations. Maneuvering around these international pressures will present entirely new challenges which must be seen, in part, in the context of our Islamic Enemy's goals. Living with mistakes, correcting them, and marching onward must be our mindset. Only when the mental battlefield is cleared of the notion that easy answers abound can we begin to embrace the real solutions and hope to advance our interests.

For any civilization, balancing the need for self-preservation with moral acceptability requires constant adjustment. Weaponry, political objectives, and technology all evolve to fit societal circumstances and requirements; so do moral principles and concepts of justice—and we will be tested in every dimension. Our most wrenching challenge may arise on the constitutional front. As we become aware of the three separate levels of threat we face, we realize the US Constitution leaves itself more vulnerable than modern America might wish. Strengthening the minds and identities of the people the Constitution protects requires our most dedicated efforts.

Ignorance and Awareness— The Three Levels of Threat

In the horror film, the characters are typically unaware of the extent of the threat they face. Later on, they often regret that they took so long to open their eyes, thereby missing the chance to deal with the threat early and swiftly while they had many tactical and strategic advantages. The same is true of America's struggle with our Islamic Enemy. It is imperative that Americans become sufficiently aware of and comprehend the details of the threat we face before the advantages we have in dealing with it are squandered. Such a dramatic race against time is entertaining in film; it is perilous in real life.

The Inner Jihad requires vigilant awareness of the ways in which our Control Factors distort our perceptions and beliefs. As in breaking any habit, we must apply consistent oversight, asking constantly, *how does this perception, belief, or characterization serve the purpose of the Control Factor? How does it interfere with the full realization that our Islamic Enemy is actively trying to destroy us? Is this thought correct or is it simply comforting me that there is no serious threat?*

Not all beliefs concerning Islam or the Islamic threat serve Control Factor purposes. However, absent constant effort, one will never learn how to tell when the Control Factor is rearing its devious head. Just as religious rituals or spiritual practices require repetition, one must practice spotting how one's Control Factor transmutes one's perceptions to give the illusion of control. The Control Factor has burrowed deep into our thought processes and must be weeded out through relentless observation. As we begin to recognize its influence, it becomes easier to diffuse its impact and reverse its effects.

Sheer *ignorance* about Islam is perhaps our biggest national handicap. It is ironic that Islam describes the state of the world prior to the deliverance of Islam to Mohammed as *al-Jahiliyah* or the state of ignorance. We must end our own ignorance before we can think cogently about the threat we face. Modern technology and connectivity have made it easy for our youth to reach voting age with few or no reference points beyond what they have acquired through television, film, and electronic games. Obama as a candidate was able to marshal this profound, zombielike ignorance to his great advantage.

Our current national educational deficiencies are readily apparent, but they are supremely magnified with respect to Islam. Secular progressive thinking has gripped large portions of Western society, destroying what used to be a shared base of religious thought. Moral relativism, rather than encouraging a wider span of curiosity and learning, has placed blinders on the West. Just as many Muslims have little idea what their religion says, very few Americans have any fundamental grasp of what they face. As in the horror film theater, we are literally in the dark.

Saudi-funded organizations and other Islamic interest groups have spent tremendous sums spreading their message to Western nations. According to the Center for Security Policy, the Saudis had spent over $70 billion from 1975-2003 on overseas "aid" of which close to 70% was estimated to have gone towards "Islamic activities" such as building mosques, religious schools, and centers resulting in over 1500 mosques, 200 Islamic centers, and 2000 schools, all in non-Islamic countries. The annual budget, both from official state funds and the private payments from the King and high level princes, has been estimated at roughly $2-2.5 billion. Alex Alexiev called it "the largest worldwide propaganda campaign ever mounted."[1]

The long arm of Saudi "propaganda" has pervaded American Islamic communities. Their point of view is promoted in most US mosques. This is accompanied by worldwide circulation of textbooks infused with violent, hateful, anti-Semitic material that will help control the minds of the next generation of Muslims.

Islamic infiltrators have systematically distributed disinformation about their true intentions in a decades-long propaganda campaign employing major lobbyists and former US government officials. Europe followed the same path in the closing decades of the 20th century, toward Bat Ye'or's "Eurabia," a Europe submissive to the Arab-Islamic world. Many who fight the disinformation, from Italy's Oriana Fallaci to Dutch Parliamentarian Geert Wilders, have faced criminal indictments. As has begun to occur in America, Islam has gained significant influence over Europe's legal and societal machinery.

Unfortunately for us, learning about our Islamic Enemy takes effort, which is not high on the current list of favorite American pastimes. Few Americans speak Arabic. Few know or have reason to be closely involved with seriously engaged Muslims. Few have any familiarity with

Islamic cultural norms or history. Nor, until recently, has investing in the Middle East offered the level of economic rewards likely to flow from investment in Asian, Indian, Russian, and other territories. As a result, much of what is necessary upon which to form a basis of understanding must be actively sought; a chore difficult to inspire in most American homes. In an environment based on rapidly acquired bite-size chunks of information, it is unlikely that citizens will invest the necessary time and thought. Instead, they will ingest the disinformation presented to them.

What's more, political pressures appear to building *against* learning about Islam and the inroads many Muslims are making in America. In March 2011, Congressman Peter King held hearings on Muslim radicalization in America. Rather than seeing this exercise as an opportunity to learn and explore, the Left-leaning press and a wide variety of liberal groups launched a campaign against Rep. King and the hearings— again displacing the enemy. On the opening day, most of the Democrats on the committee, who themselves were members of minorities, attacked the exercise for not examining other terror groups such as the KKK and neo-Nazis. These same members insisted that singling out Muslims was either racist (although Islam is not a race) or defamatory of a community. This same attack was launched again during the second round of hearings focusing on prison radicalization in June 2011. While the other members used the time to ask meaningful questions, the Democrats generally demagogued, attacking both the hearings and the witnesses while displaying most clearly their lack of interest in learning anything real.

Learning about Islam, its core ideas, its history, its laws and how our Islamic Enemy operates is essential to combating the voluminous disinformation that has been foisted upon the West. Similarly, learning about the life of the Prophet Mohammed, the highest standard of Muslim behavior, illuminates how seriously-engaged Muslims aspire to conduct themselves. Becoming familiar with the Meccan and Medina Periods and the concept of abrogation, arms one against many deceptive descriptions of Islam which are intended to defuse Western resistance to it.

The Medina Period marks the point when *jihad* emerged as a martial undertaking with the aggressive spreading of Islamic law. Understanding these two periods is crucial to understanding our Islamic Enemy as it shows how Islam expresses itself one way when it is in the minority and another when it is in control. These two different behaviors continue today, and are evidenced around the world. Determining what Islam will do when it is in control cannot be gauged from observing how westernized Muslims act when they exist as a small minority and are seemingly "assimilated" into the surrounding culture.

Peter Hammond's *Slavery, Terrorism, and Islam* analyzes trends in Muslim behavior based upon the Muslim population in a particular territory. For instance, in countries such as the United States, Canada, Australia, China, where the Muslim population is less than 2 percent, Hammond suggests that Muslims will be regarded as an unthreatening, peaceable minority. When the population jumps closer to 5 percent, such as in the United Kingdom, Spain, Denmark, Thailand, and Germany, we begin to see proselytizing and recruiting, mainly from gangs and jail populations. As in America today, the power of the "Assimilation" fantasy on behalf of the host still allows for a peaceable relationship between the Muslim and non-Muslim populations. At 5 percent, Muslims start to exert pressure for greater influence, demanding the introduction of Islamic standards such as *Halal* foods. They begin to pressure local governments to permit some degree of self-rule under *Shariah* and often resort to violence to assert their presence. This was seen in Amsterdam following the famous Mohammed cartoon incident. Russia, France, Israel, India, and Kenya are 10-20 percent Muslim. A level of 20 percent, as in Ethiopia, tends to spawn formation of militias and more frequent killings, as well as desecration of Christian and Jewish sites. Hammond suggests that at 40 percent, as in Bosnia, Chad, and Lebanon, there is widespread violence and attacks. At 60 percent, *Shariah* is implemented along with sporadic ethnic cleansings and the enforcement of *dhimmi* taxes. At 80 percent, we are warned to expect repeated violence against non-Muslims, state-authorized ethnic cleansing, and the full domination of *Shariah*. Hammond's conclusions mirror the very principle Mohammed lived—force *Shariah* only as your relative strength in a territory permits. Consequently, the behavior of Muslims in the United States today is not indicative of the ways in which Islam would express itself once it obtains greater influence or control. Remember, Hitler changed his behavior and system once he used his "lawfully" acquired power to destroy the law.

Awareness of the very major differences between beliefs, ideas, and concepts held by our Islamic Enemy and us is also crucial. "Peace," "freedom," and "civilian" have different meanings for our Islamic Enemy. For the devout Muslim, "justice" is consistent with and occurs by virtue of the application of *Shariah*. When our enemy talks of "peace with justice," "just peace," "restoring justice," or "fighting injustice," he means something radically different from that which we would assume: he is calling for the establishment of Islamic law.

Similarly, much that we would consider unethical is sanctioned in Islam if it furthers the spread of the religion. Hence, deception and various forms of lying have, over many years and through various tribal adjustments, become commonplace. Our enemy has no separate relationship with "the truth" that compels him to uphold it. Allah's purpose supersedes everything else. Nor is there much room for "playing by the rules." Since equality between Muslims and non-Muslims is non-existent within Islam, rules for conduct between the two are asymmetrical just as different standards are applied to addicts and enablers.

Just as in the horror film, most Westerners choose to live in nearly complete denial of any threat. They may recognize a problem for a limited time, but quickly choose to shift their focus away from it. On a moment-to-moment basis, their minds may rationalize that they have too much else of immediate concern, the government is assuredly on top of the situation, it will all work out eventually, it cannot be as bad as suggested, it will never come close to harming me, and so on. The essence of the Control Factor is to rush in whenever fear calls and find a means to shift focus away.

Others, although willing to take a closer look, are comfortable deluding themselves that the threat posed by our enemies lies in foreign lands, locations from which we can remove ourselves if necessary. But the War of the Houses has, for quite some time, been developing in our homeland. Europe is well on its way to being transformed into "Eurabia," meaning that in a few decades we may be likely to visit the Notre Dame Mosque.

The horror film is rapidly progressing in America. America is following Europe in large government expenditures resulting in crippling public debt and entitlement obligations that will keep deficits large for years to come. Such economic weakness, coupled with a variety of social conditions and global pressures leads to a vulnerability easily exploitable by a conscientious and well motivated foe. Much like a biological or viral threat that secretly infects the body of the main character, America's Islamic Enemy has been invading America quietly and without triggering any significant alarm—at least until the Ground Zero Mosque and the Egyptian Muslim Brotherhood made headlines. Just as a biological agent develops the ability to bypass the body's immune system, our

Islamic Enemy has studied and quickly and quietly perfected the use of our freedoms to establish a foundational presence within our borders. And at the appropriate time, its destructive "genes" can be switched on. If so, those very freedoms will be the first victim.

The Three Levels of Threat

Jihad is the primary and all-consuming duty of the seriously engaged Muslim until it is fully accomplished. As quoted earlier, *The Quranic Concept of War* defines it as "a continuous and never-ending struggle waged on all fronts including political, economic, social, psychological, domestic, moral and spiritual to attain the object of policy. It aims at attaining the overall mission assigned to the Islamic State, and military strategy is one of the means available to it to do so. It is waged at individual as well as collective level; and at internal as well as external front."

The strategies to advance *jihad* are consequently numerous. They can be usefully sorted into three groups or levels of threat: the Violent Jihad, the Civilization Jihad, and the International Institutional Jihad:

The Violent Jihad

The *jihad* that most of us are familiar with is the violent one of terrorism. The two World Trade Center attacks are symbols for many acts of the Violent Jihad that have occurred in America. Most of us are well familiar with the variety of violent acts that have taken place in the past few decades, both connected with al-Qaeda and not. Most of us also have a sense that we are vulnerable to many more and with even more devastating damage.

Much of what we have experienced is believed to have originated from "over there," the Middle East and parts of Asia with assistance at times from Europe. We are only now starting to realize how our own hemisphere is being used by operatives not just for means of transport but for extending the reach and bases of Violent Jihadists. Former Assistant Secretary for Western Hemisphere Affairs, Roger Noriega, testified to the House Homeland Security Subcommittee on Counterterrorism and Intelligence that more than 80 Hezbollah operatives have been identified across at least a dozen South American countries." As reported by the Investigative Project (7/8/11), Noriega warned of "an attack on US personnel, installations or interests in the Americas as soon as Hizballah operatives that they are capable of such an operation without implicating their Iranian sponsors in the crime." Ken Timmerman and others have also written extensively about other terrorist buildups, whether Middle Eastern, Albanian, or otherwise, in Latin America.

Our Mexican and Canadian borders are so porous that it is reasonable to suspect that terror cells (whether al-Qaeda, its affiliates, Hizb ut-Tahrir, Lashkar-e-Taiba, etc.), assisted by easy illegal immigration and gangs such as MS-13, have established themselves in the US and await further orders. At the same time, drug and gang wars have spawned a prison population of Muslims poised to engage in violence upon release. Given the intensive radicalization in mosques and Islamic communities, coupled with easier and more dangerous weaponization, it is only reasonable to suspect that the risk of severe violence has greatly increased since 9/11. In short, we know there is a major risk of continued terror attacks and hope our law enforcement is up to the task of keeping us protected. The overarching thinking (read hope) has been that the number of terrorists is relatively small and generally manageable by the techniques and competency our excellent professionals have demonstrated to date.

Separately, most of us are unaware that more than 35 terror training camps, modeled after the terror guidelines taught by radical Pakistani Sheikh Mubarak Gilani, who founded the Muslims of America, have been established in the United States. Gilani was the sheikh whom *Wall Street Journal* reporter Daniel Pearl set out to interview before he was kidnapped and beheaded, presumably by 9/11 organizer Khalid Sheikh Mohammed. Many people suspect Gilani was an accomplice in the murder although he denies any connection.

Gilani leads a Pakistani terror group, Jamaat al-Fuqra and formed Muslims of America as an American front. According to the Christian Broadcast Network reports, both shoe bomber Richard Reid and DC sniper John Allen Mohammad are said to have been his followers. The MOA compounds are situated deep in rural areas, presumably to avoid outside scrutiny and law enforcement. Many of the members are thought to have converted to Islam in prison. Gilani demands that 30% of their income be sent to him in Lahore, Pakistan. He supposedly then uses the money to fund local operations in support of the Taliban and others. In years past, MOA members have been involved in firebombing Hindu and Hare Krishna temples, assassinating rival Muslim leaders, and possessing illegal weapons.

The documentary, *Homegrown Jihad,*[2] produced by the Christian
Action Network, shows some of the terrifying activities that take place in
the camps, including a compound called "Islamberg," in Hancock, New
York, and one in Red House, Virginia. Guns, bombs and other weapons
are fired, hand to hand combat is taught, platoon maneuvering is practiced, and survival skills are rehearsed. American flags are mutilated and
used for target practice. Personal exchanges caught on film show hate-
filled members physically and verbally attacking the film makers to stay
off of their property. These camps evidence an extremely frightening
trend. While many Americans have some awareness of the Muslim con-
versions and accompanying rage against America taking place within our
prison system, these camps demonstrate the very same dynamics smack
in the middle of our communities. It is now believed that the camps have
been instructed to tone down any violent behavior, as they have come
under law enforcement scrutiny. Still, they sit lying in wait, longing for
the time when their members can be unleashed.

This "homegrown terror" is expanding as Muslim US citizens become terrorists connected to global or foreign groups. In 2009 and 2010
alone US Army Major Nidal Hasan, the "Times Square Bomber" Faisal
Shahzad, and the "Christmas Underwear Bomber," Umar Farouk
Abdulmutallab emerged with great publicity. Many others who have been
apprehended or foiled escaped public notice. While up until now many
of them have made mistakes, the next iteration of terrorists will be more
dangerous, as they will better understand our language, customs, and
routines. Their greater sensitivity to the nuances in our behavior will
necessarily assist their secrecy and success.

While the Violent Jihad has been, in part, curtailed in the United
States due to the Brotherhood's desires to not stir reaction and, instead,
to follow its "phased plan," certain changes in this approach are appearing. The new Brotherhood Supreme Guide, Mohammad Badie, has declared it is time to wage *jihad* against America and Israel and that this
jihad is "Allah's commandment."[3] In addition, a January 2011 fatwa
was issued by an al-Azhar professor that essentially gives permission to
offensive *jihad* in non-Muslim lands solely to expand Islam. According
to the *Jerusalem Post*'s Barry Rubin, Dr. Imad Mustafa said that two
Islamic schools of law have ruled offensive *jihad* permissible "in order
to secure Islam's border, to extend God's religion to people in cases
where the governments do not allow it, such as the Pharaoh did with the
children of Israel, and to remove every religion but Islam from the Ara-

bian peninsula."[4] Rubin suggests that this opens the floodgates for *jihad* against any government that does not act in accordance with *Shariah* including in such areas as child marriage, polygamy, Islamic dress, mosque building, and workplace privileges. Rubin admits that many Muslims may not yet accept this new position. Nonetheless, and especially for those otherwise inclined to the Violent Jihad, this fatwa can serve as incentive and license.

Documenting the Civilization Jihad— The Project and the Explanatory Memorandum

Saudi Arabia funds an estimated 80% or more of the mosques in the United States in exchange for their adherence to its particular Wahhabi "brand" of radical Islam.[5] Consequently, according to the Center for Security Policy's *Mapping Shariah* survey conducted by Mordechai Kedar and David Yerushalmi, in excess of 80% of the mosques promote *Jihad* and *Shariah* with over 50% distributing literature "severely advocating violence."[6] In addition, funding of many of our major universities by the Saudis, the United Arab Emirates, and other Middle Eastern doners has ensured that the message of our Islamic Enemy is being delivered directly to those most susceptible to carrying out its goals. More than $300 million has been spent on Islamic Study Centers such as Harvard University, the University of California at Berkeley and at Santa Barbara, Rice University, and the University of Arkansas, to name a few. President Obama's Middle East mentor, Rashid Khalidi, alleged to have had close connections with the PLO, was awarded the Edward Said Chair at Columbia University, itself endowed through similar funding. US politicians have been greatly influenced by Saudi funding for decades. Those who cooperate with the Saudis find money and jobs waiting for them when they step down from office.

Equally powerful is the propaganda campaign underway on our campuses as promoted directly by front organizations for Muslim Brotherhood. The Muslim Students Association expressly identified in the recent Holy Land Foundation trial materials, along with its sister organization, the Muslim Student Union, act nationally to further disseminate propaganda and spread the Saudi-funded curriculum. These grassroots organizations greatly impact students who are unaware of the true facts and intentions of our Islamic Enemy. Pounding away at the students over decades will guarantee deeper infiltration throughout our society and our government in the future.

This is only a sample of the circumstantial evidence of a carefully constructed plan to infiltrate and ultimately move America toward becoming an Islamic land—the Civilization Jihad. The reader is encouraged to examine the works of Steve Emerson, Andrew McCarthy, The Center for Security Policy and many others cited in the bibliography including the Investigative Project's film *Jihad in America, Part 2, The Grand Deception*. It must be understood that the Muslim Brotherhood, perhaps the largest and most powerful Islamic organization in the world, declares in its constitution that one of its primary goals is

> . . . establishing an Islamic state that will apply Islamic law in a practical way, and the Muslim Brotherhood will be the guardian inside the territory of this Muslim state, *and the Muslim Brotherhood will work to export this Islamic system internationally."* (Section 2, article 2, paragraph F from Gabriel translation) (italics added)

Just as the constitutions and charters of the Islamic Republic of Iran, Hamas, and Fatah articulate their respective goals, this fundamental document makes the Civilization Jihad clear.

The Society of Muslim Brothers, better known as the Muslim Brotherhood, was founded in Egypt in 1928 by a government employed schoolteacher, Hasan al-Banna. Inspired by earlier "Islamist" writers such as Jamal ad-Din, later referred to as al-Afghani ("the Afghani"), his primary student, Mohammad Abdul, and Rashid Rida, al-Banna initially sought to fortify moral and spiritual efforts among ordinary Egyptians that he observed had waned under British rule and Egyptian corruption. Central to all of these theorists was the notion that Islam needed to unite and strengthen itself to overcome the oppressive forces that had led to the decline of the Ottoman Empire followed by the secularization of Islam in Turkey under Mustapha Ataturk.

Al-Banna's organization initially sought to combine Islamic religious instruction with technical training and social benefits. The Brotherhood grew quickly during the 1930s with close to five hundred branches. In 1938, it called for Egypt to become an Islamic state. Structurally, it distributed authority among "battalions" which consisted of "clans" which in turn were comprised of "families." While initially not emphasizing violence (as with Mohammed himself, the use of violence is dependent upon the power to be successful, something that had not accrued in the early years), the Brotherhood later developed its militant arm in creating the "Secret Apparatus" which specialized in political assassinations. Besides having murdered various lower level British and Egyptian officials and soldiers, in 1948 a Brother assassinated then Prime Minister Mahmoud Fahmi Nuqrashi. After conspiring with Gamal Abdul Nasser to overthrow King Farouk in 1952, however, the Brotherhood soon targeted President Nasser himself. Following a failed assassination attempt on Nasser, the Brotherhood faced a powerful clampdown. Nasser jailed and killed many Brothers while others fled to expand the Brotherhood outside of Egypt.

The Brotherhood has developed through different iterations, stressing violence at certain times and renouncing violence—at least appearing to act cooperatively with local authorities—at other politically opportune times. Subsequent to al-Banna's murder in 1949 by Egyptian security services, Sayyed Qutb emerged as the prominent Brotherhood voice only to be jailed and killed by Nasser. His writings are of major influence around the world today among Islamists. The Pakistani-born Abdul A'la Maududi also founded an offshoot of the Muslim Brotherhood known as Jamaat e-Islami, whose purpose was to establish an Islamic state, first for what had been Indian Muslims, and later globally.

As the Egyptian Brotherhood members dispersed, armed with financial assistance from Saudi Arabia and other Arab lands, they spread variations of Brotherhood principles, including the works of Qutb and Maududi, into Europe and eventually the United States. The Muslim Students Association was formed at the University of Illinois which, over time, formed hundreds of chapters across the nation. The MSA subsequently helped establish the North American Islamic Trust which funds many of the mosques across the country. Over time, as various Brothers learned new ways to survive and relate in non-Muslim lands, a wide variety of groups and organizations developed. Just as Wittgenstein described the meaning of words as having "family resemblances," so too do the numerous organizations that have emerged worldwide under the umbrella of the Brotherhood.

In short, it may or may not be accurate to refer to the Brotherhood as a pure legally coherent singular global entity. Instead, as used here, phrases such as Muslim Brotherhood "-associated' or "related" or "-front" entities are intended to refer to the deep relationship of overlapping persons, ideas, funding, resources, and intentions. References to the

Brotherhood's motivations, goals, strategies, and so forth are intended as a distillation for simplicity's sake, as opposed to any legally demonstrable conspiracy. That being said, the family resemblances point to much more than a "loose" relationship, and the ultimate unity of vision among the various factions around the world is not debatable.

Al-Banna had famously said, "It is the nature of Islam to dominate; to impose its laws on all nations and extend its power to the entire planet."[7] The Brotherhood's own Bylaws make clear its unifying goals today. It refers to itself as "an International Muslim body which seeks to establish Allah's law in the land by achieving the spiritual goals of Islam and the true religion. . . . "[8] Those goals include establishing an Islamic state and garnering global cooperation and support as *Shariah* proscribes. In carrying out these goals, it seeks to do all it can to establish "educational, social, economic, and scientific institutions" and "mosques, schools, clinics, shelters, clubs, as well as the formation of committees to regulate *zakat* affairs and alms."

The Brotherhood may best be understood by its motto: God is our objective; the Koran is our law; the Prophet is our leader; *jihad* is our way; and death for the sake of Allah is the highest of our aspirations."[9] And the Bylaws make clear the commitment of the Brotherhood to violence or otherwise, stating that the "Islamic nation must be fully prepared to fight the tyrants and the enemies of Allah as a prelude to establishing the Islamic State."

The Control Factor tends to focus on violence as the critical criterion for determining our Islamic Enemy. Violence is familiar and easy to recognize. A morally acceptable response can also be more comfortably targeted against violence. Indeed, Osama Bin Laden himself postulated that violent acts of terror, executed well, generate a disproportionately greater response of fear than the act itself costs—a sensible tradeoff in his view. Nonetheless, the Violent Jihad is not the primary method of choice for our Islamic Enemy when it is operating within territories that have never been under Islamic control. While violence was a central aspect of Arab tribal culture during the early years of Islam, our Islamic Enemy has developed more modern, civil, sophisticated, and "moderate" strategies to advance its agenda—ones which later can more easily lead to its enemies' surrender simply through submission. While the West wishes our Islamic Enemy to become more "moderate," it is only the methods for Islamic expansion that have truly done so.

Hudson Institute writer and scholar Hillel Fradkin sums this up by succinctly distinguishing between "moderate" and "cautious." The Brotherhood, Fradkin likes to say, is cautious in how it accomplishes its goals. In no way, however, can these goals be considered moderate.

Three critical sets of documents spell out in detail the Muslim Brotherhood's plan to Islamize America and the rest of world. First, documents discovered by Swiss authorities in late 2001 reveal what has been called "The Project." It was first publicized by French writer Sylvain Besson in his book *The Conquest of the Occident*, and subsequently by writers, researchers, and investigators including Patrick Poole and Scott Burgess. The Project outlines the goals of the Muslim Brotherhood as it sets out to overtake Western nations. Since its formation, the Brotherhood has been at the center of many significant political steps taken on behalf of Islam. Its global tentacles have actively challenged and opposed Arab governments for failing to live up to Islam's commands.

The Project shows that the Brotherhood has embarked on a systematic plan to spread Islam throughout European and American lands. Written in Arabic in 1982, it sets out the goal to "establish an Islamic government on earth." Persons seriously interested in *their* Inner Jihad should familiarize themselves with the strategies outlined in the Project, as summarized by Patrick Poole in a 2006 article at Frontpagemagazine.com:[10]

- Networking and coordinating actions between like-minded Islamist organizations;
- Avoiding *open* alliances with known terrorist organizations and individuals to maintain the appearance of "moderation";
- Infiltrating and taking over existing Muslim organizations to realign them towards the Muslim Brotherhood's collective goals;
- Using deception to mask the intended goals of Islamist actions, as long as it doesn't conflict with *shari'a* law;
- Avoiding social conflicts with Westerners locally, nationally or globally, that might damage the long-term ability to expand the Islamist powerbase in the West or provoke a backlash against Muslims;
- Establishing financial networks to fund the work of conversion of the West, including the support of full-time administrators and workers;

- Conducting surveillance, obtaining data, and establishing collection and data storage capabilities;
- Putting into place a watchdog system for monitoring Western media to warn Muslims of "international plots fomented against them";
- Cultivating an Islamist intellectual community, including the establishment of think-tanks and advocacy groups, and publishing "academic" studies, to legitimize Islamist positions and to chronicle the history of Islamist movements;
- Developing a comprehensive 100-year plan to advance Islamist ideology throughout the world;
- Balancing international objectives with local flexibility;
- Building extensive social networks of schools, hospitals and charitable organizations dedicated to Islamist ideals so that contact with the movement for Muslims in the West is constant;
- Involving ideologically committed Muslims in democratically-elected institutions on all levels in the West, including government, NGOs, private organizations and labor unions;
- Instrumentally using existing Western institutions until they can be converted and put into service of Islam;
- Drafting Islamic constitutions, laws and policies for eventual implementation;
- Avoiding conflict within the Islamist movements on all levels, including the development of processes for conflict resolution;
- Instituting alliances with Western "progressive" organizations that share similar goals;
- Creating autonomous "security forces" to protect Muslims in the West;
- Inflaming violence and keeping Muslims living in the West "in a *jihad* frame of mind;"
- Supporting *jihad* movements across the Muslim world through preaching, propaganda, personnel, funding, and technical and operational support;
- Making the Palestinian cause a global wedge issue for Muslims;

- Adopting the total liberation of Palestine from Israel and the creation of an Islamic state as a keystone in the plan for global Islamic domination;
- Instigating a constant campaign to incite hatred by Muslims against Jews and rejecting any discussions of conciliation or coexistence with them;
- Actively creating *jihad* terror cells within Palestine;
- Linking the terrorist activities in Palestine with the global terror movement;
- Collecting sufficient funds to indefinitely perpetuate and support *jihad* around the world;

This list is a roadmap for much of what is taking place in America. It needs to be fully digested by everyone seeking to manage their Inner Jihad.

During the 2008 Holy Land Foundation trial in Texas, which determined that the Holy Land Foundation was a financing front for Hamas, additional documents were revealed that had been seized by the FBI in 2004. The most important was entitled "An Explanatory Memorandum on the General Strategic Goal for the Group in North America."[11] This 1991 strategy paper was written by Mohamed Akram, then a Muslim Brotherhood Director, a member of its Shura Council, and a senior Hamas leader in the United States, and currently the secretary general of Qaradawi's International al-Quds Foundation based in Lebanon. The Explanatory Memorandum further exposes the Brotherhood's plans as they exist today, specifically for America. While there appears to be no separate evidence that the Memorandum was formally adopted by the Brotherhood, its authenticity and veracity went unchallenged in court. It states (italics added) that the "process of settlement is a *Civilization-Jihadist Process* with all the word means." It continues by saying that the Brotherhood "must understand that their work in America is a kind of grand Jihad in eliminating and *destroying the Western Civilization from within* and 'sabotaging' its miserable house by their hands and the hands of the believers so that it is eliminated and Allah's religion is made victorious over all other religions." And further: "The strategic goal of the Muslim Brotherhood in North America is multifold: the destruction of Western Civilization through a long-term *civilization-killing Jihad* from within ("by their [our] hands") and through sabotage ("the hands of the believers") and, secondly; to support the global Islamic movement to establish an Islamic super-state, the 'Caliphate'."

At the beginning of the Explanatory Memorandum, the goals of enabling Islam in North America are described as "establishing an effective and a stable Islamic movement led by the Muslim Brotherhood which adopts Muslims' causes domestically and globally, and which works to expand the observant Muslim base, aims at unifying and directing Muslims' efforts, presents Islam as *a civilization alternative*, and supports the global Islamic State wherever it is." In short, the goals are to establish the global Islam Nation which will require the destruction of Western Civilization from within and substitute Islam as the "civilization alternative."

Elsewhere, the Memorandum says, ". . . the Movement must plan and struggle to obtain 'the keys' and the tools of this process in carry out this grand mission as a *Civilization Jihadist* responsibility which lies on the shoulders of Muslims and—on top of them—the Muslim Brotherhood in this country."

The Memorandum goes on to explain that the Brotherhood must settle in North America to carry out its mission. Importantly, it contains a "list of our organizations and the organizations of our friends." No fewer than twenty-nine organizations are on the list including ISNA, MSA, NAIT, IIIT, and CAIR's predecessor IAP.

Uncovered along with the Explanatory Memorandum was a third paper entitled, "Phases of the World Underground Movement Plan." This document outlines a series of phases through which the Brotherhood will move as it accomplishes its Civilization Jihad in North America. Interestingly, it has since been called "the phased plan" as was Yasser Arafat's decades long strategy for destroying Israel.

The phases are described as follows:12

I. Discreet / Secret establishment of elite leadership
II. Gradual appearance on the public scene & utilizing various public activities
III. Escalation phase, prior to conflict/confrontation with rulers, utilizing mass media
IV. Open public confrontation with the government through political pressure approach
V. Seizing power to establish the Islamic Nation

The Center for Security Policy's Team B report adds comments about these steps opining that we are in Phase III, escalation, while "aggressively implementing" phase IV by ". . . training on the use of weapons domestically and overseas in anticipation of zero-hour." The comments add that Phase II "succeeded in achieving a great deal of its important goals, such as infiltrating various sectors of the Government." It adds that the phase gained "religious institutions," and "public support and sympathy" while also "embracing senior scholars." All of this along with ". . . re-establishing a shadow government (secret) within the Government."

Team B summarizes the activities employed by the Brotherhood in America in pursuit of its Civilization Jihad goals:

- Expanding the Muslim presence by birth rate, immigration, and refusal to assimilate;
- Occupying and expanding domination of physical spaces;
- Ensuring the "Muslim Community" knows and follows MB doctrine;
- Controlling the language we use in describing the enemy;
- Ensuring we do not study their doctrine (*Shariah*);
- Co-opting key leadership;
- Forcing compliance with *Shariah* at local levels;
- Fighting all counterterrorism efforts;
- Subverting religious organizations;
- Employing lawfare—the offensive use of lawsuits and threats of lawsuits;
- Claiming victimization / demanding accommodations;
- Condemning "slander" against Islam;
- Subverting the US education system, in particular, infiltrating and dominating US Middle East studies programs;
- Demanding the right to practice *Shariah* in segregated Muslim enclaves;
- Demanding recognition of *Shariah* in non-Muslim spheres;
- Confronting and denouncing Western society, laws, and traditions; and
- Demanding that *Shariah* replace Western law.

Note that many of the foregoing techniques entail, in one way or another, influencing and neutralizing the American government at all levels.

These three sets of documents articulate the Civilization Jihad, the goal of which is to promote *Shariah* Law and all the cultural aspects of Islam into Western life, including legal proceedings, family life, financial and business dealings, education, politics, health care, and dietary customs. It is understood as a long-term endeavor (even envisioning a 100-year plan), and its patient advocates have endless faith in the value of the undertaking, planning to advance this *jihad* step by step. Nor is the goal a secret. Imams and other Islamic speakers around the world—not to mention those engaged in the Violent Jihad—regularly pronounce in mosques and on Islamic television channels that the West will sooner or later submit to *Shariah*.

Civilization Jihadists use many different approaches. One pattern involves a provocative act, followed by a claim of victimhood or assertion of rights, and then a retreat until the next round. This cycle trains our Control Factors to adjust gradually, as does a frog to slowly heating water. Muslims in the American Midwest have sought to push through various aspects of *Shariah* law, one at a time. In 2006 and 2007 we saw Muslim taxi drivers refuse to accept passengers carrying alcohol. During the same period we saw the effort to turn facilities at the Minneapolis airport into Muslim prayer sites. Detroit has become a major center for Muslim immigration, and now boasts many traffic and other signs written in Arabic. In 2010, Muslim organizations, claiming only the best of intentions, sought to build The Ground Zero Mosque at the site of the World Trade Center; an insult given with a smile. The project was fronted by the "Cordova Initiative," whose name speaks to different audiences. To the Control Factor, it speaks of tolerance and bridge building between the West and the Islamic world. To the Islamic world, however, it demonstrates an Islamic victory and conquest under the guise of "religious freedom."

The list is long, but the carefully calibrated "moderate" approach that gradually unfolds each act makes it all appear acceptable, if not innocuous. Awareness is the initial antidote.

Using the Law to Destroy the Law

"Lawfare," the systematic use of Western courts to help protect and further advance Islamic infiltration, is being used more frequently by our Islamic Enemy. Often funded by Brotherhood-associated entities or other well-capitalized Islamic "charitable" organizations, lawfare entails, in part, going to court under the pretense of having been victimized by some form of anti-Islamic act. The primary intent of lawfare is to silence the defendant. Perhaps the signature case involved the Saudi billionaire, Khalid bin Mahfouz, who sued writer Rachel Ehrenfeld for libel based on her assertions of his terrorist connections. This case of libel tourism (in which the suit was brought in the United Kingdom rather than the United States because British law makes it harder to fend off a claim) is meant to deter journalists from probing the behavior of our Islamic Enemy. Fortunately, backlash from this case caused New York and other states to adopt laws which led to federal legislation to protect US citizens from judgments from foreign jurisdictions which do not apply US First Amendment principles.

The more frequent tactic in the United States is to make claims in court concerning acts which extend the Civilization Jihad. These claims are intended to cost the defendants large and unaffordable sums simply to protect themselves. The well-funded plaintiffs know all the while that if the case proceeds to discovery—which could expose their internal workings and communications—they are free to drop it.

Lawfare has been an effective tool in advancing what has been labeled "creeping *Shariah*." Instead of conquering non-Muslim lands first and then mandating *Shariah*, much of modern Islam's advance has been incremental. In its move toward Eurabia, for instance, numerous courts in the United Kingdom have allowed *Shariah* to be applied in some disputes involving Muslim parties. Pressure is similarly being placed on other European countries and even Canada to do the same.

Daniel Pipes, for example, has voiced particular concern about a trend toward polygamy. Courts in the United Kingdom have begun to tilt toward recognizing polygamy if all the spouses contracted their marriage in a country where polygamy was legal. The original case concerned extending a tax exemption on husband-to-wife bequests to extend to more than one wife. The judgment likely involved fairness: Why discriminate among wives and deprive a second or third wife of tax-free payments if the original marriages were acceptable in their jurisdictions? UK government agencies later recommended full recognition of polygamy.

Over time, however, these occasional instances serve as a Trojan Horses that introduce problematic conflicts between *Shariah* and the law of the non-Muslim land, resulting in the subsequent conformation of the host country's law to *Shariah*. As with a Florida and New Jersey case in which *Shariah* was ordered even though one party was seeking for it not to be applied, it does not take too long for the Civilization Jihad to spread successfully.

Similarly, US law is expanding both to accommodate Muslim behavior and to restrict anti-Muslim expression. A 2011 study[13] by the Center for Security Policy, *Shariah Law and American State Courts*, examined 50 *Shariah* cases in appellate courts across 23 states, including six in New Jersey, five in California, and four each in Florida, Massachusetts, and Washington. The cases covered *Shariah* marriage, child custody, contract, property, and due process law. The study found that 15 trial court cases and 12 appellate court cases had declared *Shariah* to be applicable.

The goal of the Civilization Jihad is the worldwide institution of *Shariah*. Compared with the Violent Jihad, it is less likely to stir resistance, is easier to effectuate (as the public with its enabling tendencies is inclined to remain indifferent or even assist), and is better armed to overturn constitutional protections by incrementally gaining control over the system itself. Awareness of the true threat of this Civilization Jihad is crucial if America is ever to defend itself adequately. The Control Factor will repeatedly question whether such an organized effort could ever truly be executed, casting doubt on one's own sensibility. Accusations of paranoia, delusion, and unreasonableness are some of the Control Factor's sharpest tools; accusing those who trumpet concern of using some of the very defenses it employs to blind us to the realities we face.

Infiltration is a frequently-practiced art throughout the Islamic world. Again, embodying a time frame normally regarded as too slow for Westerners, our Islamic Enemy is strategizing for the long war. The Egyptian-based Muslim Brotherhood and related groups, for instance, have spent decades placing members within all levels of Egyptian institutions, including critical posts at universities, professional associations, media, and so forth. As noted previously, even following the fall of Mubarak, the Brotherhood has been careful not to push too hard and has initially declined to offer its own candidate for the presidency. Instead, realizing that the first president to follow Mubarak will likely fail to satisfy the populace, the Brotherhood is more wisely focused on gaining control of parliament positions and critical ministries that it can manipulate to even greater effect.

Turkey, having been essentially secularized under Ataturk following World War I, is a critical indicator of "Islamist" affairs and progress. We see today a forceful rise in Islamist presence in the Turkish government and social institutions which has resulted from a skillfully implemented campaign over years to stack government positions. Consequently, as Turkey, under Prime Minister Erdogan, senses its growing influence and threatens war with Israel, it is fast moving toward becoming an outright Islamist state.

Similar measures are being executed throughout Europe and America. And in America, our government has arranged for itself to be taught about Islam by many of the very Muslims who are advancing the Civilization Jihad including prominent figures from many of the entities associated with the Muslim Brotherhood. Due in part to political correctness, alliances with Far Left causes and activists, and Control Factor maneuvers themselves, we have opened our most critical government institutions to the multifarious tactics of our Islamic Enemy. Conversely, Major Stephen Coughlin was famously repositioned within the Pentagon in 2008 precisely because he presented a thorough and uncensored—and undisputed—analysis of Islamic law. Because the Pentagon and others were unable and/or unwilling to see our Islamic Enemy for what it truly is, Coughlin became the displaced enemy himself and was handled accordingly. His presentation, *To Our Great Detriment: Ignoring What Extremists Say about Jihad*[14] is a must-see for anyone seeking an education about our Islamic Enemy.

Europe is, perhaps, the leading indicator of what is to come for America. Buying into the "Assimilation" fantasy early on, Europeans expected a successful Muslim integration into European culture. Yet, as vast Muslim immigration occurred over the past decades, separate unassimilated communities developed. In many areas, these communities have become significant threats to their surrounding populations while simultaneously claiming apartheid victimhood. They also do their best to implement *Shariah*, weakening the surrounding rule of law.

Free speech is perhaps the most active area of lawfare, precisely because eliminating the ability to criticize eliminates the ability to resist. In Europe, generally, an attempt has been made to distinguish speech that attacks Islam from speech that is seen as insulting to Muslims. Yet, when applied, the laws have taken significant detours from common sense.

An Austrian court in 2011 convicted Elisabeth Sabaditsch-Wolff of "denigration of religious beliefs of a legally recognized religion."[15] Sabaditsch-Wolff merely described in a seminar a story of a discussion with her sister over how another woman was being pressured for questioning Mohammed's engagement to Aisha at age six and consummation of the marriage at age nine. She asked her sister, "A 56-year-old and a six year old? . . . What do you call it if not pedophilia?" In another seminar, she described how Mohammed is the perfect Muslim to be copied but that his behavior is not in keeping with today's standards because he "had had plenty of women, to put it this way, and he had a thing for children." According to her lawyer, while the judge exonerated her on the charge of incitement and found her statements on Islam permissible as they were not actually made in a provocative manner, she was guilty of denigrating of religion because that law is abstract and merely requires the possibility to cause an offense. Incredibly, the judge felt compelled to declare that Mohammed was not a pedophile because he continued his marriage to Aisha until his death.

Much of this trend in Europe started post World War II. As described in full by www.LegalProject.org, the European Convention on Human Rights in the early 1950s sought to balance free speech rights with protections of the rights and reputations of others. Subsequent international conventions then penalized the expression of ideas based on racial superiority or hatred and, later, "any advocacy of national, racial, or religious hatred that constitutes incitement to discrimination, hostility, or violence."

Interestingly, never missing an opportunity to attack Israel, the Muslim world joined with the Soviet Union and other third world countries in 1975 in a "Zionism Equals Racism" strategy passed at the UN. This approach to de-legitimizing Israel has since expanded to Europe and elsewhere. Targeting *racism* in such contexts is applied to protect Islam alone.

The European Union's 2008 Framework Decision on Combating Racism and Xenophobia seeks to punish expressions (or any other behavior) that incite violence or hatred against a group or members of a group based on race, color, descent, religion, or belief, or national or ethnic origin. In addition, it punishes any dissemination of pictures or other material containing expressions of racism or xenophobia as well as any public condoning or grossly trivializing genocide or other war crimes which, when carried out, is likely to incite violence or hatred against such a group. Prosecution under the Framework is not dependent upon any accusation or report by a victim; rather such conduct can be actionable whether or not it actually offends or incites violence or hatred. While its reach is wide, commentary by the Council which drafted the Framework humorously states "the Framework Decision is limited to crimes committed on the grounds of race, colour, religion, descent, or national or ethnic origin. It does not cover crimes committed on other grounds e.g. by totalitarian regimes. However, the Council deplores all of these crimes."

It is clear that what began as an attempt to instill sensitivity about racism and xenophobia has turned into an attack on that which can not be easily regulated—thoughts and feelings. Worse, this evolution results in transferring responsibility for one's behavior and feelings onto others. That is, if a Muslim acts violently and such act can be tied to a non-Muslim's words, it is the latter's crime. And when the law seeks to regulate feelings—a Muslim is insulted, or a non-Muslim expresses hate—it is the hate that is the crime. This is the Control Factor's "Attack Emotions" discussed earlier. The balance between freedom and injury has "crept" so far toward protecting any form of victimhood that freedom already has been severely curtailed, even if most have yet to notice. The exclusion of crimes committed by totalitarian regimes is comical precisely because this type of control on subjects' thoughts and feelings is exactly what totalitarian regimes seek. The laws that derive from this Framework need not have any victim so long as a prosecutor can make a case for, essentially, a theoretical violation.

Lars Hedegaard, the president of the Danish Free Press Society and the International Free Press Society, was found guilty of violating a provision of the Danish penal code (§266b) which states: "Whoever publicly or with the intent of public dissemination issues a pronouncement or other communication by which a group of persons are threatened, insulted or denigrated due to their race, skin colour, national or ethnic origin, religion or sexual orientation is liable to a fine or incarceration for up to two years." Hedegaard's actionable speech was, ". . . girls in Muslim families are raped by their uncles, their cousins or their dad."[16] His crime was to discuss "the great number of family rapes in areas dominated by Muslim cultures in Denmark."[17] Hedegaard was originally acquitted not on the finding that his statements were legally acceptable (the court found them to be insulting) but that they were not intended for public dissemination. His conviction on appeal was based on the finding that he knew his statements would become public.

Hedegaard will likely appeal. His latest book entitled *Muhammad's Girls: Violence, Murder and Rape in the House of Islam* was released the day of his conviction.

Perhaps even more threatening to American free speech principles is seen in a related action brought against Danish MP Jesper Langballe. Langballe was also concerned about honor killings and said sarcastically in support of Hedegaard, "Of course Lars Hedegaard should not have said that there are Muslim fathers who rape their daughters when the truth appears to be that they make do with killing their daughters (so-called honor killings) and leave it to their uncles to rape them."[18] Rather than withstand a trial, Langballe pled guilty, making a profound statement that pointed out how serious an issue honor killings are and, more importantly, how the truth of statements is not a defense and is irrelevant in Danish speech litigation. To exaggerate, but not by much, if someone is offended or merely thought to be offended, nothing else matters.

In a March 3, 2011 interview[19] with Ann Snyder, Hedegaard expressed concern over the trend of these laws. He argues it is "not irrational to fear Islam" and that it has "come as a shock to Danes that we really do not in fact have free speech. There is no prior restraint, but then they'll get you afterwards." Hedegaard describes the manner in which Muslims have brought *Shariah* into Europe, pointing out the 700 No-Go Zones in France where police do not enter and the "writ of French law does not reign." He counsels that the first step "is to understand what Islam is, and people do not realize what we are up against. They do not realize what a pernicious ideology we are facing, even an ideology that does not really demand any sort of formal leadership." Snyder writes additionally that Hedegaard "went on to add that unlike totalitarian ideologies like Communism and Nazism that were largely defeated when the states advocating those ideologies fell, Islam, without a formal head, is different."

Hedegaard warned that the United States should be seriously concerned about free speech rights in Denmark. "We live in an increasingly internationalized, globalized order where people look to other countries for guidance and inspiration. Of course, where Europe goes the United States may well go. You see the same pattern in Canada and other places. *I don't think you should believe that the US can remain an island of freedom in a world of suppression and dictatorship.*" (italics added)

Other European countries have similar laws. France has long treated criminally the incitement to racial discrimination, hatred, or violence on the basis of the same groupings. As the Legal Project.org reviews, Michel Houellebecq was prosecuted for calling Islam "stupid" and "dangerous." France does not even require that the dissemination be public. While he was acquitted, it was not on grounds of free speech. More famously, actress Brigitte Bardot was convicted of inciting racial hatred in criticizing the slaughter of sheep in Muslim feasts. The Netherlands, as described below with Geert Wilders, prohibits public intentional insults, while the United Kingdom's Sec. 18(1) of the Public Order Act of 1986 states, "A person who uses threatening, abusive, or insulting words or behaviour or displays any written material which is threatening, abusive or insulting, is guilty of an offence if: a) he intends to thereby stir up racial hatred, or b) having regard to all the circumstances racial hatred is likely to be stirred up thereby." Section 5 criminalizes the use or display of such words "within the hearing or sight of a person likely to be caused harassment, alarm, or distress thereby." These standards, especially when placed in the hands of a progressive judiciary, can wreak havoc on long-held freedoms.

The case against Dutch parliamentarian Geert Wilders demonstrates much of the dynamics currently playing out across Europe. Wilders was charged with insulting a group, hate speech, and incitement to discrimination, under two articles in the Dutch penal code[21] that date back to an effort to block Nazism's growing anti-Semitism in the 1930s. Specifically, Wilders was charged with crimes under the code for anyone who "publicly, verbally, or in writing or image," (in the case of article 137c) "deliberately expresses himself in any way insulting of a group" or (in the case of 137d) "incites hatred against or discrimination of people or violent behavior against person or property" (in both cases) "of people of their race, their religion or belief, or their hetero- or homosexual nature or their physical, mental, or intellectual disabilities. . . ." The specific speech centered upon his production of the film *Fitna* which simply juxtaposed passages from the *Koran* with imagery of Islamic terrorism. In addition, Wilders made roughly fifty statements concerning Islam including, "The heart of the problem is the fascist nature of Islam, the sick ideology of Allah and Mohammed as laid down in the Islamic Mein Kampf: the Koran"; "We have a huge problem with Muslims which crosses boundaries in every field, and we come up with solutions that wouldn't make a mouse go back into its cage"; and "Islam is a violent religion. If Mohammed were living here today, Parliament would instantly agree to chase him out of the country in disgrace."[22]

Initially, the public prosecutor refused to bring charges citing that Wilders' speech occurred in the context of a public debate and was acceptably critical of Islam as a set of ideas as opposed to Muslims for something intrinsic to them as people. A critic, however, appealed to the Court of Appeal which, as permitted by Dutch law, ordered the prosecutor to bring the case. In the October, 2010 case, three charges were brought against Wilders. As historian Thierry Baudet has described, the prosecutor continued to demand acquittal on each of the charges. He concluded that while insulting a group can be prohibited, it had to be aimed at individuals, had to be directed to "intrinsic" qualities of the individuals, and must be "unnecessarily grievous" with respect to its contribution to public debate. The prosecutor concluded that most of Wilders' statements were not about individuals and those that were dealt with behavior, not "intrinsic" qualities. A similar distinction applied to the hate speech charge. The prosecutor argued that a forbidden incitement to hatred needed to point to something with respect to the basic and intrinsic nature of the victims, not their conduct or ideology. Wilders had made clear that his objection was to the religion and ideas, not the people and that if Muslims assimilated he would have no objection at all. Finally, the prosecution argued he had no case against Wilders on the basis of incitement to discrimination because Wilders had called on the legislature, not any individual, to act. As the trial neared closing, however, and after various incidents occurred suggesting bias on behalf of judges, Wilders filed for dismissal and won. It was only a temporary victory for Wilders, however, as a new panel of judges was assigned.

Perhaps signaling a pivotal reversal in European legal judgments, in June, 2011, Wilders was ultimately acquitted of the new charges. The presiding judge said that while Wilders' remarks have been "hurtful," "shocking," or "offensive,"[23] they were still legally permissible, even if "at the edge."[24] Judge Marcel van Oosten commented that while some of Wilders' speech was "crude and denigrating," it did not constitute incitement to hatred and must be viewed in the context of a "national debate over immigration policy and multiculturalism."

While this decision was certainly the correct result, Wilders' comments are still considered "borderline." The verdict demonstrates the power of Control Factor tendencies to attack emotions; to try to enforce a ban on emotions such as hatred. The law is pointed at an emotional state of the defendant (hatred) and reflexively relies upon evidence of the emotional state of the alleged victim (fear, humiliation, etc.). While the recognition of the horrors of Nazism in the 1930s is clear justification for laws attempting to stop any similar reoccurrence, the application of these laws is susceptible to manipulation by those who might have exactly the opposite motivation. This is best seen in some of the responses of those disappointed by the Wilders acquittal. Gilbert Kreijger and Aaron Gray-Block reported in *Reuters* 6/23/11 that an Amsterdam Free University political scientist said, "This means that his political views are condoned by law, his political rhetoric has been legalized."[25] A member of the SMN association of Moroccans in the Netherlands responded, "You see that people feel more and more supported in saying that minorities are good for nothing." "The acquittal means that the right of minorities to remain free of hate speech has been breached" declared a member of the National Council for Moroccans. The idea that political rhetoric was ever to be deemed illegal—that even if Wilders himself did believe that minorities are "good for nothing"—he should be punished under the law for holding or expressing that belief, or that there was ever a "right" to remain free of hate speech, are all concepts that should be foreign to anyone who ever came to understand the principles underlying US law.

Ayaan Hirsi Ali, herself a former member of Dutch Parliament and now in America under strict security arrangements, has also been pressured for her participation in a film entitled *Submission*, which was notable for inspiring the murder of its creator Theo Van Gogh by a Muslim attacker. Hirsi Ali, in a 10/11/10 *Wall Street Journal* opinion piece,[20] explains the Wilders prosecution as a result of three factors. First is the Left's discomfort with anyone who stands up to the European "tolerance" of Muslim immigration.

Second, Hirsi Ali notes the rise of Muslim power as a voting bloc. Just as Peter Hammond correlates the tradeoff between Muslim population percentages and Muslim behavior in a particular territory, Ali ominously points out that in 2006 local elections, Muslim immigrants for the first time acted as a bloc that could wield power.

Finally, Hirsi Ali describes the influence of the OIC's efforts to "silence the European debate about Islam." Referencing various strategies of what is called here the International Institutional Jihad, Ali writes, "One strategy used by the 57 OIC countries is to treat Muslim immigrants to Europe as satellite communities by establishing Muslim cultural organizations, mosques, and Islamic centers, and by insisting on dual citizenship. Their other strategy is to pressure international organizations and the European Union to adopt resolutions to punish anyone who engages in 'hate speech' against religion. The bill used to prosecute Mr. Wilders is the national version of what OIC diplomats peddle at the United Nations and the European Union."

Nor are the losers ready to pack their bags. Remember, the "War of the Houses" is set to continue until final victory. Various Islamic minority groups claimed that they need to take this ruling to the United Nations Human Rights Committee on the basis that the Netherlands had, according to Kreijger and Gray-Block, failed to protect ethnic minorities from discrimination. It is unclear what act of discrimination specifically occurred other than that which goes on within the mind of the accused. In a move suggestive of "norming," these groups are now looking to international institutions to enforce what a domestic European court finally was willing to turn down—just as Hirsi Ali suggested.

And the press campaign started immediately as well. In a June 24, 2011 *Arab News* editorial, "Freedom to Abuse?" bemoaning the acquittal contained all of the elements of "switching identities." The paper referred to a "vicious war on a religious minority in the heart of Europe"26 as if Europe for decades had not bent over backward in dhimmitude to accommodate a vast wave of Muslim immigration. The paper argues that Dutch laws deal with attacks against the views of the majority but fail to protect minorities. As pointed out earlier, Islam expresses itself differently when it is a minority than when it is in the majority; all the while waiting for it to become the dominant force. In the interim, the paper seemingly demands the minority to be treated as the majority. The paper alludes to fascism and claims that if Wilders tried this against "the Jews," he "wouldn't know what hit him."

Playing victim in this context and hostilely claiming the "war" is fostered by Wilders when "war" is the essential activity promoted by Islam is just another example of projection gone awry. The editorial accused Wilders and "his ilk" of conducting a "fascist crusade" against Muslims with an at least subliminal identification of current Muslim conditions with those of Jews during the Nazi period. Switching identities is even more pronounced in the paper's adoption of precisely what Wilders was doing—warning about going too far. The editorial exclaims, "How much more do the Muslims have to suffer at the hands of lunatics like Wilders before Dutch courts decide that enough is enough? What else do you require to pose a clear and present danger to a civilized society?" It was Wilders who has been warning Europeans and Americans of precisely this.

Wilders gave a speech in May, 2011 in a church in Nashville, Tennessee, in which he warned, "My dear American friends, you cannot imagine how we envy your First Amendment. The day when America follows the example of Europe and Canada and introduces so-called 'hate speech crimes' which is only used to punish people who are critical of Islam, that day America will have lost its freedom."[27]

While similar laws have not as yet been enacted in America, similar behavior is beginning to emerge in American Muslim communities. Just as Mohammed's Treaty of Hudabiya served as a temporary standoff until enough power was acquired to complete a military coup, *the promise of assimilation* into a non-Islamic culture is simply that—a deceptive promise, good only for as long as it is useful. Muslim leaders generally understand it as a temporary moratorium until the establishment of separate Islamic communities capable of developing their own power base steeped in *Shariah*. And, just as the Quraysh tribe of Mecca bought into Mohammed's promises, much of America and the West readily indulge the "Assimilation" fantasy for all it pretends to offer.

There is some evidence that Europe is beginning to process its own Inner Jihad and suppress its Control Factors, Mr. Wilders' efforts being a prime example. James Kirchick's 10/12/10 *Wall Street Journal* piece[28] lists various efforts that suggest a partial awakening from the slumber induced by decades of Eurabian *dhimmi* agreements. Of Swiss voters, 60 percent voted to ban the construction of all minarets everywhere. Burqas have been banned in France, and Belgium's lower house also voted for such a ban. (Oddly, France hit a roadblock when a defendant refused to take off her burqa in court, saying that was "non-negotiable." French police were under strict orders not to remove coverings. The case was "abandoned" so that prosecutors could determine how to deal with this type of challenge). Anti-immigrant parties are gaining strength in Sweden, the United Kingdom, Austria, France and Germany. (Kirchick is careful to note that the anti-immigrant sentiment is not limited to Muslims but in some cases extends to Jews as well). It is possible that some of the trends beginning to show in Europe will take shape in America before America buries itself more deeply in its own slumber.

Fortunately, at least, some European leaders have begun to object to the claims of assimilation. German Chancellor Angela Merkel stated in October 2010 that Germany's attempt to create a multicultural society has "failed, utterly failed."[29] These comments were separately echoed by France's President Nicholas Sarkozy. Similarly, British Prime Minister David Cameron stated in early 2011 that Britain's policy of multiculturalism has led to the thriving of Islamic extremism. He referred to the country's "hands-off tolerance," and warned that "Europe needs to wake up to what is happening in our own countries."[30]

As "sweet" a fantasy as multiculturalism may seem, it also functions as an act of appeasement when kindness is mistaken as weakness. It has essentially constituted a longterm offer from the West to negotiate with our Islamic Enemy. The result for our Islamic Enemy, however, has been to extract what amounts to an intermittent "peace" in the midst of a grander "invasion" into Europe. Like all horror film attempts to negotiate, it was ultimately doomed to fail and it has.

Infiltration

Faculties and administrations in the United States have for decades blamed Western civilization for all that is wrong with the world. This bias helps ally the Far Left with our Islamic Enemy, and, not surprisingly, colors the way in which Islam is taught in our schools. Not only do university faculties, school boards, and the US Department of Education encourage pro-Islam and pro-*Shariah* curricula, but we also see leaders of other religions actively supporting such efforts in the name of promoting "mutual" acceptance and "interfaith" community.

The Civilization Jihad is influencing primary and secondary education as well. As Ryan Mauro pointed out on *Frontpagemagazine.com*, New York State's high school Regents exam requires students to regurgitate the "Party-Line" on Islam. Mauro writes: ". . . the lesson for impressionable children taking the exam is clear: Islam is historically tolerant, progressive, and admirable, whereas modern extremism has more in common with Christianity."[31] The exam avoids any reference to *jihad* and includes a reading from apologist Dr. John Esposito, who has associated himself with many of the figures in the Civilization Jihad having served with Qaradawi on the Steering Committee of the Circle of Tradition and Progress and with Azzam Tamimi on the advisory board of the Institute of Islamic Political Thought, among others. Further, Esposito heads the Center for Muslim Christian Understanding funded in part by Saudi Prince Awaleed bin Talal. Mauro describes how the correct answer for describing Islam's expansion into Africa avoids any reference to aggression or forced conversion.

Mauro also cites textbooks which treat aspects of Christianity as subject to belief whereas similar aspects of Islam are treated as fact. *Global History and Geography* describes Christians as *believing* Jesus was the resurrected Messiah whereas Muhammad is simply referred to *as* the Messenger of Allah. Another text, *World History*, states that Jesus' followers "proclaimed" that He had risen, whereas the revelations of Allah are simply accepted as written down in the *Koran*, not qualified as asserted by Mohammed. *The Western Heritage* says the Gospel authors "believed Jesus was the son of God" but Mohammed "began to receive revelations from the angel Gabriel, who recited God's word to him at irregular intervals."

Mauro further notes that when the director of the American Textbook Council examined ten textbooks, he found that many did not mention that 9/11 terrorists considered themselves Muslims or that *jihad* and *Shariah* have violent applications. "The textbooks even advocated policy, diagnosing terrorism as a symptom of poverty, ignorance, and anger over the Israeli-Palestinian conflict," the director adds. Author Robert Spencer is quoted in the article saying that this is the extension of a "multiculturalist" ethos which in theory posits that all cultures are equal, but in practice holds all non-Western cultures superior to Judeo-Christian culture. . . . "Whole generations of students are being taught to despise their own culture and civilizational heritage. Why, then, should they bother to defend it?"

Shariah is also being significantly advanced through the financial community's promotion of "*Shariah*-Compliant Finance." Billions, if not trillions, of dollars have been funneled into products created to maneuver around *Shariah* restrictions on the payment of interest and limitations on what kinds of investments are permissible. Sold by our biggest banks and investment banks, these financial products ultimately lack transparency as to where the funds are placed. And the most obvious movement of funds is as *zakat*, the Muslim's charitable duty.

Critical to the financing structure are the advisory boards stacked with "scholars" qualified to confirm and approve *Shariah* compliance. Perhaps the most notable has been Mufti Taqi Usmani who served as lead expert for the products of Dow Jones, HSBC, and others and whose son serves as well on AIG's Shariah Finance Board. Usmani reduced his presence after his jihadi devotion was given more attention by those seeking to alert the world to the dangers of *Shariah* finance. Now, much of his background is easily obtainable. As described by *Shariahfinance watch.com*, Usmani is a prolific jihadist writer who has been a vocal supporter of the advancing offensive *jihad* against non-believers "in order to establish the supremacy of Islam" throughout the world. Having been a *Shariah* judge sitting on the Supreme Court of Pakistan for two decades, he was instrumental in introducing *Shariah*'s punishment code referred to as the *Huddud Ordinance* as well as strengthening other *Shariah* laws. He is steeped in anti-Christian, anti-American sentiment, having stated "For a non-Muslim state to have more pomp and glory than a Muslim state itself is an obstacle, therefore to shatter this grandeur is among the greater objectives of *jihad*."[32] Despite his having stepped off advisory boards, Usmani continues to chair the Accounting and Auditing Organization for Islamic Financial Institutions, one of the major financial industry bodies.

Another major player is Muslim Brotherhood spiritual leader Sheikh Yusuf al-Qaradawi, reportedly chairman of more than 50 Muslim charities. Qaradawi, referring to *Shariah* Finance, told BBC Panorama in 2006 "I don't like this word 'donations,'" and "I like to call it jihad with money because God has ordered us to fight our enemies with our lives and our money."[33] With huge sums being steered by *jihadists* to fulfill *zakat* duties, among other concerns, Western financial institutions are underwriting substantial portions of our Islamic Enemy's attack against us. There is less need in the West for the Violent Jihad today when the keys to the Civilization Jihad are being handed to those best able to carry it out. Well into our horror film, the threat has already moved deep into what had been our safe and private territory. It has breached our defenses. It has begun to infect our national fabric.

Similarly alarming is the rate at which the American government and institutions are being infiltrated. Many members of our intelligence, security, and political establishment have been fed deceptive perspectives about Islam, are deeply infused with political correctness, and suffer powerful Control Factors themselves so that their true function in protecting us is often compromised. As detailed in *The Grand Deception* and many books including *American Jihad* and *Jihad Incorporated,* by Steven Emerson, *The Muslim Mafia*, by P. David Gaubatz, and *Infiltration*, by Paul Sperry—to name just a few—our law enforcement agencies, including the FBI, have been breached by operatives connected with Muslim Brotherhood associated groups. Examples abound of Muslim outreach efforts undertaken by our government which are executed or supervised by the very Muslims that have ties to the Muslim Brotherhood, and groups that seek to radically change America.

The Civilization Jihad seeks to place sympathizers into all levels of each branch of our government. Bearing in mind that the essence of infiltration is disguise, the suspicions against many specific individuals are based on statements made and connections and associations with others clearly rooted in the Civilization Jihad. Belonging to the Brotherhood-associated organizations or participating at the many conferences given by these groups is far from actionable; yet this is precisely the way much of the Civilization Jihad operates and communicates. Accordingly, the suspicions are raised not by facts that would necessarily survive in a court of law. Rather, the guilt by association is meant to stand or fall in the court of common sense.

President Obama has, rightly or wrongly, surrounded himself with many such Muslims. Like his predecessor, he has brought leaders of the "Muslim community" into government positions, flaming the fantasy that this will help facilitate common understanding. But the less visible effect has been to give legitimacy to many Civilization Jihadists. Bush seemed to be genuinely motivated by the quest for common understanding. It is unclear whether Obama—who famously said, "Islam, has always been part of America"[34]—is more interested in giving legitimacy to Civilization Jihadists.

A few of those surrounding Obama may give clues to his intentions. Historically, presidents have been held to high standards with respect to the people they choose to surround themselves with and to take advice from. The Obama campaign's Muslim outreach coordinator, Mazen Asbahi, resigned after he received email inquiries from the *Wall Street Journal*[35] concerning his short-term membership on the board of Allied Assets Advisors Fund. The fund is a subsidiary of the North American Islamic Trust, the cornerstone financing entity which was founded by Muslim Brotherhood members in the United States. NAIT, an unindicted co-conspirator and/or joint venturer in the Holy Land Foundation for Relief in Development trial, is also found on the "List of our organizations and the organizations of our friends" in the Explanatory Memorandum. The Allied Assets Advisors Fund board also seated a radical Chicago imam, Jamal Said, who, among his other activities, was an active fundraiser for families of martyrs. It was the appearance of a relationship with Mr. Said that seemingly led to Mr. Asbahi's resignation.

Obama appointed Rashad Hussain as the White House's special envoy to the OIC. Hussain found himself in controversy when he was accused of supporting Palestinian Islamic Jihad operative Sami Al-Arian by describing the trial against Al-Arian as "politically motivated." Hussain originally said he did not remember making the statement. Later, he wisely retracted it. Separately, he has suggested that the United States used the 9/11 attacks to justify broad enforcement against Muslim immigrants, while referring to internment camps. And, in a 2008 Brookings Institution paper, Hussain advocated replacing terms such as "Islamic terrorism" and "Islamic extremism" by the more narrow "al-Qaeda terrorism."[36]

The Global Muslim Brotherhood Daily Report 2/14/10[37] noted that many of the policy recommendations that Hussain published in the paper "match the agenda also being pushed by the US Muslim Brotherhood including: 'The primary cause of broad-based anger and anti-Americanism is not a clash of civilizations but the perceived effect of US foreign policy in the Muslim world.' Linking terrorism to US foreign policy and 'legitimate grievances' has been another longtime goal of the US Brotherhood." In the paper, Hussain also pressed the United States to encourage the development of "mainstream Muslim organizations and moderate institutions" referencing the work of the Brotherhood's Fiqh Council of North America. Critical to the Civilization Jihad is the Brotherhood's ability to cast its organizations as "moderate" and thus, because it is the most organized, best be able to represent Islam in the United States, Hussain's placement in the administration is perfect for the task.

As suggested earlier, the effort to limit the Violent Jihad to al-Qaeda is a transparent tactic of both the Control Factor and the Obama administration.

Dr. Islam A. Siddiqui was appointed by Obama as the Chief Agricultural Negotiator for the Office of US Trade Representative. He had served in the Clinton administration as well. Siddiqui had served on the board of advisors for the American Muslim Council under Vice President Jamil al-Amin, Treasurer Sayyid M. Syeed, along with fellow board member Siraj Wahhaj. Al-Amin, a former Black Panther, was convicted of killing a Fulton County sheriff's deputy and wounding another.[38] Syeed was director of outreach at the International Institute of Islamic Thought which, founded in 1980 by US Brotherhood leaders including Jamal Barzinji, had various connections with the World Islamic Studies Enterprise, an alleged "front group" for the Palestinian Islamic Jihad, according to the US government. As seen in *The Grand Deception,* Syeed stated, "Our job is to change the constitution of America."

Wahhaj, imam of the al-Taqwa mosque in Brooklyn, hosted speeches by the famous "blind sheikh," Omar Abdel Rahman. Wahhaj, a former Nation of Islam member who trained in Saudi Arabia, was close enough to Rahman to be one of his witnesses at his 1995 trial. Wahhaj has been the focus of many, including New York Senator Charles E. Schumer, for his radicalism. He has labeled the CIA and FBI as the "real terrorists," advocated a Shariah Society in which adulterers are stoned to death and thieves have their hands cut off as superior to the democracy in America, and stated "In time, this so-called democracy will crumble, and there will be nothing. And the only thing that will remain will be Islam."[39]

Others, including Obama's long-time friend and Palestinian advocate Rashid Khalidi, may be assisting him in wading through the Israeli-Palestinian conflict (the Arab war against Israel). And Egyptian-born Dalia Mogahed, who serves on Obama's Advisory Council on Faith-Based and Neighborhood Partnerships, is also a member of the Department of Homeland Security's Advisory Group's Countering Violent Extremism Working Group. She is the executive director of the Gallup Center for Muslim Studies. Her resume includes a book co-authored with Muslim apologist John L. Esposito, *Who Speaks for Islam? What a Billion Muslims Really Think*, which concludes that Muslims and Americans share similar values and asserts—perfectly in line with Control Factor sentiments—that radical Islam is of minimal danger and that US foreign policy has caused the anti-Americanism in the Muslim world. Robert Satloff of the Washington Institute for Near East Policy charged in the *Weekly Standard* (May 12, 2008): "Mogahed publicly admitted they knew certain people weren't moderates but they still termed them so. She and Esposito cooked the books and dumbed down the text. Apparently, by the authors' own test, there are not 91 million radicals in Muslim societies but almost twice that number."[40] According to the Global Muslim Brotherhood Daily Report, Esposito "has at least a dozen past or present affiliations with global Muslim Brotherhood/Hamas organizations including having served on the advisory board of the Institute of Islamic Political Thought in the U.K. headed by Azzam Tamimi, a leader in the U.K. Muslim Brotherhood and often described as a Hamas spokesman."[41] He has also served with and defended global Muslim Brotherhood leaders such as Youssef Qaradawi.

Mogahed's research is less worrisome than her role and influence in shaping policy. Posted by Robert Spencer on *Jihad Watch* 10/15/09, she has described her efforts with Obama "to convey . . . to the President and other public officials what it is Muslims want,"[42] not, as Spencer points out, anything concerning what Americans might want from Muslims. She as well has argued for curtailing such language as "Islamic terrorism," suggesting that Muslims who support terrorism do not do so in the name of Islam but rather are motivated by a political agenda. She has said that the phrase justifies the charge of "Islamophobia," and has concluded that data show a greater percentage of Americans support the idea of targeting innocent civilians than do Muslims.

Mogahed has frequently attended and spoken at conferences sponsored by Muslim Brotherhood-related groups such as ISNA, the Muslim American Society, and the Islamic Circle of North America. She has been a defender of CAIR and ISNA. When asked about the connections between them and radicals, she replied that it would be unfair to have those groups "disenfranchised" because of "misinformation." This was before the Holy Land Foundation trial concluded. Jumping right into Control Factor victimization, she added, "There is a concerted effort to silence, you know, institution building among Muslims. And the way to do it is to malign these groups. And it's a kind of witch-hunt."[43]

Projection has reared its head again as these are precisely the groups that set out to malign anyone who speaks out against them or the Civilization Jihad and often use lawfare and other means to silence them.

Mogahed was initially reported to have stated in a television interview following the Egyptian revolution that "Washington has no worries concerning the Muslim Brotherhood in Egypt."[44] This was subsequently revised when the Brotherhood's website claimed it had relied on inaccurate points.[45] The original 4/8/11 Globalmbreport.org post, however, had characterized her as saying in an interview that the Obama administration "respects" the Brotherhood and that, after Egyptian elections, "the relationship between the two countries will be much more that of equals rather than of a client state which had dominated the connection before."

Homeland Security Department Secretary, Janet Napolitano, has herself made appointments that have raised concerns with some. Arif Alikhan, who worked for the Bush administration as well, was appointed Assistant Secretary for Policy Development. Alikhan, who helped the LAPD remove its plan to map Muslim communities, reportedly helped raise funds for and speak at conferences assembled by the Muslim Public Affairs Council. While MPAC claims Islam is consistent with American values, its founder and senior advisor, Maher Hathout, espouses Wahhabism and called Israel a land of butchers. MPAC's own magazine, *Minaret*, describes Hathout as "a close disciple of the late [Muslim

Brotherhood founder] Hassan al-Banna of Egypt."[46] MPAC has described Hezbollah as a "liberation movement" and Hezbollah's 1983 terrorist attack on US Marine barracks in Lebanon as a "military operation." Hathout claimed "Hezbollah is fighting for freedom . . . this is a legitimate target against occupation . . . this is legitimate, this is an American value—freedom and liberty." MPAC has also called Israelis "the worst terrorists in the world" and co-sponsored in 2000 pro-Palestinian rallies where speakers were reported to have chanted "Khaybar, Khaybar, oh Jews, the Army of Mohammed is coming for you!"[47]

Napolitano also appointed Syrian-born Kareem Shora as a member of the Homeland Security Advisory Council. Shora had been National Executive Director of the American-Arab Anti-Discrimination Committee, resigning to join DHS. The ADC, with ties to Rashid Khalidi, is openly anti-Israel whose former president, Hamzi Moshrabi refused to call Hamas a terrorist or violent organization. Moshrabi's successor Hala Maksoud said he found it "shocking that [one] would include Hezbollah in . . . [an] inventory of Middle East 'terrorist' groups." Its subsequent president, Hussein Ibish referred to Hezbollah as "a disciplined and responsible liberation force."[48]

A web of relationships on the surface does not amount to anything actionable beyond a charge of shared ideas. But that is precisely the point. Again, while guilt only by association is a relevant *defense* in a court of law, it often raises relevant *concerns* elsewhere. The concern with these and many other associations is not about legal guilt at all but rather the influence of ideas upon our government leaders, policies and instrumentalities.

These are just a few of the relationships or affiliations that surround Obama. Many others exist with other branches of the government; perhaps that is why Obama directed that even NASA's highest priority should be "to find a way to reach out to the Muslim world and engage much more with dominantly Muslim nations to help them feel good about their historic contribution to science . . . and math and engineering."[49] Even a minor exploration of the material on the subject will reveal how deeply entrenched our government and legal system are becoming with Brotherhood associated persons.

Nor do these relationships arise solely on the Democratic side of the aisle. New Jersey Governor Chris Christie, for instance, disappointed some of his followers when he appointed immigration lawyer Sohail Mohammed to a state judgeship. Some have suggested that Christie was pandering to the Muslim community connected with the Islamic Center of Passaic County and the American Muslim Union when he supported Sohail Mohammed's client Mohammed Qatanani in fighting deportation. Qatanani, imam of the Center, the largest mosque in New Jersey, was a Muslim Brother who admitted to being a member of Hamas and who had defended a charity that provided funds to the families of Islamic martyrs. The Center's previous imam, Mohammad el-Mezain had been found guilty of moving funds to Hamas.

The Department of Homeland Security sought to deport Qatanani primarily for lying on his paperwork by failing to disclose that he had been convicted by an Israeli military court for his membership in and support of Hamas. Mohammed had represented Qatanani in the proceedings. Christie, who was not a US attorney in the case, nonetheless, allowed one of his assistant US attorneys to testify as a character witness on behalf of Qatanani whom Christie had separately characterized as "a man of great goodwill." The judge came out in favor of Qatanani and stated that he was impressed by the "law-enforcement officers that took time from their respective duties to appear before the court."[50]

As counsel to the AMU (which itself had various leaders connected to Hamas fundraising), Mohammed (who publicly defended convicted Sami al-Arian and refuses to connect "Islam" with "terrorism") represented clients alleged to have terrorist connections. Obviously, lawyers not only have the right but some consider the ethical responsibility to represent clients who are so accused. And obviously, lawyers, for instance a Mafia lawyer, can not be attributed with the crimes of the client. Yet, it is this very "obviousness" that the Civilization Jihad banks on. Similarly, the Control Factor implores us to consider (as did Christie) such connections as paths to "common ground." Yet, just as the appointment of a well entrenched Mafia lawyer to the bench would raise eyebrows, it is precisely the deep network of connections between members and representatives of all of these associations that, while lawful, makes the Civilization Jihad so very dangerous.

Congress' first Muslim Representative, Keith Ellison, has garnered affection from many whose Control Factors favor building bridges with "moderate Muslims." Yet Ellison, who cried tears at the House hearing on Muslim radicalization, seemed to show a more truthful side of his views two days later. As reported by the *Investigative Project* on 4/13/2011, he gave a speech in Michigan in which he disgracefully attacked three witnesses who appeared at the hearings. Marvin Bledsoe's son Carlos is accused of firing his weapon outside of an army recruiting office in Little Rock, killing one soldier and seriously injuring another. He had been indoctrinated into Islam during his college years, dropped out in 2004, and traveled to Yemen to study under a radical imam by the urging of Muslim leaders in Nashville. Referring to Islam, Marvin, the father, had correctly stated at the hearing that "There is a big elephant in the room, but our society continues not to see it."[51]

In his speech days later, Ellison amazingly transferred responsibility for young Bledsoe's radicalization from Islam to his father, remarking that Carlos "was in that man's house all his life. He's a Muslim for a few years. Enough said." Bledsoe, upon hearing of Ellison's revealing remarks responded, "They stole my son. They raped his mind. They changed his thought, his behavior. They changed him from Carlos to Abdulhakim. I asked God to give me my son back. . . . Ellison is a 'fool' and 'liar' when he tries to deny the insidious nature of jihadist recruiting that is occurring in this country."

Ellison also went after another witness, Somali-American Muslim Abdirizak Bihi, whose teenage nephew, Burhan Hassan, was among at least 20 teenage boys from Ellison's state of Minnesota who were lured into traveling to Somalia to join the terrorist group al-Shabaab. Hassan died from gunshots in Somalia in June 2009. Ellison, whose tearful recitation of his "moderation" at the hearing may have convinced some of his sensitivity, stated heartlessly days later that the "only reason" Bihi was included in the hearings was "because he's willing to diss the Somali and Muslim community in Minneapolis."

According to the Investigative Project's report, Ellison directed his strongest vitriol at witness Dr. Zudhi Jasser. A scholar, a medical doctor, and Founder and President of the American Islamic Forum for Democracy whose record is impeccable, Jasser is difficult to condemn. Nonetheless, Ellison provocatively suggested he'd been invited to the hearing "because he fits the narrative of people who want to defame you." He further attacked Jasser as one who will do anything for money, wisecracking, "Why should Ayaan Hirsi Ali [be the only one to] make all the money" in criticizing Islam—a twofer attack. Ellison called Jasser an Islamic "Uncle Tom" and accused him of Muslim bashing: "I think you give people license for bigotry. . . . I think people who want to engage in nothing less than Muslim-hating really love you a lot because you give them freedom to do that." Ellison, when his crocodile tears failed to sustain his narrative, resorted to typical attack the messenger strategy. In doing so he sounded more like a sleazy race hustler than a respectable legislator looking to find "common ground." Projection was again active here, as Jasser never seemed to exhibit any hatred. Ellison, on the other hand, was a different story. Like his fellow Democrats looking to prevent or disrupt the hearings, Ellison wasted a perfect opportunity to elicit for the American people valuable testimony from the witnesses. Instead he chose the tactics that happen to be fully consistent with the agenda of the Brotherhood and the Civilization Jihad.

Ellison's remarks should not be that surprising, given his connection with Muslim Brotherhood associated groups. Robert Spencer reported in *Human Events* 9/21/10 that the Muslim American Society paid for Ellison's *Hajj* to Saudi Arabia costing in excess of thirteen thousand dollars.[52] The *Hajj,* the pilgrimage to Mecca, is one of the five requirements (in addition to one's duty to *jihad*) of Islam. Spencer refers to the MAS as the Muslim Brotherhood's "chief operating arm in the United States" and properly notes that if a Christian Congressman took a trip paid for by a Christian group that, in its own words was dedicated to "eliminating and destroying the Western civilization from within and 'sabotaging' its miserable house by their hands and the hands of the believers so that it is eliminated and God's religion is made victorious over all other religions," we would hear a great deal more about it.

On April 14, 2011, Patrick Poole posted an extraordinary article at *Pajamasmedia.com*.[53] His sources implicate the Department of Justice, and possibly Obama himself, in shutting down the prosecutions of leaders of CAIR and other Muslim Brotherhood associated groups for political reasons. Poole and his sources describe how as a result of the 2008 Holy Land Foundation trial, "mountains" of evidence were obtained for follow-up trials of many of the previously unindicted co-conspirators/ joint venturers.

While the internally stated reason for not proceeding was the possibility of "jury nullification," Poole's sources attribute it to White House politics: these leaders are White House "interfaith allies" who would arrange for charges of "Islamophobia" and "war against Islam" and make Obama and Holder "look like absolute fools." During the Muslim radicalization hearings, Los Angeles County Sheriff Lee Baca, a friend of CAIR who has spoken at many CAIR fundraisers, laid down a challenge to those who supported the hearings to prosecute CAIR if they believe it is a criminal organization. Yet, while Baca is presumed to be a friend of the administration, the administration is making sure that can not happen.

Poole continues with reports of how powerful the DOJ's evidence was. He notes how CAIR and others had previously had their ties to the FBI cut because of evidence presented at the original trial. Additionally, the trial judge, Jorge Solis, refused to remove them from the list of unindicted co-conspirators and/or joint venturers citing the presence of evidence which creates "at least a prima facie case as to CAIR's involvement in a conspiracy to support Hamas" and "the Government has ample evidence to establish the associations of CAIR, ISNA, and NAIT with HLF, the Islamic Association of Palestine (IAP) and with Hamas."

Perhaps Holder's motivation is *only* political in nature. That would be damning enough. But the relations between the administration and the unindicted co-conspirators and/or joint venturers appear deeper. Poole's DOJ source says "many of the people I work with at Justice now see CAIR not just as political allies but *ideological* (italics added) allies. They believe they are fighting the same revolution. It's scary. And Congress and the American people need to know this is going on."

If true, Frank Gaffney and others have suggested this portends a possible inquiry into whether Holder, and possibly Obama and others, could or should be charged with misprision of treason, defined under US Code Title 18, Part I, Chapter 115, sec. 2382 as:

> Whoever, owing allegiance to the United States and having knowledge of the commission of any treason against them, conceals and does not, as soon as may be, disclose and make known the same to the President or to some judge of the United States, or to the governor or to some judge or justice of a particular State, is guilty of misprision of treason and shall be fined under this title or imprisoned not more than seven years, or both.

Concealing the giving of aid to a terrorist organization which threatens the security of the United States or its nationals would appear to fit squarely within the scope of this statute.

While many members of the Civilization Jihad owe no allegiance to the United States, Eric Holder and Barack Obama do. And if, as the DOJ source suggests, they share ideological aims with the unindicted co-conspirators and/or joint venturers, they may have knowledge above and beyond what the evidence on hand shows. After all, the essence of the Civilization Jihad is, simply put, the destruction of constitutional America.

Nonetheless, due in part to politics and in part to the US Constitution's weakness in protecting itself, it is unclear whether this issue will ever be considered, much less pursued. To imagine it true is to beg every Control Factor attack to dismiss it as a paranoid delusion. But the power of the Civilization Jihad's infiltration is already plain to observe.

The Crafting of the "Moderate Muslim"

As we've seen, Westerners are eager to believe that there is no serious problem with Islam because most Muslims are "moderates." Many Muslims present themselves as "moderates" to assuage Westerners' fears. While it is quite possible that many or most Muslims might prefer a life with limited violence and do not wish to kill others, this fact is simply irrelevant. Seriously engaged Muslims still share the ultimate goal of spreading *Shariah* worldwide.

The media image of the "Moderate Muslim" fuels the Civilization Jihad. It has been carefully nurtured over decades based on public relations and media advice bought with Arab Islamic money. Consequently, the media now present us with well-turned-out, articulate, emotionally intelligent figures who aim to calm our fears by showing us exactly how much like us they are.

Prominent among these carefully constructed media characters are the leaders of major Muslim organizations, including those affiliated with the Muslim Brotherhood. They are the talking heads we see on television and hear on the radio. They are quoted in print. They work in government outreach programs, community relations projects, and as advisers to our police, FBI, CIA, and local government bureaucracies. They carry the bullhorns at rallies and may be found wherever someone is needed to calm the masses, re-establish the narrative of the Muslim as victim, and attack, alienate, and discredit anyone who is either angry at or afraid of Muslims. Their job is to silence objections. In short, they seek to make non-Muslims the issue.

The "crafting" has been abetted not just by Western media but by Western governments. The Bush administration took great pains to distinguish "extremists" from the rest of the Muslim world and promoted many Muslim Brotherhood-associated entities. Yet, even following the information disclosed from the Holy Land Foundation trial, the Obama administration has carried this effort forward to a much greater degree. In 2009, for example, Valerie Jarrett, Senior Advisor to the President, appeared as the keynote speaker for ISNA's annual convention, a stamp of support that spoke volumes to those looking for signals. By gracing these organizations, the administrations have given legitimacy to the notion that these organizations represent the "Moderate Muslim" for which so many are looking. In fact, to repeat Hillel Fradkin, while they might represent moderate methods, their underlying goals appear anything but moderate.

In truth, today's media-ready "Moderate Muslim" is not the nice, sociable, westernized fellow he appears to be who practices his prayers and other rituals in private and otherwise "fits in with the rest of us." He is a well-trained propagandist and Civilization Jihadist who has been elevated with the collusion of the press and culture to serve a need imposed by our Control Factors.

Consider Imam Feisal Abdul Rauf, the original face of the Ground Zero Mosque project. Rauf often refers to himself as a "bridge-builder," one uniquely gifted to bring Muslims and non-Muslims together by emphasizing what is good and common among us all. The title of his well-crafted book, *What's Right With Islam Is What's Right With America*, conveys the essence of his endeavor: to show us that Islam and America are intimately compatible and embrace many of the same fundamental principles. He masterfully seeks to accomplish the Civilization Jihadist's primary concern: comfort Americans that they have nothing to fear from Islam, which offers much of what Americans value. Mutual respect is not only called for, it virtually comes naturally once one understands Islam as portrayed by Rauf. He does the job so well that the book belongs on the Control Factor's final exam.

Accordingly, for Rauf's narrative, *jihad* is truly a spiritual struggle. He acknowledges the *lesser jihad* but describes it as "what Christians call a 'just war'"[54]—a powerfully packed equivalence between the Violent Jihad and Christian concepts of justification, but one which is not borne out by history in modern times. For Rauf, following the *hadith* of Mohammed, the real *jihad* is the *greater jihad* which he defines as "the psychological war we wage within ourselves to establish the kingdom of God in our behavior and to build a lifestyle that reflects God's commandments, both in our individual life and in our collective communal lives. *Jihad* is about building what Western philosophers would call 'the good society'." At the very least, it is uncertain whether this definition could sustain a defense in the face of 1400 years of Islamic history.

Rauf suggests that *jihad* is that which our common God requires of each of us through each of his religions. Additionally, Islam and America are fully compatible, and it is only America's misunderstanding of Islam that prevents a successful integration of the two. In his assumption of the mantle of the "Moderate Muslim," Rauf's strategy, consistent with the Civilization Jihad, is to align with and identify himself as an American Everyman, in order to isolate and differentiate the "violent extremists." Rauf correctly proclaims that wherever Muslims are a minority community they are required by *Shariah* to follow the laws of the land; seemingly to allay any concerns that *Shariah* could ever threaten American jurisprudence. Critical to the Civilization Jihad, however, is the skill and ability to use the host nation's laws to implant *Shariah*, more specifically to follow *Shariah* by following the laws of the land in order to use (and transform) those laws in the service of *Shariah*. Rauf's choice of words is exquisite.

In an on-the-record talk[55] to the Council on Foreign Relations in September 2010, at a time in which rising animosity against the Ground Zero Mosque project was being voiced nationally, Rauf displayed some of what might be considered his well-practiced techniques. He commenced with a prayer:

> It is customary for Muslims to begin by first invoking the name of the all-merciful and all-compassionate creator, the creator of the heavens and the earth and all that is between them, the God of Abraham, the God of Ishmael and Isaac, the God of Moses and Aaron, the God of Jesus Christ and his mother, Mary, and the God of Mohammed. Peace and blessings upon all of these noble prophets and messengers.

Common ground indeed. As discussed previously, Islam "hijacks" the "God" of its predecessor religions, taking *Him* for its own on the one hand, and rewriting theirs on the other. Other Civilization Jihadists will say that Christianity, Judaism, and Islam all share the same God. While Islam has tried to import into Allah the identity of God of the People of the Book, Allah was, prior to Islam, one of 360 pagan gods in Mecca—and the largest of all. Mohammed negotiated with the pagan leaders to adopt many of their rituals in exchange for their worshipping only Allah. "Allahu Akbar" is the declaration that Allah is greater than all of the others.

Contrary to Rauf's implication, few Christians or Jews would associate their God with this formerly pagan figure. Nonetheless, Rauf's words certainly calm an unknowing audience into thinking this is a call for unity and a demonstration that Muslim practices are no threat to others. After all, the pitch suggests, we all really share the same God as well as the same motives and religious principles, with just different means of expression. His words demonstrate anything but; they are simply a move to establish rapport using questionable definitions and explanations.

Rauf adds his support for those Americans who responded to the Mosque debate peacefully: "And for all of those who have voiced their objections to our plans with civility, with respect and with open minds and hearts, I am also grateful. You affirm my belief in the decency and morality of the American people." Somehow, he has become the arbiter of American behavior and presents the image that while perhaps he was losing faith in Americans as a peaceable population, his faith has luckily been restored. Here we see many of our Control Factor vulnerabilities being exploited. It should be made clear that Rauf speaks in a well-tempered and practiced voice trained to convey deep understanding and emotional resonance. By elevating himself above—and then conferring positive judgments upon—non-Muslim Americans, Rauf assumes a role of authority similar to that of the modern media. This is a core characteristic of today's media-savvy "Moderate Muslim."

Similarly, by "approving" of the criticisms by virtue of the fact that they were civil, Rauf subtly slows some of the momentum of those who object. By seemingly aligning himself with opponents in terms of their choice of tactic, he reduces their resistance to him and places himself in a better position to influence their agenda. He is additionally suggesting that so long as one's approach is civil, we need not worry; many of us hear "as long as the Muslim is not engaged in the Violent Jihad, he is ok."

Part of the media-savvy "Moderate Muslim's" game plan requires grabbing the narrative of Muslim victimhood whenever possible. Rauf tries to peddle an absurd comparison:

There's a history of the last century where we've had secular regimes really pushing religious voices out of the—out of the—away from the—from the boardroom. These are among the—among the issues that have—that have fueled this crisis—the sense of alienation among Muslim minorities is more so in Europe than in—than in this country—and the sense that—you know, that we Muslims have to—have to help each other, just like during the communist regime American Jews were supportive of Soviet Jewry and their plight. There's a sense of a common bond.

Forthright Muslim Brothers would marvel at the way Rauf attacks the Near Enemy of Arab secular rulers in front of the Far Enemy audience. What better way to establish victimhood than travel the globe across a century. Ridiculously equating Western treatment of Muslims—whether in Europe or America—with the plight of Soviet Jewry, however, shows exactly what the exercise is about.

One of Rauf's stated objectives for his talk was to "explain and share his love of America" to his Muslim brothers and sisters all over the world. A Kuwaiti, born to an Egyptian father who graduated from Al-Azhar, Rauf himself was sent to the United States by Al-Azhar to lead a Muslim community in New York. It is difficult to be under the guidance of Al-Azhar, the center of the Arab-Islamic world, and not be steeped in the expression of Islam it promotes. Rauf obtained a physics degree at Columbia and became a naturalized US citizen in 1979. Sharing that he had a number of jobs, Rauf declares "I'm a typical New Yorker, ladies and gentlemen. I am an American."

Rauf describes himself as a "devout Muslim," citing the fact that he prays five times or more a day and observes the requisite rituals. Again, this is the Civilization Jihadist "moderate's" claim regarding Islam and religion in general—that it is, as most modern Americans tend to agree, a private activity with private practice and thoughts. Al-Azhar would likely have much more to add to the equation if discussed in Arabic.

The overarching theme of Rauf's talk is to bolster the Civilization Jihadists' most critical talking point: the idea that Islam and America are fully compatible. He has previously asserted that America *is* "*Shariah* compliant,"[56] an absurd proposition on its face, and a call for America to gradually make room for more and more *Shariah* at its core. Curiously, in a 2006 radio interview[57] with Mark Sommer, Rauf stated "I founded the Cordova Initiative in 2002. We have given ourselves 'til the year 2015 to bring about what we would call a tipping point in the relationship between the United States and the Islamic World on all the various fronts." Requiring more than a decade to force things to a tipping point, suggests significant, if not insurmountable, conflicts—not compatibility or compliance, between America and *Shariah*. And what happens in 2016 if he has failed?

Interestingly, following the interview when he was offline, Rauf gave further color to his vision. As posted in Pam Geller's *Atlas Shrugs* website on 9/27/10, he compared his role to that of a football coach who looks at others as the players he manipulates: "I'm the head coach of this strategic initiative, and the President of the United States, or the President of Malaysia, or the President of England is like a player you want to bring in for particular plays." So goes the notion that the Civilization Jihad is not a well-orchestrated effort.

He had an interesting slip when he continued, "So if we have strategic action plays, designed plays in the area of foreign policy, in the area of healing the divide, and then you unpack and *give up Israel* (italics added) and then what you do, what are the specific actions that you might do, because things are always moving, things are always happening."

Contrary to compatibility, Rauf also made his real intentions clear years ago as shown in the documentary by the Christian Action Network, *Sacrificed Survivors*, "Those who are hostile to us now will see their children and grandchildren become Muslims in the future."[58] This is compatibility only in the sense that America is ripe to become a compatible *dhimmi* within a future Islamic World.

Rauf continues his seeming *taqiyya* in his Council on Foreign Relations talk, "So for me, Islam and America are organically bound together." Further,

> I discovered that the country that at first had seemed so anti-religious in fact has a profoundly spiritual base and a religious purpose. The Founding Fathers of this nation were men of faith. Within the governing documents they created, the Declaration of Independence and the Constitution, they affirmed their most sacred spiritual values. These documents are legal expressions of in fact a religious ideal, non-parochial but substantively religious, that is rooted in the commandments and principles of the three faiths practiced by the People of the Book—Jews, Christians and Muslims.

Later, in response to a question as to the compatibility of *Shariah* with American constitutional law, he responds that they are "Absolutely coincident . . ." and continues:

The fundamental rights of—the opening lines of Declaration of Independence, "We hold these truths to be self-evident, that all men are created equal"—the equality of human creation is a fundamental principle of the Abrahamic faiths—"endowed by their Creator with certain inalienable rights"—the fact the creator gave these rights to us, not any government or man-made agency, is a religious concept among which our life, life and property, then changed to life, liberty, pursuit of happiness.

Seven centuries before these words were penned by Thomas Jefferson, Muslim jurists said all of shari'a law, all of Islamic law is intended to uphold six fundamental objectives: the protection of life, of human dignity, which (can?) relate to liberty, to religion, to family, to property and the intellect. And what do we do (after?) life to pursue our happiness? We get married to our loved ones, we seek material well being, we seek our intellectual pursuits and we seek to practice our faith religions.

In many respects, yes, there are aspects of shari'a law which we ourselves have trouble with. But in many respects we practice shari'a already when we practice—when we—when we—when we adhere to our dietary laws, we are practicing shari'a law. When we bequeath our estates to our children in accordance with the dictates of shari'a, we are—there are—we are consistent with American law and consistent with Islamic law. And when we pray, when we (fight?), these are all commandments of shari'a law. So 90 percent of shari'a law is fully compatible, and not only—not only compatible, is consistent or compatible with American constitutional law and American laws. The areas of difference are small and minor.

First, an appeal to the Founding Fathers abuses the reality that separation of church and state is a critical difference—if not the critical difference—between *Shariah* and American constitutional law. This is particularly true for Jefferson who, in drafting the Virginia Statute for Religious Liberty submits that such separation comes out of Judeo-Christian thought, not apart from it. Islam commands no such separation; the two are intimately and inseparably bound.

As noted in the Center for Security Policy's treatise written by Frank Gaffney and his "Team B," *Shariah: The Threat to America*—perhaps the most important book for commencing one's Inner Jihad—Jefferson was fully aware of the realities of Islam and would certainly dispute any claim of compatibility between it and the America he helped found. After meeting with the Ambassador representing the demands of the Islamic Barbary pirates, Jefferson wrote:

> We took the liberty to make some inquiries concerning the Grounds of their pretentions to make war upon Nations who had done them no Injury, and observed that we considered all mankind as our friends who had done us no wrong, nor had given us any provocation.

> The Ambassador answered us that it was founded on the Laws of their prophet, that it is written in the Qur'an, that all nations who should not have acknowledged their authority were sinners, that it was their right and duty to make war upon them wherever they could be found, and to make slaves of all they could take as Prisoners, and that every Musselman who should be slain in battle was sure to go to paradise.[59]

The Center's treatise continues by excerpting John Quincy Adams' essays on Islam which again shows how well understood Islam was during the early years of America and how distinguishable it was from the Christian foundations of America. To repeat a few:

> . . . [Mohammed] declared undistinguishing and exterminating war, as part of his religion, against all the rest of mankind. . . .The precept of the Quran is, perpetual war against all who deny, that [Mohammed] is the prophet of God.

> The vanquished [*Dhimmi*] may purchase their lives, by the payment of tribute.   ·

> As the essential principle of [Mohammed's] faith is the subjugation of others by the sword; it is only by force, that his false doctrines can be dispelled, and his power annihilated.

> The commands of the prophet may be performed alike, by fraud, or by force.[60]

Secondly, Rauf's answer also flipped America's legal system on its head. By asserting that since one can observe most *Shariah* rituals privately in America, *Shariah* is compatible, he avoids the critical paradoxical point of dispute: which law is supreme? If everything Islam commanded were limited to that in Rauf's list, there would not only be no problems between Islam and America; there would be no problems with

Islam anywhere. It is precisely Rauf's avoidance of the tensions between the two bodies of law—the fact that *Shariah* demands it is the supreme law of that land and that only Allah, not man, may make laws—that betrays him as a Civilization Jihadist.

Finally, it is simply insulting for Rauf to in any way suggest that *Shariah* embodies the fundamental precept of the Declaration of Independence—that all men are created equal and therefore should be treated equally. *Shariah* is founded upon the asymmetry between Muslims and non-Muslims and expressly discriminates against the latter. It was noted previously how Keith Ellison disingenuously tried to suggest verse 5:32, which was intended to forbid Muslims from killing other Muslims, was to apply to non-Muslims as well. Here as well, Rauf is taking a notion of equality that applies only within the Ummah and suggesting it applies equally to non-Muslims outside of the Ummah. Little is more revealing than the fact that in Malaysia and elsewhere in the Muslim world, Rauf's book was published under a different title: *A Call to Prayer From The World Trade Center Rubble: Islamic Dawa In The Heart of America Post 9/11*. Little could better describe Rauf's true sentiments and intentions than heralding the power of the 9/11 "rubble" as well as building the Ground Zero Mosque to serve as a victory symbol enhancing the Muslim world's ability to recruit more soldiers through *jihad* by *dawa*.

The perfected manipulation of the realities of Islam by a media savvy "Moderate Muslim" in a Muslim-minority territory is precisely "coincident" with the "Trojan Horse" strategy of the Civilization Jihad.

The International Institutional Jihad

The third level of threat which is beginning to receive more attention gives an overarching context to both the Violent and Civilization Jihads—the International Institutional Jihad. Perhaps its greatest and best-orchestrated push comes from the Organization of the Islamic Conference. This confederation of 57 members (which includes the non-state, Palestinian Authority) wields the tools of statehood to pursue the vision of a global Caliphate to rule a global Ummah. It is the vanguard of the International Institutional Jihad and is already hugely influential on a global basis.

Bearing in mind the *hadith* in which Mohammed certifies that only the one sect (out of seventy-three) which holds the majority will end up in Paradise, there is much perceived value in unifying Muslims across the world. As a pool of state governments with all the tools of statehood available to it, the OIC is, when it obtains consensus, best able to coordinate and execute many parts of the agenda also shared by the Muslim Brotherhood.

Created by the Saudis in 1969 with the initial mission of "protecting" Jerusalem's Al-Asqa Mosque from the Israelis, the OIC is premised on the idea that *Shariah* is the ultimate and sole determiner of human rights. Along with related organizations such as the Islamic Educational, Scientific, and Cultural Organization, the OIC has become the most powerful bloc within the United Nations and dominates the General Assembly.

The OIC is the group best positioned to institute—under the banner of opposition to "Islamophobia"—a global ban on any criticism of Islam enforced by international prosecution. It can lead the charge to create further limitations on cherished American First Amendment rights. The OIC's *Third Observatory Report*[61] defines the problem: "Islamophobia has been described as 'fear or suspicion of Muslims and Islam and matters pertaining to them,' and as such Islamophobia is prejudice, intolerance, and discrimination against Muslims and Islam." Discrimination, which under US law is tied to discreet acts, is here extended to cover, and therefore regulate, the thoughts, attitudes, and emotions of non-Muslims.

As commentator Andy Rooney and others have observed, somehow an opinion, in this case about Islam, has been turned into a phobia, all to help facilitate our Islamic Enemy. In typical Control Factor fashion, blame is placed on the enabler's thoughts, transferred away from Islam itself. The OIC, here, is seeking to regulate *the non-Muslim's hatred* while the essence of the addiction/enabler dance is to transfer to the enabler responsibility for *the Muslim's hatred*. In another case of projection, Islam, as expressed throughout most of the Arab world, is replete with indisputable prejudice, intolerance, and discrimination against Jews. Do Muslims or the United Nations ever intend to address their Judeophobia? Needless to say, as the old adage suggests: Just because you are paranoid does not mean they are not out to get you.

The OIC is also available to assist the United Nations with its own corrupt Human Rights Council. After the United States blocked Iran's acquisition of a seat on the UN Human Rights Council, the United Nations, strongly influenced by the OIC, gave a seat (by "acclamation" as opposed to a vote) to Iran on its Commission on the Status of Women, affording Iran the oxymoronic position of monitoring the global treatment of women. Similarly, Syria was headed for a seat until its brutal efforts to forestall its own 2011 revolution forced it to defer its efforts at least until 2013. The United Nations has sought to substitute Kuwait in Syria's place.

Furthering the objectives of Civilization Jihad, the OIC and its associated organizations will look to extend and implant Islamic cultural identities throughout the non-Muslim world. It will function more and more as a central base able to educate Muslims all over the world via Islamic centers, mosques, schools, and other institutions. It can organize mass movements of immigrants where desired, and create—through laws and enforcement—blanket protections for Muslims worldwide. Centralizing communications to Muslims throughout the non-Islamic world will also significantly advance the creation of a global Ummah. Utilizing Israel as a unifying enemy, it is positioned to become a tremendous power over time. Unifying countries controlling over 70% of the world's oil and gas resources places the OIC and our Islamic Enemy itself in direct conflict with the Western world.

The OIC's Charter[62] demonstrates these objectives. Beginning with, "In the name of Allah, the most Compassionate, the most Merciful," some of its "Determinations" include:

- To be guided by the noble Islamic values of unity and fraternity
- To preserve and promote the lofty Islamic values of peace, compassion, tolerance, equality, justice, human dignity
- To endeavor to work for revitalizing Islam's pioneering role in the world while ensuring sustainable development, progress and prosperity for the Peoples of the Member States
- To enhance and strengthen the bond of unity and solidarity among Muslim peoples and Member States
- To foster noble Islamic values concerning moderation, tolerance, respect for diversity, preservation of Islamic symbols and common heritage and to defend the universality of Islamic religion
- To advance the acquisition and popularization of knowledge in consonance with the lofty ideals of Islam to achieve intellectual excellence
- To support the struggle for the Palestinian people, who are presently under foreign occupation, and to empower them to attain their inalienable rights, including the right to self-de-

termination and to establish their sovereign state with Al-Quds Al-Shariff as its capital, while safeguarding its historic and Islamic character, and the holy places therein

- To safeguard and promote the rights of women and their participation in all spheres of life, in accordance with the laws and legislation of Member States
- To create conducive conditions for sound upbringing of Muslim children and youth, and to inculcate in them Islamic values through education for strengthening their cultural, social, moral and ethical ideals
- To assist Muslim minorities and communities outside the Member States to preserve their dignity, cultural and religious identity

Many of these resolutions would sound benign, even noteworthy, if we were not aware that words have different meanings in the Western and Muslim worlds. The deceptive uses of "tolerance," "peace," "freedom," "dignity," "equality," "justice," "respect for diversity," would be alarming enough. So too with Jamaat-e-Islami which, according to the Investigative Projects News (6/28/11) asserts that secularism, nationalism, and democracy "are wrong. Not merely wrong, rather we believe with full confidence and certainty, that they are indeed the root cause of all those calamities and troubles in which humanity is involved today. . . . As a matter of fact, we are opposed to these principles and wish to fight against them with all our strength."[63] This view underlies the positions of many of the OIC nations as well. The charade of protecting women's rights and creating appropriate conditions for raising children insults the foundational principles of the Western world. Further, by elaborating conditions for a settlement of the Palestinian issue—such as establishing a Palestinian capital in Jerusalem—this document should render obsolete any State Department plan for settling that conflict if it does not incorporate those conditions as the fifty-seven OIC members have already agreed to them.

Theoretically, a state can become a member of the OIC only if the majority of its population is Muslim. Yet in 11 OIC member states Muslims are a minority—including Gabon, where the Muslim share of the population is only about one percent. The OIC very conveniently overlooks its majority requirement and buys UN votes by inducing compliant, poverty-stricken states to join, as the large Islamic states including

Turkey, Iran, Saudi Arabia, Pakistan, and Indonesia call the shots. A large OIC voting bloc at the United Nations is evidently more important than the actual presence of Muslims.

President George W. Bush created a US special envoy to the OIC. His intention appeared to be to listen and learn about Muslim values while sharing American values as well. President Obama's envoy, Rashad Hussain, seems to have a more focused mission: to work with the OIC on the issue of defamation of religion, particularly in Europe. A noted Hafiz (a Muslim has memorized the *Koran*) Hussain is more likely to share the views and goals of other seriously engaged Muslims.

Perhaps even more indicative of the OIC's intentions are certain "Objectives and Principles" in its Charter:

8. To support and empower the Palestinian people to exercise their right to self determination and establish their sovereign State with Al-Quds Al-Sharif as its capital, while safeguarding its historic and Islamic character as well as the Holy places therein;

9. To strengthen intra-Islamic economic and trade cooperation, in order to achieve economic integration leading to the establishment of an Islamic Common Market;

11. To disseminate, promote and preserve the Islamic teachings and values based on moderation and tolerance, promote Islamic culture and safeguard Islamic heritage;

12. To protect and defend the true image of Islam, to combat defamation of Islam and encourage dialogue among civilizations and religions;

16. To safeguard the rights, dignity and religious and cultural identity of Muslim communities and minorities in non-Member States;

These are all elements of a would-be worldwide Muslim Ummah, and many OIC members are already involved in fulfilling these and other objectives, including controlling the spread of Islamic education and fighting "defamation" around the globe through "libel tourism."

The OIC has steadily pushed to implant *Shariah* principles into international precepts, if not law. For instance, in 1948 the General Assembly of the United Nations, along with all Muslim states excluding Saudi Arabia, formulated the Universal Declaration of Human Rights.[64] In

1990, the then forty-five members of the OIC created the Cairo Declaration on Human Rights in Islam[65] which, embodying *Shariah* principles, declared that all rights are derived from Allah. In 2007 a failed effort was made to reference the Cairo Declaration as complementing the Universal Declaration, the result of which would be to submit the latter to further requirements of Islamic law.

In essence, the effort sought to subordinate the principles of the Universal Declaration to those arrived at by the OIC. In fact, because of the inherent conflicts between the two declarations, by adopting and promoting the Cairo Declaration, the Islamic states are reneging on their commitments to the Universal Declaration, a slow but unceasing effort to push *Shariah* onto the non-Muslim world.

The Cairo Declaration elevates Islam above other religions. It makes *Shariah* the ultimate arbiter; all rights and freedoms are made subject to it, and it is the final point of reference for "explanation or clarification." Meanwhile the Ummah, the community of Muslims, is set out as the best example for creating a "well-balanced civilization" whose function is to "civilize" the world. The Cairo Declaration presses for Islamic treatment of women, which differs greatly from the Universal Declaration's more Western vision of equality between sexes. Religious freedom is further limited as Islamic states impose, sometimes through capital punishment, restrictions on leaving Islam or apostasy. *Shariah* will dictate what acts are crimes—including acts which insult Islam in any manner, something that would not be considered as such under the Universal Declaration. Punishment, too, is to follow *Shariah*, in conflict with many fundamental precepts of Western propriety.

Certain non-Islamic religious expression is further restricted as blasphemy under the Cairo Declaration, and other laws that prevent criticism of religion would overrule any liberty permitted in the Universal Declaration. Note that the *Koran*, itself replete with what could (should) be considered blasphemous statements about Christianity and Judaism, would be exempted by such an interpretive exercise. As Dutch Parliamentarian Geert Wilders discovered, the mere use of the *Koran* to demonstrate its own "insults" and "blasphemy" against Christians and Jews and its murderous essence is met with the full force of the international Islamic tantrum. It is the power of the coordinated OIC Members that allows such clear breaches of true universal rights as recognized by the West to take place under the banner of Islam.

In 1981, the OIC created the Islamic Fiqh Academy, which gave a platform to scholars representing 43 of the 57 Member states. According to Lahem Al-Nasser, as of 2009 it had issued 185 resolutions during 19 sessions.[66] The essential goal of the Academy, according to the human rights activist, theologian, and Fellow of the Australian Academy of the Humanities Dr. Mark Durie, is "to unite the Ummah, the Nation of Islam, by conforming conduct to the norms of Islam at all levels. . . . Their goal is to work toward a true Islamic conduct in accordance with the principles of Islam at every possible level . . . and also specifically to apply Islam to contemporary problems."[67] It seeks to give guidance for living in the modern world, dealing with a vast array of issues including *Shariah* finance, marriage, inheritance, Muslim minorities, medical applications, and apostasy.

The Fiqh Academy is a potent tool in bringing Muslims together in a manner that charts a path toward a single Islamic nation, a global Caliphate. As discussed elsewhere, there could be benefits to the Western world from a unified representation of Islam. It would supply a much-needed locus that could be held responsible for acts it proscribes. It could provide an ear to which Western grievances could be voiced and with which negotiations could take place. And under certain leadership it could be a tool for true reform. Yet given the history of the OIC, as the Ummah becomes more singularly defined by this Academy, the power of the International Institutional Jihad will likely become all the more pronounced. Worse, a global Caliphate would represent the concentration of Islamic forces empowering each level of Jihad beyond which the West currently appears unable to withstand.

The OIC is certainly not the only way its members pursue *jihad's* march of *Shariah*. The twenty-two member Arab League has had significant influence in representing Arab interests, not the least of which was demonstrated in its effectively granting Obama "permission" to enter into a military operation against Libya. Formerly controlled in large measure by Egypt whose post-Mubarak shift toward Iran and Hamas has caused great concern among Saudi Arabia and its nearby Persian Gulf states, the Arab League is facing a loss of consensus. As Saudi Arabia and Iran, along with Turkey, battle for dominance in the region, the League has lost some cohesion. In its place, the Gulf Cooperation Council, dominated by Saudi Arabia, is ascending. Formed in 1981 to provide mutual security against an Iranian attack and to lend support to Afghanistan's *jihad* against the Soviet Union, the Council recently expanded by taking in two members from outside its original sphere of concern—Jordan and Morocco. The GCC has become all the more important to Saudi Arabia in protecting it from the increasing influence of Iran in the region. While tension between and among Islamic countries exists and is accentuated during the recent revolutions as each reassesses with whom to ally, the central thrust of the International Institutional Jihad remains intact.

Most of the wealthy Muslim states also act independently to support the same aims expressed by the OIC. We have noted massive Saudi funding of educational programs, for instance. More insidiously, under the banner of *zakat* or charitable giving (one of the five "pillars" of Islam), powerful people in Islamic states have established foundations and made individual grants that effectively further *jihad* in America and the West.

Saudi Arabia's Prince Alwaleed bin Talal, for instance, who is a major shareholder in large Western-controlled media companies such as NewsCorporation and TimeWarner, has made significant donations to institutions such as CAIR. He gave $500,000 to CAIR in 2002 according to *Arabiabusiness.com*.[68] In 2006, CAIR announced it was planning to meet with Alwaleed to finance a five year $50 million media campaign "to create a better understanding of Islam and Muslims in the US" according to Javid Hassan in *Arab News* 6/21/06.[69] Alwaleed has given sizeable sums to US educational institutions as well. He gained national notoriety when, following 9/11, his $10 million "gift" to New York was ripped up by then-Mayor Rudy Giuliani because the Prince had attributed the Trade Center attacks to America's pro-Israel policies. Dore Gold's *Hatred's Kingdom* tracks a wide variety of examples of Saudi and other Arab Islamic funding of Violent and Civilization Jihadists.

Gaubatz and Sperry's *Muslim Mafia* and Sperry's *Infiltration* detail many other sources of funding, such as Saudi Prince Abdullah bin Mosa'ad, as well as endowments from the rulers of the United Arab Emirates, including the Al-Maktoum Foundation controlled by Dubai's Sheik Mohammad bin Rashid al-Maktoum.

Ken Timmerman, by way of small example, has alleged at *Newsmax.com* and elsewhere that the Office of Her Highness, Sheikha Mozah Bint Nasser al-Missned, wife of the ruler of Qatar, has financed the "Al Fakhoora Project" which aims at de-legitimizing Israel and supporting Hamas.[70] In her work she is assisted by the US public relations firm Fenton Communications. Researcher/writer Rachel Ehrenfeld has shed light on various other international financing sources that all contribute to the march toward *Shariah* in the West.

The role of Israel as a uniting force for the International Institutional Jihad can not be overstated. The Arab League was formed to coordinate Arab nations in their response to the UN's approval of the State of Israel. The Arabs immediately set out to reverse what they have called the Nakba or catastrophe of such statehood. They went to war against Israel and encouraged Arabs to leave Israel 's land anticipating they could easily return upon victory. They lost that war and continued to do so again in 1967 and 1973. Nonetheless, the goal for most has consistently remained to ultimately drive Israel out of the region.

The Arab League, and later the OIC, have sought about to turn the UN away from Israel and toward their favor as a primary step in advancing the International Institutional Jihad. They have for more than 60 years been extremely successful, steering the UN to act in obvious contravention to the very principles upon which it was founded. While they have yet to seize control of the Security Council, the General Assembly is generally at their beck and call when needed. And with Hezbollah controlled Lebanon soon to preside over the Security Council and elevated status having been given Iran, the Council will come under added pressure to conform to these nations' demands.

As Prime Minister Netanyahu charged in his September 23, 2011 speech there, the UN has become the "theatre of the absurd." Netanyahu pointed as well to the oxymoronic result of Libya under Qaddafi chairing the UN Commission on Human Rights while Saddam Hussein was allowed to lead the UN Committee on Disarmament. Douglas Murray often makes note of how the UN's 1975 "Zionism Equals Racism" resolution was introduced by the Ugandan dictator Idi Amin and celebrated at a party thrown by Kurt Waldheim. These are just a few. The UN has become a sanctuary for lies and institutionalized taqiyya. To paraphrase Netanyahu, we couldn't make this stuff up!

Yet these absurdities are not the result of random quirks in the bureaucratic system; they are clear expressions of how the UN has been hijacked as an instrumentality in service of the long term objectives of the International Institutional Jihad. And Israel has been the battleground upon which the original admirable principles of the UN have been systematically turned on their heads by this hijacking.

Regardless of conflicts between Islamic nations, most can always find "common ground" in hating Israel. One central organizing movement has been that of the Durban Declaration. Embodying the most extreme examples of projection and introjection (along with many other Control Factor moves), this effort commenced in 1975 when the UN General Assembly equated Zionism with racism. While subsequently reversed in 1991, Muslim states worked together to create the Durban Declaration in 2001 which condemned only Israel for racism and declared Palestinians as victims of this racism. While the absurdity of this conference did not escape notice (the Durban Conferences have been famously labeled as "racist anti-racism conferences") and while the US walked out, Muslim nations still pressured the UN Human Rights Council and General Assembly to hold Durban II in 2009. While Mahmoud Ahmadinejad was the only world leader to appear, the UN High Commissioner of Human Rights, Navi Pillay, declared the conference a success because it reaffirmed the Durban Declaration and Palestinians as victims.

It is a measure of the power of the International Institutional Jihad that so many Islamic nations congeal around such absurdity. Yasser Arafat had declared at Durban I, "Israel represents racial discrimination in its ugliest form and images" and Mahmoud Ahmadinejad stated at Durban II, "The word Zionism personifies racism that falsely resorts to religion and abuses sentiments to hide their hatred and ugly faces. . ."[71] Over 80% of all UN Emergency Sessions have concerned Israel while none have dealt with the genocides in Cambodia, Rwanda, or Sudan. In 2010 alone, 78% of the member states condemned only Israel for human rights violations. The fact that Palestinians enjoy more rights and freedoms in Israel than in any other Middle Eastern Islamic nation is irrelevant. Rather, anything that contributes to the destruction of Israel takes precedence as it furthers the goals of the International Institutional Jihad. (Anne Bayefsky's www.EYEontheUN.org is an excellent source for information on the Durban Conferences. Bayefsky also successfully organized an anti-Durban III conference in New York in 2011 which overshadowed a contemporaneous failed Durban III exercise.)

Support for the addiction/enabling dance through the "Arab-Israeli conflict" is perhaps the central indice of the OIC's power over the UN. The conflict, to paraphrase Harvard Professor Ruth Wisse, is more accurately described as the Arab war against Israel as it has been the Arabs' persistent cause since 1947. Any notion of equivalence between the two sides is intentionally distortive. While the OIC nations are stuck with important resolutions supporting Israel , they have successfully managed in recent decades to cause the UN to place all demands on Israel and virtually none on the Palestinians. As described earlier, the UN's Relief and Works Agency for Palestine Refugees (UNRWA) was originally designed in 1948 to assist for three years those who fled what became Israel in response to Arab calls and warnings. The UN did nothing for the similarly numbered of Jews who involuntarily were forced to leave their homes in neighboring Arab countries at the same time. The OIC nations have ensured UNRWA's continued existence for over 60 years, complete with alleged mismanagement and assistance to Israel's enemies while perpetuating the narrative of victimized "refugees" for International Institutional Jihad purposes.

The International Institutional Jihad seeks to coordinate what has been developing in Islamic countries for decades. It is important to remind ourselves that some Islamic nations have constitutions that either expressly or implicitly adopt *Shariah* as their law, or embody various *Shariah* principles. Recognizing differences between the various countries, the OIC demands that each Member State not interfere with the private affairs of the other Member States. The coordination among the Member States toward common goals, however, does not require new ideas or concepts.

The institutionalization of *Shariah* has made significant progress in modern times. Obviously, there is often much tension and conflict between many member states of the OIC, with Sunni-Shia differences being the most obvious. Competition between Saudi Arabia and Iran is pronounced as countries in internal turmoil look to align themselves with whichever power they anticipate will dominate in the future. There are clearly areas in which agreement among all of the parties is or will be difficult to obtain. For decades, the OIC has had difficulty resolving certain disputes between Muslim countries yet it has always been able to demonstrate unity by showing solidarity with the Palestinian "cause." Nonetheless, the overarching goals of the OIC fuse many of the most disparate elements within our Islamic Enemy, uniting them as an Ummah against the non-Muslim world. Conflicts between Muslims and non-Muslims always take precedence over intra-Islamic disputes.

The International Institutional Jihad is intended to prepare the world for Islam. It attempts to firm up acceptance of Islam, placing greater pressure on non-Muslim countries to yield eventually in compliance with it. It also attempts, through "norming," to force into Western nations Islamic principles that would never evolve from within. Thus if blasphemy laws cannot be instituted within a Western legal system, it is hoped that international blasphemy laws, made part of treaties and other international agreements to which America and Europe become parties, will eventually be made to bind Westerners.

As an example of potential "norming" into the United States, in mid 2011, it joined 152 other countries endorsing a UN Arms Treaty Resolution which, while appearing to merely regulate international arms trading has a wider objective. According to former Ambassador John Bolton, "there is no doubt that the real agenda here is domestic firearms control."[72] As described by Larry Bell on *Forbes.com* 6/7/11, if passed by the UN and ratified by the US Senate, the agreement will, among other things, force the United States to "[e]nact tougher licensing requirements, creating additional bureaucratic red tape for legal firearms ownership . . ." "[c]onfiscate and destroy all 'unauthorized' civilian firearms . . ." and "[c]reate an international gun registry, clearly setting the stage for full-scale gun confiscation."[73] The Second Amendment debates in the United States are very dear to those on both sides of the issue. Passing those decisions off to an international body is a significant infringement on US sovereignty. While this example is not directly related to Islam (at least currently), the norming precedents bode poorly for that time when provisions more easily attributable to our Islamic enemy are proposed.

Unlike other international institutions that might seek a way in which different civilizations can learn to live and compromise with each other, the International Institutional Jihad aims to use institutions to transform Western Civilization into an Islamic one. This is a triumphalist operation, in service of a global Ummah.

Oil power has concentrated the economic interests of many of the OIC Member States. OPEC's ability to wield power over the West during the 1970s awoke many Islamic-controlled countries to their ability to advance Islamic goals. Bat Ye'or's *Eurabia* details how Arab nations used such leverage to extract extraordinary concessions concerning Islam from European governments. OPEC and the OIC have intimately overlapping interests, and OPEC often serves as an OIC tool when the issue at hand is not inconsistent with the interests of non-Islamic OPEC members. This is particularly significant in light of the recent appointment of Iran's oil minister to become Chairman of OPEC in 2011. OPEC might lose, at least temporarily, some of its unity in adjusting to Iran's influence. Nonetheless, while the West and others attempt to exert sanctions and other pressures on Iran, Iran will be uniquely situated among those powers that hold great leverage over the West.

As revolutions occur across the Islamic Middle East, many existing relationships will be challenged. An "Arab Spring" fantasy has tried to suggest that new democratically based leaders will emerge who will guide their countries away from any Islamist or radical strategy. Yet, when the Control Factor is stripped away, one can see that the Muslim Brotherhood and related groups are best suited to take control in many areas. The previous group of tyrants who shared some common interests will be replaced by new leaders who share much more—in particular an interest in spreading *Shariah* worldwide. Institutions such as the OIC are then even more likely to marshal their power to advance the International Institutional Jihad.

Level Confusion and Convergence

Violent Jihad, has been used for decades as an agitating tool. Often carried out by diverse groups such as the PLO and al-Qaeda, fulfilling the Koranic command "to strike terror into the hearts of the enemies of Allah," it has powerfully impressed the Western world with its ability to inflict harm in order to extract major concessions. It has grown and evolved into various forms, and presents the West with a daunting challenge, especially if it becomes easy for terrorists to acquire weapons of mass destruction.

Yet, as we've seen, making terrorism the central and exclusive focus when confronting our Islamic Enemy is dangerously naive. While this distortion can provide subtle comfort that the problem we face is not very different from violence as employed by the Mafia or groups such as the KKK or neo-Nazis, it blinds us to the comprehensive threat we face. While Obama approaches the conflict as a legal one in which prosecution and penalties are the primary tool, countering such a strategy is child's play for our true Islamic Enemy.

Civilization Jihad that chips at cultural institutions from within might appear difficult to accomplish, but it has regularly scored major victories. The Muslim Brotherhood's progress throughout Europe and America has been both stealthy and swift. As it uses our laws to protect its advance, the Civilization Jihad is deliberately non-violent. Violence or terrorism would betray Islam's intentions. Yet the Control Factor keeps us engaged in what might be called "level confusion"—the failure to distinguish the Civilization Jihad from terrorism. As the Ground Zero Mosque proposal became a matter for public debate, many supporters of the mosque defended Imam Rauf on the basis that he was not engaged in terrorism. Yet terrorism is not the criterion for the Civilization Jihad; rather, we should ask Imam Rauf what his acts and intentions are with respect to spreading *Shariah*. Since we have little in the way of constitutionally acceptable solutions for the Civilization Jihad, it is easier for us to move back to something we believe we can better control—terrorism. Nonetheless, we must always be on the lookout for level confusion, constantly asking ourselves "What level of threat are we discussing here?"

Finally, when nation-states join to force Islam and Muslim culture into the non-Muslim world while simultaneously uniting the activities of Muslims within their own territories, we face a seemingly insurmountable force—the third level of International Institutional Jihad, bent on creating an Islamic super-state. This third level is only beginning to rear its head in public. Arab uprisings might create some interim conflicts and may pressure for intra-Islamic realignmnts. But as uprisings topple Arab authoritarian rulers, or force them to accept systemic changes in favor of Brotherhood or al-Qaeda objectives, the OIC and other International Institutional Jihad organizations will attain greater prominence.

The ultimate coordination of Islamic countries with the OIC's vast resources and unitary goals may well enable it to emerge from obscurity within the UN as a force with which the West would not wish to be at war, even if it could withstand such a war. As with the horror film, the critical moment arrives when survival appears impossible, and this third level will perhaps deliver that message perfectly.

Joel Gilbert described the "Diplomatic Strategy against Israel"[74] as the Arab-Islamic world's staged approach to destroying Israel. While that strategy is based on time—first containing Israel, then working within and without to delegitimize and de-Zionize it leading toward eliminating it—its foundation encompasses all three levels of Jihad discussed here. That strategy recognized the limits of military efforts which had led to defeat and focused equal or more efforts on chipping away at Israeli society both from within as well as through international institutions. In thinking about the three levels, it is helpful to examine what has happened to Israel over the past century.

Furthermore, this analysis must not leave out an additional critical aspect well described by Jamie Glazov in *United in Hate*, by David Horowitz in much of his work, and by Andrew McCarthy in his invaluable analysis of our conditions today, *The Grand Jihad*. Our Islamic Enemy has forged an alliance with the radical Left of the Western world, one that greatly facilitates the destruction of Western institutions and culture and helps pave the way for our enemy to march forward. Sharing a deeply held hatred for America, seemingly odd combinations of characters are able to "come together." For example, as an early step in working together, in January 2011, the Muslim Brotherhood, leftist labor advocates, and youth opposition groups combined to launch the Egyptian protests which led to the deposing of Mubarak. Similarly, US labor coordinators allegedly later appeared in the Middle East, perhaps dividing up the spoils and future responsibilities of nations going through "revolutions" while Western Leftists are even alleged to be instigating protests in Israel to further the chaos in the region. In addition, radical Leftist Bill Ayers and his wife have alleged ties to a contemplated launch of the threatened second Hamas flotilla. Unfortunately, hatred has, throughout history, been a more effective unifying force than the pursuit of freedom.

Each of the three levels of Jihad stirs specific and distinct fears. The Violent Jihad obviously centers around fears of physical harm and death. The Civilization Jihad, in contrast, plays upon notions of what we believe is socially fair and just and challenges our commitments to our many freedoms. The International Institutional Jihad focuses upon concerns about being accepted in the so-called "international community," about our ability to protect our bargaining power in global affairs, and our need to maintain some form of "Superpower" status. Accordingly, each level can evoke different Control Factor responses.

The Control Factor encourages us to treat each level as if unrelated to the others. There is nothing wrong with the OIC's efforts to expand Muslim outreach, the Control Factor tells us, as there is no terrorism or violence involved. Indeed, to the Control Factor, it seems a sign of America's strength that Barack Obama can reach out as America's "Educator-in-Chief on Islam." Similarly, the lack of violence encourages the Control Factor to welcome all dealings with "peaceful" American Muslims engaged in the Civilization Jihad. Just as Islam expresses itself differently depending upon whether it is in the minority or majority, the Violent Jihad waxes and wanes depending upon the opportunities available and the weaknesses in the host territory. During periods of lull in terrorism, which must not be mistaken as a measure of the real war, the

Control Factor pressures us to overlook what else is occurring on the other levels.

Still, as Islam gains more power, the three levels also tend to converge in various ways. We are just beginning to identify some of the connections among the three levels. Frank Gaffney refers to the Civilization Jihad as simply the "pre-violent" stage of Islamic takeover (reminiscent of the old "joke" that defines a "moderate Muslim" as a "Muslim without ammunition"). While the Civilization Jihad tries to criminalize "insults" to the Prophet, violent riots (framed by media manipulators as spontaneous public reactions) are ordered by those more closely associated with the terror level. It must be noted that the riots in Europe over the Mohammed cartoon incident followed months after the publication of those cartoons, allegedly on orders from the Muslim Brotherhood, which makes clear that orderly coordination, rather than emotional reaction, was at work.

For years, the OIC and Arab League have prevented any sensible definition of "terrorism" to be created for international institutional purposes. As Anne Bayefsky of the Hudson Institute has pointed out, the Arab Terrorism Convention, for instance, has exempted from the definition "all cases of struggle by whatever means . . . against foreign occupation and aggression for liberation and self-determination."[75] Consequently, regardless of tactical suicide bombing, flying airplanes into buildings, etc., if the political motivation of the actors fits this exemption, they would escape any consequences from international institutions.

This assistance from these institutions to the Violent Jihad was further embellished following the killing of bin Laden. As Bayefsky also pointed out, the UN High Commissioner of Human Rights, Navi Pillay, aided by two professors, sought to pursue the United States for violations of human rights in killing bin Laden instead of capturing him and affording him due process. The presupposition was that international law of warfare did not apply so that bin Laden was not a "combatant." Rather, they insisted that "the norm should be that terrorists be dealt with as criminals, through legal processes of arrest, trial and judicially-decided punishment." Interestingly, while the Obama administration has also advocated this approach, the killing of bin Laden was an act outside its scope.

Apologists for the Brotherhood like to refer to the "battle" between former Brotherhood activist—and now, following bin Laden's death, al-Qaeda leader, Ayman al-Zawahiri—and the Brotherhood. Zawahiri has criticized the Brotherhood for its use of non-violence as a strategy and its participation in seeming democracies such as Egypt. Yet this dispute is much overstated, as the goals of al-Qaeda and the Muslim Brotherhood almost fully overlap. The Brotherhood motto—dating back to al-Banna himself—holds that a Muslim should love death more than life, a principle that connects directly with al-Qaeda's use of violence and suicide bombing. And, the new Brotherhood leader, Mohammed Badie, has been direct in his response to al-Qaeda's prodding that it is time for Muslims to wage *jihad* against the West.[76]

Lawfare as a tactic is similarly shared across all three levels of threat. The "offensive" use of domestic and international courts to replace Western notions of justice with Islamic justice affords opportunities for parties working at each level to assist each other. The Lawfare Project defines at least three goals:

1. To silence and punish free speech about issues of national security and public concern;
2. To delegitimize the sovereignty of democratic states such as the United States and Israel; and
3. To frustrate and hinder the ability of democracies to combat and defeat terrorism.

The *Lawfare Project* (www.LawfareProject.org) lists "Case Examples" of legal actions which we can readily match with the different levels of threat:[77]

Violent Jihad:
"Attempts by terrorist organizations such as Hamas to impede the free movement of democratic state officials and achieve legitimacy by hiring lawyers and instituting "human rights" litigation abroad."

Civilization Jihad:
"Predatory defamation and 'hate speech' lawsuits filed against anyone brave enough to speak publicly about radical Islam, terrorism, and its source of financing."

International Institutional Jihad:
"Efforts at the United Nations to exclude attacks on American and Israeli civilians from any international definition of terrorism, and to enact a global ban on the 'defamation' of religion."
"The Goldstone Report and similar flawed and politicized documents masquerading as legitimate legal analyses and created solely to give legal patina to military and political goals."
"The lack of legal accountability demanded of theocratic states that recruit their own children as suicide bombers and child soldiers."

In no sense do complementary actions constitute a global conspiracy. Rather, different actors with overlapping interests pursue their own agendas and learn to work together when it is mutually beneficial. Iran and al-Qaeda have enough shared interests for Iran to have assisted the transit of many of the 9/11 terrorists and to have offered refuge to the family members of Bin Laden and al-Zawahiri if not more. The Brotherhood is actively engaged in assisting Hamas, as is Iran. The different actors try new tactics and strategies and learn from each other what works.

It is true that the level of terrorism employed by al-Qaeda is anathema to many prominent members of the ruling class of the OIC, such as the Saudi royal family, which assists the United States with anti-terror intelligence operations. The Brotherhood has always been hostile toward tyrannical Arab rulers and regimes that do not promote Islam in the way the Brotherhood demands.

Yet terrorists guided by the principles of prominent Islamists such as Sayyed Qutb and Syed Abul A'ala Maududi are looking to erase the borders of the nation-state within the greater united House of Islam. Meanwhile, Saudis bankroll the Civilization Jihad in America, promoting principles very much in agreement with those of the terrorists. As work toward Islamic supremacy progresses—whether through terror groups, the Muslim Brotherhood, or the OIC—the points of disagreement among these different groups will begin to fade.

In September 2010, The American Islamic College in Chicago held a conference allegedly planned by the Muslim Student Association entitled "Islam and Muslims in America." The conference brought together participants affiliated with both the Muslim Brotherhood and the OIC, including H.E.(His Excellency) Dr. Ekmeleddin Ihsanoglu, Secretary General of the OIC; Ambassador Ufuk Gokcen, Ambassador of the OIC to the United Nations; Ambassador Rashad Hussain, Special Envoy of the

White House to the OIC, Ambassador Sada Cumber, First Special Envoy of the White House to the OIC; Safaa Zaraour, Secretary General of the Islamic Society of North America (ISNA); Ahmed Rehab, Executive Director of The Council on American Islamic Relations (CAIR).

According to Bat Ye'or, the OIC is "close to the Muslim World League of the Muslim Brotherhood" and shares its "strategic and cultural vision, that of a universal religious community, the Ummah, based on the Koran, the Sunna, and the canonical orthodoxy of shari'a."[79] A conference does not a conspiracy make; nonetheless, the event presages a growing cooperation between the Civilization and International Institutional Jihad levels in their American operations.

It is also clear that the different levels communicate with each other in other ways. Anwar al-Awlaki, presumably speaking on behalf of al-Qaeda, spoke through al-Qaeda's own July 2010 issue of *Inspire Magazine*: "We invite Muslims worldwide to stand up in defense of the Messenger of Allah" and pushed them to have "their efforts manifest in all appropriate means."[80] Similarly, in the same issue, Shaykh Abu Basir stated, "My advice to my Muslim brothers in the West is to acquire weapons and learn methods of war. They are living in a place where they can cause great harm to the enemy and where they can support the Messenger of Allah." These comments have been interpreted by some intelligence experts as, in part, a "prod" to the Muslim Brotherhood to move from "pre-violent" to Violent Jihad.

The prodding appears to have worked well. On September 30, 2010, the recently elected Supreme Guide of the Muslim Brotherhood, Muhammad Badie, announced that "[t]he US is now experiencing the beginning of its end and is heading toward its demise. . ."[81] He further proclaimed, "Resistance is the only solution against the Zio-American [*sic*] arrogance and tyranny and all we need is for Arabs and Muslim peoples to stand behind it and support it."

On one hand, there is little philosophically new for the Brotherhood here; on the other, the hostility to America is more blatant and violent than in prior Civilization Jihad pronouncements. While Badie, the eighth Supreme Guide, is the first to not have had a relationship with al-Banna, he had a close one with Sayyed Qutb. Badie was arrested with Qutb in 1965 and jailed for nine years accused of being part of the Brotherhood unit that attempted to assassinate Nasser. Qutb's hatred for America is the foundation which sprung him to become the effective spiritual leader of the Brotherhood even through today.

Again, Badie announced that Allah's mandatory commandment to wage *jihad* has been disregarded by Muslims worldwide. (This came after he had claimed that Arab and Muslim rulers had been aiming their weapons at their own people rather than at Israel—hardly the words of an internal spiritual struggle). Badie continued that Arabs and Muslims "crucially need to understand that the improvements and change that the Muslim nation seeks can only be attained through *jihad* and sacrifice and by raising a jihadist generation that pursues death as the enemies pursue life."

Revolutions in Tunisia, Egypt, Libya, and Syria, in early 2011, were followed by major unrest in other Islamic lands. These uprisings could ultimately deliver state territories to the Muslim Brotherhood. Westerners deep in the spell of their Control Factors bought into the narrative the "Arab Spring" fantasy that the Egyptian revolution was created by and for modernized secular youth, and that the Brotherhood was just along for the ride. Quite the opposite was true. The Brotherhood was deeply entwined from the start and, once Mubarak was deposed, grabbed the reins, albeit behind closed doors, to effectively control the process of amending the constitution, and to cement its relationship with the previously dominant military regime. If, as appears likely, power becomes concentrated in the hands of the Brotherhood, the force of these and other countries applying *Shariah*-based pressure through international organizations will be greatly enlarged.

In turn, the Brotherhood's ability to advance the Civilization Jihad through the West will also be significantly enhanced. And as it acquires more power, it appears to be moving from the "pre-violent" into the Violent Jihad as well. Barry Rubin, in a 10/9/10 Gloria-center.org post, suggests that Badie is moving the Brotherhood "from the era of propaganda and base-building to one of revolutionary action."[82] His call, as Rubin characterizes, that "Palestinians should back Hamas in overthrowing the Palestinian Authority in the West Bank and unite in waging war on Israel," along with his announcement that the Palestinians are preparing for a third intifada and urging that all Arabs and Muslims support this fight is further evidence of his move toward violence.

In recent years, America has realized that dependence on foreign oil is a major threat. We need to become equally aware of how denial under the influence of the Control Factor is enabling our Islamic Enemy's advance—whether through terror carried out by individual groups small and large, or through the deeply implanted tentacles from the Civilization Jihad of the Muslim Brotherhood, or through the international directives being proffered by the OIC at the United Nations. We must awaken to all that is unfolding around us if America is to have any real chance to survive.

Chapter 11

The Inner Jihad—Fighting the Control Factor

Because the Control Factor exploits the idiosyncrasies of each mind, each individual's Inner Jihad must take its own unique course. Even so, once we begin to become aware of the depth of the threat we face, how it organizes itself, and what it is doing, certain principles apply to guide all of us in battling the Control Factor.

Transfer of Responsibility— Put it Back Where it Belongs

All behavior is instructive. Each of us is constantly teaching others through the messages our behavior sends. We continually teach people who we are, what we accept, what we do and do not tolerate, and so on. To right the dangerous imbalance between ourselves and our Islamic Enemy, we must change our ways and *teach* responsibility to the enemy. We must transfer back to Islam the responsibility we have grabbed for our own comfort.

One cannot avoid teaching those around oneself. When we as a nation retreated from Lebanon, as Reagan ordered following an attack on our Marine base there, we taught a lesson. When we bomb Afghanistan following 9/11, we teach. When we send back a bust of Sir Winston Churchill that had been a gift from the United Kingdom, we teach. When we beg our enemies to "engage" with us, we teach. When we push aside Hosni Mubarak who had been an ally and state that Muammar Qaddafi, who had given up his nuclear program "must go" while refusing to take any serious action against Iran who is seeking nuclear weapons, we teach. When protesters are supported simply because they are protesting, we teach. When we restrict our use of words so as not to upset Muslims, we teach. In short, we have helped to teach our Islamic Enemy to act the way it does. We must therefore begin to instruct otherwise.

We must demonstrate that we will no longer accept responsibility for hatred and unacceptable behavior. Instead we must hold our Islamic enemy fully responsible for its actions and emotions. Our challenge is to undo our own patterns of behavior that have been so deeply entrenched and practiced over the years. We must resist the impulse to act as if we are guilty of some injustice to the Muslim world. We must avoid making excuses for the enemy's behavior.

We must accept that our anger for the Muslim world's failure to share and demonstrate the same values that form the foundation for the West is justified and not aim that anger at ourselves or otherwise deflect it from its proper focus. We have very different values. Our anger is appropriate and pales in comparison to our Islamic Enemy's hatred of us. Pretending otherwise is naively self-destructive.

Responsibility is a central concept in political thought. How responsibility is allocated within a polity greatly defines that polity. In American politics, conservatives generally argue for some abridged notion of "individual responsibility," while liberals and progressives generally lean toward transferring to the government responsibility for many aspects of individual lives. Is the polity seeking to promote the individual or some iteration of the collective? With our Islamic Enemy, we must realize we are confronting notions of responsibility that do not conform to *any* of our traditions or comport with our long-term survival. Their responsibility is to advance *Shariah*'s march, whether by *dawa* or the sword, on behalf of the collective Ummah. That is the behavior they have been taught to cherish and which they try to teach the world. We must work to hold them accountable by teaching otherwise.

While we are quick to blame ourselves for the world's problems, we feel great resistance to holding our Islamic Enemy responsible for anything. After Hamas won elections in the Gaza strip in 2006, the Bush administration ostensibly cut off communications with it. This was an important first step in demanding accountability for the consequences of that election; if you elect a terrorist organization you must suffer the consequences of such vote. The refrain often heard, however, was to question how America could first push for democracy but then turn its back on a democratically-elected organization. Yet this apparent conflict is no conflict at all. Democracy is not simply the act of voting; it requires the voter to understand whom they are voting for and to accept all of the consequences of their choices. Responding forcefully to Hamas was part of that teaching process.

In no case is it America's responsibility to alter its actions in order to let the Palestinians off the hook for their election results. "Elections have consequences," and the Palestinians, as with the Iraqis and Afghanis, must learn this lesson. Unfortunately, the Bush administration lost its will to hold Hamas accountable, eventually permitting funds to flow into Gaza, against the spirit if not the letter of our own terror finance laws.

In contrast, Obama has made clear, both in his second Middle East speech and other actions, that he will support the results of the elections in Egypt and Tunisia. Even if the Brotherhood were to control the entire outcome, Obama has signaled that these countries will not be held responsible should they vote in our Islamic enemy.

In the same speech, after blaming Israel for the lack of peace and pressuring it to make major concessions of territory, Obama made only one demand of the Palestinians: to explain with a "credible answer" how Israel could be expected to transact with them if they would not recognize Israel's right to exist—another invitation to a land-for-false-rhetoric deal. Obama is back to teaching our enemy that it controls the game.

Control Factor slaves often tie themselves in knots over responsibility. In discussing the blockade of Gaza by Israel and Egypt, liberal writers have argued that the Palestinian people should not be "punished" because they elected Hamas. Rather, they hold Israel at fault for allowing Hamas to be on the slate in the first place.

Responsibility has been turned inside out in international institutions such as the United Nations. Much of the effort of so-called "human rights" activists is based upon trying to asymmetrically hold the West to standards of warfare that the United Nations decides are appropriate. A 2010 UN report suggests that US Predator drones are problematic because they will lead to a "PlayStation mentality."[1] We are all too familiar with the separate and unequal treatment the United Nations affords Israel—most recently observed in the Goldstone Report[2] (from which Goldstone has subsequently retracted his support) and the responses to the "Flotilla attack"—no matter what action Israel takes. Due in large part to the power of the OIC, little to no international effort is devoted to confronting, much less punishing, the many war and human rights crimes committed by our Islamic Enemy.

And yet, in recent years many US Democratic candidates campaigned on propositions that give international institutions greater influence over our foreign policy decisions. (Indeed both Bushes also aggressively sought international coalitions to support their forays into the Arab world but more as a strategic benefit rather than a policy necessity). Obama has gone to great lengths to condition his use of force on the participation of the "international community." Supporting a policy which furthers our dhimmitude, he has to some degree subordinated our sovereignty to the will of that "international community" which, due to the power of the OIC, is becoming increasingly aligned with our Islamic Enemy.

At the most basic level, our Islamic Enemy must at least be held accountable for its words. Despite utilizing a sophisticated web of deceptions for certain purposes, the enemy often says exactly what it means and means exactly what it says.

Part of the Inner Jihad requires our resisting the temptation to airbrush away that which we find undesirable. While Hitler frequently made clear his intentions, Stalin and the Western Allies—not to mention much of Germany—refused to believe him, with tragic consequences. When the Islamic Republic of Iran says it is at war with America and seeks the eradication of Israel, believe it. When Muslim Brotherhood front groups spew venom against Western culture, Jews, and infidels and announce plans to destroy America from the inside out, they must be taken seriously and held to their statements. Words do Matter!

The Control Factor makes taking our enemy's words seriously extremely challenging for many of us. It tempts us with a palette of shadings and colorful excuses, assuring us with, "What he really meant was . . . ," "That is just to build his political constituency . . . ," or "The crowd knows what he is really saying . . . ," or "The translation is faulty," and so on. Instead, we must believe what they say! And then formulate thinking consistent with that belief.

This struggle with words became critical in the march toward the Iraq War in 2003. Saddam Hussein had spoken and acted in ways that suggested he had at least some weapons of mass destruction and was seeking others. Intelligence agencies around the world were also convinced, as were world leaders, US presidents, senators, and congressmen, both present and past. Nonetheless, many Westerners today have convinced themselves that Saddam not only misspoke or (as he later testified) was posturing to scare off Iran and other challengers. The implication from those who opposed the war is that somehow it was the West's responsibility to ignore Saddam's words and actions, to somehow divine his true meanings, and to resist doing what it deemed necessary to protect itself.

Consequently, the responsibility was transferred from Saddam onto President Bush, via the bizarre narrative, against all evidence to the contrary, that Bush lied about Saddam's weapons. This demonstrates how potent, insidious, and overwhelming a force the Control Factor can be. Saddam's actual lie was projected onto Bush. While Bush may have progressed on his own Inner Jihad, much of the country was not adequately prepared for theirs. Instead, they resorted to Control Factor enabling behavior. The real shame of the Iraq war was not that we wrongly entered the war. It was that once we started to teach our Islamic Enemy that we will hold them to their words and actions, we gave up and attacked ourselves under pressure from our own Left. Instead of teaching a new lesson, we reinforced the old.

The Control Factor never quits; it will even rewrite history. Years after Saddam's death, the suggestion is sometimes made that, if left alone, he would have become a "moderate" and, because he had no nuclear program, he could have been a useful instrument for the West in dealing with Mahmoud Ahmadinejad. The Control Factor uses the frailty of memory to rinse the past of its terrifying aspects as it transfers responsibility for any continuing anxiety, in this case onto America's failure to comprehend who Saddam truly was.

Similarly, many "intellectual" voices in the West frequently describe the Palestinian "problem" as really a secular one. That is, they construe the struggle as one in which Abbas (and Arafat before him) has used a religious conflict for his own purposes—securing power for himself. It is certainly true that many leaders of Islamic countries or territories are not what we would consider "religious." Saddam Hussein was often described as a secular tyrant who used Islam only when needed to secure allegiance, as when he announced he was writing a *Koran* using his own blood.

Arafat was often described as a secular communist, only secondarily interested in Islam. Abbas is sometimes argued by Western writers to be far more interested in lining his pockets and maintaining power rather than in any advancement of *jihad*. Nonetheless, they both talk to their people in powerfully religious terms, spewing hate and the need for *jihad*.

More significantly, they use the Palestinian Authority's media to brainwash the next generation with *jihad*-driven and hate-filled ideology. Palestinian Media Watch (PMW.org) has catalogued endless examples to demonstrate the Palestinian Authority media's use, cynical or not, of *jihad* and Islam as rallying cries for their people. Western policy, however, while paying lip service to stopping the behavior, has again and again failed to require any true cessation of the incitements and brainwashing campaign. Only by holding them to their words will Westerners either force them to change positively, or to cease fooling the West about their true objectives.

Our words matter as well. For example, America essentially told the Afghan fighters who opposed the Soviet Union's war there throughout the 1980s that it would remain in Afghanistan to assist them after victory. Following a Soviet retreat, however, we betrayed our words and pulled out without contributing to the very effort that now, many decades later, is needed in order to prevent a return of the Taliban. We teach with our conduct.

Similarly, conducting military actions in both Iraq and Afghanistan while verbally making clear that we are prepared to withdraw at a date certain regardless of conditions, is yet another way American leaders have failed to give their own words the attention they are due.

Human rights violations as Westerners define them exist throughout many Islamic-controlled countries, particularly in nations where the populace is treated brutally by a tyrannical regime. In certain cases, however, it is not simply brute force that keeps the abuses in place. Islam is a major contributor, especially when mixed with age-old cultural practices. Islam's treatment of women in territories dominated by *Shariah*—from simple prohibitions against driving or leaving the house unescorted to stonings for adultery after being raped—has resulted in some of the most horrific acts ever seen, and should give rise to forceful action in response.

The United Nations promotes itself as the appropriate global body to address human rights concerns. It holds out the promise that human rights violators will be held liable for their acts. Apart from scolding Israel, however, it is unable to meaningfully address any human rights violations. The influence of the OIC and many of its member states ensures that no meaningful action will ever be taken against Islamic abuses.

This sham, evidenced by the presence on the shameful Human Rights Council of some of the Muslim world's worst violators, is given legitimacy by President Obama, his State Department, and his inner circle of advisors. Writers including Anne Bayefsky of the *Eye on the UN* website and Claudia Rosett have tracked the "good intentions" of Obama's efforts at influencing the Council. Secretary of State Hillary Clinton suggested that to encourage reform the United States join in order to be able to work from within and participate in its formal review process. Yet, the joint sessions, as Bayefsky reported on 3/25/11, "produced six resolutions condemning Israel, one resolution each on four other states, and nothing at all on the remaining 187 countries."[3] In addition, of the 42 reform proposals the United States put forward, only three inconsequential procedural ones were accepted. Certainly Islamic countries commit some of the most insidious human rights atrocities. Nonetheless, as long as Islam controls such a powerful bloc, no serious reform will ever occur. The Western world, ultimately, cannot be effective in this context. At some point, responsibility for Islamic human rights abuses must be returned to Islam and its victims. How Islam evolves is primarily the responsibility of Islam. Once again, when we continue to support the UN in and despite these endeavors, we teach.

Some Muslims, under the heading of "Reform," have created the illusion that they desire to Westernize or modernize Islam. What they actually are attempting is the converse—to Islamicize the West. While many Westerners wish to believe that the immutability of the *Koran* can somehow be overlooked—and that Islam can be reshaped to fit modernity—there is a converse trend which carries substantial weight in the Islamic world. This effort attempts to conform Western notions of modernity to Islam, rather than to have Islam retreat from modernity. At the absurd extreme, the results are displayed in ridiculous fatwas covering such issues as "adult breastfeeding." To overcome the bar against women co-existing in public with men to whom they are not related, permission has been given for the women to share their breast milk with such men in order for them to qualify as properly related. This is a curious example not of destroying modernity to bring back the conditions of Mohammed's times, but rather of reforming modernity in order to have it comply with the demands of *Shariah*.

More characteristic, however, is the path of Civilization Jihad. We've seen a litany of attempts to force Western laws and customs to accommodate Islamic practices. From prayer rooms and dress codes, to allowing taxi drivers to refuse passengers, to separating men and women in normally unisex activities, the Civilization Jihadists are out to press every "cultural button" they can. While advocates of "moderate Islam" seek to demonstrate that Islam fits in with American culture and democracy, its goal is the converse—to reshape America and the West to accommodate Islam. Step by step, Western institutions bend to conform to this "creeping dhimmitude."[4] In Minnesota, for instance, state agencies have made "Islamic mortgages" available in order to allow home sales to comply with *Shariah*. Essentially, the state purchases the targeted home and then resells it to the buyer at a higher price which effectively accounts for the interest the Muslim otherwise is forbidden to pay. Numerous private lenders provide similar products as well which helps make such conformities to *Shariah* more common.

Perhaps the oddest example comes from the Liberal Democrat-run Stockport Council in Greater Manchester, UK, where a café owner was ordered to remove an extractor fan because the smell of bacon cooking was offensive to passing Muslims, and because a neighbor asserted that his Muslim friends refused to visit him because they "can't stand the smell of bacon."[5] A lower court judge ruled against the café, and although the judgment was overturned by a higher court, the fact that the case was brought at all is emblematic of the tactics of Civilization Jihad.

Among the ever-increasing examples of governmental complicity, was one cleverly packaged by Obama himself during his "Apology Tour." In his Cairo speech to the Muslim world (the front rows for which he had reserved for Egyptian Muslim Brothers), Obama said: "In the United States, rules on charitable giving have made it harder for Muslims to fulfill their religious obligations. That's why I'm committed to working with American Muslims to insure that they can fulfill *zakat*."[6]

Most Westerners have no idea what this means. *Zakat* is the Muslim obligation to pay a proportion of one's wealth to approved classes of recipient. According to *Reliance of the Traveller: A Classic Manual of Islamic Sacred Law*,[7] the most useful compendium of Islamic law for interested Westerners, there are eight and only eight categories of recipients of *zakat* that qualify. (In three of the four Sunni schools of law, one eighth of the donation is to go to each; the Hanafi school permits the giver to allocate his total *zakat* amount however he chooses.)

The categories are of particular interest. The poor, those short of money, those in debt, and travelers in need of money—all of these are understandable in the modern world as worthy recipients. None of these categories is inherently Muslim in nature. These, therefore, should not present Obama with any particular issue as no Muslim would be prevented from helping them. The fifth category is slaves purchasing their freedom from their owners, a criterion generally irrelevant in the modern Western World.

The three remaining *zakat* categories, however, are specifically tied to Islam. One is *zakat* workers—those engaged in collecting *zakat* itself. Another is those whose hearts are to be reconciled, which, according to *Reliance of the Traveller* includes "(1) the chief personages of a people (O: with weak Islamic intentions) whose Islam may be expected to improve, or whose peers may be expected to enter Islam; (2) or the heads of a people who collect *zakat* for us from Muslims living near them who refuse to pay it, or who fight an enemy for us at considerable expense and trouble to themselves."

The final category is most problematic: those fighting for Allah. *Reliance of the Traveller* defines this category as:

> . . . people engaged in Islamic military operations for whom no salary has been allotted in the army roster (O: but who are volunteers for jihad without remuneration). They are given enough to suffice them for the operation, even if affluent; of weapons, mounts, clothing, and expenses (O: for the duration of the journey, round trip, and the time they spend there, even if prolonged. Though nothing has been mentioned here of expense involved in supporting such people's families during this period, it seems clear that they should also be given it). [Note: "O" represents commentary from Sheikh Umar Barakat.][8]

Are these three categories the ones that Obama claims are difficult to support under US charitable giving rules? US terror finance laws? Those fighting *jihad*, those veering away from Islam and *jihad*, and those who enforce the efforts to secure funding for these groups? Perhaps that is exactly what Obama meant for seriously engaged Muslims throughout the world to hear, knowing full well that Westerners would have no clue as to what he intended. Will we soon witness Civilization Jihad efforts to modify US charitable giving rules to accommodate terrorists and others involved in "military operations"?

This tension between Islam and modernity creates the means by which responsibility can be transferred. It raises the brutally provocative question of whether Islam should be treated as a "religion" at all for purposes of Western freedoms and laws. Revisiting Wittgenstein's notion of "family resemblances," Islam certainly contains many features commonly associated with religion—the presence of a God, the requirements of rituals and devotion, a narrative addressing the afterlife, the purpose of life, and certainty, and a tradition stretching back 1400 years. Most importantly, over a billion adherents call it a religion.

But just as our traditional concept of "marriage" as the union of opposite sexes is being transformed, so might our concept of "religion" have to change drastically to deal with the threat of a political ideology that is adverse to our founding principles and that seeks to impose itself worldwide.

As we have seen, Islam, in mirroring Mohammed, is a full political system. Should the inability to separate church and state disqualify it from being afforded the protections and benefits of a religion? Does a political system that hides within a religious wrapping deserve the benefits of protection under the very Constitution it sets out to destroy? Responsibility for these decisions must be taken.

Similarly, if Islam does not constitute a religion for these purposes, does being a Muslim deserve the benefits of a protected class? Many civil rights advocates (to expand their list of claims) improperly frame Muslims as a race. Yet it has nothing to do with race any more than other protected classes that are not defined by choice such as age and sex. Choice has become a tool, however, as modern liberal judicial trends have expanded protections, for instance to gays and lesbians, by relying in part on the notion that they essentially have no choice in their sexuality. Perhaps the same liberal thinking will be applied here. That is, given the realities of Islamic apostasy laws which do not permit adult Muslims to leave, would we extend protection to Muslims on the basis that they can be deemed to have no choice? Either way, responsibility for clarity on these issues has, by default, been given to our Islamic Enemy who takes full advantage.

The Control Factor vigorously and frequently displays its assumption of responsibility in its compulsion toward diplomacy. Our State Department operates on the principle that diplomacy is the only effective answer to disputes. In *Surrender is Not an Option,* former US Ambassador to the UN, John Bolton, points out that, for the State Department, diplomacy and the consummation of "the deal" are ends in and of themselves. This proclivity has historically reinforced the Control Factor's notion of the "business transaction model" even for dealing with problems that are otherwise insoluble without the willingness to use force.

The State Department is an unchanging institution, in part because of its size, its deeply entrenched philosophical biases, and because the Secretary of State has only limited control over other officers. When a new Secretary enters, the department in many ways "controls" the Secretary, who is often denied any substantial power to bring about meaningful change. It becomes difficult to change the institutional principles, biases, and motivations that have been deeply embedded over the course of decades. Consequently, we see endless reworking of diplomatic solutions that have repeatedly failed in the past, for example, those concerning the Israeli-Palestinian situation and those used with Iran and North Korea.

This compulsion toward diplomacy derives in large part from of our firmly held belief in "reason" as the ultimate tool of persuasion. In *The Suicide of Reason*, Lee Harris argues that much of the world today still remains in a "tribal" culture where the "law of the jungle" ultimately rules. America, he maintains, arose through a unique set of circumstances, and its success in constructing its culture around reason is somewhat of an historical novelty growing out of the European Enlightenment. Reason—which informs our culture, values, and politics—does not provide the same function in tribal cultures. Ultimately, as Harris describes in detail, what we face today is the conflict between these two worlds, and the culture of reason sadly may lack the tools to enable it to navigate successfully through the waters that lie ahead.

Other writers have taken similar approaches when describing this tension—most famously, Samuel Huntington's *The Clash of Civilizations*, as well as Middle East scholar Daniel Pipes' conflict between civilization and barbarism. While these narratives have their differences, in reference to the Control Factor, they both identify a critical weakness in Western psychology.

The compulsion to diplomacy brought on by the Control Factor is a by-product of this culture built around reason. Diplomacy is valuable for one party when mirrored on the other side by a similar set of values and assumptions—when *both* come from similar belief systems based upon faith in reason as the ultimate tool for conflict resolution. The law of the jungle, however, is based on, and places its ultimate faith in, strength and force. Of course, the law of the jungle has its own "reasonable" basis (as Westerners would understand it), and those utilizing it are often fully capable of "reasonable" justifications and explanations for their actions. Indeed, 1400 years of Islamic thought have produced some of the most "well-reasoned" writings and scholarship from brilliant and powerful minds. These writings have delved as deeply into examination of their beliefs as have any writings from other religions or political systems.

It would be unforgivable naïveté to equate Islam with thoughtlessness, superficiality, or illogic. "Reason," however, is not elevated in Islam to the highest priority, a position reserved solely for Allah, not man. For our Islamic Enemy, reason, a faculty of man, can never challenge the knowledge of Allah. Accordingly, primary faith in reason ultimately becomes un-Islamic and a threat to Islam. Therefore, no matter how often Muslims and non-Muslims might find "common ground," some circumstance will inevitably bring forth this conflict. *Allah can not be reasoned with.*

As a result, to survive in "the jungle," even for those compelled to "reason," one must not only be unafraid to deploy force, but must also do so from time to time to counter the challenges that others raise. The compulsion to diplomacy, when acted upon in the jungle, can only be interpreted as a sign of weakness: the fear of deploying power. Little else is as inviting to those who rely on force.

Conversely, diplomacy is a valuable substitute for force that can benefit both parties only when *both* overwhelmingly wish to avoid the consequences of force. When one party does not share that wish, and, in fact, understands only militaristic engagement, diplomacy becomes not only ineffective but also suicidal. For instance, mutual assured destruction, though ultimately effective in neutralizing Soviet aggression, will have no effect against an Iranian regime that values the afterlife more than this one and lives, ultimately, by the law of the jungle. The Control Factor will attempt to pin responsibility for failures to resolve such asymmetrical conflicts on the party relying upon diplomacy, blaming that party for failing to close the deal even though failure was dictated by the asymmetrical rules and belief systems themselves.

No better example exists than Israel which is endlessly blamed for the failure of any "peace." Despite giving back land in Lebanon and Gaza (essentially land-for-false-rhetoric transactions) and despite offering virtually everything Palestinians representatives could ever expect to receive, Israel has once again been treated by Obama as if it were the party at fault. In his second Middle East speech,[9] Obama continued to use the word "occupation" to define Israel's presence in its own land. He also describes the Palestinian condition as one of humiliation, something that has been pushed upon them. Obama, in that "daddy" style of his, declared: "The international community is tired of an endless process that never produces an outcome. The dream of a Jewish state and democratic state cannot be fulfilled with permanent occupation." Subsequently, in a speech to AIPAC,[10] Obama continued, "There's a reason the Palestinians are pursuing their interests at the United Nations. They recognize that there is an impatience with the peace process, or the absence of one, not just in the Arab world—in Latin America, in Asia, and in Europe. And that impatience is growing, and it's already manifesting itself in capitals around the world." (This, despite the fact that the unrest around the Arab world had nothing to do with Israel). The media has also long piled on in blaming the lack of peace on Israel's continued building of settlements.

Netanyahu, in his historic speech to the US Congress,[11] set the record straight. "You have to understand this," he said. "In Judea and Samaria, the Jewish people are not foreign occupiers." He made clear that of the 300 million Arabs in the Middle East, only the one million living in Israel are truly free, enjoying real democratic rights. Netanyahu continued, "This startling fact reveals a basic truth: Israel is not what is wrong about the Middle East; Israel is what's right about the Middle East."

Not only did Netanyahu refuse to accept the blame, he returned the projection to where it belonged, "Militant Islam threatens the world. It threatens Islam." And perhaps his most significant rejection of Control Factor maneuvering was this: "You see, our conflict has never been about the establishment of a Palestinian state; it's always been about the establishment of the Jewish state. This is what the conflict is about." That demonstrates a well practiced Inner Jihad!

We frequently have been told in regard to Saddam Hussein, Kim Jong-Il, and the Iranian regime that while they may be more than tough negotiators and even, perhaps, a little "crazy," they ultimately will act "reasonably." This facilitates the never-ending push for never-ending diplomacy. Instead, the central issue is responsibility: these leaders have rarely been held to their declarations, whether or not they were reasonable persons or crafty negotiators.

For instance, our Control Factors have stripped the Islamic Republic of Iran of responsibility for thirty years of "Death to America" chants and declarations of war, a constitution implicitly calling for the support of those who stand against America, not to mention its connection to almost every act of terror against the United State since their revolution. Yet, most destructively, whenever these leaders offer us some crumb of rational and reasonable behavior, the Control Factor snaps it up like a starving dog. It immediately dismisses all previous uncooperative behavior and marches forward in temporary relief with its fantasy of successful diplomatic resolution to come (the "Let's Start From The Beginning Rally Call" fantasy).

Unfortunately, the futility of this behavior has been demonstrated over and over. When we do not wish to hear what they say, we convince ourselves they do not mean what they say. Bush was incessantly crucified for his "Axis of Evil" reference to Iraq, North Korea, and Iran, yet none of those enemies had been held responsible for its words.

Teaching responsibility requires following through on threats. Just as punishing a child might cause his parent pain, it is nonetheless necessary to establish rules and order. Barack Obama convinced those who voted for him that he was strong enough to be commander-in-chief of our armed services, in part by stating that Iran must never become a nuclear power. Later, while offering his hand to the Iranian Regime, he set a deadline of end of year 2009 for obtaining significant reciprocal action. Well past that expired deadline, he failed to carry out his threat to get tougher—despite his eventual push for stronger sanctions. When handed the gift of the Green Revolution, in which the people of Iran rose up as best they could to protest the fraudulent 2009 Presidential election results affording Ahmadinejad an additional term, Obama turned his back on them, refusing to offer any publicly perceptible assistance to the uprising.

Echoing the Control Factor's preoccupation with the enemy's opinion, Obama said at a press conference, "It's not productive, given the history of US-Iranian relations, to be seen as meddling . . . the US President . . . meddling in Iranian elections."[12] As the people reached out for Obama, Obama turned away.

Remarkably, Obama subsequently leaked descriptions of his administration's switch to a policy of "containment" with Iran, in which America will fool itself and its Arab and Israeli "friends" that it will be able to defend against an Iranian nuclear capability. By applying a distorted history of US-Soviet Cold War realities, he is handing our Control Factors the flawed notion that a religiously motivated regime can be deterred by the concept of "mutual assured destruction." Once so enabled, the Control Factor will quell our fears so that what eventuates will be exactly what we set out to avoid—an Iranian regime armed with nuclear weapons. Failing to follow through on threats does not teach responsibility. Rather, it teaches our Islamic Enemy to march onward without hesitation. Just as the Left in America undercut Bush's ability to follow through on the transfer of responsibility he had started in Iraq, many have sought to attack and neutralize Netanyahu for his articulate placement of responsibility where it truly belongs. When an addict is challenged, he fights with everything he has.

In today's environment, with its ubiquitous access to information, it sometimes appears difficult to determine whether another party operates from a "tribal" or "reasonable" set of principles. Our Islamic Enemy (both on the Civilization and International Institutional Jihad levels) often intentionally creates such confusion for us. It has learned to sound and act convincingly like a responsible member of the world of reason. The UN podium is constantly visited by representatives who know how to use "reason-speak" while their nations are simultaneously strategizing for war, conducting horrendous human rights violations, and engaging in other law-of-the jungle behaviors.

This conflicting-message approach is a vital enemy tactic. Being on record with statements, gestures, and actions that convince us the enemy shares our modern-day reasonableness has helped satisfy our need to believe the enemy is just like us. Once that projection is accepted, the Control Factor takes over, explaining away any evidence to the contrary. When Mahmoud Abbas, duplicating exactly the behavior of his predecessor Arafat, addresses reasonable sounding statements to the West, many Westerners become unable to hear any of the calls for the destruction of Israel he simultaneously makes in Arabic to his people. Nor do they reflect upon the fact that Abbas controls Palestinian Authority television, which runs programs teaching children the hatred of Jews and that martyrdom is the highest moral act guaranteeing a place in Paradise after this life. According to the Palestinian Media Watch's paper, importantly entitled *Aspiration not Desperation*,[13] at least 70 percent of Palestinian children aspire to become *Shahids* or martyrs. Palestinian media almost daily incite violence, spread the idea that Israelis are Nazis, and exclude Israel from all maps of the region. When an Iranian ambassador sounds so reasonable to Americans, or American journalists and elitists make claims such as "Iran just wants, . . ." or "Ahmadinejad really has no power, . . ." the Control Factor comfortably hits the mute button on Ahmadinejad's calls for Israel's destruction.

An interesting variation has appeared in the split between the Palestinian factions Hamas and Fatah. Fatah can adopt the posture of reason while Hamas holds firmly to its "jungle" war agenda. Our Control Factor kicks in to push us to honor and chase after Fatah, seemingly to reduce the threat from Hamas. But Fatah's actual goals, as opposed to its tactics, are no different from those of Hamas. Both parties' core documents make clear that the destruction of Israel is their ultimate goal. And, as seen throughout Islamic history, differences among Muslims are easily deferred in the face of a common non-Muslim enemy: "Conquer first, settle differences later," is the rule most often applied.

Conflicting messages are part of the Civilization Jihad's twists on language as well. Dr. Salah Sultan, identified as president of the American Center for Islamic Research and a member of the Muslim American Society signed a fatwa[14] from the Fiqh Council of North America condemning "terrorism." The 2005 fatwa was heralded as a display of moderate Islam by moderate Muslims. Later, however, Sultan showed how disingenuous this motion was, making clear his vision was "To live happily. To die as a martyr." He also stated on Saudi television that he believed the United States, not al-Qaeda, caused 9/11 in order to bring about a war upon the as-yet-undefined "terror."[15] His resumé also indicates connections to a variety of Brotherhood associated organizations.

Ultimately, the Control Factor demand that Muslims "renounce violence" is worthless. Words have been rendered useless by our Islamic Enemy. Nonetheless, during the initial phases of the Cairo protests, when the most likely successor to Egypt's military regime seemed to be the Egyptian Muslim Brotherhood, Secretary of State Hillary Clinton stunningly suggested that as long as the Brotherhood renounces violence, it can be an acceptable partner. In a conflict in which "war is deceit," reliance upon any proclamation without firmly holding the party to his words is a formula for defeat.

Teaching responsibility and accountability is a vast departure from the policies and biases that have become deeply implanted in the American liberal agenda over the past century. As with tough love toward an addict, transferring responsibility back to our Islamic Enemy will initially feel uncomfortable, even reprehensible. Refusing to take on Western Guilt; forgiving ourselves for any past indiscretions; ceasing to apologize unduly; maintaining great pride for all of the good that America has stood for and provided to the rest of the world; living up to our own words, threats, and promises alike; taking others' words seriously and at face value; accepting that there is clearly defined good and evil in the world; and realizing that there is no other choice but to confront evil—especially that embodied in our Islamic Enemy; we must firmly apply these actions early, often, and continuously to establish proper boundaries and return responsibility for our enemy's behavior to our enemy, where it belongs.

The Turnaround Moment

Let's return to the horror film. As the film progresses, efforts to mollify the threat are ineffectual and resisting with insufficient weapons proves useless. The protagonists' options run out. By this point vast destruction has typically been wrought, many peripheral characters have been killed, and we are left with the main character or small group of characters. Even more alarming, the Enemy has grown in size, learned more about us than we have about it, and adapted to all efforts used against it. Every strategy tried to date has backfired and little hope remains.

Having apparently reached the end of the line, the climactic pivot is due to take place—called here the "Turnaround Moment." This is generally the "Make My Day"; "I'll be back"; "Hasta La Vista, Baby," turning point in which the main character finally *gives himself the license* to value himself more than he does the Enemy, and becomes willing to use anything and everything necessary to win. It is the moment when Sigourney Weaver's character in "Alien" blows the alien out of the spaceship. It is also the moment when Adrienne gives Rocky permission to fight and "Win," the emotional and moral permission he needs to unleash his full power and determination. It is the point that Todd Beamer aboard Flight 93 on 9/11 shouted "Let's Roll!" It is precisely because we secretly desire to experience these moments that Hollywood is able to capitalize on their emotional significance.

Two critical elements of the narrative have typically taken place before this Turnaround Moment. First, the world has divided itself into clear demarcations of good and evil. The threat has created so much destruction and demonstrated sufficient unwillingness to stop or be stopped that it can comfortably be considered evil. Meanwhile, the main character, while full of flaws and weaknesses, has demonstrated sufficient virtue that all of his actions will now be deemed acceptable by the audience. He has essentially earned a moral license. He has won the audience's affection and identification in large part because he has—to satisfy our diplomacy compulsion—tried first to use the tools of the world of reason to confront a threat from the jungle, and failed.

Secondly, what makes such a film compelling is that the audience is ahead of the main character. We know more about the danger he faces than he does. An effective film creates in the audience a powerful desire for the main character to wake up and find some overwhelming force to end the nightmare. Having placed the good character at such a disadvantage and with much suffering, damage, and injury, the film then shifts the rules so that he is allowed greater latitude in action. Like Rocky's Adrienne, the audience gives the main character permission to do anything and everything to survive and win.

This license is the essential goal of the Inner Jihad. Lee Harris describes it as license to *be willing to do* what is necessary to eliminate the threat we face. He suggests that we must ultimately be willing to be as ruthless as the enemy—as ruthless as the war of the jungle requires. Importantly, *it does not necessarily mean* we behave as ruthlessly. It is not a license to become an uncontrollably vicious killing machine for its own sake. Rather, the *willingness* to be focused, determined, strong, and ruthless often communicates all that is necessary.

On the other hand, this new condition cannot be faked. It is a mental state, and is also an indication of the state of war on the internal battlefield. The Control Factor—amplifying deeply infused notions of Western Guilt, political correctness, moral platitudes, radical-leftist intellectual formulations, and the restriction of aggressive acts solely to self-defense—is designed to do all it can to delay the Turnaround Moment. The structure of the horror film suggests how difficult it is for Westerners to reach the mental clarity necessary to allow themselves to fight whole-heartedly. Yet, as the film also demonstrates, if the West is to survive, it must eventually reach and pass through the Turnaround Moment.

This willingness to do what is necessary flashed for brief moments in the months following 9/11. It also burst forth in Bush's "Axis of Evil" speech, which convinced the Iranian regime that Bush was serious about accomplishing his objectives, no matter what was required. For much of the liberal West, however, the flash ignited a strong countervailing reaction. Unfortunately, following the poor execution of the post-invasion transition in Iraq combined with pressure from the Control Factor-dominated Congress and media much of the political will collapsed. The West became less committed to doing what was necessary then, and under Obama's watch remains deeply reluctant to pass through the Turnaround Moment.

That post 9/11 willingness began to show itself in the US attack on Afghanistan, the use of Guantanamo to hold enemy combatants, covert operations, indefinite detentions, enhanced interrogations, black prisons, etc. Against all these salutary measures, the Control Factor reasserted itself, causing many Americans to become uneasy with what they considered new, unnecessary, or inappropriate activities, all of which became subject to overwhelming attention and scrutiny. Such sentiments are among the most potent weapons in the Control Factor's arsenal. Remember, when one takes the substance away from the addict, the addict kicks and screams and does all he can to return to the equilibrium he had known before.

The significance of the Turnaround Moment is that we are *not* living in a film. We need not wait an inordinate amount of time to see good and evil clearly as they manifest themselves. Similarly, we need not wait to know that we are good. We do not have to convince an audience (ours exists only in our minds) that we are justified. While our Control Factors are secretly geared to make that literally an *endless* task in a war that clearly has an end, we must do all we can to recognize the Turnaround Moment and move through it with clear purposeful intent. This is the lesson of all horror films

Mirroring

The Turnaround Moment gives rise to a critical countermeasure: the use of "mirroring." One of the most effective ways to return responsibility to where it belongs is to be willing and able to mirror what the party rejecting responsibility actually does. If an addict fails to relate responsibly, do not relate back. If he is unable to give, do not give to him. Just as if an actual mirror were held up, the addict is given a new perspective on his own behavior as he begins to see it in the enabler.

On the geopolitical level, mirroring is a more malleable concept but no less effective. Mirroring is not a prescription for any specific policy, plan, or action. Rather, it first exists as the mental flexibility to explore and pursue an expanded set of possibilities for action. If attacking Israeli civilians is acceptable for Hamas and the Palestinians, one way they may change is when their civilians are actually victimized by Israel. Only when the Palestinians themselves are made to understand who is truly victimizing them will they learn to hold Hamas and Fatah responsible. Similarly, when our Islamic Enemy defines "civilians" to exclude all

Zionists and Americans, we should be free to make similar exclusions with their civilian population.

Playing under identical rules is essential to a fair fight. Much of the modern world's attempt to constrain warfare rides on the hope and wish that all parties will ultimately abide by the same rules. Since our Islamic Enemy does not like to voluntarily submit to the rules of Western Civilization, we must be mentally flexible enough to adopt and match theirs when useful. The problems the West encounters with asymmetrical warfare have, incredibly, led it to search for rules to constrain itself in the hope that its enemies would be encouraged to reduce that asymmetry by joining the game. Mirroring suggests an alternative route to reducing the asymmetry by letting the enemy help set the rules and then applying them symmetrically.

This is not a frivolous call to bomb innocent civilians or to start beheading Muslims in central squares or on widely released videos. Nor is it a call to violate "international norms" of warfare for its own sake. It is, however, a call to wake up, realize that we are in a real war whether we like it or not, and adjust our attitudes and perceptions to be willing to do what is necessary to win. It is a call to get on a "war footing" as urged by Frank Gaffney in his eponymous book. The Turnaround Moment occurs when the key character mirrors the mental state of the threat—that critical singularity of purpose crucial for victory.

Mirroring demands that the same moral and ethical code be shared by both opponents. If deception is a core strategy for one, honesty and moral sanctity need not be as constraining for the other. If one side is incapable of treating the other as an equal, the other need not be burdened by such restraint. If boundaries are not respected by one, the other need not respect them either. If asymmetrical warfare is acceptable for one side, disproportionate warfare should be permissible in return.

Throughout much of US history, mirroring has taken place "underground." We have handled the perceived conflict between doing what is necessary and maintaining our "reasoned" sense of moral decency by splitting off the "ruthless" function to some covert agent such as the CIA or Special Forces. We would metaphorically look away because to do so was possible. Some things just needed to be done. And then, of course, after the fact the nation would face pressure and guilt and often seek to punish those who had saved us by acting outside our moral scope. Given today's more open world with global news services and sources such as WikiLeaks that endeavor to expose anything possible, such splitting and subterfuge is more difficult to execute. Consequently, the perceived conflicts will have to be resolved in new ways which may result in more varied forms of mirroring.

The West's Self-Destructive Failure to Mirror

History is replete with sophisticated philosophies concerning war, its efficacy and how to conduct it. Today, the traditional principles of "just war" as embodied in a variety of international agreements (including the various Hague and Geneva Conventions and the 1948 Convention on the Prevention and Punishment of the Crime of Genocide) occupy a great deal of attention. Much of the "civilized" world prides itself on its desire to reduce the occurrence of war as well as the destruction it creates. Indeed, as we have seen, the "End of War" fantasy plays a big role in the Western mind. After 9/11, we saw how problematic issues such as preemptive war can become in the face of modern thinking, weapons, and terrorism.

As in the horror film, how long does one have to wait or how much damage does one have to endure before one is effectively granted permission to go to war, *jus ad bellum*? Enormous effort has been expended in an attempt to delineate acceptable rules, attempting to refine and position concepts such as just cause, the proportionality of ends, right intention, military necessity, reasonable prospects of success, last resort, peace as the primary end, and so on. Time will tell whether the "civilized" world is better off for the delay.

For decades Israel has been criticized for its defensive responses in Lebanon and Gaza—as well as in connection with the Gaza Flotilla—as having violated international principles of conducting warfare, *jus in belo*; specifically constraints that war should not be conducted indiscriminately or disproportionately. These challenges have distorted the traditional idea of "disproportionate" military response. Originally intended to require some connection between the unintended harm to civilians as a result of an attack and the military value to the attacker, "disproportionate force" has mutated into a ridiculous notion that often compares the number of casualties (military and civilian) and number and power of weapons on each side.

The United Nations and other anti-Israel international institutions have attempted to use this and other bastardized concepts to transfer responsibility for the lives of civilians under the control of Hamas and

Hezbollah back to Israel. Muslim apologists have even made straight-faced arguments that since only a tiny percentage of missiles launched into Israel from Gaza actually caused injury, and have affected only small portions of Israeli territory, they present no real threat and do not warrant retaliation. And while much has been written about Israel's intensive effort—greater than that of any other military in history—to accommodate the needs of the enemy's civilian population, such information falls on deaf ears among a Western public dominated by its own Control Factors. (Also worth noting is the simultaneous failure to recognize Israel's frequent and generous acts of charity in international disaster cases such as the 2010 Haiti earthquake, as well as Israel's other "disproportionately" influential contributions to innovation.)

There is no consistency between the principles applied to Israel and those applied everywhere else. This is the addiction of our Islamic Enemy, and those who share the view that the creation of the state of Israel was a "catastrophe." While libraries are filled with books discussing the unique treatment of Israel, it is relevant here to give us insight into how powerful the Control Factor has become in keeping us trapped in place.

"Disproportionate" on the surface appears to demand equality on each side. Instead of being applied to numbers, however, mirroring could require equality of strategy. One example could be that where one side is advantaged by the use of unpredictable attacks, as with Hamas' seemingly random and intermittent launching of rockets into Israeli civilian territory without a specific context of war, Israel should be "proportionally" free to strike at unpredictable times without any necessary condition. Just as "fair" can mean many different things even in a single context, so can the notion of "fair fighting" disguise a preconceived bias to protect one side or the other. UN attempts to regulate the Arab war against Israel generally boil down to a political decision: to handcuff Israel.

Nor is mirroring a foreign notion to our Islamic Enemy. Osama bin Laden made clear that he believed the Islamic world has the right to match the number of Muslims America has killed. That is, he believed Islam entitled him to kill 4 million Americans in return for America having killed that number in the Middle East and Eastern Europe.[16] This is a fundamental rationale for his desire to acquire nuclear weapons. Obviously it had been his inability to carry out such an act out during his life that stopped him, not the decision that mirroring is an inappropriate approach to determining strategy.

While the effort to establish international standards for warfare may be admirable, it has gone so far as to be self-destructive. It has taken too seriously the pleasant Western notion that it is not whether you win or lose but how you play the game. Unfortunately, as "nice" as the adage is, at some point it becomes fatal. War is about winning and losing, and only that. As Daniel Pipes likes to say, wars are ended by winning or surrender, when one side has had enough. Getting there is the point, and as Vince Lombardi famously said, winning is "the only point." It might be pleasant to wish that global conflicts could be resolved by a panel of Olympic or American Idol judges independently scoring the individual performances of the parties, but the reality more closely resembles a no-holds-barred Ultimate Fighting Challenge. And just because the West might not wish to be in a war, it *is* in one because its Islamic Enemy has declared it so.

One premise to this book stated at the beginning is that the threat we face today is in large part new to America . Having been protected by its borders, its power in the world, its ability to retreat or remain isolation-ist, its threat of retaliation, and the stalemate so long enjoyed by mutually assured destruction, America has had the illusory luxury of accepting constraints on its use of force that had for years not significantly im-peded its national security. That luxury is quickly fading and these pas-sive protections must be substituted with new active and aggressive ones.

This is particularly significant today, given the potential of the Inter-national Institutional Jihad. As global organizations become more sub-ject to the demands of their Muslim constituents, "rules" will become even more constrained to fit Islamic needs, all to the benefit of *jihad*.

Mirroring can offset the compulsion to over-regulate war. Argu-ments against disproportionate force and pre-emptive war are based on the assumption that both sides are similarly motivated. This might make sense when the conflict is between civilized nations. Presumably it would never apply to two barbaric nations since, by definition, they do not follow any rules beyond necessity. It might also make sense between parties engaged in a territorial war, but falls away when one party is using territory to advance an ideological war within. It is partially re-sponsible for the perpetual inability of the United Nations to settle upon a definition of "terrorism." Consequently, it makes no sense between a "civilized" party and a "barbaric" one. For that same reason, it makes little sense between the House of Islam and the House of War.

A more effective way to teach responsibility and accountability is to show our Islamic Enemy who he is by reflecting his behavior back to him. He understands the messages intended by his own behavior, will project those motivations onto us, and will have no choice but to get the message when that behavior is mirrored back to him.

In one sense, the Hiroshima and Nagasaki bombs were disproportionate and barbaric. They did, however, mirror the ferocity with which the Japanese were fighting, and demonstrated a willingness to do whatever was necessary to win. And they were successful. While many Western liberals castigate the United States for the use of such weapons, its post-World War II conduct toward both Japan and Germany—including extensive and costly rebuilding efforts as well as the investigation and punishment of misdeeds by the United States—demonstrated that far from the fear expressed, America did not "lose itself" by employing such overwhelming force upon innocent civilians. Rather, the use of those bombs enabled America to demonstrate after the war exactly who and what it always was and continues to be.

The 2011 killing of Osama bin Laden is another example of mirroring. The intention to kill was clear from the start; early Obama administration suggestions that the mission was to kill OR capture were highly suspect given its own misgivings with detaining enemy combatants. The action involved surprise and invasion into sovereign territory and private property. No regrets followed as most of the nation was overjoyed with the success. Once again, the nation will follow up with investigations and efforts to right any collateral wrongs to ensure that it did not "lose itself." Since the mission occurred under a liberal administration however, the country is less likely to rebel against itself and offer the enemy concessions as is often to be expected when a step is taken out of the addict/enabler dance.

Again, mirroring is primarily an internal process to counter the effects of the Control Factor. It does not dictate any particular policy or action on the external battlefield. It can, however, express itself in a wide variety of policies. It covers behavior from the seemingly "acceptable" to the grossly "unacceptable," and can challenge much of what we would commonly identify with. For instance, if American symbols of great value, such as the World Trade Center, are considered proper targets for disrespect and terror, perhaps so should sacred sites at Mecca and Medina. If Hamas, under Iranian directives, continues to launch random missiles into Israel , perhaps Israel should do similar bombing of

Gaza or target the sacred Imam Ridha Mosque in Iran . If the Palestinian Authority threatens to make a Palestinian state Judenrein by expelling Jews, perhaps Israel should consider doing the same with its Muslims. Mirroring begs the age-old ethical struggle over how much "better than" we really are if we ultimately forfeit our own survival to prove ourselves?

If *dhimmi* rules are applied throughout the Islamic world to limit the freedoms of non-Muslims abroad, perhaps we should consider limitations on the exercise of Muslim practices in the West. If apostasy or leaving the "religion" is a capital offense, perhaps deserting American constitutional principles in favor of certain expressions of Islam should be equally punishable as sedition. In short, if our Islamic Enemy values death more than life, views women with deep disgust, uses children as sacrificial soldiers, and sees itself engaged in perpetual war, mirroring allows our Islamic Enemy to be similarly devalued and denigrated.

"Freedom of religion" in US tradition embodies a notion of "religion" very different from that of Islam. Pakistani Koranic scholar Abdul A'la Maududi, who along with Qutb have been unparalleled spiritual guides for much of our Islamic Enemy, wrote in *Jihad in Islam*:

> But the truth is that Islam is not the name of a 'Religion,' nor is 'Muslim' the title of a 'Nation.' In reality, Islam is a revolutionary ideology and programme which seeks to alter the social order of the whole world and rebuild it in conformity with its own tenets and ideals.[17]

Perhaps such differences should be taken into account when granting Muslims their "religious freedoms."

There are many obvious reasons not to blow up the Imam Ridha Mosque or bomb Mecca including restrictions in international agreements to not bomb religious buildings not themselves used for military purposes. (Given the commandments to go to war and other pronouncements so often made at these sites, they could reasonably be argued to have been used for military purposes). Many feel disgust even reading such a proposal. And that is the point: our disgust is a measure not only of our moral sense, but with the grip our Control Factors have on us as well. That disgust is exactly what needs to be identified in our Inner Jihad.

Mirroring makes us fully comfortable with a state of mind that can better guide us to more suitable rules, regulations, or other actions. The scope, means, and authority for any particular policy are often complex decisions in need of careful multi-faceted thought. Only when enough Western minds begin to share a common understanding of the threat posed, however, will they successfully generate the most appropriate responses.

The Chinese and other non-Western actors are notorious for mirroring any Islamic violence by swiftly killing the perpetrators and detaining the families of anyone associated with any terror incident. No trials. No concerns about the abuse of defendants' rights. No human rights activists. No war crimes charges. Russia has approached its Chechen terrorists in somewhat similar fashion. No international outbursts or rush to the International Criminal Court over that! Just as Mohammed extinguished parts of Jewish tribes for standing up to him, these authoritarian states have no problem treating uncooperative Muslims with brutality.

Imagine if Israel were permitted similar privilege by the "international community." The greatly desired "peace" likely would have occurred decades ago and, by now, the Palestinian people would be a thriving population—even if Israel never behaved as such.

Mirroring is not simply repeating similar behavior. It establishes rapport—a deeper link—between the parties through the similarity of rules and communication. It also helps eliminate disparities caused by doublespeak and conflicted messaging. By equalizing the behaviors, it destroys the inequalities that allow the victim-victimizer, addict-enabler, cause-effect relationships to develop.

If a party wishes to appear offended at insults to its religion or leaders and to use that as a reason to initiate violence, the other party must be free to do the same. Otherwise, "Death to America" and "Jews are pigs and monkeys" chants, and burning Bush effigies are excused, while cartoons depicting Mohammed and insults to Ahmadinejad become excuses for terror campaigns. Sadly, only when all are symmetrically considered as either justified provocations for war or acceptable exercises of freedom will there be a basis for an alternative to violence to emerge.

Returning All Projections

Mirroring literally reflects expressions that our Islamic Enemy seeks to project. It makes it more difficult for those projections to stick to us and helps offset the enabler's temptation to absorb the addict's projection. Hatred, envy, and barbaric instincts are returned to their source. Western Civilization does its best to restrain its hostile and aggressive impulses, seeking to substitute other behavior for force in conflict resolution. It fails, however, to deal effectively with parties who do not share this goal. Instead of similarly subjugating these impulses, our Islamic Enemy projects them outward onto its enemies (us) who, in order to avoid confrontation, collude by accepting these projections. We then punish ourselves (including for our own natural instinct to mirror) in various ways, attempting to close the door on the conflict. This acceptance of responsibility for the continued conflict merely causes the conflict to escalate in ever harsher form. Mirroring, instead, rejects such responsibility and lays it back at the enemy's door. It demonstrates to the enemy that he will get what he gives.

In the internal theater, merely stopping the initial transfer of responsibility is an act of force. The West must learn to reject responsibility for Islamic conditions. Israel (with the assistance of its "allies") must refuse the projections that make them into hateful, barbaric "Nazi Occupiers" who took away land from a supposed Palestinian "people" and now operate an "apartheid" state. Any argument or explanation that accepts such projections is poisoned from the start. The adamant refusal to accept projections is the critical first step toward mirroring, and provides the fortitude and clarity necessary to continue the fight.

The Control Factor puts up many forms of resistance to mirroring. Perhaps the most common, as noted above, is the demand that we not become like our enemy, not lower ourselves to his standards, and not "lose our soul" in order to obtain victory over him.

Resistance takes subtler forms as well, including the compulsion to envision a complete solution before feeling free to pursue a given path. Mirroring Hamas' call for "Death to Israel" by taking a step toward destroying Hamas leads to the sophomoric question, "What are you going to do, commit genocide in Gaza?" A similar response marks the debate over what to do with twelve million illegal aliens in the United States. The Control Factor often tosses out, "You cannot deport twelve million people!" and the mind accepts that as obviously true. But the power of mirroring lies partially in the messages it telegraphs. As my brilliant, commonsense father observes, "Start deporting one million and watch what the other eleven do!"

The failure to return all illegitimate projections opens the door to suicidal appeasement. My grandfather, a successful trial lawyer and businessman, used to repeat the adage: "Don't mistake my kindness for weakness." He was often conciliatory as a first step toward resolving a conflict. But it was meant as a first step, intended to evoke a matching response. He was happy to make the first generous move toward resolution with the expectation that the other party would recognize his generosity, appreciate his willingness to "go out on a limb," and reach a matching (or mirroring) conclusion that resolution is better than continued conflict.

This series of expectations defined his act of initial generosity. While the West has a history and place for this type of action, it appears largely lacking with our Islamic Enemy. Instead, our enemy fails to operate from the same assumptions, opting instead to regard first moves as indicators of defeat. Kindness is perceived as weakness and, accordingly, as an invitation to pounce.

Our Islamic Enemy operates from the premise that if it has the power and strength to win, it will do so. It pulls back in its perpetual war only when it assesses that it lacks the requisite power. Projecting such thinking onto us comes naturally. If we are not fighting our side of the war, it must be because we really lack the necessary strength and power.

We distort reality equally on our side of the dance. While the "Lone Superpower" fantasy attempts to convince us we can handle any threat, so that it is in everyone's best interest for us to exhaust all other approaches before resorting to fighting, the Control Factor is merely covering up overwhelming fear. We repress our weakness with kindness.

The paradoxical result is that while we see our Islamic Enemy as *mistaking our kindness for weakness*, it sees us as *masquerading our weakness as kindness*. The solution to the paradox is to stick a mirror in the middle so that each side learns to see itself and the other clearly.

Israel, for example, has unilaterally withdrawn from Lebanon and Gaza. These are moves interpreted by Palestinians not as encouragement for similar efforts on their part to seek genuine peace but as proof that their violence has been successful. Still many Western "elites" echo the Palestinian call for Israel to continue again and again to make conciliatory gestures while the Palestinians do not change anything. As with the game of guilt, this routine does not end on its own; only a conscious, focused effort can end it.

This difference in perceptions and projections is so pronounced that diplomatic "experts" and trained negotiators call for "confidence-building measures." This is a Western attempt to make a "process" out of holding our Islamic Enemy's hand while demonstrating that he need not be afraid that we will take advantage of him. Some diplomats even go so far as to interpret terrorism as a "call for help," a childlike request for a mature response. Again, it is the non-Muslim's responsibility, these elites presume, to help the Muslims and commence negotiations for their sake. And, as usual, it is our Islamic Enemy who will take advantage of weakness in its enemies.

Mistaking kindness or reasonableness for weakness is the primary consequence of the West's endless acts of appeasement. Much of the history of the Israeli-Palestinian conflict can be viewed as a never-ending series of one-sided compromises—the effect of the ongoing "Extortion Process" described earlier. This has been Fatah's strategic goal—to diminish Israel step by step until the complete takeover can be accomplished with the weaponry available. And in fact, this is very much the foundational strategy of the Civilization Jihad throughout the rest of the West as well.

Obama fueled this process with his second Middle East speech.[18] After describing America's interest in the region, he tried to "show the world" by acknowledging that America's narrow interests do not fill empty stomachs or create freedom of speech. He asserted that US failure to address the "broader aspirations" of Arab populations has sowed suspicion and mistrust, and added appeasingly, "a failure to change our approach threatens a deepening spiral of division between the United States and the Arab world."

So-called "confidence-building" fails with our Islamic Enemy precisely because it neither lacks "confidence" nor cares to build it. It knows the West better than the West knows itself. What might appear as a lack of trust is a carefully developed negotiating style engineered to extract as many concessions as possible. In fact, the one thing the Palestinians *do* trust is the West's Control Factor and its inability to mirror back. The endless sequence of appeasing gestures serves only to reinforce our enemy's conviction that his methods work well. That is not the "confidence" the experts think they are building.

A basic tenet of communication theory is that there must be rapport between parties for any successful resolution to emerge. Rapport is greatly assisted through mirroring. That is, when the parties reflect similar attitudes, ethics, assumptions, and points of view back to each other, they can be more easily reach agreement. Often Westerners regard their own appeasing acts as a step toward such rapport. This completely mistakes—and disrespects as well—our Islamic Enemy's true world view, as it presumes it desires what we desire. Hence, weakness is *the only* conclusion our Islamic Enemy can draw.

Furthermore, a basic (and over generalized) tenet of many psychological theories of change is that the therapist must first pace and mirror the patient's beliefs and perceptions in a wide variety of ways in order to establish rapport with him. Once this rapport is grounded, the therapist is then able to take control and lead the patient into different ways of thinking and acting. If we are to have any effect upon our Islamic Enemy and lead it toward a better interaction with us, mirroring is an important tool to use.

If rapport is truly sought, it must be the West that aligns itself presumptively with our Islamic Enemy, joining in the essential notion that strength is to be used when available to advance one's efforts in the War of the Houses. Essentially, only through true mirroring at the level of our assumptions will sufficient rapport ever lead the West to the peace it truly seeks.

On May 26, 2010, John Brennan, President Obama's Assistant for Homeland Security and Counterterrorism ridiculously described *jihad* as "meaning to purify oneself of one's community."[19] Brennan is correct that "purification" is a part of *jihad*—it is the *greater jihad* once referenced by Mohammed. However as we have seen, the overwhelming use of the concept involves the notion of purifying the earth of non-believers, with one's blood in martyrdom if necessary.

Interestingly, at the end of his talk, Brennan warned against our returning to a "fearful position," a version of the Control Factor's attack on emotions discussed earlier. As we have seen, however, fear is fully appropriate in response to our Islamic Enemy and it is the Control Factor that has allowed us to become so detached from it. Only by reversing the Control Factor and experiencing our fear will we be able to confront the threat at hand.

Tough Love

Mirroring is a core aspect of the tough love necessary to break the addict-enabler dance. Addicts typically take advantage of enablers' goodwill and treat them without respect. Tough love requires the enabler to set new rules which mirror back in the addict's mind the same lack of respect for his inappropriate behavior and desires. The addict will become shocked and enraged by the enabler's change in behavior as the enabler implicitly takes away the asymmetric advantage the addict had previously maintained.

Nor is it ever helpful for the enabler to financially support the addict. Any money given an addict will be likely used to advance the addiction, regardless of what the addict says or even believes. Similarly, financial assistance given our Islamic Enemy in any form only contributes to the danger we face. This process is now better understood, as evidenced by the recent upsurge in calls for energy independence as a means to combat terror financing. The same principle needs to be applied even more widely, so that we cease to fund any of the enemy's activities, directly or indirectly though middlemen such as the United Nations and the IMF. Any form of support which accrues to the financial benefit of our Islamic Enemy must be fully withdrawn.

Of course mirroring initially feels awkward to an enabler, as he must cross familiar boundaries of ethical and moral behavior. It exposes the very panic that control has been lost; the panic the Control Factor is tasked to hide. That panic will tell us in a multitude of ways not to go down this path, not to allow the addict to rage wild and so forth. Our uniquely Western impulse to accommodate leads us into unfamiliar feelings and self-images when we shift focus and begin to return responsibility where it belongs. Westerners will experience this same awkwardness if they begin to mirror our Islamic Enemy. Whether mirroring results in more aggressive military behavior, denying the enemy freedoms on the basis that they pose unnecessary dangers, or refusing to tolerate dangerous behavior, it is certain to evoke loud objections. It will upset our national self-image. That is, however, to be expected—it is always hard to administer and stick with tough love.

An addict will assuredly kick back hard when those around him change their routine-enabling behaviors. An interesting example could be seen during the initial attacks by British, French, and US forces against Libyan sites to bring about a ceasefire. Strained by the outbreaks of revolt in Tunisia, Egypt, Libya, Bahrain, and Syria, all of which demonstrated that tyrannical rulers, not Israel, were the source of much Arab frustration and conditions, Hamas could not quit its addiction "cold turkey." It was compelled to immediately bomb Israel from Gaza in an attempt to bring Israel immediately back into play. It is a hard habit to kick.

A similar response was seen in connection with Congressman Peter King's House Committee hearings on Muslim Radicalization in America. This small step toward exposing one of our Islamic Enemy's most potent weapons inevitably induced "withdrawal symptoms." Responding immediately, Senator Richard Durbin—a devotee of Obama and a friend of CAIR—could not resist the impulse to set up a Senate Hearing on Protecting the Civil Rights of American Muslims.

Yet, as mentioned previously, the severity of the addiction can be measured by the intensity of the withdrawal symptoms. As reported by the FBI as well as Clare Lopez and other analysts at the Center for Security Policy, hate crimes against Muslims in America are a fraction of those against Jews and Christians.[20] During essentially the first decade of the century (excluding the weeks following 9/11 when a reaction could be anticipated), Jewish victims of hate crimes outnumbered Muslim victims by a factor of eight—just one of many data points that support the conclusion that the outcry and projection by Brotherhood associated groups and the media over violence against Muslims has been a red herring. Was Durbin not aware of this?

Mirroring means reflecting back intolerance for the intolerance Islam shows us. It also acknowledges the behavior Islam displays when it is in control. Consequently, mirroring means objecting forcibly to Islam's intolerance in Western-controlled lands where the West is best able to exert state power. Mirroring its various asymmetrical concepts back upon it will more likely compel Islam to clarify its true intentions.

For enablers, "tough love" is difficult to deliver precisely because it "feels" contrary to moral instinct. (It even feels uncomfortable to many to adopt an "arrogant" analogy involving addiction, therapy, and rehabilitation in the Inner Jihad).Yet, as discussed earlier, the pain of such empathy is often its own defense for keeping the enabler trapped in the addict's dance. The enabler, in some manner, wishes to see the addict through "loving eyes" and do what he thinks he would most desire if he himself were the addict. In this way, the enabler justifiess his response as following some iteration of the Golden Rule. The result, however, is a strengthening, not a lessening, of the addictive behavior. And this is precisely what Western Guilt prescribes. Only by allowing the addict to "hit bottom" will the enabler contribute to the actual healing of the addict. The same must occur with our Islamic Enemy, which, despite all scruples of the West, must be allowed to face the consequences of its behavior. When the West ceases to project, introject, and apply all the other tools used by the Control Factor, these expressions of Islam will be exposed to either fight or reform.

It should be understood that there are many possible positive outcomes. In successful rehabilitations, the addict and enabler are eventually able to attain greater rapport through mirroring. Once they can share rules and expectations, they can return to more tolerant and congenial styles of relating. This time, however, they will be wearing similar shoes, so that they can dance a new and very different step.

This occurred between America and its enemies following many of our wars. With Germany, Japan, Vietnam, and others, war served the function of breaking down the processes that were previously in place—war is often the most straightforward, if least attractive, form of mirroring. Once there was a winner and a loser, an opportunity was created both for America to address its own concerns about winning and to "show the world" it had not "lost itself," and for the losers to address what had gotten them into the situation in the first place. Relationships were allowed to evolve differently. Consequently, important and strong alliances emerged from the change, to the benefit of each side.

The defining characteristic of the Turnaround Moment is the singularity of purpose, focused intention, and complete comfort with and confidence in the license to act in that moment. Clint Eastwood's trademark line, "Go ahead, make my day," is a declaration of attitude and intention. Because we instinctively know how important intention is, a film audience at the Turnaround Moment understands that the story has reached a critical point and the action is about to change. Any moral hesitancy has been eliminated in order to allow a forceful response. This is precisely the power expressed by those extraordinary United Flight 93 passengers on 9/11 as they told one another, "Let's roll."

In Iraq, America experienced the consequences of uncrystalized intention in its first encounter against insurgent forces in Fallujah. Having closed in on enemy terrorists who had based themselves in the town, US forces were encouraged by the State Department to retreat in the interests of "showing the world" peaceful intentions. The result was predictable: the enemy interpreted the retreat as weakness and re-armed, leading to even greater violence. Only when US forces were given the full go-ahead to clear the town was any semblance of an ultimate "peace" obtained. The film *The Last 600 Meters: The Battles of Najaf and Fallujah* shows the effects of intention put into action.

The pre-eminent historian of Islam, Bernard Lewis, expresses this best. After 9/11, when many Americans were asking, "Why do they hate us?" Lewis instead made clear the more appropriate question is, "Why do they not fear us?" Certainly the jihadists' victory over the Soviet Union in Afghanistan showed that superpowers are not invincible. Osama bin Laden believed he destroyed the Soviet Union. In subsequent decades, America has shown many of its weaknesses including its unwillingness to protect its borders or enforce its immigration laws, its insistence on "politically correct" policies that assign rights to its enemies that few, if any, other countries would consider doing, its low tolerance for conflict, much less battle or war, its difficulty in using counterterrorism and counterinsurgency strategies, as well as its trouble in hunting down jihadists and eliminating dictators such as Qaddafi. As made clear by Osama bin Laden, many in the Arab world and certainly in Iran awakened to the reality that America, in its partially paralyzed state, is less threatening than the already demolished Soviet Union. Why do they not fear us? The answer lies in large part in our Control Factors' dominance, which compels us to make every effort to alleviate the enemy's fear of us. Clarity of intention, focused attention, and the freedom to mirror help create the proper environment to resolve our external conflicts with our Islamic Enemy most effectively.

Again, the Inner Jihad to tame our Control Factors is not to be confused with a bias against "love," "compassion," or "forgiveness." Our hearts might tell us that what is important is to act peaceably and to avoid conflict or violence. This is attributable in part to the Judeo-Christian tradition that informs Western Civilization. Our values and ethics might dictate certain responses to our Islamic Enemy and rule out others. None of this conflicts with the fundamental concepts of the Inner Jihad. In fact, such responses are perfectly appropriate so long as one is free to *choose* them rather than being forced to do so through the workings of fear and one's Control Factor.

Just as a Muslim is given the freedom to choose to wear a burka even in jurisdictions where Muslim dress is not required, Westerners must be free to choose how to engage in the external battlefield with our Islamic Enemy. What we have seen, however, is that when fear pulls the strings of the Control Factor and permits only limited choices—choices that our Islamic Enemy knows how to game—we have no real choice at all. That is a prescription for defeat.

The consequences of teaching responsibility and accountability, mirroring, and crystallizing intention are frequently more favorable than ever initially anticipated. In the face of consolidated and focused power, many enemies collapse. Merely setting foot on that path will drastically change the dynamics between ourselves and our Islamic Enemy. This certainly does not preclude the possibility of firm and disastrous reactions from the enemy, but such is not a pre-determined outcome. As with Saddam's Hussein's threat that the first Iraq War would become the "mother of all wars" which became an epic defeat for him after the United States developed a clarity of purpose, our actions can greatly alter the range of response.

Speak Up

Free Speech is, perhaps, the West's most powerful weapon—both offensive and defensive. It is also critical for each of the other elements of the Inner Jihad. Awareness requires each of us to discuss, argue, and debate openly the issues related to Islam and our Islamic Enemy. The Control Factor maneuvers are so compelling that only an aggressive effort can hope to diminish their power, so verbally struggling through those issues is essential. To learn about Islam, one must voice, argue, and defend positions, discover their strengths and weaknesses, fine-tune them, practice them, and then start over again.

One must be free to explore positions in order to discover and appreciate more fully the gravity of the threat we face. One must be free to verbalize criticism as part of determining what one believes is true or false, useful or irrelevant, accurate or simply emotionally charged. Speaking freely and actively does not merely apply to reporting but an entire range of activities that furthers understanding, learning, and identifying one's own Control Factor processes.

Speaking up is also essential for teaching responsibility and mirroring. Each lesson requires new behaviors, and such acts require speaking out to supply a context that provides meaning. Demonstrating that one no longer accepts an enabling role (*dhimmitude*), demands purposeful confrontation supported by rational explanation. Speaking out again and again is part of the process of solidifying such intentions as well as communicating firm resolve.

To secure Western Civilization, nothing is more fundamental than fully protecting the right to free speech. Once the ability to express—particularly the "darker" range of speech that involves insulting, criticizing, demeaning, blaspheming, etc.,—is curtailed, the West is on the road to destruction. History proves that once free speech is impaired, the ride toward tyranny accelerates. If limits on free speech are not con-

fronted and defeated early, the situation becomes more difficult to reverse without violence and warfare.

A Control Factor fantasy suggests that America's free speech rights
are unassailable. They are, after all, provided for in our founding documents. Yet the reality is far different. There are plenty of limits on the
right to free speech, including slander and defamation laws, censorship
and obscenity laws, political and campaign finance restrictions, broadcast license restrictions, just to name a few. We have also witnessed a
slow but effective effort by the secular Left to eliminate as many indications of our Judeo-Christian roots as possible from public expression;
school prayer and the use of "God" in any governmental function or
context to name a few. Limitations are placed on a few in specific circumstances, only to creep into public activity over time—in much the
same way that a frog loses its life when it does not notice that the slowly
heating water in which it swims has now come to a boil.

There has been pressure to bring European style hate speech laws to
America. We believe that no matter what has occurred in Europe, it can
not happen here. Those laws, in large part, originated from the fear of a
return to horrific anti-Semitism and the possibility of another holocaust.
They eventually became more restrictive, such as bans against mere insults. This change crept into the law due to complacency and the unwillingness to see and say what was happening. For America, the best way
to prevent this and to protect our precious right to free speech is to use it
boldly, again and again, to establish and reinforce that such right is an
intrinsic part of our society.

We have a dangerous tendency to permit our Islamic Enemy to advance—step by step—restrictions on our ability to speak freely about
Islam. While terrorists frequently cite anti-Islamic speech as the cause
and rationale for their violent acts, Civilization Jihadists are actively
working to have us willingly adopt restrictions that limit our ability to
discuss Islam freely. The extensive use of intimidation has worked well
in the absence of laws on the books; so much so that we decline to speak
in ways that might insult or demean Muslims. Any cursory review of
news stories shows how the "Peaceful Muslim Disclaimer" has become
a regular part of our dialogue. Just as Mayor Bloomberg refused to initially identify the Muslim Times Square bomber as a terrorist, Fox News
declined to call the French rioters "Muslims." In terror and similar incidents, most news organizations are reluctant to ever refer to any perpetrator as Muslim and those few that do wait until irrefutable confirmation

has been made. Our Islamic Enemy is fully aware that self-imposed limitations are the most difficult to reverse. Once we have allowed our beliefs and emotions to be so manipulated, it becomes difficult to return to the *status quo ante*. Preying upon Western Guilt, bad faith, enabling tendencies, and all of the other Control Factor tools, Civilization Jihadists are pressing for cultural and legal restraints on all aspects of speech concerning Islam. Speaking out strongly is the best antidote to such efforts, and must be pursued actively and continually.

And while our legal history has built significant barriers to some of the limitations on free speech that have taken hold in Europe (such as "defamation of a religion or ethnic group" laws), the International Institutional Jihadists are using "norming," through treaties and international standards, as a tool to advance these limitations. As Daniel Huff of the Middle East Forum has warned in a variety of articles, the groundwork was laid in 1986 by the DC Circuit US Court of Appeals, citing a "compelling government interest" to override the First Amendment provision for free speech.[21] The case in question, *Finzer v Barry,* involved a treaty which restricted displays of critical messages within a certain distance of an embassy. The treaty was found to trump any domestic law which would allow such behavior. Essentially, international treaties that cite such a "compelling government interest" can be used to restrict speech that would be freely permitted absent such treaty. Treaties can therefore be used to force restrictions at home that could not otherwise be approved through that nation's regular legislative or judicial processes.

Huff has pointed to UN resolutions, orchestrated by the OIC, banning "hate speech" or proscribing "defamation of religions" as critical examples of such efforts to impose external restraints on the United States. The Obama administration has announced that it will "work together" with Islamic nations "on the issue of defamation of religion." It has worked with Egypt on a resolution that denounces "incitement to discrimination," "negative religious stereotyping," and "promotion by certain media of false images and negative stereotypes." And, as Huff concludes, the standard reservation in a treaty that states that nothing in the agreement shall require the United States to restrict the right of free speech would not defeat a "compelling government interest" argument since the latter is also a part of US law. By way of example, Huff queries whether General David Petraeus' admonition that *Koran* burnings in the United States will set back American efforts in Afghanistan can be considered a "compelling government interest" that could be used to restrict otherwise-protected speech at home.[22]

Speaking up has required great courage. Indeed, the 1948 Universal Declaration of Human Rights[23] states in its preamble, ". . . a world in which human beings shall enjoy freedom of speech and belief and freedom from fear and want has been proclaimed as the highest aspiration of the common people." Nonetheless, the OIC and many of its member states and associated institutions have been engaged in exactly the opposite: seeking to ensure that all forms of criticism of Islam are stopped worldwide.

As far back as 1988, the OIC condemned and banned in Muslim countries the famous book, *The Satanic Verses*, written by then London-based secular Muslim author Salman Rushdie. As Lorenzo Vidino retraces in *The New Muslim Brotherhood in the West*, initial indirect attempts by an Indian Maududi-based group to have the book banned failed, leading to numerous protests. Subsequently, a book-burning rally was organized in the United Kingdom. When the publisher still resisted, appeals were made to various Muslim countries including Saudi Arabia, at which point the OIC acted. The following year Iranian leader Ayatollah Khomeini (not to be outdone by the Sunni Saudis) issued a fatwa calling for the "execution" by "all zealous Muslims" of those who were involved with the publishing of the book. The Supreme Leader noted that those who die in such a mission would be considered martyrs deserving of all the benefits associated with such status.

Many other similar events have taken place since Rushdie's fatwa. Vidino suggests the Rushdie incident set an example to guide the Muslim world for decades. Former Indian Muslim Ibn Warraq, who grew up in Pakistan, and who authored *Why I Am Not A Muslim* and other important books, left Islam when he began to see it as a totalitarian system and concluded "the effects of the teachings of the Koran have been a disaster for human reason and social, intellectual, and moral progress."[24] Ibn Warraq has named as one of his goals to "win the right to criticize the religion without fear of retribution"[25] from those who would be labeled here as our Islamic Enemy. As discussed previously, Ayaan Hirsi Ali and Geert Wilders have faced extreme pressure from Muslims as well as European institutions—acting as *dhimmis* in relation to our Islamic Enemy. Authors Oriana Fallaci, Mark Steyn, Rachel Ehrenfeld, and Elisabeth Sabaditsch-Wolff are just some of those who have faced Lawfare legal actions in foreign jurisdictions for speaking out. And the publication of the "Danish Mohammed cartoons" in the newspaper *Jyllands-Posten* resulted in numerous deaths, forcing some of the artists and publishers into hiding under police protection.

In *Victims of Intimidation*, Douglas Murray and Johan Pieter Verwey have compiled stories from twenty-seven politicians, journalists, activists, writers, academics, and artists who fought against the intimidation brought to bear by European Muslim communities. Their speaking up should serve as a model for all of those engaged in the Inner Jihad. Speaking up means being vigilant against all efforts to restrict speech. Although it used free speech as a banner for rebellious activities in the 1960s, the Left has now traded away this cause as it relates to Islam in exchange for the apparent comfort offered by the Control Factor as well as an alliance of convenience with our Islamic Enemy. This parallels the bargain that European nations made with the Arab-Islamic World in order to obtain energy security for "Eurabia," as described so well by Bat Ye'or in her book of that title. Our Inner Jihad requires that this temptation be resisted at all costs and freedom of speech be protected aggressively and advanced as widely as possible.

Support True Reform

Many observers hope that Islam will go through its own "Reformation." Courageous Muslim speakers and writers such as Irshad Manji, Dr. Zuhdi Jasser, Mona Eltahawy, Dr. Wafa Sultan, Asra Nomani, Dr. Tawfik Hamid, and others have been vocal in calling for reforms that would take Islam out of the seventh century and allow it to join modernity. In an intriguing contrast, many former Muslims who either converted to Christianity—such as Mark Gabriel and Nonie Darwish—or became atheists—such as Ayaan Hirsi Ali—tend to doubt that Islam is capable of reform.

The Hudson Institute's Zeyno Baran edited *The Other Muslims: Moderate and Secular*, an excellent collection of works by other Muslims who see Islam as fully compatible with universal human rights and Western democracy, categorizing the heart of Islam as "peaceful" while maintaining that "a Muslim can be both pious and secular." Baran's authors fully recognize the formidable forces behind those "extremists" who control the face and agenda of most of the distinct expressions of Islam today—the Saudi Wahhabis, the worldwide Muslim Brotherhood, al-Qaeda, and Hizb ut-Tahrir, the secretive network of cells operating throughout Europe, the United States, and headquartered in the United

Kingdom—but remain optimistic that with great effort over time, Islam can emerge as fully congruent with Western democracies.

In a *Wall Street Journal* piece of 5/7/2011, Irshad Manji wrote:

> It is time for those who love liberal democracy to join hands with Islam's reformists. Here is a clue to who's who: Moderate Muslims denounce violence committed in the name of Islam but insist that religion has nothing to do with it; reformist Muslims, by contrast, not only deplore Islamist violence but admit that our religion is used to incite it.[26]

Baran's group does this and more.

There is a commendable intention that underlies the effort to reform Islam, and Manji, Dr. Jasser, and the other courageous reformers should be widely encouraged and celebrated. They may represent the best hope for the future. There is, however, a major paradox in the hope of Islamic Reform. It is not simply that the religion is "used to incite;" the religion *embodies* that which incites. For Islam to be truly reformed, much has to be eliminated, not merely re-interpreted, and that act alone violates Islamic law.

The notion of reformation is often tossed about, but few have been able to describe what exactly such an Islam would look like, or how it could be realized. There have been attempts throughout Islamic history to accomplish such a goal with very limited success. Sufis have survived a long history but constitute a small percentage of Muslims, and not all Sufis are "peaceful" and "moderate"—Sheikh Gilani, whose Muslims of America compounds in the United States were mentioned earlier, is a Sufi.

The Ahmadis have had an even more difficult time. Founded in the 1800s by Mirza Ghulam Ahmad and led by successors to their version of the Mahdi, Ahmadis attempted to take the violence out of Islam, alter the notion of immutability, and have a Mahdi figure that cancelled many prior commands. Unfortunately, this group is today considered apostate by most Muslims, and its followers are considered "lower than" *dhimmis*. Being so despised and rejected throughout the Muslim world, over one hundred Ahmadis were slaughtered in Pakistan in 2010 by other Muslims.

It is not uncommon for Westerners to fantasize about an Islamic Reformation as an intellectual exercise. Some fantasies carry a buried presupposition that people are free to reconstruct their beliefs as they choose. Others seem reminiscent of a 1960s adolescent's approach of taking college courses in comparative religion to choose which parts of each religion one wishes to keep. Yet true reformation butts against 1400 years of culture and practice. More importantly, there is, worldwide, a collection of millions of religious authorities, scholars, experts, and the like whose existence is based upon ensuring that no meaningful reformation can take place. Similarly, the tools of communication and propaganda primarily reside under the control of those with aims in partial or complete conflict with reformation.

And, as with other fancies of the young, the dream of reformation simply imagines that 1400 years of intensive religious scholarship should be discarded in favor of what seems to be new and original ideas, as if the issues that face us today have not been considered and explored throughout most of Islamic history. That body of work must be acknowledged and addressed directly because that same history teaches that any attempt to disregard it results in a backlash that is often violent and followed by severe consequences. Many of the beliefs and concepts are so deeply embedded in all facets of Muslim life and cultures that a substantive reformation may only be able to occur at a glacial pace.

In such a reformation, when the political, discriminatory, intolerant and freedom-restricting features of *Shariah* are deleted, little likely is left beyond ritual and various cultural traditions. This is not to demean the rich Islamic ritual life. Rather, it is to question what the foundational narrative which ties all these behaviors together would then promote.

Would Reform Muslims stress their forgiveness, the Golden Rule, or their call to good works? Those primarily characterize Christianity and Judaism. As described earlier, Mohammed had the benefit of coming later than the other two monotheistic religions so that he could define Islam around them, in terms of them, and in opposition to them. From the perspective of reformation, however, this timing becomes a detriment, as much of what Mohammed used to create an identity for Islam is precisely what reformers would seek to extinguish. When the call to spread *Shariah* is eliminated, what becomes the essential identity of a "reformed Islam?" To what, exactly, is unquestioned submission now owed?

One approach might include treating the Meccan period of Mohammed's life as the dominant element of Islam—a form of reverse abrogation. Some explanation would be required to discount or expunge the later Medina years. However, as discussed previously, the Meccan

years were those in which Mohammed had little power and minor success in recruiting followers. It is difficult to see how the early years as
the centerpiece could demonstrate the glory required of a great religion.

The fantasy of a Reformed Islam is held most often by those non-
Muslims who are wishing that Muslims were much more like them, ex-
cepting the decision to engage in specific private rituals. For them, it
attempts to institutionalize the activities and beliefs of what Mark Gabriel
labeled "Liberal" and "Secular" Muslims. That is, the Muslim would
essentially integrate into all of Western culture yet retreat to perform his
religious practice in private, much as do Christians, Jews, Buddhists,
and those of other faiths in America.

That wish, unfortunately, again erases much of what makes Islam
unique. As we have seen, that public aspect is founded on discrimination
and superiority bound with a political dimension which gives Islam a
distinctive identity and would be difficult to wring out of the religion. It
is simply problematic for a seriously engaged Muslim to declare—apart
from *taqiyya*—"I am American first, Muslim second!" (Note: Muslims
are commanded to obey and submit to the local authority when in a non-
Muslim dominated territory such that this would not appear as un-Islamic. That command, however, is only meaningful in the context of a
larger submission to Allah, not in lieu of such submission).

Further, any such "Reformation" would require at least some separation of mosque and state, which would be antithetical to Islam itself.
The religion is to be the state; therefore it determines state functions. It is
the legal code for the complete life of the Ummah. American democracy
originated in the midst of religious principles—God was central to many
of the Founders. Nonetheless, religion was subjected to the higher tests
included in the Constitution—accommodated and even preferred, but re-
strained from controlling state functions. European democracies have
accommodated religion in slightly different fashions. In no case, however, does any religious formulation become the supreme law of the land
commanding the state, as Islam requires.

Historians such as Daniel Pipes have held out hope that some reformation might occur. Perhaps some version of Ataturk's model of Islam
would, over the long term, merge into Western culture. Reference is
made to the Christian Reformation, which saw the Church begin to be
removed from most state activities. But the Church was created separate
from and long after the life of Christianity's center—Jesus Christ. Generally speaking, Jesus recognized the same separation of power ("Give

unto Caesar . . . .") which allowed a variety of expressions of Christianity to emerge consistent with His teachings. Mohammed commanded the opposite, creating major roadblocks for the would-be reformist. Nonetheless, it is Muslims that must make it happen, all the while maintaining vigilance against the threats that accompany the abuse of the commands of Islam as actually written. Muslims decide what Islam is and is not; they determine Islam's many expressions.

To be clear: there is no theoretical reason why Islam cannot be reshaped into something fully acceptable to and easy to integrate with the West. Islam can evolve to express in any form Muslims choose. If Gabriel's estimates of the number of "Liberal" and "Secular" Muslims are even close to accurate, there is a significant worldwide potential. The issue, however, is that, even if desired by the majority of the 1 to 1.5 billion Muslims worldwide, such change would be monumental and require deep penetration into and fundamental reorientation of the vast number of Islamic cultures and identities throughout the world. It also requires a reframing of Islamic history and law to integrate such change. This effort, even if deliberately executed, would take time and effort on an epic scale.

On the other hand, we must diligently monitor our temptation to exaggerate the number of Muslims actually prepared to reform. The hope for a transformation more likely insults hundreds of millions of Muslims across the world. The 2011 Cairo protests led many Westerners to imagine the majority of Egyptians as if they were Westerners trapped under an authoritarian rule. Given freedom, many believed they would turn away from those Islamic expressions the West does not favor. Nonetheless, polls showed quite the opposite: most Egyptians favored the establishment of some form of *Shariah* in Islamic lands, desired stonings for adultery, etc. A 2010 Pew Research Poll[27] about Egypt, reported by Dr. Richard Swier, showed that 85% of Egyptians believed that Islam's influence over political life is positive for the country and should play a "large role in politics;" 82% believe adulterers should be stoned; 49% believe that Islam played only a small role in the country; 84% believe apostates should be executed; while 77% believe thieves should be flogged or have their hands cut off as prescribed by *Shariah*. Also, 54% supported gender separation in the workplace. These and other results suggest that Egyptians were not the young, Westernized, secularists that Western media sought to find. (Nor are these numbers unique to Egypt. A 2007 University of Maryland Poll[28] of over 4,000 Muslims across the

Muslim world showed that over 65% (and 67% in Egypt) wanted to unify Islamic countries under a Caliphate).

As the Muslim Brotherhood creeps into control in Egypt, it paves the way to satisfy these desires. After securing its place in the process of amending the Egyptian Constitution following the fall of Mubarak, the Brotherhood ensured that Article 2 was carried forward, securing *Shariah* as the principle source of legislation and Islam as the religion of the nation. At the same time, it has made an alliance with at least part of the military to help facilitate both groups' objectives while leaving in place both the declared state of emergency and secret police. Meanwhile, many Islamist prisoners have been released, adding strength to the Brotherhood's cause. This put quite a damper on any Western illusion that a radical transformation is likely to occur.

Nor did the elimination of Mubarak open Egyptian Muslims to make peace with Coptic Christians—something that might be anticipated if the revolution constituencies were so "Westernized." Rather, church burnings and other tensions have continued in full force. As reported in *The New York Times* on May 9, 2011, when Hussein Qheder, who considered himself an "extremist" and had been recently released from a fourteen year prison term for his Islamist political work was solicited to join a Muslim riot against Christians, he declined stating, "In this period we are in, we cannot bear this kind of talk. . . . This could kill the revolution."[29] Knowing how to intelligently hide their true ultimate intentions for the revolution is a sign of how well organized and prepared the Brotherhood is.

As for those "young" activists who supposedly had a Western style vision of freedom, there has been instead a resurgence of anti-Israel sentiment. Threats abound that Egypt will break its treaty with Israel. This is not simply a view held by a few outnumbered "extremists." Rather, as Andrew Bostom reports, crowds in Alexandria marched to the Israeli consulate chanting "With our souls, with our blood, we redeem you Palestine." Bostom quotes Mohammad Abdel-Salam, a 22-year-old activist announcing, "We are here today to show our support for the Palestinian cause. The victory will not be complete without the liberation of Palestine."[30]

Since the fall of Mubarak, unemployment has risen drastically while the economy has ground down. The country has had to eat into significant portions of its foreign reserves while food and other shortages plague the region. The only unifying idea of the original protests was to get rid of Mubarak. The only unifying idea post-Mubarak has been some form of "social justice" yet to be clarified but consistent with the socialism espoused by the Brotherhood and by Leftist protesters who helped initiate the revolution. The military, now consisting mainly of bureaucrats, is organized by experience and history but internally consists of individuals with disparate interests. Mubarak had kept the lower class Salafists under wraps; now they (perhaps 10% of the population) are attacking the Copts. Meanwhile, the more educated middle class Brotherhood members, bent on securing power above all else, are both the ones with the most at stake and best organized to assert themselves.

Egypt, the fertile land of the Nile, is certainly more fertile for extreme rather than reformed expressions of Islam. While many in the West cling to the notion that a Western democracy leading to Western notions of freedom will emerge, the early indications suggest that is merely the "Arab Spring" fantasy.

Even so, according to Manji and others, many Muslims who live quietly under threatening Islamic cultural conditions are crying out for new expressions of Islam. Reformation is a powerful force that needs extensive nourishing. The paradoxes inherent in such an effort need not prevent new forms of expression so long as Muslims themselves choose to create such expressions and they themselves are prepared to defend, strengthen, and reinforce their choices. And that will take assistance from the non-Muslim world.

Dr. Jasser has worked tirelessly for a Reformed Islam. He suggests that he already practices such an expression, and that most American Muslims are of similar inclination. He cites "political Islam" as the culprit which distorts and prevents the free practice of the "spiritual Islam" that he and his family follow diligently, and with appropriate pride. Jesus has been interpreted to have so distinguished the mundane and political "Caesar" from the spiritual that Christians are well able to describe separate domains. Dr. Jasser similarly seeks to isolate and cauterize the "political" out of Islam, i.e., to compartmentalize. Because Mohammed, as deputy of Allah, assumed authority over all domains of life, this surgery is uniquely more life threatening (both to Islam and to Dr. Jasser). In some sense, it is easier for God himself (in Christianity's case, Jesus) to authorize compartmentalization than it is for an agent (Mohammed) who would otherwise be performing the greatest of sins in excluding Allah from anything.

As discussed early on, the phrase and language of "Political Islam" is the first step in this isolation. As goes the language, so goes the expression. Dr. Jasser likes to point out that *Ummah* has two meanings, one as a religious community and another as "the state," and that he seeks to eliminate the latter. The more Dr. Jasser and others are able to speak about and to reinforce such separations, the more "real" they can make the distinctions they wish to see.

Dr. Jasser, like Manji, is compelling, extremely competent, intelligent, well schooled, heartfelt, and determined to lead the noble effort of bringing Islam into a more acceptable partnership with Western modernity. He describes himself as fully American and recognizes that the American Constitution must remain the supreme law of the land, and advocates that American principles of democracy, non-violence, pluralism, and freedom must be fully supported in order to properly allow his "spiritual Islam" to flourish. Unlike Imam Rauf and others foisting the Civilization Jihad, Dr. Jasser has distinguished "under God" from "under Islam."

The Syrian psychiatrist Dr. Wafa Sultan expresses a different angle. As fellow reformer Asra Nomani wrote in *Time* Magazine, Dr. Sultan, like Dr. Jasser, seeks to "take the politics out of Islam,"[31] but also views many Muslims as having been brainwashed, a process she hopes to reverse. Sultan says of herself, "I even don't believe in Islam . . . but I am a Muslim."[32]

As discussed earlier, escaping the compulsion to define what Islam "is," is the first step in beginning to allow Islam to become something else. Such a process, however, first requires an understanding of the variety of ways Islam has expressed itself throughout history, in order that reformers may comprehend what kind of new creation is necessary.

This is no simple task. Concepts and principles based on 1400 years of Islamic law must be addressed. Conscious choices must be made to accept this, throw away that, diminish this, magnify that, invent this, and give new meaning to that. Pretending Islam is something that it is not and has never been, is doomed to failure. Actively choosing a new expression of Islam, with worldwide support, can very possibly succeed, but it will be a mammoth task.

Reformation can also be assisted by distinguishing the religion from the cultures in which it has been grounded. Parts that are undesirable can be split off and attributed to the cultures in which Islam developed as opposed to Islam itself. For those looking for significant change, the brutal treatment of women, the use of terror, battle, and barbaric means to interact with non-Muslims, the lack of mutual respect and tolerance for others, and the aversion to change that so extensively defines many expressions of Islam, can all be cited as features of tribal societies that birthed Islam but need not be carried forward. Islam, instead, can be presented as embodying principles that seek to break with these out-of-date customs.

Reformers such as Manji and Dr. Jasser are extremely courageous. They are fully aware of the difficulties of reconciling Islam with modernity. They enrage many Muslims and have had to stand all but alone in the face of tremendous adversity. Their views differ in critical fashion from and cannot be reconciled with those of typical "moderates." Remember, however, the "moderate Muslim" is largely a creation of non-Muslims.

"Moderates" are still stuck in what Islam "is" and attempt to reconcile the irreconcilable. Reformers place more emphasis on making Islam become fully compatible with Western modernity through new expressions rather than defending the old ones. This does not mean that reformers freely create against the express word of the *Koran*. Nor does it mean they do not make every effort to draw legitimacy from the texts and history of Islam and Islamic cultures. Rather, Manji, Dr. Jasser, and others are fully able to find support for their expressions in the texts and certain periods of history. And they do so with the clear understanding that the needs for new expressions outweigh the benefits of other textual and historical continuity. In Wittgenstein's words, they seek to "breathe a new kind of air" and take full responsibility for doing so, and for leading others to join.

In short, the efforts of these reformers identify and define themselves. This reverses the Control Factor's transfer of responsibility for reforming to non-Muslims that keeps us so trapped in the addiction-enabler dance. The reformers themselves are taking on the burden of unwinding this dance. They are truly the heroes of this modern day effort.

The Arab revolts of 2011, which began in Tunisia, spread to Egypt, exploded in Libya, and, as of this writing, are percolating in Syria, Jordan, Yemen, Bahrain, and elsewhere, represent a crossroads for the possibility of reformation. George W. Bush's Freedom Agenda, widely castigated by the Left, heralded the universal principle that if man is able to taste freedom he will seek to secure it. By "freedom," Bush meant the Western concept which affords the individual the ability to choose and simultaneously take responsibility for most aspects of his life largely free of government intervention.

And this freedom must first be kindled. That is, perhaps, the greatest contribution the Irshad Manjis of the Muslim world are making. By example over the past decade she has developed a large following of Muslim youth throughout the world who crave something different but have been kept silent by a culture of fear. And many of these youths have in turn become leaders within the "undergrounds" that have sprouted across the Islamic world.

The internet, satellite television, and various forms of social media have also made it impossible for these youths to remain ignorant of life elsewhere in the world. To most of them, those lives are better and more desirable. It is not necessarily clear what ultimate "Islam(s)" these seekers would craft but it is clear that the flames Bush referred to are being kindled and stoked worldwide, awaiting sufficient fuel to flare out fully.

The revolutions of 2011, in part, may represent this igniting—"in part" because they appear to result from the confluence of different and incompatible directives. To much of the Arab world, as discussed previously, "freedom" refers to the liberation from government tyranny which fails to comply with Islamic precepts,—which is also, by definition, liberation from those who seek Western "freedom." That is certainly what the Muslim Brotherhood and al-Qaeda mean when they refer to "the near enemy"—the tyrannical rulers who have blocked the freedom of the Ummah to submit to an Islamic state.

The Cairo protests appear to have started with the joint efforts of the Left, worldwide labor groups, Google executives, and Muslim Brotherhood representatives. Tunisia and Libya have their own diverse actors, reportedly including the Brotherhood and al-Qaeda. From a distance it appears that some want variations of the Western notion of freedom while others want a government that provides for the submission to either Islam, some Leftist vision of socialism/Marxism, or some combination of the two. Who wins out in each case and what the future is to look like is up for grabs. For true reformation to occur, the ultimate winners of these revolutions must choose more of the Western "freedom" and forfeit more of the Islamic "freedom." Only time will tell which way history will move.

Significantly, however, if this is to be a march to Western "freedom," it must follow a progression. Life under tyranny embeds fears deeply within the populace. Westerners tend to project onto these subjects a familiarity with democratic institutions, rule of law, and freedom of speech. The unquestioned expectation of Westerners is that once the tyrant is deposed the people will immediately know how to construct their states more in accord with Western principles—as if they are in some sense being "restored."

Unfortunately, these "subjects" have no experience with what has taken the West centuries to create and shape. As Bush warned, freedom takes time and results from a lengthy and sustained process. What we see now is that, step by step, those who live under Islamic tyrannies, Arab and Persian, taste more and more of it. As they taste, they learn. During the 2009 Iranian election protests, many in the streets learned that they could say more than they had previously imagined. Westerners, Muslim and non-Muslim, now send television programs into Iran with political messages as well as comedies that mock and humiliate the regime. Some get through. Some of the dissenters are punished or killed while others survive and learn new techniques. As more and more step outside and experiment with speech and tolerance and religious expression, even more will take up the invitation.

Eventually, a tipping point may be reached. In the "Hundredth Monkey" story, a troupe of monkeys on an island mysteriously learn a behavior once a certain number of monkeys (100) on the distant mainland have been taught that same behavior. So may Western freedom be learned across the Islamic world. The learning will expand exponentially as those Muslims fighting for reformation create new ways to satisfy their desires to both modernize and participate with the Western world, while maintaining and bolstering their Islamic identities. If we are at such a crossroad, the outcome will be determined by which "freedom" the more powerful Muslims choose and which Islam(s) the more powerful Muslims decide to express.

On the other hand, up until now, the Arab Muslim experiments with importing communism, fascism, socialism, and other political forms have all failed. And Iran's experiment with revolution in 1979 pushed away the Leftists—who believed they brought it about in the first place—as control was assumed by those who sought to destroy any evidence of Western "freedom." Both Leftist and Islamic visions, sharing a similar hatred, start with the demise of the West. For 1400 years, however, the Islamic world has developed and rehearsed a vision of what is to replace the West. No such competing vision of the future is offered by Far Left ideologies. If the Muslim Brotherhood and other leaders of the three

Jihads surface with the power in these "revolutions," anything but a reformation is likely to take place. This is why it is so necessary that Western powers have clarity on the pervasiveness of these Jihads, who is leading them, and what their goals are. Supporting the Muslim Brotherhood so long as it "renounces violence" (as Hillary Clinton advocated) or disposing of tyrants with no clear understanding of what or who will take their place (as Barack Obama did), is not only bad policy, it likely will set back the path of reformation.

Supporting a "Reformation" in any manner is the Inner Jihad's positive counterbalance. A focus upon what Islam can become in the modern world can afford a valuable relief from the anxiety the Control Factor seeks to quell. It offers the vision of an alternative to the "War of the Houses."

Such an alternative may or may not turn out to be feasible. We would be negligent, however, not to give it its best shot. Ultimately, however, the choice is only that of the Muslim world itself. If it is able to give up its addiction to hate, intolerance, grandiosity and its underbelly of prejudice, and allow its profound attraction to submission to be, at least in part, transferred to the pursuit of freedom, reason, and the rule of law of man, mutual tolerance, and the acceptance of responsibility, the world has a magnificent future. If not, the "war of the Houses" will have to be played out until one side eventually wins.

Finally, supporting "Reformation," along with the other elements of the Inner Jihad, is an important piece in helping us handle the problem of how to identify and distinguish our Islamic Enemy.

When we:

- Admit that we don't have an easy answer;
- Make great efforts to learn about the enemy and the threats he poses;
- Begin to act in ways that teach and transfer back responsibility;
- Demand that the enemy prove his own identity;
- Mirror the behavior that conflicts with our normal demands and expectations;
- Voice our concerns loudly; and
- Side with those who are courageously working to apply the banner of Islam to something truly mutually tolerant;

we will have gone a long way toward creating conditions where it is substantially easier to determine:

- Who is using taqiyya;
- Who is the so-called moderate—who, instead of conforming Islam to Western Civilizational demands, seeks to do the reverse; and
- Who is truly working to impose *Shariah* worldwide.

When we do our part in the Inner Jihad, our Islamic Enemy will more readily appear to float to the surface and crystallize, becoming easier to spot. As stated previously, as much as we realize that reality creates perception, perception, in turn, helps create reality. When we remove much of what distorts our perception, the reality of what we see becomes clearer. Just as a war on the physical battlefield will ultimately force everyone involved to choose sides, so will the Inner Jihad in the mental theater perfect our ability to perceive, (to paraphrase President George W. Bush), who is truly with us and who is against us.

And this is what is necessary to accomplish the next aspect of the Inner Jihad.

Understand, Respect, and Care for the Limits of Western Civilization

Some writers have framed the battle with our Islamic Enemy as one threatening our civilization, or civilization in general. Different formulations of the battle have been proposed, including Huntington's "Clash of Civilizations" or Pipes' war between barbarism and civilization, or Wafa Sultan's "clash between a mentality that belongs to the Middle Ages and another that belongs to the 21st Century . . . a clash between freedom and oppression."

Alternatively, as the Muslim Brotherhood's own Explanatory Memorandum describes it, the struggle pits Western Civilization against Islam as the "civilization alternative." Whether the phrase describes an alternative civilization or an alternative *to* civilization is worth pondering.

Strong arguments can be made to support any of various descriptions, perhaps none better than Islam's own "War of the Houses."

Nonetheless, a critical concept animates most discussions over the issue: the embedded fear that modern Western Civilization can "lose itself" if it stoops to any form of aggression that might resemble barbarism—either through the possibly excessive use of force or other constitutionally questionable acts—to protect itself. Intellectuals, politicians, and pundits often stress that we must be careful not to become that which we are fighting. This is a compelling thought which carries a veneer of simplicity, rationality, and moral superiority. It is, however, one of luxury—one which can easily be followed only as long as our fundamental existence faces no true challenge.

Instead, America faces "losing itself" precisely through what the Control Factor has urged. Entrenching itself in the game of guilt, with political correctness and self-hate guiding its enabling roles, it becomes ever more difficult to remember what the country was meant to be. America has historically always "found" itself when it took pride in itself; when it stood up for itself and fought for its principles. Pride is achieved through correctly and honestly perceiving the threats we face and then, in the face of obstacles, working to eliminate those threats. Pride is achieved when we stretch to demonstrate the greatness we all know is there; not when we bend over backwards to apologize for a deficiency we invent to appease those whom we fear. Pride is achieved through practicing pride, not self-hate. Pride is achieved when we stop romancing multiculturalism, the paradoxical attempt to place value above all else upon our not valuing our civilization over others. And pride is what makes it impossible for us to "lose ourselves" even in the most difficult of struggles.

Simply put, America is not capable or equipped to become uncivilized "butchers," not because we fear becoming so. Instead, it is simply not part of the makeup of the nation.

This fear of "losing ourselves" is based in part on the idea that modern Western Civilization objects to the use of force, particularly unrestrained and excessively cruel force, other than in self-defense. The term "civilization" embodies an agreement to use every effort to settle conflicts by other means, typically economic, and within some diplomatic framework. This approach is mutually understood to enjoy a morally higher status than the unchecked use of force, and the civilized world compliments itself on its ability to follow it.

President Obama often demonstrates the deeply embedded liberal instinct that we can solve our problems by rising above them. Indeed, the resolution of many seemingly irreconcilable disputes begins by first identifying on a more general level something to which both sides can subscribe (often described as rapport and confidence-building measures). The notion is that we can somehow step up to a "meta-level" to be able to reframe the conflict in such a way that both parties can find agreement and common ground. Once reached, it is taken for granted that some reasonable solution or allocation of responsibilities will be forthcoming. And all will be in service of avoiding the use of force.

This process generally requires a neutral third party to sit as mediator, construct the reframing, serve as a substitute to allow grievances to be voiced without inflaming the other party, and to remind each party of the consequences of failure. Part of the vision of the United Nations is that it can play this role. Unfortunately, its neutrality has been elusive, if not a joke. Obama himself, however, has staked out this "higher than" position for himself, earning him such derogatory descriptions as "The Anointed One," "President of the World," or "The Messiah."

Obama has expressed this notion in various statements to the Islamic world. He has diminished any notion of American exceptionalism by stating that America is exceptional just as every other nation presumably views itself as exceptional. By jumping out of his role as American advocate and acting as fair advocate for all parties, Obama subtly suggests he more accurately represents the world rather than America. He has stated, for instance, that no single nation should be in the position to be able to decide which nations should be permitted nuclear weapons. While insisting that he is not "naïve," this voluntary surrender of authority, whatever his intention, has eroded American self-respect, American exceptionalism, and, above all, American and Western values. He simply cannot protect America by elevating himself above American values.

The core assumption here is that we can be both player and referee. This capability can sometimes be effective within the modern civilized world. Parties to a dispute can appear to rise to a sensible level at which a non-coercive means of resolution presents itself. Nonetheless, despite appearances to the contrary, resolution of this sort ultimately arises from each party's taking inventory of its relative strengths, war-gaming what can be achieved, and agreeing quickly to forego any use of force to generate a better outcome.

However, when civilization meets barbarism seeking its destruction or submission, or mutual tolerance meets intolerance, it is impossible to be both referee and player. It is only our grandiosity that masks this common-sense fact. We can pretend to appeal to or identify with some "higher" level of justice—whether religious, moral, or simply some notion of global wisdom to which one aspires—but this is just another fantasy that prevents us from protecting ourselves.

Ironically, whereas the fundamental fear is that civilization risks losing itself by stooping to barbaric means, civilization will actually self-destruct if it fails to do all it can to protect itself—another case of a defense creating that which it seeks to avoid. While Bush was castigated for simply being a player under the principles he enumerated, Obama risks much more by deluding himself and the rest of us that he can somehow rise above our "differences" with our Islamic Enemy in an effort to reach a peace. Here, in action, is the suicidal tendency of a civilization that Lee Harris describes.

One World, One Government

Obama also appears to be attempting to create the initial foundations for a one-world government. His approach with respect to the initial no-fly zone in Libya in March 2011 was, to some degree, to turn American foreign policy over to the United Nations and NATO. International approval was all that counted. He acted upon a UN resolution without obtaining any meaningful authorization from the US Congress. Having been elected president in large part due to his being the "un-Bush," he was well aware of the domestic dismay over going to war, commencing a pre-emptive war, and the excessive use of executive power to lead the country into war without knowing or defining the mission or exit strategy. Yet, he seemingly had made no preparation for the future of the land he helped attack after Qaddafi. He also seemingly had no clear idea of whom we were supporting (or worse, did). These, along with commencing a war, were major issues during the Bush presidency. But none of it mattered to Obama when he was given the opportunity to engage under the shield of NATO in a semblance of unified global action with the support of international institutions and, in particular, the Arab League.

This is not merely Obama's ego as some critics suggest. Rather, Obama is advancing powerful long-held Leftist goals of transferring sovereignty to the so-called "international community." This is not unlike more recent efforts promoted by the Far Left to consolidate and subordinate the US financial system to a global monetary authority under rules generated by the Bank of International Settlements, the IMF, the World Bank and other forums of major central bankers.

In exercising his power, Obama has promoted and then relied upon the "Responsibility to Protect" doctrine developed by his inner circle, including his National Security Special Adviser Samantha Power, and financed in large part by George Soros though the Global Centre for Responsibility to Protect. This doctrine essentially establishes the international community (read "United Nations") as the ultimate arbiter, usurping a targeted nation's sovereign right to determine how it treats its own people. Sovereignty is considered an earned responsibility which can only be earned protecting one's own people, according to UN standards. In other words, this is no sovereignty at all. If the United Nations disapproves of a leader's actions, it authorizes itself to interfere on behalf of a victimized populace that requires protection.

Obama made clear two elements of this approach in responding to Libya's revolution: America has a moral duty to protect victims of brutal national leaders, and the performance of this duty is subject to the approval of the international community. For any such remedial action, international approval is presumably obtained through a vote in the UN Security Council. In the case of the NATO intervention "Operation Unified Protector" in Libya, that hurdle was met primarily because the Arab League desired it.

Obama's policy will no doubt serve many functions for him going forward. It gives him a way out of what had been a difficult political dance—how does he reconcile his need to "show the world" he is as tough and unafraid to use force, while confirming for his Far-Left base that America is a source of fundamental evil in the world, and requires substantial handcuffs? The doctrine also gives him an out he will need in future conflicts—the lack of international approval. Should the Iranian people, for instance, rise up in revolt again and provoke a brutal inhumane response from the regime, Obama knows that Russia and China will not permit military action on behalf of the United Nations. Obama, who appears uninterested in attacking Iran to halt its march to nuclear weapons, faced complaints when he failed to support the Iranian people in their Green revolution in 2009. Next time, he will be able to claim that while there might be a humanitarian crisis—not to mention a danger to the entire world—international support could not be secured.

The same response will likely shelter Obama in other Middle Eastern territories as well, except one—Israel. Responsibility to Protect appears to have been motivated to assist many of those influencing the UN in one of its primary efforts: disempowering or even destroying the nation of

Israel. It is no coincidence that, as investigator Aaron Klein reported in
World Net Daily in 2011,[33] Hanan Ashrawi served on the advisory board
of the International Commission on International and State Sovereignty
which birthed the Responsibility to Protect doctrine. Ms. Ashrawi was a
former deputy of Yasser Arafat and is the daughter of PLO co-founder
Daoud Mikhail. She served the PLO in various functions, has defended
the legitimacy of Hamas, is a Holocaust denier, and refers to Israel's
creation as "al Nakba" or "the Catastrophe." She has served as a spokes-
person for the Arab League, whose recent Secretary General, Amre
Moussa, also served as adviser to the same 2001 Commission.

From its inception, the doctrine was developed by some steeped in
anti-Israel motivations. It is possibly being positioned now for use at the
point when war breaks out and Israel can be accused of failing to protect
and intentionally abusing the Palestinian people. In one scenario Iran,
through its proxies Hamas and Hezbollah, provokes Israel into some
form of intensive military action in self-defense. This becomes the pre-
text for sending UN forces into Israel, re-assessing Israel's membership
in the UN, and establishing a Palestinian state not through negotiation
with Israel, but through UN action, on terms which Israel would otherwise never approve.

Consistent with trying to be both referee and player, Obama is, despite the verbiage about pursuing US interests, *redefining* US interests as
those of the "global community" and laying the groundwork for the eventual transfer of power to the UN to pursue those interests. One could see
this as a shrewd Far-Left agenda to transfer sovereignty to that organization, but executed via a stratagem that might even satisfy right wing and
"Neocon" interests through an apparent willingness to use force to advance freedom.

The obvious consequence is that we cannot remain a referee while
giving up sovereignty to the UN, especially when no other powerful
competing nation is doing it. In its pure form, the doctrine is based upon
the fantasy of a one-world government which strips America of all that
defines it. Yet, as we have seen, the General Assembly is becoming a
wholly-owned subsidiary of the OIC, and has much of the agenda of the
International Institutional Jihad that is seeking our transformation or demise. Our advance, even one small step in this direction, is one giant
leap toward the destruction of everything Western Civilization holds dear.

Obama's approach is evidence of how his administration has been
somewhat aligned with our Islamic Enemy, not fighting against it. Our

Islamic Enemy will never subject the supreme law of Allah to any international institution unless that institution itself is subject to Islamic law. If that would ever happen, it would constitute a *de facto* transformation of the UN into the long-desired world Caliphate.

Nor is this matter restricted to issues involving the use of US force. Rather, US sovereignty is increasingly being handed over to the "international community" through the deterioration of the US economy. As US debt and deficits grow wild—seemingly without foreseeable end—dollar issuance fast becomes the only weapon left in the Federal Reserve's arsenal. Ultimately, as with past declines of "empires," the dollar's role as the world's reserve currency may be challenged both by enemies of the United States as well as by allies who must nonetheless protect their own asset values. Iran has called out for the end of the dollar and various Gulf States have been evaluating strategies to transact oil sales without using the dollar. Destroying the US economy through destroying the value of the dollar sits high on the agenda of our Islamic Enemy. Transferring more of its sovereignty and ability to act independently within the "international community" will simply handcuff the United States, making it unable to deal effectively with such a challenge, precisely at the time it will need flexibility the most.

Within America, Obama is labeled a "redistributionist" for his interest in, as he put it, spreading "the wealth around" through increasing taxes to fund large social programs. Yet Obama's interests, in full conformity with the radical Left, are much grander than mere domestic budget considerations. His policies, on a global level, seek to redistribute to the world much of what Americans value in their nation—its wealth, power, charity, sovereignty, leadership and exceptionalism. Emanating in large part from the narrative that America illegitimately obtained its status, Western Guilt and other Control Factor mechanisms contribute to the goal to move America out of being the world's richest and most powerful singular leader in the world to simply becoming one nation among many—the planned obsolescence of American greatness which the Far Left despises; all toward a vision in one way or another of a one world government. While some today debate America's "decline" and others define a new era of "Post-America," the objective of this "Global Redistributionism" is clear and it is influencing in the most dangerous ways our ability to adequately confront our Islamic Enemy.

Perhaps the Wilsonian progressive inclination to legislate brute force out of world conflict will finally prove achievable. The UN, with all its efforts at regulating warfare and installing a global justice system to which parties will eventually surrender their sovereignty, is the modern embodiment of the longed-for notion of global peace. While the development of the UN has mostly failed up until now, it continues in large part because the Control Factor has patience. This Control Factor fantasy is that "civilization" is so compelling that it will naturally spread the values of self-preservation to the point that it will be able to sustain itself without any recourse to force.

The fantasy shares certain features with the various paradises that Leftists have dreamed of for centuries, and helps us understand the ever-more noticeable convergence of interests between the Far Left and our Islamic Enemy. The foundations of the systems valued by the Far Left and the expressions of Islam favored by our Islamic Enemy all rest on the promise of a collective future world of splendor. However, as cogently explained by Jamie Glazov in *United in Hate,* and by Andrew McCarthy in *The Grand Jihad*, this paradise first requires the full destruction our existing society. That is the proximate objective of these policies, which are too dangerous for us to ignore. Western Civilization is still too frail and fragile to survive by itself.

The Fragility of Western Civilization

Western Civilization, and particularly the United States, is often mistakenly taken for granted. Their uniqueness and the special circumstances from which they were created are gifts we need to cherish.

Benjamin Franklin understood this in the case of America in his essay *What July 4th Means to Me*[34] as he wrote, "The manner in which the whole of this business was conducted was such a miracle in human affairs, that if I had not been in the midst of it, and seen all the movements, I could not have comprehended how it was effected." Franklin attributed the miracle to God and implored us, "may our future conduct manifest gratitude."

Franklin continued, "It is a singular thing in the history of mankind that a great people have had the opportunity of forming a government for themselves. We are making experiment in politics." He also recognized America's exceptionalism continuing, "Only a virtuous people are capable of freedom. As nations become corrupt and vicious, they have more need of masters. But America is too enlightened to be enslaved."

Yet, is the Control Factor endangering that enlightenment? The greatness that Western Civilization has conferred upon generation after generation often disguises the frailty that exists just below its surface.

Principles are critical to all civilizations. Yet those principles are fragile in the face of contrary ideas embedded in various expressions of Islam that seek a "civilization alternative." Like a biological threat in a horror film, thought forms that hold sway over our Islamic Enemy require extraordinary measures to be uprooted and defeated. They are virulently contagious, especially when propagated by well-funded and motivated community leaders through culturally attuned families of young, impressionable subjects. The virus is especially deadly when seeded within communities that follow the directive to reproduce as rapidly as possible to spread through demographic warfare.

Again, this is to distinguish Muslims as human beings from the viral ideas that some of them spread. A civilization can travel the long route to recognize the value of each and every human being regardless of religious belief. It tends to falter, however, if it values mortally destructive and virulent belief systems more than it values its own protection. Like a dedicated medical practitioner, it can make every effort possible to differentiate the living body from its viral invader. At some point, however, destroying the virus must take precedence, and that often requires destroying infected bodies.

Western Civilization has only been able to sustain itself *because* of the use of force. Andrew Bostom's 6/5/11 post[35] (pointing out how historically the mosque has served as Islam's barracks and recruiting office) reminds us of John Quincy Adams' take on Western Civilization's vulnerability to our Islamic Enemy. Adams, recognizing in 1829 what the Control Factor today struggles to have us forget said, ". . . he [Muhammad] declared undistinguishing and exterminating war, as part of his religion, against all the rest of mankind. . . . The precept of the Koran is, perpetual war against all who deny, that Mahomet is the prophet of God."

And in 1916, Theodore Roosevelt described the history as:

The civilization of Europe, America, and Australia exists today because of the victories of civilized man over the enemies of civilization . . . [including] those of Charles Martel in he 8th century [over Arab jihadists] and those of John Sobieski in the 17th century [over Ottoman Turkish jihadists]. During the thousand years that included the careers of the Frankish soldier [Martel] and the Polish king [Sobieski], the Christians of Asia and Africa proved unable to wage successful war with the Moslem conquerors; and in consequence Christianity practically vanished from the two continents; and today nobody can find in them any "social values" whatever, in the sense in which we use the words, so far as the sphere of Mohammedan influence [is] concerned. . . .

It is force, not some higher concept or principle, which has kept civilization intact and preserved it under threat. Denying this is the Control Factor's formidable foolery, and will ensure the destruction of civilization as we know it. Michael Oren's book *Power, Faith, and Fantasy*, reminds us of America's own choice in the early 1800s to employ force when it stood up to militant Islamic forces in North Africa. Then as now, the Barbary pirates were obeying the instructions of Islam. From Thomas Jefferson to Winston Churchill, some of the modern West's greatest minds have seen clearly the threat we face today, and have understood the necessity of fighting forcefully and promptly. They needed no Inner Jihad to grasp the obvious. Nor did basic principles of religious freedom and democratic principles serve to inhibit their actions.

Western Civilization could be viewed as utilizing the "suspension of force," a voluntary pause, for as long as it can until it is challenged. This is not very different from the Roman notion of "bellum interruptus" or that period between wars which itself implies that war is a permanent part of life. In this sense, civilization's intermittent periods of peace are luxuries that never last long enough not to be defined by force. This concept seems little different from the Islamic "War of the Houses," in which the war is inevitable, the "natural and permanent relationship" as Bernard Lewis has said, and merely managed through intermittent periods of ceasefires on the model of the Treaty of Hudabaya. Nonetheless, common uses of the term *civilization* tend to value the periods of suspension of force.

The suspension of force as a means to resolve conflicts becomes increasingly attractive as new generations forget or never learn for themselves the realities of the law of the jungle and the barbarism experienced by their ancestors. This is evident among modern European and American youth. The luxury of periods of peace is taken for granted. Civilization is forced to forfeit more and more in an effort to sustain these periods. America in particular has become so accustomed to this luxury, regarding itself first as a superpower, and then as *the* superpower, that it has forgotten how easily its good fortune can be lost. Just ask the United Kingdom or other empires—including Islam of centuries past—that have fallen into decline.

Mark Steyn deftly speaks of how Americans delude themselves that the coming "decline" of the West will occur in slow, comfortable stages that will be easy for us to adjust to, similar to what the British experienced in the twentieth century. What we might call the "Easy Decline" fantasy is recklessly dangerous, since all indications are that if we do not fight with all our power to preserve our civilization, the havoc we will face will be quick, severe, and irreversible as our power is transferred elsewhere—more like the Japanese earthquake and tsunami of 2011 than the eons of erosion required to wear down the Rocky Mountains.

From a different angle, the connectivity and technological advances in a more globalized community have led to an increasingly volatile "marketplace of the political." More people than ever are able to evaluate and consume the competing ideas of democracy, capitalism, socialism, Marxism, Islamism, and all the other available *isms*. Just as Islam uses its *dawa* to recruit converts, so too does Western Judeo-Christian civilization use its assets to help bring in new "customers."

Yet as these tools—which include wealth, resources, educational superiority, and opportunities for advancement—begin their decline on the world stage, many customers will look elsewhere. Major businesses that were the household names of yesterday have now vanished from the scene. There is no law of physics that prohibits Western Civilization from surprising us with an abrupt and ominous fall if we fail to do what is necessary to support it.

The House of Islam tends to avoid war or rebellion when it has no power. It takes the long view and retreats, only to rise again when victory becomes possible. After the collapse of the Ottoman Empire at the end of World War I, Islam was left with limited power. The discovery of vast oil reserves in Islamic lands at the same time that Western industrial countries required ever-greater supplies of it, coupled with a population explosion, the availability of weapons, and intercommunication with the civilized world, put Islam on the rise throughout the latter half of the twentieth century.

One of the values of the Turnaround Moment in the horror film lies in the opportunity for the audience to identify with the hero and feel along with him that it has actually confronted and defeated a threat. It allows the audience to displace its own personal threats and momentarily seem to rise above them, affording a sense of great victory and power at its conclusion. The audience knows there is an end to the film. It knows that no matter how frightening the scenes become, the end will arrive, and it can walk out of the theater unscathed.

The Control Factor, however, does all it can to delay the real Turnaround Moment. It attempts to sell the notion that there is no serious threat, or that if there is a threat, it can be addressed when necessary, and that avoiding any Turnaround Moment maximizes the chance for a successful final act of cherished "peace." It simultaneously gives us the same comfort provided the cinema audience that eventually this horror will end and all will be fine.

From a different perspective, pain in its various forms is a necessary part of life. According to well-known adages, avoiding dealing with pain most often results in greater difficulties later. In a fiscal analogy, the Austrian School of economic theory suggests that—contrary to the Obama administration's assertions—anesthetizing the pain of a recession with excessive government spending and money creation will only increase the injurious effects, and lead to an even more devastating, even deferred, depression. Extending the analogy to international conflicts: the failure to confront an enemy that seeks our annihilation will only magnify the inevitable destruction. Delaying the Turnaround Moment may temporarily avoid pain, but carries a much greater long-term cost.

Western Civilization is facing another form of decline through demographic change. A popular YouTube video entitled "Muslim Demographics in Europe"[36] has been widely circulated. It must be made clear that sources for the data cited are missing and open to question. Nonetheless, the fundamental point is relevant, regardless of the specific numbers.

The video argues that no civilization can sustain itself with a fertility rate less than 2.1 children per woman, and that the European population is collapsing, as its rates are well below this target. Meanwhile, European Muslim fertility rates are significantly greater than 2.1. Eventually, therefore, European countries will have Muslim majorities and be under Islamic control.

Demographics as a weapon is a potent and time-hallowed component of *jihad* by *dawa*. The Palestinians have also used the threat of their eventual demographic takeover of Israel to affect Israeli policymakers. Libyan leader Colonel Muammar Qaddafi has famously stated that "We have 50 million Muslims in Europe. There are signs that Allah will grant victory to Islam in Europe without swords, guns, or conquest. We don't need terrorists or homicide bombers. The 50-plus million Muslims in Europe will turn it into a Muslim continent within a few decades. . . . Europe is in a predicament and so is America. They should agree to become Islamic in the course of time, or else declare war on the Muslims."[37]

While America is far behind Europe in Muslim population levels, it seems to have started down the same path. And powerful deleterious effects emerge at population levels much lower than a majority: the power of a negative voting bloc; the ability to organize vociferous masses of people to claim victimhood; the wherewithal to target, isolate, and chip away at specific communities; and the push to commandeer legislative, lobbying and lawfare activities. All of these tactics can be marshaled at relatively low group population levels.

Regardless of numbers, however, the point is that Western Civilization is more fragile and vulnerable than we would like to think.

Current technology and global connectivity have granted smaller and less organized armies and collections of individuals the capability of inflicting massive damage on far greater powers. The threat of an Electromagnetic Pulse (EMP) as a weapon has moved closer to center stage in the arsenal of some of our enemies. One form of EMP attack occurs when a nuclear device is detonated at high altitudes. Energy waves are spread across the area below resulting in the destruction of all unprotected electronic equipment and electrical grids. If, for instance, Iran or some al-Qaeda group were to anchor a small boat twelve miles off America's east coast, launch from it a primitive scud missile with a nuclear device, and cause it to detonate many miles above, the eastern half of our nation could lose much of its modern technology. We could literally be sent back to the early nineteenth century, with no electricity, cars, modern communications, etc.,—just as committed Muslims desire. Additionally, because death would result only indirectly from the loss of modern life (as opposed to the radiation itself) greater support for such an attack could be obtained from imams who might otherwise oppose any unprovoked offensive *jihad*.

It should be noted that in the summer of 2010, Iran tested a missile which exploded in mid-air. The press described the test as a failure. That would be true if the goal was a traditional missile test. The same facts, however, support a very successful test, however, of an EMP device detonating at high altitudes. As Ken Timmerman describes in his 6/16/11

Newsmax article,[38] North Korea has been miniaturizing its nuclear warhead design so that it can be placed on a ballistic missile. It is alleged that this Russian technology had leaked to North Korea and that it has tested it in 2006 and 2009. Iran is North Korea's nuclear development partner and many suggest that Iran has obtained and tested a very "super-EMP" technology.

Alternatively, the possibility of a suitcase nuclear device or powerful chemical or biological agents falling into the hands of terrorists has become much more plausible in the years since 9/11. The profound power of connectivity lowers the barriers to entry for any motivated terrorist or activist. As witnessed in the Arab protests in 2011, previously unnoticed leaders can more easily bring about unpredictable and overwhelming change—for good or ill.

The status of "superpower" loses much of its relevance in the face of these kinds of modern technological advances. Nonetheless, a superpower becomes accustomed to the belief (the "Lone Superpower" fantasy) that when its back is against the wall and the Turnaround Moment arrives, it will have the capability to manage the outcome. The Control Factor goes to extraordinary lengths to ensure that Western thought takes this capability for granted.

This idea, however, is proving increasingly false every day. American offensive and defensive superiority over much of the rest of the world is evaporating. As distasteful as it may be to progressives, American dominance has been established and enforced by fear—the communication of a capability to exert overwhelming force in our national interests.

Our efforts to obtain international approval coupled with our difficulties in combating terrorism and rising rogue states have severely diminished our ability to wield such a powerful sword today. A similar phenomenon may be observed in the revolutions spreading across the Arab world. As soon as the people see that their despot—Ben-Ali, Mubarak, Qaddafi, to name a few—has difficulty standing up to a challenge to his authority, his ability to wield power immediately vanishes. Chinks in his armor prove inviting to those who would unseat him.

America's 2008 "financial crisis" exposed the lessons of "moral hazard"—that failing to address and absorb the consequences of a risky situation leads to greater risky behavior and more devastating consequences in the future. Similarly, our failure to deal with the realities of the "War of the Houses" is raising the stakes of continued failure to existential levels. What we have not addressed for decades will hurt us in exponentially greater ways in the future. The sooner we face the challenge and endure whatever consequences arise, the greater our chances for survival.

To protect against the "civilization alternative" from within, much of the nation must simultaneously comprehend the threat and elect leaders who will guide the nation through the fight, a lengthy process requiring significant effort and funding, which is, of necessity, difficult to assemble. The luxury of suspending the use of force—martial as well as that required to fight the Civilization Jihad—will inevitably disappear. This ominous prospect should re-ignite an old common sense principle: fight sooner rather than later, while Western Civilization still has the advantage.

Like the horror film in which the threat invades one's house or body, the greatest tragedy lies in the failure to summon the will to fight when the odds are in one's favor. Western Civilization, so taken for granted, is truly vulnerable in today's world. Its frailty must be quickly recognized and all efforts mobilized to protect it.

Chapter 12

Finale

A month or so after the Cairo protests of 2011, a progressive young American from New York City said, "I've been thinking about the Muslim Brotherhood, and it's not so bad." Nothing sums up the Control Factor at work more concisely. The young woman knew little about the subject; she had merely heard others discussing whether the Brotherhood would drive Egypt's future and had assumed it was simply just one of many groups doing what groups do—supporting its own cause. When she learned that the Brotherhood might represent an ominous threat, her fear came up and her Control Factor kicked in. It "thought" about it and concluded that the Brotherhood is "not so bad."

Like any religious or spiritual discipline, the Inner Jihad must be exercised constantly. We must become as relentless in its pursuit as our Islamic Enemy is in its own. The Inner Jihad must be tended to over and over again until it has become habit and second nature. Learning to say "No" to everything the Control Factor proposes is the most critical weapon we must develop to win on the internal battlefield.

Remember, the Control Factor is an active and continuous process. It is active in that it constantly attempts to formulate our perceptions and beliefs in order to allow us to feel more in control or that control is easily obtainable. It is continuous in that, even if combated, it rises again at every opportunity to accomplish its purpose. In this sense, the Inner Jihad resembles the game "whack-a-mole:" just when one thinks he has addressed one Control Factor maneuver, another is sure to pop up in its place.

The Inner Jihad is practiced in layers. We reach one level of under-standing and think we have grasped the issues in full. Then the Control Factor forces itself upon us in new and more devious ways, and the Inner Jihad is required in even deeper form. At times the battle seems manage-able, at others more daunting. Like most progress, the Inner Jihad pro-ceeds in steps, forward and backward, until we become comfortable with our increasing understanding of the threat facing us.

The Control Factor exists to convince us we are in control of that which we are not. That is its mandate. The Control Factor will only lead to more chaos, disorder, and our eventual destruction if it is not carefully understood, monitored, and managed. Our Islamic Enemy will not stop, has endless patience, and desires nothing short of our submission or demise. Just as in the most terrifying horror film, it keeps coming at us, and it confounds our efforts to find a civilized way to make it disappear.

The Inner Jihad is focused on the internal battlefield, the mental theater. Our temptation is to dismiss its relevance by jumping directly to questions such as, "What policy or military strategies are being sug-gested here?" or "Forget all of this mental focus, what actions are being promoted?" or "Isn't 'soft power' preferable to 'hard power' in these cases?"

As sensible as this focus might seem, it can be one of the Control Factor's most devious and compelling maneuvers. Continually asking, "What do we do?"—obviously the most relevant question on the external battlefield—can be part of the Control Factor syndrome in the mental theater. This question reinforces the idea that there is something wrong with wholeheartedly fighting for our own survival, thus causing us to search for a different response.

The Control Factor ensures that strategies that involve transferring responsibility back to its proper place are perceived negatively. When any act of mirroring is considered, it will often appear extreme, discon-nected from all prior acts, and dangerous. Strategy considerations that might arise with a more tamed Control Factor might include:

- Whether pre-emptive war should be US policy with Iran
- Whether to abandon the United Nations or at least force major reforms upon it
- Whether to establish true energy independence immediately
- Whether to place restrictions on Muslim activities and/or pres-ence in the United States

- Whether to investigate all aspects of the Civilization Jihad being conducted in America today and pass laws to prevent its operations
- Whether to terminate relations with countries that embody our Islamic Enemy

It is important to re-emphasize that the effective conduct of the "war" on the external battlefield is not the subject here. That issue is fraught with complexity and, as is often the case with wars, much of what is initially planned will prove ineffective, and much of what was never foreseen may prove vital. This is especially true when dealing with institutional perspectives, such as those long held by the State Department, the Pentagon, and the CIA. To push any meaningful changes through such institutions takes time and will, two of the scarcest resources available when most needed. When a "free" press is added to the equation, adjustment is all the more difficult.

President Bush had great difficulty, and faced political sabotage and many other obstacles from all organs of the government, when he tried to put the nation on a "war footing." History shows that severe hardship is required before the nation can marshal the nerve to make the policy changes necessary to confront the threats we face. This is precisely why the Inner Jihad on the internal battlefield is so relevant: it seeks to strengthen our will sooner rather than later, preferably before irreversible destruction has awakened us. It simply took too long for Westerners to realize Sir Winston Churchill was correct about the Nazi threat.

It is critical to remember that the two battlefields are intimately connected. The best strategies in the external theater will emerge *only after* the mental theater is well purged of the effects of the Control Factor. Otherwise, any policy will be interpreted under the same Control Factor perspectives and thus be infected by the same distortions and denials. Indeed, until a critical mass has developed, and enough of our Control Factors have been held in check, the viable support system necessary to maintain consistent action will not emerge. As more and more of us become properly prepared by our Inner Jihads and attain a commonality of purpose, *how* to act will be much easier to address. Absent a Pearl Harbor or 9/11 to "bring us together," this process must evolve naturally.

Unfortunately, we cannot rely on a slow evolution to save us from the next event. The enemy is progressing too rapidly and becoming exponentially more dangerous. And America's many other struggles-economic pressures, drug and energy dependence, border invasion to name a few- its vulnerability is greatly increased. Accelerating the process through the Inner Jihad has become a necessity.

Western political directives have assiduously avoided any language of "Holy War," as it is believed that such references would only incite anger and hatred throughout the Islamic world. President Obama has insisted that America is not and will *never* be "at war" with Islam.[1] This is pure Control Factor logic at work which can only lead us toward dhimmitude. To declare we will never be at war with Islam is an announcement of unconditional surrender. To the contrary, we are "Dar al-Harb," the "House of War," because *they* say we are. It is a "Holy War" because *they* attach it to Islam and to "religion." We must be able to mirror their language of war and operate within it rather than hide from the facts and pretend something else is meant by it.

The simple reality is that we are locked in a long-term Holy War precisely because Islam commands and claims a Holy War, and war leads only to victory or surrender. We have the responsibility to make sure it is not our "end times" precisely because our Islamic Enemy says and wills it to be "end times" for themselves.

Two very different gods are leading much of the world today. One of them—whether understood as a religious figure, as a set of values, as governmental principle, or even as a morality drawn from atheism—places value on individual efforts to embody the values of love, forgiveness, redemption, pluralism, tolerance, freedom of conscience, and mutual respect for all, even those of other faiths. The other places value only on his community, and is hateful towards those who fail to submit to him. While Islam argues that submission is the highest of all principles, and therefore it is most "loving" of Allah to insist on such submission, this logic is out of step with the non-Islamic world. And since Islamic scripture portrays these two visions of god at war with each other, there is no avoiding "Holy War." To be blunt: Get used to it!

In effect, the two gods are battling over two documents: The US Constitution versus the *Koran*. Each instructs its adherents on how to construct and maintain full polities. One document serves the individual, while the other pits the Ummah in service to Allah. One favors life, liberty, and the pursuit of happiness in this life; the other submission, the spreading of *Shariah* and the afterlife in Paradise. One leans toward capitalism and the right of the individual to succeed or fail; the other places ultimate value in the collective Ummah. One promotes the freedom of the individual to make decisions; the other commands submission to decisions Allah has already made. One looks to the consent of the governed to protect the inalienable rights granted by the Creator; the other deems all authority as the realm of Allah, with consent required but utilized simply to enforce the rights of Allah.

From an alternate perspective, this battle reflects the age old conflict between the individual and the collective. The US Constitution seeks to protect the rights of the individual with certain agreed upon limitations to respect certain needs of the collective. Over centuries, interpretations have expanded the rights of the collective but the clear power of the Constitution lies in its promotion of the individual. Islam, on the other hand, remains fully subservient to Allah's wish to create one worldwide collective. The individual has meaning only in so far as he furthers this ultimate vision.

Various compromises can be made by either god to partially accommodate the other but these efforts are just that: accommodation. There is no way to reconcile the two while remaining true to one or the other.

It would be foolish, however, to overlook what is common to both—devotion. The extent to which each is adhered to is a measure of the impossibility of true reconciliation. Should such devotion to principle ever recede, one side or the other would become open to integration into the other. In such a case, however, we would no longer be dealing with one or the other god as they have expressed themselves to date.

The US Constitution states in Article 6 that it (and the laws and treaties which emanate from it) is the "Supreme Law of the Land." It also adds that no "religious test shall ever be required as a Qualification" for office. For our Islamic Enemy, however, only *Shariah* can be the supreme law of the land and, by definition, this is a religious test. There is no room to compromise despite all the efforts the Control Factor makes to reconcile. And just as any challenge to *Shariah* is deemed blasphemy, and sometimes punishable by death, any attempt to supplant the US Constitution as America's Supreme Law is seditious. *Shariah* does not merely present "unconstitutional" elements; it *is*, as Frank Gaffney says, "anti-Constitutional."

The critical impasse can be stated simply: Western Civilization is based in part on the belief in permanent, pluralistic, mutual tolerance of each other. In contrast, Islam is intolerant of anything other than Islam. The West is thus left with the paradox that it must tolerate the intolerant and foolishly hope the intolerant will tolerate what it finds intolerable.

This paradox also expresses itself in the notion that the West must afford Islam the freedom to deny freedoms to others. The Civilization Jihad demands that our Constitution give freedom to that which seeks to destroy it and end the freedoms it bestows upon us. Our constitution simply lacks the necessary protections against those who cleverly seek to use it to destroy it.

As George Santayana famously summarized, "The overarching duty of a tolerant man is to be intolerant of intolerance."[2] The paradoxical implication is that our civilization may ultimately be forced to use near-barbaric means to protect itself against barbarism.

The game itself is asymmetrical. Tolerance is weaker and less assertive than intolerance. Throughout history, intolerance has been able to eradicate tolerance but it has yet to be shown that tolerance can eradicate intolerance over the long term.

Multiculturalism, a fantasy that has gripped the West for decades, embodies this very paradox. A culture defines its own boundaries, that which it accepts and that which it forbids. A culture may incorporate a wide variety of tastes and styles, art forms and beliefs. It may place value on the vast societal expressions taking place around the globe and import and integrate whatever aspects it chooses. It may even take pride in its "openness." Any true integration, however, must necessarily take place under an overriding set of principles and identity. A culture cannot become many cultures and simultaneously express contradictory premises. And it cannot tolerate that which *fails* to tolerate these core principles.

Our culture takes great pride in advancing the concept of "diversity" and all of its related forms. A nadir of ghoulish "diversity"—its virtual parody—was reached when General George W. Casey Jr., responding to the Fort Hood terror attack, was more concerned that a backlash might be a greater threat to our diversity than even the carnage wreaked by Major Hasan. Casey said, "Our diversity, not only in our Army, but in our country, is a strength. And as horrific as this tragedy was, if our diversity becomes a casualty, I think that is worse."[3]

Premised on the equality of all, this ideal of "diversity" conflicts directly with Islam which favors Muslims and only Muslims. While the Western Left idolizes diverse lifestyles and belief systems, including those of gays, atheists, communists, and socialists, our Islamic Enemy would destroy each of these diverse "idolators." Opening our system equally and evenly to those who wish it closed arrives at the same paradoxical end.

America has accomplished much along the long march to eliminate discrimination, so much so that any suggestion of discrimination today is frowned upon, even if constitutionally acceptable. Islam, conversely, is premised on discrimination based upon religious identity. Irrespective of apologists' sugar coating, Islamic history is a tale of fundamental hatred for all kuffar, a hatred embedded in its teaching, and embellished by the many cultures which Islam has dominated. Some hypothesize that the hatred manifested by its discrimination arises in part from envy of the surrounding world—from Mohammed's time through to modern times—and in part from the comfort and identity it provides. Not only has there been no comparable long march to dispel this hatred in the Islamic world; modern Islamic trends show a worldwide strengthening not just of anti-Semitism, but of the essential loathing of all non-Muslims as well. The Muslim world would have to become very different, entailing a monumental effort, if it were ever seriously to attempt to rid itself of this fundamental hatred which has yielded so much for it.

Nor is this tension new. More of the excerpts from John Quincy Adams' essays on Islam as cited in the Center for Security Policy's *Shariah: The Threat to America,* are self explanatory:

> This appeal to the natural hatred of the Musselmen towards the infidels is in just accordance with the precepts of the Quran. The document [the Quran] does not attempt to disguise it, nor even pretend that the enmity of those whom it styles the infidels, is any other than the necessary consequences of the hatred borne by the Musselmen to them. The paragraph itself, is a forcible example of the contrasted character of the two religions.

> The fundamental doctrine of the Christian religion is the extirpation of hatred from the human heart. It forbids the exercise of it, even towards enemies. There is no denomination of Christians, which denies or misunderstands this doctrine. All understand it alike—all acknowledge its obligation; and however imperfectly, in the purposes of Divine Providence, its efficacy has been shown in the practice of Christians, it has not been wholly inoperative upon them. Its effect has been upon the manners of nations. It has mitigated the horrors of war—it has softened the features of slavery—it has humanized the intercourse of social life.

> The unqualified acknowledgement of a duty does not. Indeed, suffice to insure its performance. Hatred is yet a passion, but too powerful

upon the hearts of Christians. Yet they cannot indulge it, except by the sacrifice of their principles, and the conscious violations of their duties. No state paper from a Christian hand, could, without trampling the precepts of its Lord and Master, have commenced by an open proclamation of hatred to any portion of the human race. The Ottoman lays it down as the foundation of his discourse.[4]

The separation of church and state lies at the core of our constitutional rights, irrespective of many of the Founders' deeply religious leanings. More specifically, it is not merely one of many principles engaged by the Founders; it is a foundational principle embedded in our modern understanding of "religion." Religion has largely evolved into a private practice as long as it does not interfere with the rights of others. Yet "religion" as a concept utilized by our Islamic Enemy is *not* a private matter but *the* central organizing principle for all of life (and death).

Even more problematic, how do we use the state to properly insulate itself from the mosque when the state is controlled by those who recognize no such difference and in fact believe it a violation of both religion and law to separate the two?

Individual rights demand individual responsibility. Responsibility, that is, must be placed appropriately. Men are responsible for their own lusts, not the women who become the objects of such lust. Individuals themselves are responsible for their own material well-being or the lack thereof, not the government or "the Jews." Local and national leaders are responsible for conditions, not Israel or America. *Where* to place responsibility is the critical dispute underlying the tension between the Islamic world and the West in modern times. It also provides another perspective on individual rights versus those of the Ummah and Allah.

Our rights, including the right to speak freely, cannot be used by those who seek to bar speech that offends or is forbidden. Allowing speech to advance the elimination of speech contradicts the core of our constitution. More significantly, how does our system, based on advancing individual rights, survive the group efforts of those who recognize no individual rights, only the rights of the Ummah to serve Allah instead?

Freedom of speech is Western Civilization's most necessary and potent weapon. Many commentaries define the struggle with our Islamic Enemy as a "battle of ideas." As long as speech is allowed to flourish, the battle is winnable. When even the smallest of ideas is denied expression, however, the balance of power is shifted significantly.

Freedom of religion must include the freedom to choose and to leave any religion, and to abandon religion entirely. As discussed earlier, the famous Koranic injunction of the Meccan period, "There is no compulsion in religion," has been used by some as commanding that Islam cannot be forced upon anyone. This does not, however, obfuscate the fact that there are clear consequences to the choice to not be a believer, including death or *dhimmi* status. In the hands of apologists, this has been twisted into more of a statement about freedom than it is about religion, as it overlooks the consequences of the failures to make the proper Islamic choice.

Even "religion" raises concern. Given that *Shariah* controls every aspect of society, including affairs of state and politics, Islam goes far beyond the modern Western concept of "religion." Since "peacefulness," "mutual tolerance," and separation from state activities are such deeply entrenched premises in our modern concept of "religion," perhaps Islam should fail to qualify as a religion at all. It may not deserve religious freedom or other constitutional protections.

The road to such a constitutional interpretation would be fraught with formidable challenges; nonetheless, it may be one of the few available approaches to resolving the paradoxes we face.

When should a call for the overthrow of the state, and the demand for a new law of the land lose constitutional protection? Why should embedding such things in a "religion" grant it immunity?

Furthermore, the Judeo-Christian notions of mutual respect, the Golden Rule, and forgiveness have served humanity well when mutually observed. Yet in the face of a more powerfully armed intolerance, they are easily vanquished.

How do Westerners, who treasure the sanctity of life, ever permit those who admittedly cherish death and hatred of others to impose such values upon us? As former Israeli Prime Minister Golda Meir famously remarked, "We will have peace with the Arabs when they love their children more than they hate us." While many Muslims certainly satisfy this condition, our Islamic Enemy is burned through with hate it knows not how to responsibly manage and is ultimately willing to destroy its children's bodies and minds to advance its cause.

"Turn the Other Cheek" is a supremely powerful spiritual principle with vast implications. It was not, however, intended as an operating principle or defense strategy for nations. Even Mahatma Gandhi recognized one's duty to serve in the military and with the police to protect the state as limitations on "non-violence."[5] And while Gandhi famously said "an eye for an eye makes the whole world blind," mirroring or a return to some form of "An Eye for an Eye" may be necessary to avoid the destruction inherent in "Submit or Give Me Your Neck."

Similarly, the compulsion to turn American decision-making over to international institutions, including even the power to opt out of such institutions, under the fantasy of creating a more unified, peaceful, and productive world will only lead to a more dangerous and impoverished one.

Our Islamic Enemy uses the temporary suspension of force to *re-arm*. The West has been using it to *disarm*, in an effort to submit itself further to global institutions that are progressively becoming the captives of our Islamic Enemy. Peace may, at least temporarily, advance this way. It would be, however, an *Islamic* peace.

These paradoxes are real. Much of the Control Factor's mission is to create the illusion that we can resolve them in one form or another in the world of thought and imagination. The wish is that if we can somehow resolve them in the arena of ideas, these incongruencies will no longer threaten us in the "real world." The problem is that they are fully *real* in the "real world." The immutable *Koran* says what it says, and the history of Islam is what it is. And most believers are carrying out the faith as they understand it: The House of Islam *is* at war with The House of War.

There is no efficient way to resolve these paradoxes without extensive compromise from one side or the other. The illusions of the Left and Obama to the contrary, there is no higher level to which to jump to create resolution. "Common ground" *cannot* be found. Our Constitution and way of life must be defended and, as we learn how to do so, we must recognize that we may be required to temporarily restrict the scope of our freedoms in order to protect our freedoms for the long term.

The fear that we might "lose ourselves" on the road to defending ourselves is just another Control Factor scheme to keep us from the difficult task of preserving our gifts: what we have and who we are. We will have plenty of time in the future to demonstrate who we are, once we secure the capacity and ability to do so. Otherwise we risk losing forever the capacity and ability to do so. For the time being, we must learn to defeat our Control Factors so that we can develop a single-minded focus on the war we are in—regardless of whether we chose it. We will lose ourselves if we do not.

These paradoxes are mirrored by a paradox of our own creation: all Control Factor attempts to create the illusion of control ensure that control is never obtained.

The conflict our Islamic Enemy poses for us is a zero-sum game and must be fought or allowed to destroy us. That simple conclusion and the clarity it embodies are ultimately what the Inner Jihad must lead us to. The sooner we get our Control Factors under our *own* control and give up our Western guilt, fantasies, and enabling roles, the better able we will be to deal competently with the threat that faces us.

The purpose of the Inner Jihad is to help us advance the Turnaround Moment so that we end the horror film sooner rather than later, limiting needless destruction as much as possible. Fighting effectively may entail certain compromises of our moral and ethical principles, as well as our beliefs about ourselves. It certainly entails forfeiting the pride we take in the illusory belief that we are devoid of any ruthless instinct. It entails understanding that ruthlessness demands an appreciation of our strengths and weaknesses, and the courage to put it all on the line.

It might further require limitations on the freedoms we take for granted and consider part of our national character. Until we eradicate the danger we face, such freedoms are a luxury we can ill afford. Our choice is no longer between the world as we once believed it to be and a long hard struggle to defeat our Islamic Enemy. The only choice remaining is whether we engage the struggle sooner, while we enjoy many advantages, or later, when we will have depleted much of what makes us strong.

Western Civilization is ill-equipped to fight on the three levels of Jihad conducted by our Islamic Enemy against us. The Violent Jihad is effective precisely because it is a difficult activity to prevent. Counter-terrorism and counterinsurgency strategies are evolving, but so are the capabilities of those in the Violent Jihad. As a "superpower," America has great confidence when fighting traditional wars against states. Non-state opponents, especially those backed by other states, present different obstacles, however. Our efforts to treat terrorism as a criminal activity forfeit many of the strengths necessary to provide us with a complete sense of security. We simply have not yet forged a successful, useful, and acceptable theory which blends war and criminal concepts to define the best ways to combat terrorism.

The Civilization Jihad uses our constitutional freedoms to destroy our freedoms. We have yet to create an effective response that secures enough popular support while passing constitutional muster; especially in an era where judicial trends are being lead by Control Factor maneuvers. Given America's hardened political polarities, speedy and effective change through judicial action, much less legislative action or constitutional amendment, is difficult to imagine.

Which value takes precedence when demographics, immigration, and *dawa* eventually lead a Western nation to face a substantial and antagonistic Muslim population: representative government or protecting the system? As the Muslim population grows, must their wishes be respected if their wish is for a "civilization alternative" to the one we now have?

Finally, as the International Institutional Jihad gathers force and the West's power begins to wane in the face of growing powers elsewhere, we are hard pressed to stand against powerful global trends institutionalizing principles that threaten our constitution. And as the Obama administration advances its "one-world" vision that is attractive to so many, which "one-world" will it ultimately turn out to be? In the face of such global movements, Western Civilization must make critical decisions about what it will and will not to be.

In short, we do not know yet how to fight—much less win—the war. We have been ignorant of the enemy and have barely begun to organize to confront it. This is the source of much of the true terror we feel that our Control Factors seek to abate. We would rather deny the war and all that fighting entails than face reality in all its horror. Until we silence our Control Factors, we will lack the conditions necessary to learn how to fight and win this war. Until enough of us have advanced our Inner Jihads will a consensus emerge to allow us to fight to win.

In 1941, Bernard Lewis was well aware of what was occurring around him in Europe. He describes the world then as extremely bleak. Yet he was more confident then than he is now. He says that back then we knew who we were, who the enemy was, and what we had to do. Today, we know so much less.

We could wait until every Control Factor denial and avoidance strategy has been exhausted and then try whatever "Hail Mary" choice remains—if any. Or we can fully accept that we do *not* control the threat we face, and refuse to entertain all thoughts that suggest otherwise.

Only then will we be able to marshal the collective will, creativity, and solidarity to formulate an acceptable path to victory. The choice is ours.

This is the call to engage in our Inner Jihads to combat the Control Factors so effective in keeping us from knowing who we are, who the enemy is, and what we must do.

We have reached our Turnaround Moment.

Any sensible audience would be exhorting us "Let's Roll!"

Endnotes

Chapter 1

1. Ayn Rand, A*yn Rand Answers: The Best of Her Q & A* (New York: New American Library, 2005), 78.

Chapter 2

1. Abudullah Yusuf Ali, *The Meaning of the Holy Qu'ran.* All Koranic citations are from this text unless otherwise noted.

2. Bill Warner, "Statistical Islam, Part 1 of 9," *Political Islam,* http://www.politicalislam.com/blog/statistical-islam-part-1-of-9/.

3. Prime Minister Recep Tayyip Erdogan, *Milliyet* (Turkey), August 21, 2007.

4. "Shahzad Gets Life Term for Times Square Bombing Attempt," *New York Times,* October 5, 2010.

5. Interview by Aaron Klein, WABC Radio, quoted in "*'Ground Zero' imam makes stunning terror comments,"* WorldNetDaily, June 20, 2010, http://www.wnd.com/?pageId=168797.

6. Mark Gabriel, *Culture Clash: Islam's War on America* (Lake Mary, FL: Frontline, 2007), viii-xvi.

7. Mordechai Kedar and David Yerushalmi, "Shari'a and Violence in American Mosques," *Middle East Quarterly* (Summer 2011).

8. Bernard Lewis, *The Political Language of Islam* (Chicago: University Of Chicago Press, 1991), 78.

9. Imam Feisal Rauf, "Letters from the Iman," *Wall Street Journal,* September 1, 2010.

10. Joel Gilbert, *Farewell Israel: Bush, Iran, and The Revolt of Islam* (Highway 61, 2007).

11. S. K. Malik, *The Quranic Concept of War* (Himalayan Books, 1986), 54.

12. Andrew G. Bostom, "Egyptian Muslim Brotherhood Democrats to Form 'Perfect Slavery to Allah Party,'" *American Thinker,* June 9, 2011, http://

www.americanthinker.com/blog/2011/06/egyptian_muslim_brotherhood_
democrats_to_form_perfect_slavery_to_allah_party.html.

13. Beverly Milton-Edward, *Islamic Politics in Palestine* (New York: St.
Martin's Press, 1996), 100.

Chapter 5

1. Mark A. Gabriel, *Islam and Terrorism* (Lake Mary, FL: Charisma
House, 2002), 148.

2. Barry Rubin, "Muslim Brotherhood Declares War on America; Will
America Notice?" *Rubin Report*, October 7, 2010, http://www.rubinreports.
blogspot.com/2010/10/muslim-brotherhood-declares-war-on.html.

3. Nihad Awad, "Muslims Pleased by Arrests, Caution Against Specula-
tions," *Islam Online*, October 25, 2002, http://www.islamonline.org/English/
News/.../article81a.shtmlþ

4. Elie Nakouzi, "Bush: All religions Pray to 'Same God,'" *WorldNetDaily*,
October 7, 2007, http://www.wnd.com/?pageId=43906.

5. Osama bin Laden, "Al Qaeda's Fatwa," *PBS NewsHour*, February 23,
1998, http://www.pbs.org/newshour/terrorism/international/fatwa_1998.html.

6. "Preamble to 1979 Iranian Constitution," Hanover College History
Department, history.hanover.edu/courses/excerpts/261ircon.html.

7. John Doyle, Sally Goldenberg, and Bruce Golding, "Defiant Times
Square Bomber Faisal Shahzad Sentenced to Life in Prison," *New York Post*,
October 5, 2010.

8. National Commission on Terrorist Attacks. *The 9/11 Commission Report: Final Report of the National Commission on Terrorist Attacks Upon the
United States* (New York: W. W. Norton & Company, 2004), 240.

9. Ken Timmerman, "Lawsuit: Iran Knew about 9/11 Attack," *Newsmax*,
May 19, 2011, http://www.newsmax.com/KenTimmerman/al-qaida-
osamabinladen-911-september11/2011/05/19/id/396993.

10. "Was Ft. Hood Shooter Taking Army-Administered Medication?"
Huffington Post, November 6, 2009 (updated March 18, 2010), http://www.
huffingtonpost.com/2009/11/06/fort-hood-shooting-provok_n_348740.html.

11. *Real Time with Bill Maher*, HBO, March 12, 2011.

12. Charles Krauthammer, "The Delusional Dean," *Washington Post*, December 5, 2003.

13. Cindy Adams, *New York Post*, August 14, 2006.

14. Andrew G. Bostom, "Jihad WarFrom the Prophet Muhammad to
Muhammad Atta," *Berean Publishers*, http://www.bereanpublishers.com/Cults/
Muslims/jihad_warfrom_the_prophet_muham.htm.

15. "Report Sheds Light on Hariri Murder," *Now Lebanon*, November 23,
2010, http://www.nowlebanon.com/NewsArchiveDetails.aspx?ID=217831.

16. Steve Emerson, "Islamists Dominate DOJ's List of Terror Prosecutions," *IPT News*, March 9, 2011, http://www.investigativeproject.org/2659/islamists-dominate-doj-list-of-terror-prosecutions.

17. Fareed Zakaria, "Al Qaeda is Over," *Time,* May 2, 2011.

18. Hillary Clinton, meets President of Pakistan Asif Ali Zardari in Islamabad, Pakistan on May 27, 2011.

19. President Barack Obama, "Remarks by the President on the Middle East and North Africa," U.S. Department of State, Washington, D.C., May 19, 2011. Full text at *TPM LiveWire*, http://tpmlivewire.talkingpointsmemo.com/2011/05/full-text-of-president-obamas-middle-east-speech.php#0_undefined,0.

20. Ayatullah Mahmud Talegani, Ayatullah Murtada Mutahhari, and Ali Shari'ati, *Jihad and Shahadat* [Struggle and Martyrdom in Islam] (North Haledon, NJ: Islamic Publications International, 1986), 21.

21. "Congressman Suggests People Will Don 'White Hoods' if Wilson not rebuked," *Fox News*, September 15, 2009, http://www.foxnews.com/politics/2009/09/15/congressman-suggests-people-don-white-hoods-wilson-rebuked/.

22. Benjamin Netanyahu. *Place Among the Nations* (New York: Bantam,1993), 130-183.

Chapter 6

1. U.S. Department of Homeland Security, The State of Environmental Justice in America 2010 Conference, December 21, 2010.

2. President Barack Obama, interview by *Al Arabiya* , January 27, 2009.

3. Sara Sorcher, "DNI Says 1 in 4 Prisoners Released From Guantanamo Bay Return to Terrorism," *National Journal,* December 8, 2010, http://www.nationaljournal.com/nationalsecurity/dni-says-1-in-4-prisoners-released-from-guantanamo-bay-return-to-terrorism-20101208.

4. Shelby Steele, "A Referendum on the Redeemer," *Wall Street Journal*, October 28, 2010.

5. *The Rachel Maddow Show*, MSNBC, March 22, 2011.

6. Terry Gilliam and Terry Jones, *Monty Python and the Holy Grail* (1975).

Chapter 7

1. Farnaz Fassihi, "Bombs Kill 39 in Iran," *Wall Street Journal*, December 16, 2010, http://online.wsj.com/article/SB10001424052748704828104576020940862594576.html.

2. Itamar Marcus and Barbara Crook, "Fayyad's Advisor Libels and Demonizes Israel," Palestinian Media Watch, October 13, 2010, http://www.palwatch.org/main.aspx?fi=157&doc_id=3365.

3. Muslim Brotherhood Supreme Guide: 'The U.S. Is Now Experiencing the Beginning of Its End'; 'Improvement and Change in the Muslim World Can Only Be Attained Through Jihad and Sacrifice,' U.S. and the Arab and Muslim World Special Dispatch No.3274. October 6, 2010.

4. David Bedein, "The PA's Fayad is No Moderate," *Israel National News*, September 25, 2009, http://www.israelnationalnews.com/Articles/Article.aspx/9075.

5. Steven Simpson, "The Truth About 'Palestine,'" *FrontPageMag.com*, July 13, 2010, http://frontpagemag.com/2010/07/13/the-truth-about-palestine/

6. Discover the Networks, profile of Mohammad Amin Al-Husseini, http://www.discoverthenetworks.org/individualProfile.asp?indid=2150.

7. Andrew G. Bostom, "Eygptian Democrats: The Victory of our Revolution Will Not Be Complete Without Liberation of Palestine," *American Thinker*, May 13, 2011, http://www.americanthinker.com/blog/2011/05/egyptian_democrats_the_victory.html.

8. President Barack Obama, "Remarks by the President on the Middle East and North Africa," U.S. Department of State, Washington, D.C., May 19, 2011. Full text at *TPM LiveWire*, http://tpmlivewire.talkingpointsmemo.com/2011/05/full-text-of-president-obamas-middle-east-speech.php#0_undefined,0.

9. Prime Minister Benjamin Netanyahu, address to U.S. Congress, May 24, 2011. Transcript published online by the *Washington Post*, http://www.washingtonpost.com/world/israeli-prime-minister-binyamin-netanyahus-address-to-congress/2011/05/24/AFWY5bAH_story.html.

10. Obama, Middle East speech, May 19, 2011. See note 8.

11. Thomas Friedman, "Bibi and Barack," *New York Times*, May 17, 2011, http://www.nytimes.com/2011/05/18/opinion/18friedman.html.

Chapter 8

1. Center for Security Policy, *Shariah Law and American State Courts: An Assessment of State Appellate Court Cases* (Washington, DC, May 20, 2011). Occasional paper series.

2. Mark A Gabriel. *Islam And Terrorism: What the Quran Really Teaches about Christianity, Violence and the Goals of the Islamic Jihad* (Lake Mary, FL: Frontline, 2002), 148-149

3. Bruce Lawrence, ed., *Messages to the World: The Statements of Osama bin Laden* (Verso, 2005).

4. Stuart Munckton, "Opinion Poll Names Chavez Most Popular Leader in Middle East," *Green Left Weekly*, May 30, 2009, http://www.greenleft.org.au/node/41750.

5. Jeff Zeleny, "Obama Clinches Nomination; First Black Candidate to Lead a Major Party Ticket," *New York Times*, June 3, 2008, http://www.nytimes.com/2008/06/04/us/politics/04elect.html.

6. Joshua Landis, "Clinton Calls Bashar al-Assad a 'Reformer'—Syria Lifts Emergency Law," *Syria Comment,* March 27, 2011, http://www.joshualandis.com/blog/?p=8822.

7. Eugene Robinson, interview on *Morning Joe*, MSNBC.

8. Thomas Friedman, "The Geo-Green Alternative," *New York Times,* January 30, 2005, http://www.nytimes.com/2005/01/30/opinion/30friedman.html.

9. Andrew C McCarthy, *The Grand Jihad: How Islam and the Left Sabotage America* (New York: Encounter, 2010), 146

10. President Barack Obama, interview on *Larry King Live*, CNN, quoted by *CBS News,* June 3, 2010, http://www.cbsnews.com/8301-503544_162-20006765-503544.html.

11. *Charlie Rose Show*, PBS, March 24, 2011.

12. Matthias Kuntzel. *Jihad and Jew-Hatred: Islamism, Nazism and the Roots of 9/11* (New York: Telos Press, 2007), 35.

13. Denis McDonough, "Partnering with Communities to Prevent Violent Extremism in America" (remarks, Sterling, VA, March 6, 2011). Transcript published online by the Council on Foreign Relations, http://www.cfr.org/terrorism/remarks-denis-mcdonough-deputy-national-security-advisor-partnering-communities-prevent-violent-extremism-america-march-2011/p24313.

Chapter 9

1. *60 Minutes*, CBS, September 30, 2001.

2. "Dr. Bill Warner Addresses Jonesboro, AR Act! for America," *Grendel Report*, June 23, 2011, http://www.grendelreport.posterous.com/dr-bill-warner-addresses-jonesboro-ar-act-for.

3. Imam Rauf, interview on *Larry King Live*, CNN, September 8, 2010, http://transcripts.cnn.com/TRANSCRIPTS/1009/08/lkl.01.html.

4. Itamar Marcus and Nan Jacques Zilberdik, "PA TV Attacks PMW: PMW Accused of 'Incitement' against the PA," Palestinian Media Watch, March 21, 2011, http://www.palwatch.org/main.aspx?fi=157&doc_id=4565.

5. The Investigative Project on Terrorism, "Brotherhood Assurances Not Backed by Track Record," *IPT News*, June 28, 2011, http://www.investigativeproject.org/3012/brotherhood-assurances-not-backed-by-track-record.

6. Ken Timmerman, "Obama Egypt Strategy Could Place US at Risk," *Newsmax*, January 31, 2011, http://www.newsmax.com/KenTimmerman/hosni-mubarak-iran-Mahmoud/2011/01/31/id/384496.

7. Alan M. Dershowitz, "Mishandling bin Laden's Body," *Wall Street Journal,* May 5, 2011, http://online.wsj.com/article/SB10001424052748703849204576303431557377492.html. See also: Anne Bayefsky, "Did the US Violate bin Laden's Rights?" *Fox News*, May 9, 2011, http://www.foxnews.com/opinion/2011/05/09/did-violate-bin-ladens-rights/, and Reuters, "Son Says bin Laden Sea Burial Demeans Family: Report," May 10, 2011, http://www.reuters.com/article/2011/05/10/us-binladen-son-statement-idUSTRE7495E720110510.

8. Andrew G. Bostom, "Did Naval Burial Ceremony for Bin Laden Curse Jews and Christians, and Confer Pardon and Paradise on the Muslim Mass

Murderer?" *American Thinker*, May 7, 2011, http://www.americanthinker.com/blog/2011/05/did_naval_burial_ceremony_for.html.

    9. Ruth R. Wisse, *If I Am Not For Myself . . . The Liberal Betrayal of the Jews* (New York: The Free Press, 1992), 122.

    10. Itamar Marcus and Nan Jacques Zilberdik, "PA: Conditions For Palestinians in Israeli Prisons Are Worse Than Jews' Conditions in 'The Auschwitzes'," Palestinian Media Watch, October 10, 2011, http://palwatch.org/main.aspx?fi=157&doc_id=5752.

Chapter 10

    1. Frank J. Gaffney Jr., "Waging the 'War of Ideas,'" Center for Security Policy, December 8, 2003, See also: "Al Qaeda's Secret Saudi Arabian Money, Influence and Money," *Al Qaeda Watch*, January 26, 2011, http://www.alqaedawatch.com/2011/01/al-qaedas-saudi-arabian-heritage-and.html.

    2. Martin Mawyer, *Homegrown Jihad: The Terrorist Camps Around the U.S.* (PRB Films/Christian Action Network, 2009).

    3. Art Moore, "Muslim Brotherhood 'Declares War' on U.S.," *WorldNet Daily,* October 12, 2010, http://www.wnd.com/?pageId=214245.

    4. Barry Rubin, "The Region Revolutions, Walk-Outs and Fatwas," *Jerusalem Post,* January 16, 2011, http://www.jpost.com/Opinion/Columnists/Article.aspx?id=203876.

    5. The Jewish Institute for National Security Affairs, "Al Qaeda, Other Terror Groups Swim in Global Sea of Saudi-Funded Wahhabi Institutions," *JINSA Online*, August 22, 2007, http://www.islamicpluralism.org/532/al-qaeda-other-terror-groups-swim-in-global-sea-of-saudi.

    6. Mordechai Kedar and David Yerushalmi, "Shari'a and Violence in American Mosques," *Middle East Quarterly* (Summer 2011).

    7. Clifford D. May, "A Hundred Years of War?" *National Review Online*, April 10, 2008, http://www.nationalreview.com/articles/224150/hundred-years-war/clifford-d-may#.

    8. Frank J Gaffney Jr., *Shariah: The Threat to America* (Washington, DC: Center for Security Policy, 2010), 74-75.

    9. Lorenzo Vidino, "The Muslim Brotherhood's Conquest of Europe," *Middle East Quarterly* 12, no. 1 (Winter 2005): 25-34. Published online by the Middle East Forum, http://www.meforum.org/687/the-muslim-brotherhoods-conquest-of-europe.

    10. Patrick Poole, "The Muslim Brotherhood 'Project,'" *FrontPageMag.com*, May 11, 2006, http://archive.frontpagemag.com/readArticle.aspx?ARTID=4476.

    11. Mohamed Akram, "An Explanatory Memorandum on the General Strategic Goal for the Brotherhood in North America," The Investigative Project on Terrorism, May 19, 1991, http://www.investigativeproject.org/document/id/20.

12. Frank J Gaffney Jr., *Shariah: The Threat to America.* (Washington, DC: Center for Security Policy, 2010), 74-75

13. Center for Security Policy, *Shariah Law and American State Courts: An Assessment of State Appellate Court Cases* (Washington, DC, May 20, 2011). Occasional paper series.

14. Stephen Collins Coughlin, "To Our Great Detriment: Ignoring What Extremists Say About Jihad" (unclassified thesis, National Defense Intelligence College).

15. Ned May, "Sentence First—Verdict Afterwards: The Persecution of Elisabeth Sabaditsch-Wolff," *Big Peace,* February 20, 2011, http://bigpeace. com/nmay/2011/02/20/sentence-first-verdict-afterwards-the-persecution-of-elisabeth-sabaditsch-wolff/.

16. International Free Press Society, "Shame on Denmark! Lars Hedegaard found guilty of hate speech," May 3, 2011, http://www.internationalfreepress society.org/2011/05/president-of-the-free-press-society-lars-hedegaard-declared-guilty-of-racist-statements/.

17. Phyllis Chesler, "Protecting Muslim Girls from Rape is Now a Crime in Europe," *NewsRealBlog,* May 7, 2011, http://www.newsrealblog.com/2011/05/07/protecting-muslim-girls-from-rape-is-now-a-crime-in-europe-1/.

18. International Free Press Society, "The Scandal of Danish Justice," December 12, 2010, http://www.internationalfreepresssociety.org/2010/12/the-scandal-of-danish-justice/.

19. Ann Snyder, "Eternal Vigilance in the Defense of Free Speech: An Interview with Lars Hedegaard," March 3, 2011.

20. Ayaan Hirsi Ali, "In Holland, Free Speech on Trial," *Wall Street Journal,* October 11, 2010, http://online.wsj.com/article/SB10001424052748704657 304575539872944767984.html.

21. Baron Bodissey, "The Dutch Law Used Against Geert Wilders," International Free Press Society, February 7, 2009, http://www.internationalfree presssociety.org/2009/02/the-dutch-law-used-against-geert-wilders/.

22. Thierry Baudet, "Thou Shalt Not Offend Islam," *City Journal,* January 19, 2011, http://www.city-journal.org/2011/eon0119tb.html.

23. Gilbert Kreijger and Aaron Gray-Block, "Dutch Populist Geert Wilders Acquitted of Hate Speech," Reuters, June 23, 2011, http://www.reuters.com/article/2011/06/23/us-dutch-wilders-idUSTRE75M10P20110623.

24. "Editorial: Freedom to Abuse?" *Arab News,* June 24, 2011, http://arabnews.com/opinion/editorial/article460891.ece.

25. See note 23.

26. See note 24.

27. Andrew G. Bostom, "A Warning to America: Geert Wilders in Nashville, Tennessee 5/12/11," *American Thinker,* May 13, 2011, http://www.americanthinker.com/blog/2011/05/a_warning_to_america_geert_wil.html. See also: Rhonda Robinson, "Geert Wilders Presents: 5 Steps Americans Must

Take to Avoid the Fate of Islamized Europe," *NewsRealBlog,* May 20, 2011, http://www.newsrealblog.com/2011/05/20/geert-wilders-presents-5-steps-americans-must-take-to-avoid-the-fate-of-islamized-europe-1/.

28. James Kirchick, "Europe the Intolerant," *Wall Street Journal,* October 12, 2010, http://online.wsj.com/article/SB10001424052748704696304575537950006608746.html.

29. Editorial, "Norway's Horror," *New York Times,* July 25, 2011, http://www.nytimes.com/2011/07/26/opinion/26tue2.html.

30. John F. Burns, "Cameron Criticizes 'Multiculturalism' in Britain," *New York Times,* February 6, 2011, http://www.nytimes.com/2011/02/06/world/europe/06britain.html.

31. Ryan Mauro, "Islamist Propaganda in the K-12 Classroom," *FrontPage Mag.com,* September 9, 2011, http://frontpagemag.com/2010/09/09/islamist-propaganda-for-american-students/.

32. Shariah Finance Watch, Center for Security Policy, "Meezan Bank holds 17th Shariah Supervisory Board Meeting–Or Is It a Jihadi Convention???" April 13, 2011, http://www.shariahfinancewatch.org/blog/2011/04/13/meezan-bank-holds-17th-shariah-supervisory-board-meeting-or-is-it-a-jihadi-convention/.

33. Rachel Ehrenfeld and Alyssa A. Lappen, "Jihad Economics and Islamic Banking," *Right Side News,* July 28, 2008, http://europenews.dk/en/node/12586.

34. Andrew Malcolm, "Barack Obama Issues Special Ramadan Message," Top of the Ticket, *Los Angeles Times,* August 11, 2010, http://latimesblogs.latimes.com/washington/2010/08/obama-ramadan-message.html.

35. Dan Slater, "Obama Advisor, Schiff Hardin Associate, Resigns Over Ties to Imam," *Wall Street Journal,* August 7, 2008, http://blogs.wsj.com/law/2008/08/07/obama-advisor-schiff-hardin-associate-resigns-over-ties-to-imam/. See also: Glenn R. Simpson and Amy Chozick, "Obama's Muslim Outreach Adviser Resigns," *Wall Street Journal,* October 6, 2008, http://online.wsj.com/article/SB121797906741214995.html.

36. Rashad Hussain and al-Husein N. Madhany, *Reformulating the Battle of Ideas: Understanding the Role of Islam in Counterterrorism Policy* (Washington, DC: Brookings Institution, August 2008), http://www.brookings.edu/papers/2008/08_counterterrorism_hussain.aspx.

37. "Exclusive: New Obama Envoy Has History of Engagement With U.S. Muslim Brotherhood; Called Al-Arian Case 'Politically Motivated Persecution,'" *Global Muslim Brotherhood Daily Report,* February 14, 2010, http://globalmbreport.org/?p=2173.

38. "Ex Black Panther Convicted of Murder," *CNN.com,* March 9, 2002, http://edition.cnn.com/2002/LAW/03/09/al.amin.verdict/index.html.

39. Paul M. Barrett, "One Imam Traces the Path of Islam in Black America," *Wall Street Journal,* October 24, 2003, http://online.wsj.com/article/0.,SB106694267937278700.00.html.

40. Robert Satloff. "Just Like Us! Really?" *Weekly Standard*, May 12, 2008, http://www.weeklystandard.com/Content/Public/Articles/000/000/015/066chpzg.asp.

41. "Obama OIC Representative to Participate in Conference with US Muslim Brotherhood," *Global Muslim Brotherhood Daily Report*, September 22, 2010, http://globalmbreport.org/?p=3474. See also: "Georgetown Academic 'Redefines' Jihad," *Global Muslim Brotherhood Daily Report*, February 24, 2008, http://globalmbreport.org/?p=582.

42. Robert Spencer, "Obama Adviser Loves Sharia" *Jihad Watch*, October 15, 2009, http://www.jihadwatch.org/2009/10/spencer-obama-adviser-loves-sharia.html.

43. "Sourcing Islam: Nuanced Reporting on a Contested Faith," panel discussion, 59th Annual Religious Newswriters Association (RNA) Annual Conference, September 20, 2008.

44. Ruth King, "Obama 'Faith Advisor' Dahlia Mogahed says US Not Worried About Muslim Brotherhood in Egypt," *Global Muslim Brotherhood Daily Report*, April 8, 2011, http://globalmbreport.org/?p=4165.

45. "Correction: Recent Post on Obama Faith Advisor Revised," *Global Muslim Brotherhood Daily Report*, April 20, 2011, http://globalmbreport.org/?cat=6.

46. Discover the Networks, profile of Maher Hathout, http://www.discoverthenetworks.org/individualProfile.asp?indid=1401.

47. Discover the Networks, group profile of Muslim Public Affairs Council (MPAC), http://discoverthenetworks.org/groupprofile.asp?grpid=6177. Also see the profile of this group by Stand4Facts: http://www.discoverthenetworks.org/Articles/mpactstand4facts25.html.

48. Aaron Klein. "Napolitano Adds Adviser with Less Ties to Terror Backers," *WorldNetDaily,* June 7, 2009, http://www.wnd.com/?pageId=100486.

49. Charles Bolden conversation with Imran Garda, Al Jazeera, July 1, 2010.

50. Andrew C. McCarthy, "Christie's 'Crazies,'" *National Review Online*, August 6, 2011, www.nationalreview.com/articles/ print/ 273865. See also: The Investigative Project on Terrorism, "Governor Christie's Strange Relationship with Radical Islam," *IPT News*, January 19, 2011, http://www.investigativeproject.org/2506/gov-christie-strange-relationship-with-radical.

51. The Investigative Project on Terrorism, "Keith Ellison's Slurs," *IPT News,* April 13, 2011, http://www.investigativeproject.org/2763/keith-ellison-slurs.

52. Robert Spencer, "The Muslim Brotherhood's Congressman," *Human Events*, September 21, 2010, http://www.humanevents.com/article.php?id=39080.

53. Patrick Poole, "(PJM Exclusive) Did Obama and Holder Scuttle Terror Finance Prosecutions?" *Pajamas Media*, April 14, 2011, http://pajamasmedia.com/blog/did-obama-and-holder-scuttle-terror-finance-prosecutions/.

54. Feisal Abdul Rauf, *What's Right with Islam: A New Vision for Muslims and the West* (New York: HarperCollins, 2005), 135.

55. Imam Feisal Abdul Rauf, remarks at the Council on Foreign Relations, New York City, September 13, 2010. Transcript posted online by the Council on Foreign Relations, http://www.cfr.org/religion/converstion-feisel-abdul-rauf/p22940.

56. Feisal Abdul Rauf, *What's Right with Islam: A New Vision for Muslims and the West* (New York: HarperCollins, 2005), 198.

57. Pamela Geller, "Atlas Exclusive: Imam Rauf Exposed Off Mic, 'I'm the Head Coach of This Strategic Initiative, and the President of the United States, or the President of Malaysia, or the President of England, is a Player to Bring in for Particular Plays,'" *Atlas Shrugs,* September 27, 2010, http://atlasshrugs2000.typepad.com/atlas_shrugs/2010/09/atlas-exclusive-imam-rauf.html.

58. Jason Campbell, *Sacrificed Survivors: The Untold Story of the Ground Zero Mega Mosque* (PRB Films/Christian Action Network, 2010).

59. Frank J. Gaffney, Jr., *Shariah: The Threat to America* (Washington, DC: Center for Security Policy, 2010), 224.

60. Ibid., 225.

61. Organization of the Islamic Conference, *Third OIC Observatory Report on Islamophobia*, presented to the 37th Council of Foreign Ministers (Dushanbe, Republic of Tajikistan: OIC, May 18-20, 2010), http://www.oic-oci.org/uploads/file/Islamphobia/2010/en/Islamophobia_rep_May_22_5_2010.pdf.pdf.

62. Charter of the Organisation of the Islamic Conference, http://www.oic-oci.org/is11/english/Charter-en.pdf.

63. The Investigative Project on Terrorism, "Brotherhood Assurances Not Backed by Track Record, " *IPT News*, June 28, 2011, http://www.investigativeproject.org/3012/brotherhood-assurances-not-backed-by-track-record.

64. UN General Assembly, Universal Declaration of Human Rights, *December 10, 1948.* http://www.udhr.org/udhr/udhr.HTM.

65. Organisation of the Islamic Conference, Cairo Declaration on Human Rights in Islam, August 5, 1990. Published online by Human Rights Library, University of Minnesota, http://www1.umn.edu/humanrts/instree/cairodeclaration.html.

66. Lahem Al-Nasser, "The Islamic Fiqh Academy," *knol Beta*, June 20, 2009, http://knol.google.com/k/lahem-al-nasser/the-islamic-fiqh-academy/jzg9so45w3jo/59#.

67. Mark Durie, "The Organization of the Islamic Conference: Fatwas on Freedom and Democracy," Hudson Institute, January 19, 2011, http://www.hudson.org/index.cfm?fuseaction=hudson_upcoming_events&id=818.

68. Robert Spencer, "Speak to Me, Ibrahim!" *FrontPageMag.com, March 10, 2003,* http://archive.frontpagemag.com/readArticle.aspx?ARTID=19370.

69. Javid Hassan, "Media Campaign in US to Dispel Islamophobia," *Arab News*, June 21, 2006, http://archive.arabnews.com/?page=1&section=0&article=84122&d=21&m=6&y=2006.

70. Ken Timmerman, "Left-Wing Lobbyists Orchestrate Gaza Campaign," *Newsmax*, June 18, 2010, http://www.newsmax.com/KenTimmerman/Al Fakhoora-Gaza-blockade/2010/06/18/id/362396.

71. *Israel and Double Standards: Durban III @ New York City*, posted on YouTube by eyeontheun, August 29, 2011, http://www.youtube.com/watch?v=5jM_UPIwNZ0.

72. Daniel New, "U.N. Agreement Should Have All Gun Owners up in Arms," UNWatch, June 7, 2011, http://www.unwatch.com/un-wants-guns.html.

73. Ibid.

74. Joel Gilbert, *Farewell Israel: Bush, Iran, and The Revolt of Islam* (Highway 61, 2007).

75. Anne Bayefsky, "Did the U.S. Violate bin Laden's Rights?" *Fox News*, May 9, 2011, http://www.foxnews.com/opinion/2011/05/09/did-violate-bin-ladens-rights/.

76. Art Moore, "Muslim Brotherhood 'Declares War' on U.S.," *WorldNetDaily*, October 12, 2010, http://www.wnd.com/?pageId=214245.

77. The Lawfare Project, "Lawfare: The Use of the Law as a Weapon of War," http://www.thelawfareproject.org/index.php?option=com_content&view=article&id=120&Itemid=74.

78. The Investigative Project on Terrorism, "House Hearing: Hizballah Threat Looms in U.S. Backyard," *IPT News*, July 8, 2011, http://www.investigativeproject.org/3028/house-hearing-hizballah-threat-looms-in-us.

79. Bat Ye'or, "OIC and the Modern Caliphate," *American Thinker,* September 26, 2010, http://www.americanthinker.com/2010/09/oic_and_the_modern_caliphate.html.

80. Shaykh Anwar al-Awlakr, "May Our Souls Be Sacrificed for You," *Inspire Magazine*, Summer 1431/2010, http://www.homelandsecurityus.com/PDF/Inspire%20Summer%202010R.pdf.

81. The Middle East Media Research Institute, "An Overview of the Egyptian Muslim Brotherhood's Stance on U.S. and Jihad; Translation of Its Draft Political Platform," http://m.memri.org/14499/show/0b5b63f3c2b8120123666c5cd4149fe1&t=20320d97cb30b6845cb6422bedb5dfbe.

82. Barry Rubin, "Muslim Brotherhood Declares War on America; Will America Notice?" Rubin Report, October 7, 2010, http://rubinreports.blogspot.com/2010/10/muslim-brotherhood-declares-war-on.html.

Chapter 11

1. UN General Assembly Human Rights Council, Fourteenth Session, *Report of the Special Rapporteur on Extra Judicial Summary or Arbitrary Executions*, May 28, 2010, http://www2.ohchr.org/english/bodies/hrcouncil/docs/14session/A.HRC.14.24.Add6.pdf.

2. *Judge Richard Goldstone,* "Report of the United Nations Fact Finding Mission on the Gaza Conflict," September 15, 2009.

3. Anne Bayefsky, "Obama's U.N. Debacle," *National Review Online*, March 25, 2011, http://www.nationalreview.com/articles/263102/obama-s-un-debacle-anne-bayefsky.

4. Jessica Mador. "New Islamic Mortgages Now Available in Minnesota, " Minnesota Public Radio, March 1, 2009, http://minnesota.publicradio.org/display/web/2009/02/28/islamicfinancing/.

5. "Café Fan Banned in Case Smell of Bacon Offends Muslims," *Telegraph*, October 22, 2010, http://www.telegraph.co.uk/.../Cafe-fan-banned-in-case-smell-of-bacon-offends.

6. Andrew C. McCarthy, "Uncharitable," *National Review Online*, April 23, 2011, http://www.nationalreview.com/articles/265437/uncharitable-andrew-c-mccarthy.

7. "Ahmad Ibn Lulu Ibn Al-Naqib," *Reliance of the Traveller: The Classic Manual of Islamic Sacred Law Umdat Al-Salik* (Beltsville, MD: Amana Publications, 1991), 266-274.

8. Ibid., 272

9. President Barack Obama, "Remarks by the President on the Middle East and North Africa," U.S. Department of State, Washington, D.C., May 19, 2011. Text posted online by the *New York Times*, http://www.nytimes.com/2011/05/20/world/middleeast/20prexy-text.html?_r=1.

10. President Barack Obama, "Remarks by the President at the AIPAC Policy Conference 2011," Washington, D.C., May 22, 2011, http://www.whitehouse.gov/the-press-office/2011/05/22/remarks-president-aipac-policy-conference-2011.

11. Prime Minister Benjamin Netanyahu, address to U.S. Congress, May 24, 2011. Transcript published online by the *Washington Post*, http://www.washingtonpost.com/world/israeli-prime-minister-binyamin-netanyahus-address-to-congress/2011/05/24/AFWY5bAH_story.html.

12. Brian Montopoli, "Obama: 'Not Productive' To Be Seen As Meddling," *CBS News*, June 16, 2009, http://www.cbsnews.com/8301-503544_162-5091640-03544.html.

13. Itamar Marcus and Barbara Crook, "Aspiration not Desperation," *Jerusalem Post*, January 29, 2004, http://www.pmw.org.il/main.aspx?fi=155&doc_id=1811.

14. Islamic Society of North America, "US Muslim Religious Council Issues Fatwa Against Terrorism," July 31, 2011, http://www.isna.net/index.php?id =316.

15. "Salah Sultan Says Zionists Make Matzoh with Christian Blood," *Global Muslim Brotherhood Daily Report*, April 26, 2010, http://globalmb report. org/?p=2907.

16. Stewart Sogel, "Bin Laden's Goal: Kill 4 Million Americans," *Newsmax*, July 14, 2004, http://archive.newsmax.com/archives/articles/2004/7/14/215 350.shtml.

17. Abdul A'la Maududi, *Jihad in Islam* (Beirut, Lebanon: Holy Koran Publishing House, 2006). An address delivered in Lahore, Pakistan, on April 13, 1939. Online at http://www.muhammadanism.org/Terrorism/jihah_in_islam/ jihad_in_islam.pdf.

18. Obama, speech on the Middle East, May 19, 2011. See note 10.

19. John Brennan, "Remarks by Assistant to the President for Homeland Security and Counterterrorism John Brennan at CSIS," Washington, D.C., May 26, 2010. Transcript at http://www.whitehouse.gov/the-press-office/re-marks-john-brennan-center-strategic-and-international-studies.

20. Clare M. Lopez, Roland Peer, and Christine Brim, *Religious Bias Crimes Against Muslim, Christian and Jewish Victims: Trends from 2000-2009* (Washington, DC: Center for Security Policy, March 9, 2011). Occasional paper series. Online at http://awaitingtheprotectorate.blogspot.com/2011/03/religious-bias-crimes-against-muslim.html.

21. Daniel Huff, "Is the First Amendment in Jeopardy?" *Middle East Forum*, July 6, 2010, http://www.meforum.org/2684/first-amendment-in-jeopardy.

22. Daniel Huff, "Why Is America Curbing Free Speech and Giving Extremists What They Want?" The Legal Project, September 24, 2010, http:// www.legal-project.org/779/is-koran-burning-protected-by-free-speech.

23. United Nations General Assembly, Universal Declaration of Human Rights, *December 10, 1948*. http://www.udhr.org/udhr/udhr.HTM.

24. Daniel Pipes, *Miniatures: Views of Islamic and Middle Eastern Politics* (New Jersey: Transaction, 2003), 97.

25. Lee Smith, "Losing His Religion: Apostate Ibn Warraq Campaigns for Right Not to Be a Muslim," *Boston Globe*, August 17, 2003. Online at Kabyle.com, http://www.kabyle.com/forum/salon-discussions-generales/16069-article-du-boston-globe-sur-ibn-warraq-auteur-de-pourquoi-je-ne-suis-pas-musulman.html.

26. Irshad Manji, " Islam Needs Reformists, Not 'Moderates,'" *Wall Street Journal*, May 7, 2011, http://online.wsj.com/article/SB1000142405274870399 2704576305412360432744.html.

27. Pew Research Center, "Muslim Publics Divided on Hamas and Hezbollah," December 2, 2010, http://pewglobal.org/2010/12/02/muslims-around-the-world-divided-on-hamas-and-hezbollah/. See also: Richard Swier,

"John Guandolo on the Muslim Brotherhood," *Boogai*, February 7, 2011, http://www.boogai.net/us-news/john-guandolo-on-the-muslim-brotherhood/.

28. Steven Kull, *Muslim Public Opinion on U.S. Policy, Attacks on Civilians and al Qaeda* (College Park, MD: University of Maryland, April 2007), http://www.worldpublicopinion.org/pipa/pdf/apr07/START_Apr07_rpt.pdf.

29 .David D. Kirkpatrick, "Clashes in Cairo Leave 12 Dead and 2 Churches in Flames," *New York Times,* May 8, 2011, http://www.nytimes.com/2011/05/09/world/middleeast/09egypt html

30. Andrew G. Bostom, "Egyptian Democrats: 'The Victory of Our Revolution Will Not Be Complete Without the Liberation of Palestine,'" *American Thinker*, May 13, 2011, http://www.americanthinker.com/blog/2011/05/egyptian_democrats_the_victory.html.

31. Asra Q. Nomani, "Wafa Sultan," *Time*, April 30, 2006, http://www.time.com/time/magazine/article/0,9171,1187385,00.html.

32. Ibid.

33. Aaron Klein, "Another Stunner Behind Obama's Libya Doctrine," *WorldNetDaily*, March 29, 2011, http://www.wnd.com/?pageId=281065.

34. Ben Franklin, "What July 4th Means to Me," *Human Events*, July 3, 2006, http://www.humanevents.com/article.php?id=15750.%20.

35. Andrew G. Bostom, "Mosques as Barracks in America," *American Thinker*, June 5, 2011, http://www.americanthinker.com/2011/06/mosques_as_barracks_in_america_1.html.

36. *Muslim Demographics (Europe, USA, Scandinavia)*, posted on YouTube by WelcometoSweden, February 18, 2010, http://www.youtube.com/watch?v=Cj-ceoxHc4U.

37. Al-Jazeera, MEMRI TV Libyan Leader Mu'Ammar Al-Quadhafi, Quatar, April 10, 2006.

38. Ken Timmerman, "North Korea Tests 'Superman-EMP' Nuke," *Newsmax*, June 16, 2011, http://www.newsmax.com/KenTimmerman/super-emp-emp-northkorea-nuke/2011/06/16/id/400260.

Chapter 12

1. Helene Cooper, "America Seeks Bonds to Islam, Obama Insists," *New York Times,* April 6, 2009, http://www.nytimes.com/2009/04/07/world/europe/07prexy.html. See also: "America will Never be at War with Islam: Obama," *Al Arabiya News*, September 11, 2010, http://www.alarabiya.net/articles/2010/09/11/119053.html.

2. Herbert I. London, "Purveyors of Political Correctness," Hudson Insitute, November 30, 2009, http://www.hudson-ny.org/939/purveyors-of-political-correctness.

3. Reuters, "General Casey: Diversity Shouldn't be Casualty of Fort Hood," November 8, 2009, http://blogs.reuters.com/frontrow/2009/11/08/general-casey-diversity-shouldnt-be-casualty-of-fort-hood/.

4. Frank J Gaffney Jr., *Shariah: The Threat to America.* (Washington, DC: Center for Security Policy, 2010), 225-226.

5. B. S. Sharma, "The Ideal and the Actual In Gandhi's Philosophy," Bombay Sarvodaya Mandal, http://www.mkgandhi-sarvodaya.org/g_relevance/chap27.htm.

Bibliography and Recommended Reading

Abou El Fadl, Khaled, Joshua Cohen and Deborah Chasman. *Islam and the Challenge of Democracy: A "Boston Review" Book*. Princeton, NJ: Princeton University 2004

Abraham, A.J. *Khomeini, Islamic Fundamentalism and the Warriors of God: An Islamic Reader*. Wyndham Hall, 2000

Ali,Yuuf, Abudullah. *The Meaning of the Holy Qur'an*. Beltsville, MD: Amana Publications, 10th edition, 1999

Baran, Zeyno. *The Other Muslims: Moderate and Secular*. New York: Palgrave Macmillan, 2010

Barnett, Roger W. *Asymetrical Warfare: Today's Challenge to U.S. Military Power*. Dulles,VA: Brassey's Inc, 2003

Bostom, Andrew G.,ed. *The Legacy of Jihad: Islamic Holy War and the Fate of Non-Muslims*. Amherst, New York: Prometheus Books, 2008

Bulliet, Richard W. *The Case for Islamo-Christian Civilization*. New York: Columbia University Press, 2006

Crone, Patricia. *God's Rule - Government and Islam: Six Centuries of Medieval Islamic Political Thought*. New York: Columbia University Press, 2006

Dashti, Ali. *Twenty Three Years: A Study of the Prophetic Career of Mohammad*. Routledge, 2007

Davis, Gregory, M. *Religion of Peace?: Islam's War Against the World*. Los Angeles, CA: World. Ahead Publishing, 2006

Delong-Bas, Natana J. *Wahhabi Islam: From Revival and Reform to Global Jihad* . New York: Oxford University Press, 2004

Dershowitz, Alan M. *The Case ForIsrael*. Hoboken, NJ: John Wiley & Sons, 2004

Emerson, Steven. *American Jihad: The Terrorists Living Among Us*. New York: Free Press, 2002

Emerson, Steven. *Jihad Incorporated: A Guide to Militant Islam in the US*. Amherst, New York: Prometheus, 2006

Esman, Abigail R. *Radical State: How Jihad Is Winning Over Democracy in the West*. Santa Barbara, CA: Praeger, 2010

Fallaci, Oriana. *The Force of Reason*. Rizzoli, 2006

Fukuyama, Francis. *The End of History and the Last Man*. New York: Avon, 1992

Gabriel, Mark A. *Islam And Terrorism: What the Quran really teaches about Christianity, violence and the goals of the Islamic Jihad*. Lake Mary, FL: Frontline, 2002

Gabriel, Mark A. *Islam And The Jews: The Unfinished Battle*. Lake Mary, FL: Frontline, 2003

Gabriel, Mark A. *Jesus and Muhammad: Profound Differences and Surprising Similarities*. Lake Mary, FL: Frontline, 2004

Gabriel, Mark A. *Journey Inside The Mind Of an Islamic Terrorist: Why They Hate Us and How We Can Change Their Minds*. Lake Mary, FL: Frontline, 2005

Gabriel, Mark A. *Culture Clash: Islam's War on America*. Lake Mary, FL: Frontline, 2007

Gabriel, Mark A. *Coffee with the Prophet*. Casselberry, FL: Gabriel, 2008

Gaffney, Frank J. Jr. *Shariah: The Threat to America*. Washington, DC: Center for Security Policy, 2010

Gaffney, Frank J. Jr. *War Footing: 10 Steps America Must Take to Prevail in the War for the Free World*. Naval Institute, 2005

Gaubatz, P. David and Paul Sperry. *Muslim Mafia: Inside the Secret Underworld that's Conspiring to Islamize America*. Los Angeles, CA: WorldNetDaily, 2009

Glazov, Jamie. *United in Hate: The Left's Romance with Tyranny and Terror*. Los Angeles, CA: WorldNetDaily, 2009

Gold, Dore. *Hatred's Kingdom: How Saudi Arabia Supports the New Global Terrorism*. Washington, D.C.: Regnery, 2004

Guillaume, A. and Ishaq, I. *The Life of Muhammad: A Translation of Ishaq's Sirat Rasul Allah*. New York: Oxford University Press, 2002

Habeck, Mary. *Knowing the Enemy: Jihadist Ideology and the War on Terror*. New Haven, CT: Yale University Press, 2007

Hamid, Tawfik. *The Roots of Jihad*. Top Executive Media, 2006

Harris, Lee. *The Suicide of Reason: Radical Islam's Threat to the West*. New York: Basic Books, 2007

Heschel, Abraham Joshua. *The Prophets*. Hendrickson, 2007

Hirsi Ali, Ayaan. *The Caged Virgin: An Emancipation Proclamation for Women and Islam*. New York: Free Press, 2008

Hirsi Ali, Ayaan. *Nomad: From Islam to America: A Personal Journey Through the Clash of Civilizations*. New York: Free Press, 2010

Jafarzadeh, Alireza. *The Iran Threat: President Ahmadinejad and the Coming Nuclear Crisis*. New York: Palgrave Macmillan, 2007

Kagan, Robert. *Of Paradise and Power: America and Europe in the New World Order*. New York: Vintage, 2004

Karsh, Efraim. *Islamic Imperialism: A History*. New Haven, CT: Yale University Press, 2007

Karsh, Efraim. *Arafat's War: The Man and His Battle for Israeli Conquest*. New York: Grove Press, 2004

Karsh, Efraim. *Islamic Imperialism: A History*. New Haven, CT: Yale University, 2007

Karsh, Efraim. *Palestine Betrayed*. New Haven, CT: Yale University, 2010

Kepel, Gilles. *Jihad: The Trail of Political Islam*. I.B. Tauris & Co. Ltd., 2002

Khomeini, Imam and HamidAlgar trans. *Islam and Revolution 1: Writings and Declarations of Imam Khomeini (1941-1980)*. Berkley, CA: Mizan, 1981

Kuntzel, Matthias. *Jihad and Jew-Hatred: Islamism, Nazism and the Roots of 9/11*. New York: Telos Press, 2007

Lawrence, Bruce, ed. *Messages to the World: The Statements of Osama Bin Laden*. Verso, 2005

Ledeen, Michael A. The *Iranian Time Bomb: The Mullah Zealots' Quest for Destruction*. New York: St. Martin's Press, 2007

Lewis, Bernard. *The Jews of Islam*. Princeton, NJ: Princeton University Press, 1987

Lewis, Bernard. *The Political Language of Islam*. Chicago, IL: University of Chicago Press, 1988

Lewis, Bernard. *The Shaping of the Modern Middle East*. New York: Oxford University Press, 1994

Lewis Bernard. *The Middle East*. New York: Touchstone, 1995

Lewis, Bernard. *Semites and Anti-Semites: An Inquiry into Conflict and Prejudice*. New York: W.W.Norton & Company, 1999

Lewis, Bernard. *The Multiple Identities of the Middle East*. New York: Schocken, 1999

Lewis, Bernard. *What Went Wrong?: The Clash Between Islam and Modernity in the Middle East*. New York: Oxford University Press, 2002

Lewis, Bernanrd. *The Crisis of Islam: Holy War and Unholy Terror*. New York: Random House, 2004

Mamdani, Mahmood. *Good Muslim, Bad Muslim: America, the Cold War, and the Roots of Terror*. New York: Pantheon, 2004

Manji, Irshad. *The Trouble with Islam Today: A Muslim's Call for Reform in Her Faith*. New York: St. Martin's, 2005

Marshall, Paul. *Radical Islam's Rules: The Worldwide Spread of Extreme Shari'a Law*. Rowman & Littlefield, 2005

McCarthy, Andrew C. *Willful Blindness: A Memoir of the Jihad*. New York: Encounter, 2008

McCarthy, Andrew C. *The Grand Jihad: How Islam and the Left Sabotage America*. New York: Encounter, 2010

Morse, Chuck. *The Nazi Connection to Islamic Terrorism: Adolf Hitler and Haj Amin Al-Husseini*. Lincoln, NE: iUniverse, Inc., 2003

Muhammad Ali, Maulana. *A Manual of Hadith*. Ahmadiyya Anjuman Ishaat, 1990

Murray, Douglas. *NeoConservatism: Why We Need It*. New York: Encounter, 2006

Murray, Douglas and Johan Pieter Verwey. *Victims of Intimidation: Freedom of Speech within Europe's Muslim Communities*. Trowbridge, Wiltshire: Cromwell Press, 2008

Nasr, Vali. *The Shia Revival: How Conflicts within Islam Will Shape the Future*. New York: W. W. Norton & Company,2007

National Commission on Terrorist Attacks. *The 9/11 Commission Report: Final Report of the National Commission on Terrorist Attacks Upon the United States*. New York: W. W. Norton & Company, 2004

Netanyahu, Benjamin. *A Place Among the Nations*. New York: Bantam, 1993

Netanyahu, Benjamin. *A Durable Peace: Israel and Its Place Among the Nations*. New York: Bantam, 1999

Phares, Walid. *Future Jihad: Terrorist Strategies against the West*. New York: Palgrave Macmillan, 2005

Phares, Walid. *The War of Ideas: Jihadism against Democracy*. New York: Palgrave Macmillan, 2008

Pipes, Daniel. *Miniatures: Views of Islamic and Middle Eastern Politics.* Edison, New Jersey: Transaction, 2003

Pipes, Daniel. *Militant Islam Reaches America.* New York: Norton, 2003

Pipes, Daniel. *Miniatures: Views of Islamic and Middle Eastern Politics* Transaction November 11, 2003

Podhoretz, Norman. *World War IV: The Long Struggle Against Islamofascism.* New York: Random House, 2007

Rand, Ayn. *Ayn Rand Answers: The Best of Her Q & A.* New York: New American Library, 2005

Rauf, Feisal A. *What's Right with Islam: A New Vision for Muslims and the West.* New York: HarperOne, 2005

Roy, Oliver. *Globalized Islam: The Search for a New Ummah.* New York: Columbia University Press, 2004

Schact, Joseph. *An Introduction to Islamic Law.* New York: Oxford University Press, 1982

Schwartz-Barcott, T.P. *War, Terror, & Peace in the Qur'an and in Islam: Insights for Military and Government Leaders.* The Army War College Foundation, 2004

Schwartz, Stephen. *The Two Faces of Islam: Saudi Fundamentalism and Its Role in Terrorism.* Anchor, 2003

Sharansky, Natan. *The Case For Democracy: The Power Of Freedom to Overcome Tyranny And Terror.* PublicAffairs, 2004

Shoebat, Walid. *Why I Left Jihad: The Root of Terrorism and the Return of Radical Islam.* Top Executive Media, 2005

Sivan, Emmanuel. *Radical Islam: Medieval Theology and Modern Politics.* New Haven, CT: Yale University, 1985

Spencer, Robert. *Onward Muslim Soldiers: How Jihad Still Threatens America and the West.* Washington, DC: Regnery, 2003

Spencer, Robert. *The Myth of Islamic Tolerance: How Islamic Law Treats Non-Muslims.* Amherst, NY: Prometheus, 2005

Spencer, Robert. *Religion of Peace?: Why Christianity Is and Islam Isn't.* Washington, DC: Regnery, 2007

Spencer, Robert. *The Truth About Muhammad: Founder of the World's Most Intolerant Religion.* Washington, DC: Regnery 2007

Sperry, Paul. *Infiltration: How Muslim Spies and Subversives have Penetrated Washington.* Nashville, TN: Nelson Current, 2005

Sperry, Paul. *Onward Muslim Soldiers: How Jihad Still Threatens America and the West.* Washington, DC: Regnery, 2003

Steele, Shelby. *White Guilt: How Blacks and Whites Together Destroyed the Promise of the Civil Rights Era*. New York, NY: Harper Perennial 2007

Talegani, Ayatullah Mahmud, Ayatullah Murtada Mutahhari, and Ali Shari'ati *Jihad and Shahadat (Struggle and Martyrdom in Islam)*. North Haledon, NJ : Islamic Publications International, 1986

Taheri, Amir. *The Spirit of Allah: Khomeini and the Islamic Revolution*. Adler& Adler, 1986

Taheri, Amir. *Holy Terror, Inside the World of Islamic Terrorism*. Adler&Adler, 1987

Taheri, Amir. *The Persian Night: Iran under the Khomeinist Revolution*. New York: Encounter, 2009

Takeyh, Ray. *Hidden Iran: Paradox and Power in the Islamic Republic*. New York: Holt Paperbacks, 2006

Timmerman, Kenneth, R. *Preachers of Hate: Islam and the War on America*. New York: Three Rivers Press, 2003

Timmerman, Kenneth, R *Countdown to Crisis: The Coming Nuclear Showdown with Iran*. Crown Forum, 2005

Vidino, Lorenzo. *Al Qaeda in Europe: The New Battleground of International Jihad*. Amherst, New York: Prometheus, 2006

Watt, W. Montgomery. *Muhammad: Prophet and Statesman*. New York: Oxford University Press, 1961

Watt, W. Montgomery. *Muhammad at Medina*. New York: Oxford University Press, 1981

West, Diana. *The Death of the Grown-Up: How America's Arrested Development Is Bringing Down Western Civilization*. New York: St. Martin's, 2007

Wisse, Ruth R. *If I Am Not For Myself . . . The Liberal Betrayal of the Jews*. New York: The Free Press, 1992

Wright, Lawrence. *The Looming Tower: Al-Qaeda and the Road to 9/11*. New York: Knopf, 2006

Ye'or, Bat and David Maisel. *The Dhimmi: Jews and Christians Under Islam*. Cranberry, NJ: Associated University, 1985

Ye'or, Bat, Miriam Kochan and David Littman. *Islam and Dhimmitude: Where Civilizations Collide*. Cranberry, NJ: Associated University, 2001

Films:

Farewell Israel: Bush, Iran, and The Revolt of Islam. Joel Gilbert, Highway 61, 2007

Grand Deception, Steven Emerson, SAE Productions

Homegrown Terror: The Terrorist Camps Around U.S. Martin Mawyer, PRB films in association with Christian Action Network, 2009

Sacrificed Survivors: The Untold Story of the Ground Zero Mega Mosque. Jason Campbell, Christian Action Network/PRB Films, 2010

The Third Jihad. Wayne Kopping and Erik Werth, PublicScope Films, 2009

Index

About the Author

Bill Siegel is a lawyer and a former executive at various public and private companies. He is a producer of several documentary films and assists numerous non-profit organizations.